Communications
in Computer and Information Science   1435

More information about this series at http://www.springer.com/series/7899

Mufti Mahmud · M. Shamim Kaiser ·
Nikola Kasabov · Khan Iftekharuddin ·
Ning Zhong (Eds.)

Applied Intelligence and Informatics

First International Conference, AII 2021
Nottingham, UK, July 30–31, 2021
Proceedings

 Springer

Editors
Mufti Mahmud 🆔
Nottingham Trent University
Nottingham, UK

Nikola Kasabov 🆔
Auckland University of Technology
Auckland, New Zealand

Ning Zhong 🆔
Maebashi Institute of Technology
Maebashi, Japan

M. Shamim Kaiser 🆔
Jahangirnagar University
Savar, Dhaka, Bangladesh

Khan Iftekharuddin 🆔
Old Dominion University
Norfolk, VA, USA

ISSN 1865-0929   ISSN 1865-0937 (electronic)
Communications in Computer and Information Science
ISBN 978-3-030-82268-2   ISBN 978-3-030-82269-9 (eBook)
https://doi.org/10.1007/978-3-030-82269-9

This Springer imprint is published by the registered company Springer Nature Switzerland AG
The registered company address is: Gewerbestrasse 11, 6330 Cham, Switzerland

Preface

The term 'Intelligence' is defined as the ability to perceive or infer information, and to retain it as knowledge to be applied towards adaptive behaviours within an environment or context. It can be the capacity for logic, understanding, self-awareness, learning, emotional knowledge, reasoning, planning, creativity, critical thinking, and problem-solving. 'Informatics,' on the other hand, is the study of the structure, behavior, and interactions of natural and engineered computational systems.It studies the representation, processing, and communication of information in natural and engineered systems. Applying both intelligence and informatics can be used to solve the most complex problems in science, engineering, real-life manufacturing, defence, management, government, and industrial domains.

The 2021 International Conference on Applied Intelligence and Informatics (AII 2021) brought together researchers and practitioners from diverse domains to share cutting-edge research results obtained through the application of intelligence and/or informatics to solve problems that it otherwise would not have been possible to solve. AII 2021 also fostered the exchange and dissemination of innovative and methodologies and the practical development of technologies with real-life applications.

The concept of the AII conference series was conceived last year when the whole world was combating the first wave of COVID-19. During that extremely challenging time, everyone, especially scientists and researchers from all disciplines, wanted to contribute in their own ways to this war against COVID-19. When cities and countries were going into lockdown, and universities and research labs were evacuated to stop the aggressive spread of the disease, computational scientists and researchers contributed significantly through developing different methods to detect and diagnose the disease, building models to help stop its spread, and facilitating the development of vaccines. However, most of these methods which were developed and published to fight the pandemic remained proprietary and had limited access for others to reproduce the results. Realising this, a set of committed academics felt the need for a dedicated avenue to discuss the reproducibility of research results through sharing the methods and the datasets. The AII conference series was born with a keen focus on the applications of Artificial Intelligence and Informatics, not only in the field of healthcare but also in all walks of life.

This first edition of AII was supposed to be held in Nottingham, UK; however, this was not possible due to the extenuating circumstances caused by COVID-19. This led to the organisation of the event in a fully virtual mode, with the hope that future editions will be held physically. The AII 2021 online conference was supported by the Applied Intelligence and Informatics (AII) Laboratory, the Web Intelligence Consortium (WIC), Nottingham Trent University, the IEEE Computational Intelligence Society UK and Ireland Chapter, and the International Academic Communication Center (IRNet).

The theme of AII 2021 was "Fostering the Reproducibility of Scientific Results." The goal was to see how best we can promote open methodological contributions to reproduce the scientific results presented in the literature. The papers presented at AII 2021 addressed broad perspectives on applied research to facilitate the reproduction of results. These papers provide a good sample of state-of-the-art research advances on applications of artificial intelligence and informatics in diverse fields and disciplines. The selected papers cover five major tracks: (1) Application of AI in Disease Detection, (2) Application of AI in Healthcare, (3) Application of AI in Pattern Recognition, (4) Application of AI in Network, Security, and Analytics, and (5) Emerging Applications of AI and Informatics.

This first edition of the AII conference attracted 107 submissions from authors in 16 countries across all five AII 2021 tracks. The submitted papers underwent a single blind review process, soliciting opinion from at least three experts: a minimum of two independent reviewers and the handling chair. After the rigorous review process, reports from the reviewers and the track chairs on the respective papers were considered and, finally, 30 full papers from authors in 12 countries were accepted for presentation at the conference. Therefore, this volume of the conference proceedings contains those 30 papers which were presented virtually at AII 2021. Despite the COVID-19 pandemic situation, it was an amazing response from the community during this challenging time.

We would like to express our gratitude to all AII 2021 conference committee members for their instrumental and unwavering support. AII 2021 had a very exciting program which would not have been possible without the generous dedication of the Program Committee members in reviewing the conference papers. AII 2021 could not have taken place without great team effort and generous support from our sponsors.

We would especially like to express our sincere appreciation to our kind sponsors, including Springer Nature and the Springer CCIS team. Our gratitude goes to the AII Lab for sponsoring 25 author registrations, which were selected based on the quality of the submitted papers and their need for financial support.

We are grateful to Ronan Nugent, Amin Mobasheri, Alla Freund, Samuel Raj, Selma Somogy, Guido Zosimo-Landolfo, and the complete Springer CCIS team for their continuous support in coordinating the publication of this volume.

Last but not least, we thank all our contributors and volunteers for their support during this challenging time to make AII 2021 a success.

July 2021

Mufti Mahmud
M. Shamim Kaiser
Nikola Kasabov
Khan Iftekharuddin
Ning Zhong

Organization

Conference Chairs

Mufti Mahmud   Nottingham Trent University, UK
Nikola Kasabov   Auckland University of Technology, New Zealand

Advisors

Amir Hussain   Edinburgh Napier University, UK
A. Bandyopadhyay   NIMS, Japan
David Brown   Nottingham Trent University, UK
Hamido Fujita   Iwate Prefectural University, Japan
Kanad Ray   Amity University, India
Martin McGinnity   Ulster University, UK
S. C. Satapathy   KIIT Deemed to be University, India
Shariful Islam   Deakin University, Australia

Program Chairs

Khan Iftekharuddin   Old Dominion University, USA
Ning Zhong   Maebashi Institute of Technology, Japan

Track Chairs

Cris Calude   University of Auckland, New Zealand
Francesco C. Morabito   University of Reggio Calabria, Italy
Joarder Kamruzzaman   Federation University, Australia
Min Jiang   Xiamen University, China
Nelishia Pillay   University of Pretoria, South Africa
Tingwen Huang   Texas A&M University, Qatar
Vicky Yamamoto   Keck School of Medicine of USC, USA

Special Session, Tutorial, and Workshop Chairs

Manjunath Aradhya   JSS S&T University, India
Noushath Shaffi   College of Applied Sciences, Oman
Tianhua Chen   University of Huddersfield, UK
Yang Yang   Beijing Forestry University, China

Local Organizing Chairs

Diana Frost	Nottingham Trent University, UK
Omprakash Kaiwartya	Nottingham Trent University, UK
Tawfik Al-Hadhrami	Nottingham Trent University, UK

Publicity Chairs

Abzetdin Adamov	ADA University, Azerbaijan
Cosimo Ieracitano	University of Reggio Calabria, Italy
K. C. Santosh	University of South Dakota, USA
M. Arifur Rahman	Jahangirnagar University, Bangladesh
Nilanjan Dey	JSS University, India
Ramani Kannan	Universiti Teknologi PETRONAS, Malaysia

Conference Secretaries

Shamim Al Mamun	Jahangirnagar University, Bangladesh
M. Shamim Kaiser	Jahangirnagar University, Bangladesh

Webmaster

Md Asif Ur Rahman	PropertyPro Plus, Australia

Technical Program Committee

A. B. M. Aowlad Hossain	KUET, Bangladesh
A. K. M. Mahbubur Rahman	IUB, Bangladesh
A. S. M. Sanwar Hosen	JNU, South Korea
Alessandra Pedrocchi	Politechnico di Milano, Italy
Alessandro Gozzi	IIT, Italy
Amir Hussain	Edinburgh Napier University, UK
Anirban-Bandyopadhyay	NIMS, Japan
Antesar Shabut	Leeds Trinity University, UK
Antony Lam	Mercari Inc., Japan
Atik Mahabub	Concordia University, Canada
Aye Su Phyo	University of Computer Studies, Kalay, Myanmar
Belayat Hossain	Loughborough University, UK
Bernd Kuhn	Okinawa Institute of Science and Technology, Japan
Bo Song	University of Southern Queensland, Australia
Cosimo Ieracitano	University of Reggio Calabria, Italy
Cris Calude	University of Auckland, New Zealand
Daniel Marcus	University of Washington, USA
David Brown	Nottingham Trent University, UK
Davide Zoccolan	SISSA, Italy

Dejan C. Gope	Jahangirnagar University, Bangladesh
Derong Liu	University of Illinois at Chicago, USA
Dimeter Prodonov	Imac, Belgium
Egidio D'Angelo	University of Pavia, Italy
Eleni Vasilaki	The University of Sheffield, UK
Ezharul Islam	Jahangirnagar University, Bangladesh
Farah Deeba	DUET, Bangladesh
Francesco C. Morabito	University of Reggio Calabria, Italy
Francesco Papaleo	University of Padova and IIT, Italy
Gabriella Panuccio	IIT, Italy
Gaute Einevoll	Norwegian University of Life Sciences, Norway
Giacomo Indiveri	University of Zurich, Switzerland
Giancarlo Ferregno	Politechnico di Milano, Italy
Giorgio A. Ascoli	George Mason University, USA
Golam Dastoger Bashar	Boise State University, USA
Guenther Zeck	NMI, Germany
Gustavo Deco	Pompeu Fabra University, Spain
H. Liu	Wayne State University, USA
Hishato Fukuda	Saitama University, Japan
Imtiaz Mahmud	Kyungpook National University, Korea
Joarder Kamruzzaman	Federation University, Australia
Jonathan Mappelli	University of Modena, Italy
Kanad Ray	Amity University, India
K. C. Santosh	University of South Dakota, USA
Khan Iftekharuddin	Old Dominion University, USA
Khoo Bee Ee	Universiti Sains Malaysia, Malaysia
Laura Ballerini	SISSA, Italy
Linta Islam	Jagannath University, Bangladesh
Lu Cao	Saitama University, Japan
Luca Benini	ETH, Switzerland
Luca Berdondini	IIT, Italy
Luciano Gamberini	University of Padova, Italy
M. A. F. M. Rashidul Hasan	Rajshahi University, Bangladesh
M. Ali Akber Dewan	Athabasca University, Canada
M. Shamim Kaiser	JU, Bangladesh
Manjunath Aradhya	JSS S&T University, India
Manohar Das	Oakland University, USA
Marco Mongillo	University of Padova, Italy
Martin McGinnity	Ulster University, UK
Marzia Hoque-Tania	University of Oxford, UK
Mathew Diamond	SISSA, Italy
Mathias Prigge	Weizmann Institute of Science, Israel
Md Abu Yousuf	Jahangirnagar University, Bangladesh
Md Ahsan Habib	MBSTU, Bangladesh
Md Badrul Alam Miah	UPM, Malaysia
Md Habibur Rahman	MBSTU, Bangladesh

Md Sanaul Haque	University of Oulu, Finland
Michele Magno	ETH, Switzerland
Min Jiang	Xiamen University, China
M. Shahadat Hossain	University of Chittagong, Bangladesh
Mufti Mahmud	Nottingham Trent University, UK
Nelishia Pillay	University of Pretoria, South Africa
Nikola Kasabov	AUT, New Zealand
Nilanjan Dey	JIS University, India
Ning Zhong	Maebashi Institute of Technology, Japan
Noushath Shaffi	College of Applied Sciences, Oman
Ofer Yizhar	Weizmann Institute of Science, Israel
Omprakash Kaiwartya	Nottingham Trent University, UK
Paolo Del Giudice	National Insitute of Health, Italy
Paolo Massobrio	University of Genova, Italy
Patrick Ruther	University of Freiburg, Germany
Ralf Zeitler	Venneos GmbH, Germany
Ramani Kannan	Universiti Teknologi PETRONAS, Malaysia
Roland Thewes	Technical University of Berlin, Germany
Ryote Suzuki	Saitama University Japan
S. M. Riazul Islam	Sejong University, South Korea
Saiful Azad	Universiti Malaysia Pahang, Malaysia
Sajjad Waheed	MBSTU, Bangladesh
Sergio Martinoia	University of Genova, Italy
Shariful Islam	Deakin University, Australia
Silvestro Micera	Scuola Superiore Sant'anna, Italy
Stefano Ferraina	University of Rome 'La Sapienza', Italy
Stefano Panzeri	IIT, Italy
Stephan Punitha	Karuna University, India
Surapong Uttama	Mae Fah Luang University, Thailand
Suresh C. Satapathy	KIIT Deemed to be University, India
T. Hashiyama	University of Electro-Communications, Japan
Tabin hassan	AIUB, Bangladesh
Tawfik Al-Hadhrami	Nottingham Trent University, UK
Themis Prodomakis	University of Southampton, UK
Thompson Stephan	M. S. R. University of Applied Sciences, India
Tianhua Chen	University of Huddersfield, UK
Tingwen Huang	Texas A&M University, Qatar
Tushar Kanti Shaha	JKKNIU, Bangladesh
Vicky Yamamoto	Keck School of Medicine of USC, USA
Wladyslaw Homenda	Warsaw University of Technology, Poland
Wolfgang Maas	Technische Universität Graz, Austria
Yang Yang	Beijing Forestry University, China

Contents

Application of AI and Informatics in Network, Security, and Analytics

Emerging Applications of AI and Informatics

Application of AI and Informatics in Disease Detection

Inference and Learning Methodology of Belief Rule Based Expert System to Assess Chikungunya

Zinnia Sultana[1] , Lutfun Nahar[1] , Nanziba Basnin[1] ,
and Mohammad Shahadat Hossain[2]([⊠])

[1] International Islamic University Chittagong, Chattogram, Bangladesh
[2] University of Chittagong, Chittagong, Bangladesh
hossain_ms@cu.ac.bd

Abstract. Chikungunya virus (CHIKV) causes Chikungunya disease in human, transmitted by the Aedes species of mosquito. To this date, no vaccines are available to cure this disease as a result doctors rely on symptomatic treatment. This treatment is significantly based on recording the observation of signs and symptoms related to CHIKV in patients before prescribing medication. However, this disease can be misdiagnosed as its signs are similar to diseases like dengue or zika. This, in turn, gives rise to an uncertain diagnosis of Chikungunya. In addition, it is necessary to develop a system that will not only ensure the accurate assessment of Chikungunya but diagnose it within its early stages of infection. Since expert systems are adequate for handling uncertain data as well as generating more precise and accurate inferences, it is applied to this research. A Belief Rule Base Expert System (BRBES) is proposed in this research for performing the assessment of Chikungunya in its early stages of infection in patients. BRBES is reckoned to obliterate human labor and is computationally faster and less expensive in implementation and inferencing the assessment of CHIKV. This research is carried out using real-world data and inference of Chikungunya has been made by using Receiver Operating Characteristics Curves (ROC). In order to increase the accuracy of assessment, an optimal learning model of BRBES is developed with respect to various combinations of sets of training perimeters. In order to prove trained BRBES is an optimal learning model, it's performance is differentiated with the initial BRBES. Further, this trained BRBES is also compared with a deep learning model such as Convolutional Neural networks (CNN) and machine learning models such as Support Vector Machine (SVM), Random Forest (RF) and Artificial Neural Network (ANN).

Keywords: Chikungunya · Belief Rule Base · Optimizations · Convolutional neural network · Random Forest

© Springer Nature Switzerland AG 2021
M. Mahmud et al. (Eds.): AII 2021, CCIS 1435, pp. 3–16, 2021.
https://doi.org/10.1007/978-3-030-82269-9_1

4   Z. Sultana et al.

1   Introduction

A most emergent vector-borne disease known as Chikungunya, caused from chikungunya virus (CHIKV) [3], which is a mosquito-borne alphavirus a member of *'Togaviridae'* family. Chikungunya was first identified through an outbreak of dengue-like disease between 1952 to 1953 in Tanzania [11]. This disease spreads when the mosquito feeds upon a viremic person (infected person), the virus then replicates in the mosquito before it can be transmitted. The infected mosquito then disseminates the virus to the next person it feeds. CHIKV, a mosquito-borne virus transmits to a new host faster in comparison to other virus-caused diseases. The vectors involved in the transmission of chikungunya are Aedes aegypti and Aedes albopictus. These vectors are also responsible for infecting people with dengue and the zika virus. Fever, joint pain and other symptoms such as heachache, muscle pain, joint swelling and rashes are characteristic manifestation of chikunguniya disease. These signs and symptoms may last for a few days, weeks, months, or even years, corresponding to chronic disease. Due to this uncertainty of diagnosis, CHIKV remains unrecognized. Common symptoms of Chikungunya are also found in dengue and zika illness, hence, it is often misdiagnosed. Moreover, no vaccine is available for immunization against Chikungunya. So treatment solely depends on observation of signs and symptoms [15]. Since signs and symptoms appear to be unreliable in the diagnosis of CHIKV, the development of a system that will address this uncertainty is necessary. For this purpose, an expert system capable of handling the uncertain nature of the signs and symptoms occurring in patients with Chikungunya needs to be developed. In addition, uncertain signs and symptoms arise as it is difficult to observe due to various factors such as miscommunication between patient and doctor, incompetence of patient to express his or her current state of health or inadequate probing by a physician, and so on resulting in uncertainty in diagnosis. Now if this deduction is used to build a rule-based system it will correspond to an ineffective and unreliable decision-making process. Hence, to address such uncertainty in clinical data BRBES is proposed to carry out this research. Moreover, BRBES is capable of dealing with any 'what if' scenarios, facilitating accurate decision-making of CHIKV in infected people. This BRBES should be developed to attain an optimal learning model which would minimize the error lying between the observed and expected level of Chikungunya.

The current section demonstrates the problem of this research. A comprehensive outline of other reviews is discussed in Sect. 2. Section 3 narrates the methodology. The experimental outcome are evaluated in Sect. 4. Section 5 concludes this research.

2   Literature Review

An expert system in [1] which is a knowledge base is developed for the diagnosis of Chikungunya to analyze the symptoms reported in patients. This system uses an input-output matrix generated from the questionnaire of patients. However, uncertainty factors were avoided as a result the output matrix corresponds to an unreliable deduction.

In [16] a fuzzy-based expert system is proposed which constitutes five layers that depict knowledge with uncertainty. Nonetheless, fuzzy-based systems depend on assumptions that are not often accepted in many cases.

A survey to evaluate different deep learning techniques on biological data from different domains is carried out in [17]. The research is aimed at inspecting the consequences of different deep learning architectures when applied to various patterns of complex biological datan [23]. However, implementing such models is tricky because of the troubleshooting errors which appear in the code. Also, it is impossible to predict the consequence of a deep learning model on a dataset prior to development. As data processing inside the model is neither transparent nor explainable.

Another survey in [18] gauges the impact of Deep Learning (DL), Reinforcement Learning (RL), and deep RL while mining features in different types of biological datasets. It was discovered that DL and RL consume immense computing power along with storage capacities. So these methods are not a good choice to be applied in a dataset of moderate size. It was also noticed, DL is not free from the problem of misclassification. Now when it comes to RL, it requires a large dataset to produce ab accurate result. For deep RL the process is complex and unstable, especially when working with nonlinear functions such as a neural network to demonstrate a specific action value.

A mobile application is developed [14] to assist industries to identify probable COVID-19 infected suspects among their staff for providing early treatment. Fuzzy Neural Network based on the industry employee database is embedded in the application. The application utilizes Bluetooth sensors, K Nearest Neighbor, and K-means modules to enable the application to tracks, trace, and notifies Covid-19 infection risk when the user is in contact with other employees. In addition, to evaluate the current health state of COVID-19 patient logistic regression, the Bayesian Decision Tree model is used. Since the app is based on industry health data, the credibility of such data cannot be guaranteed to address all uncertainties. Moreover, the use of geo-location by the app raises concerns about the privacy of individuals.

Here, air pollution is evaluated using a BRB-DL model in [13]. Two datasets obtained from sensors are used to train the model. However, BRB-DL was not trained against diverse datasets such as biological data which are complex and uncertain.

Different types of optimization models, namely single and multiple-objective non-linear problem-solving model is proposed in [27] for locally training the BRB. To train the initial BRB systems, optimization models are developed where attribute weight, rule weight, and belief degrees are utilized for learning parameters. This combination has been formulated using the nonlinear objective function to reduce the gap between the initial system and the BRB that has been implemented. However, not much error gap was reduced because the method used fewer learning parameters and did not perform any type of fine-tuning.

Another research in [20] is carried out to investigate different deep learning algorithms used in different domains to achieve success in accomplishing specific tasks. Deep Belief Networks (DBN) are also explored by pre-training them. Here, a layer after layer approach for learning significant weights is undertaken, with the top two hidden layers. Although DBN is able to gauge the difference between erroneous and real data, the hidden layers correspond to implicit training parameters which are not explainable. Furthermore, apart from high computational cost, the model resorts to ineffectiveness since the auto encoders are present in the first layer. This means any error from uncertain data will affect the rest of the layers. Thus, requiring reconstruction of the model [25].

Furthermore, BRBES [2, 4–8, 10, 12, 19, 21–23] works efficiently in dealing with uncertain clinical data. Thus, it is adhered as the main module to carry out the detection of CHIKV in patients.

3 Methodology

This section demonstrates the methodology used in developing an expert system which will enable the handling of uncertainty to assess Chikungunya. It provides a description of various components and tools, deployed to build a expert system. For the development of this BREBS based expert system [10], HTML, JavaScript, and PHP have been used. The training module which forms a core part of this system has been introduced and implemented in MATLAB. In order to decrease the error between the experimental and estimated results, an optimal learning model is built. Three distinctive combinations of training parameter sets have been considered while developing this optimal learning model. To construct the optimization model, an objective function is utilized to set the constraints required for the training parameters. Three training parameters namely, rule weights, belief degrees, and attribute weights are applied. This research work presents the design, development, and application of a BRBES which may assist the physicians to provide early treatment and accurately identify the CHIKV.

3.1 BRB Expert System Methodology

An inference mechanism is employed to construct a Belief Rule Base system. There are several steps in inference procedures that are describing below:

3.1.1 Input Transformation

Input transformations administers input values on top of attributes of referential values. For example, Chikungunya assessment belief rule Rk: IF Fever is Medium AND Joint Pain is High AND Muscle Pain is High, AND Headache is Medium AND Joint Swelling is Medium THEN Chikungunya (High, 0.8), (Medium, 0.2), (Low, 0.0). Where "High" = 80%, "Medium" = 20%, "Low" = 0%. Since the summation of the belief degree is $(0.80 + 0.20 + 0.00) = 1.00$, this demonstrates the completion of Belief Rule.

3.1.2 Activation Weights Calculated

The activation weight is calculated for individual rules in the BRB using the following formula:

$$\alpha_{k_i} = \prod_{i=1}^{T_k} (\alpha_k^i)^{\delta_{k_i}}$$

Where α_k = joint matching degree, T_k = antecedent attributes of k-th rule [10]. Once the k-th rule becomes active, its weight of activation, is calculated by using the formula below.

$$\omega_k = \frac{\theta_k \alpha_k}{\sum_{j=1}^{L} \theta_j \alpha_j} = \frac{\theta_k \prod_{i-1}^{T_k}(\alpha_i^k)^{\delta'_{ki}}}{\sum_{j=1}^{L} \theta_j [\prod_{i-1}^{T_k}(\alpha_i^j)^{\delta'_{ji}}]}, \delta'_{ki} = \frac{\delta_{ki}}{\max_{i=1,\ldots,T_k} \delta_{ki}}$$

3.1.3 Belief Degree Update

For the missing or ignored input data in antecedent, the belief degree related to every rule base should be updated using the following formula

$$\beta_{ik} = \bar{\beta}_{ik} \frac{\sum_{t=1}^{T_k} (\tau(t,k) \sum_{j=1}^{J} t\alpha_{tj}}{\sum_{t=1}^{T_k} \tau(t,k)}$$

(t, k) = {1 if P_{ik} is used in defining R_k(t = 1, ..., T_k) 0, otherwise}
Here, β_{ik} = updated belief degree, while $\bar{\beta}_{ik}$ = initial belief degree. α_{tj} = denotes the degree where the value of input is a part of an attribute belief degree inclusive of possible consequences in the activated rules, updated in the rule base.

3.1.4 Rule Aggregation

Here all rules are arrogated. Using the analytical ER [26] algorithm, the final belief degree β_j is calculated using the following expression.

$$\beta_j = \frac{\mu[\prod_{k-1}^{L}(\omega_k\beta_{jk} + 1 - \omega_k \sum_{k-1}^{N}) - \prod_{k=1}^{L}(1 - \omega_k \sum_{j-1}^{N} \beta_{jk})}{1 - \mu x[\prod_{k-1}^{L} 1 - \omega_k]}$$

$$\mu = [\sum_{j-1}^{N} \prod_{k-1}^{L}(\omega_k\beta_{jk} + 1 - \omega_k \sum_{j-1}^{N} \beta_{jk}) - (N-1) \prod_{k-1}^{L}(1 - \omega_k \sum_{j-1}^{N} \beta_{jk}]^{-1}$$

β_j is the belief degree, linked to one of the consequent values. These values are calculated in an analytical format of the ER algorithm. ω_k is the activation weight.

3.1.5 Optimal Learning Model

To determine the optimal value of rule weights, attribute weights; and Consequent belief degrees in a BRB system optimal learning module is introduced. To minimize the error gap between the experiential and estimated these learning parameters can be learned from domain experts. These parameters may also be produced randomly. But these may not be exact in 100%. To get the accuracy we have to create trained BRB and for this here use historical data [9]. Figure 1 illustrates the optimization model framework.

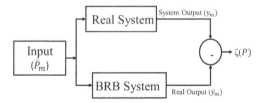

Fig. 1. Optimization model

FMINCON function is used for optimization in Matlab to solve the single-objective model. Construction of optimal learning model has the following steps: 1. Construction of an objective function namely "ObjBetaOneAll.m" 2. Constraints have to set for the training parameters. 3. For finding optimal parameter set training module to have to be developed (Fig. 2).

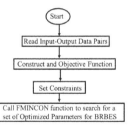

Fig. 2. Flowchart of BRB learning module

3.1.6 BRBES Architecture

The organization of the system component can be defined as system architecture. The system architecture consists of an input and a BRB module to develop a BRBES, and a training module as shown in Fig. 3. Data is collected from different sources based on signs and symptoms of Chikungunya to provide to the input module and process in the BRB main module to predict the risk of Chikungunya. The training module receives training data and initial values from the input module. The trained learning parameters generated from the training module are stored as data in the Knowledge Base. Afterwards, the learning parameters are used to generate the rule base. Then the optimal value for the training parameters is attained by setting parameters to resort to original value. MATLAB is used for high performance to integrate calculation, conception and programming.

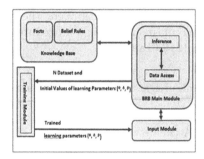

Fig. 3. BRBES architecture

4   Experimental Result

In order to perform validation on the result generated by the BRBES, the data is collected from numerous hospitals of Dhaka and Chittagong in Bangladesh. 250 patients are interviewed, with questions regarding their signs and symptoms of CHIKV. Then a databse is formed from the answers recorded of patients. Table 1 represents samples of the collected data, where in column 1, for the patient Rubi Akter whose age is 35 years and occupation is a Housewife suffers from symptoms like high fever, high joint pain, medium headache, medium muscle pain and high joint swelling. On the basis of these symptoms, according to Table 1 the BRBES system outputs a 75.443% chance of CHIKV which is seen to closely match to the opinion of the Physician/Expert who states a risk of 75% of the patient.

Table 1. Collected data from patients

Patient			Signs and Symptoms					Result	
ID	Name	Age	Fever	Joint pain	Headache	Muscle pain	Joint swelling	BRBES output	Expert opinion
1	Ruby Akter	35	High	High	Medium	Medium	High	75.4430%	75%
2	Shamsul Islam	52	High	High	High	High	High	84.7135%	85%
3	FazlaAzim	68	Low	Low	Low	Low	Low	27.8756%	29%
4	Nilufar Begum	42	High	High	High	High	High	71.8900%	73%
5	.Zobaer Hasan	48	High	High	Medium	High	High	59.2996%	53%

Three distinct sets, namely R1, R2 and R3 of training parameters are developed to train the BRB module [24]. Where, R1 are trained with rule weights, antecedent attribute weights, consequent belief degrees. R2 are trained alongside rule weights and antecedent attribute weights. R3 are trained with antecedent attributes weights and consequent belief degrees.

Optimal learning procedures are applied to obtain optimal values for the three learning parameters in R1. So, for training procedures, data from 200 patients are taken into account. The aim here is to transform the initial BRB into a trained BRB, so that the accuracy of the model is increased along with the correctness in prediction of CHIKV infection in patients. For instance, when R1 set of training parameters are applied, the total number of learning parameters with their optimal learning procedure, appears to consist of $((243 + 243 + (243) * 3) = 1215$ (Table 2).

Table 2. Training with rule weights, antecedent attribute weights and consequent belief degrees

Sl. no	Rule weight	Attribute weight	Belief degree	High	Medium	Low
0	0.056	1	0.4667	1	0	0
1	0.3	1	0.0667	0.95	0.05	0
2	0.3443	1	0.7333	0.9	0.07	0.03
3	0.456	1	0.8667	0.85	0.15	0
4	0.0567	1	0	0.7	0.3	0
5	0.3967	1	0.3333	0.7	0.1	0.2
6	0.5	1	0	0.9	0.08	0.02
...	...	...	...	...	...	...
243	0.75	1	0.214	0.2	0.3	0.5

Table 3. Training with rule weights and antecedent attribute weights

Sl. no	Rule weight	Antecedent attribute weight	High	Medium	Low
0	0.056	0.4667	1	0	0
1	0.3	0.0667	0.95	0.05	0
2	0.3443	0.7333	0.9	0.07	0.03
3	0.456	0.8667	0.85	0.15	0
4	0.0567	0	0.7	0.3	0
5	0.3967	0.3333	0.7	0.1	0.2
6	0.5	0	0.9	0.08	0.02
...	...	...	...	...	...
243	0.75	0.214	0.2	0.3	0.5

Similarly, the learning parameter sets of R2, which consists of rule weight and antecedent attribute weight is optimized by applying optimal learning procedure. The same number of training data found in R1 is used in R2. The optimal values obtained from both rule weight and antecedent attribute weight for each of the 243 rules are illustrated in Table 3. The rule weight and antecedent attribute weight of rule "1" which are 1 and 1 is converted to 0.056 and 0.4667 after training. So that the total number of learning parameters in R2, consists of $243 + 243 = 486$. Likewise, the training parameter sets of R3 comprising of rule weight and belief degrees. Table 4 illustrates the optimal values for the learning parameters of R3. In Table 4 the value of antecedent attribute weight and belief degree of rule 1 are changed to 0.578 and 0.466 respectively. The total number of learning parameters considered in case of R3 consist of $(243 + (243 * 3)) = 972$.

Table 4. Training with antecedent attribute weights and consequent belief degrees

Sl. no	Antecedent attribute weight	Consequent belief degree	High	Medium	Low
0	1	0.4667	1	0	0
1	1	0.0667	0.95	0.05	0
2	1	0.7333	0.9	0.07	0.03
3	1	0.8667	0.85	0.15	0
4	1	0	0.7	0.3	0
5	1	0.3333	0.7	0.1	0.2
6	1	0	0.9	0.08	0.02
...	...	...	...	...	...
243	1	0.214	0.2	0.3	0.5

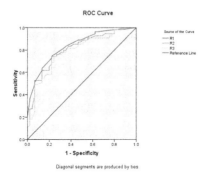

Fig. 4. Reliability comparison among R1, R2 and R3

4.1   Reliability of Trained BRBES

The ROC curves for each of the training parameters (R1, R2, and R3) are developed from the data of 100 patients (Fig. 4) as well considering initial BRB and Trained BRBES as illustrated in Table 5. The Area under the curve (AUC) against R1, R2, R3 training parameter sets as well as BRBES which uses initial

BRB is also demonstrated in Table 5. It is observed in the table that the value of AUC (0.837) for R1 training parameter sets is 1275, as it uses more number of learning parameter sets. The AUC value for R3 training parameter is the second largest (0.808) because it uses less number of umber learning parameters (972). In addition, the AUC for the R2 parameter sets (0.785) uses the least number of learning parameters. Thus, it can be deduced that number of learning parameters increases the accuracy. Moreover, the BRBES which uses initial BRB obtained less AUC value than trained BRBES. This is because the initial BRBES based on the survey is not much reliable. Thus the BRBES should persist to learn and train in order to generate more accurate prediction.

Table 5. Parameters R1, R2 and R3 for trained BRB

R. no (1)	(2)	(3)	(4)	(5)	(6)	Training parameter R1 result (%) (7)	Training parameter R2 result (%) (8)	Training parameter R3 result (%) (9)	Benchmark (10)
1	97	96	93	80	92	78.98	92.27	80.57	1
2	90	25	36	55	97	90.27	48.35	88.75	1
3	55	86	65	75	95.5	67.57	84.63	69.64	1
4	49	68	83	76	95	72.34	49.05	62.79	1
5	18	60	87	12	69	40.87	36.28	21.4	0

4.2   ROC for Trained BRB

The data of 250 patients have been obtained from various hospitals located in Dhaka and Chittagong. In the beginning, an interview was carried out where the patients questioned about their signs and symptoms of Chikungunya (Table 6).

Table 6. Reliability comparison among R1, R2 and R3

Test result	Area	Asymptotic 95% confidence interval	
		Lower bound	Upper bound
R1	0.837	0.760	0.914
R2	0.808	0.724	0.893
R3	0.785	0.694	0.875

4.3   Comparison of Accuracy of Trained and Non-trained BRBES Using Test Data

250 data is divided into a split ratio of 8:2 for training and testing, so that 200 and 50 data are allocated for training and testing the method. Data for testing

is applied to the initial BRBES as well as trained BERES, in order to enable comparison of accuracy. Figure 5 compares the original obsered output with that of the obtained from the initial BRBES, where it is noticed that the original data is significantly greater than that of the output of the initial BRBES. Figure 6 illustrates the real output data with the output obtained for trained BRBES, where the original output data is seen to lie closer to the output data of BRBES. Thus, from the two figures, it is deduced that the accuracy of trained BRBES is greater than that of the non-trained BRBES. For instance, the real output data of a patient can be deduced from the trained BRBES, to be under a 95% risk of Chikungunya. In contrast, from the initial BRBES for the same patient, is shown to have 90% chance of Chikungunya. Therefore, it can argued that better results are obtained from the trained BRBES compared to that of the non-trained BRBES.

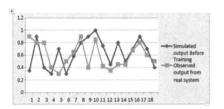

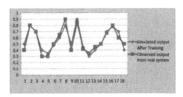

Fig. 5. Comparison among real system observed output and BRB (Before training)

Fig. 6. Comparison among real system observed output of the and BRB (After training)

4.4   Comparison among Deep learning and other Machine Learning Algorithm with BRBES

CNN, SVM, and RF are applied to compare the performance of BRBES. Each layer of CNN has two parameters, weights, and biases but BRBES uses three learning parameters namely, belief degree update, attribute weight and rule weight. BRBES produces better results than that seen in CNN. SVM is used to find optimal separating hyperplane that outputs the highest value for the training data. Without distributing input data this algorithm uses input data directly for prediction. As a result, SVM is unable to handle any kind of uncertainty. On the other hand, the use of RF resulted in an overfit model. This is because a large number of trees from the aftermath of uncertain data hindered the performance of RF.

Table 7 demonstrates the AUC's of Trained BRBES is 0.891, Non-trained BRBES is 0.878, CNN is 0.820, SVM is 0.810, and Random Forest is 0.744. By considering 95% CI, The lower limits and upper limits of AUC, where the CI occurs to be 95% for Trained and Non-Trained BRBES are 0.825-0.950 and 0.770-0.921 where CNN is 0.728-0.887, SVM is 0.716-0.878 and for Random Forest the value is 0.630-0.758.

Table 7. Comparison of AUC of distinctive learning techniques

Results	Trained	Non-trained	CNN	SVM	Random Forest
AUC	0.891	0.878	0.820	0.810	0.744
CI	0.825–0.950	0.770–0.921	0.728–0.887	0.716–0.878	0.630–0.758

4.5 ROC for Trained BRB

Figure 7 represents the ROC curves for Non-Trained BRBES, Trained BRBES, ANN, SVM, and Random Forest. Hence, from ROC it is observed that Trained BRBES gives more accurate output than ANN, SVM, and Random Forest. Not only that, but it also performs better than Non-trained BRBES.

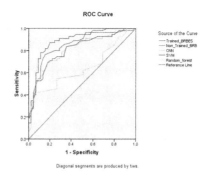

Fig. 7. Reliability comparison among BRBES, and other ML algorithms

5 Conclusion and Future Work

Chikungunya is still a concern worldwide, because of no vaccine. It is often misclassified as the signs and symptoms of Chikungunya are similar to other mosquito-borne diseases. The BRBES system proposed in this research will assist countries like Bangladesh where doctor to patient ratio is abysmally low. The goal of this particular research was to deduce a reliable system to accurately diagnose Chikungunya disease from uncertain clinical data in order to provide early treatment. This research work demonstrates the design, development, and application of a BRBES to assist patients alongside physicians to early detect CHIKV so that patients can attain accurate treatment. Moreover, the research outputs a trained BRBES which is able to handle various uncertainties associated with this disease. Also, it was observed that the optimal learning model minimizes the error between the observed and expected level of Chikungunya. The trained BRBES was also compared with initial BRBES and other deep learning and machine learning algorithms. Where the trained BRBES provided more accurate results compared to other methods.

In the future, this research aims to build larger real-time data gathered from wider geographical zones as well as increased referential value. An increased referential value will also ensure greater system validation and better performance of the system. Furthermore, to add a new dimension, other methods such as Transfer Learning will be introduced.

References

1. Adams, J., Brückner, H.: Wikipedia, sociology, and the promise and pitfalls of big data. Big Data Soc. **2**(2), 2053951715614332 (2015)
2. Ahmed, T.U., Jamil, M.N., Hossain, M.S., Andersson, K., Hossain, M.S.: An integrated real-time deep learning and belief rule base intelligent system to assess facial expression under uncertainty. In: 2020 Joint 9th International Conference on Informatics, Electronics & Vision (ICIEV) and 2020 4th International Conference on Imaging, Vision & Pattern Recognition (icIVPR), pp. 1–6. IEEE (2020)
3. Hossain, M.S., Akter, S.: Analyzing the repercussions of climate change on the outbreak of chikungunya in Bangladesh. J. Earth Sci. Geotech. Eng. **9**(1), 15–31 (2019)
4. Hossain, M.S., Ahmed, F., Andersson, K., et al.: A belief rule based expert system to assess tuberculosis under uncertainty. J. Med. Syst. **41**(3), 43 (2017)
5. Hossain, M.S., Al Hasan, A., Guha, S., Andersson, K.: A belief rule based expert system to predict earthquake under uncertainty. J. Wirel. Mob. Netw. Ubiquit. Comput. Dependable Appl. **9**(2), 26–41 (2018)
6. Hossain, M.S., Habib, I.B., Andersson, K.: A belief rule based expert system to diagnose dengue fever under uncertainty. In: 2017 Computing Conference, pp. 179–186. IEEE (2017)
7. Hossain, M.S., Khalid, M.S., Akter, S., Dey, S.: A belief rule-based expert system to diagnose influenza. In: 2014 9th International Forum on Strategic Technology (IFOST), pp. 113–116. IEEE (2014)
8. Hossain, M.S., Monrat, A.A., Hasan, M., Karim, R., Bhuiyan, T.A., Khalid, M.S.: A belief rule-based expert system to assess mental disorder under uncertainty. In: 2016 5th International Conference on Informatics, Electronics and Vision (ICIEV), pp. 1089–1094. IEEE (2016)
9. Hossain, M.S., Rahaman, S., Kor, A.L., Andersson, K., Pattinson, C.: A belief rule based expert system for datacenter PUE prediction under uncertainty. IEEE Trans. Sustain. Comput. **2**(2), 140–153 (2017)
10. Hossain, M.S., Rahaman, S., Mustafa, R., Andersson, K.: A belief rule-based expert system to assess suspicion of acute coronary syndrome (ACS) under uncertainty. Soft. Comput. **22**(22), 7571–7586 (2018)
11. Hossain, M.S., Sultana, Z., Nahar, L., Andersson, K.: An intelligent system to diagnose chikungunya under uncertainty. J. Wirel. Mob. Netw. Ubiquit. Comput. Dependable Appl. **10**(2), 37–54 (2019)
12. Jamil, M.N., Hossain, M.S., ul Islam, R., Andersson, K.: A belief rule based expert system for evaluating technological innovation capability of high-tech firms under uncertainty. In: 2019 Joint 8th International Conference on Informatics, Electronics & Vision (ICIEV) and 2019 3rd International Conference on Imaging, Vision & Pattern Recognition (icIVPR), pp. 330–335. IEEE (2019)
13. Kabir, S., Islam, R.U., Hossain, M.S., Andersson, K.: An integrated approach of belief rule base and deep learning to predict air pollution. Sensors **20**(7), 1956 (2020)

14. Kaiser, M.S., et al.: iWorksafe: towards healthy workplaces during Covid-19 with an intelligent pHealth app for industrial settings. IEEE Access **9**, 13814–13828 (2021)
15. Karim, R., Hossain, M.S., Khalid, M.S., Mustafa, R., Bhuiyan, T.A.: A belief rule-based expert system to assess bronchiolitis suspicion from signs and symptoms under uncertainty. In: Bi, Y., Kapoor, S., Bhatia, R. (eds.) IntelliSys 2016. LNNS, vol. 15, pp. 331–343. Springer, Cham (2018). https://doi.org/10.1007/978-3-319-56994-9_23
16. Lee, C.S., Wang, M.H.: A fuzzy expert system for diabetes decision support application. IEEE Trans. Syst. Man Cybern. Part B (Cybern.) **41**(1), 139–153 (2010)
17. Mahmud, M., Kaiser, M.S., McGinnity, T.M., Hussain, A.: Deep learning in mining biological data. Cogn. Comput. **13**(1), 1–33 (2021)
18. Mahmud, M., Kaiser, M.S., Hussain, A., Vassanelli, S.: Applications of deep learning and reinforcement learning to biological data. IEEE Trans. Neural Netw. Learn. Syst. **29**(6), 2063–2079 (2018)
19. Mazumder, S.H., Hossain, M.S., Andersson, K.: A belief rule-based expert system to assess multiple human reaction in the context of Facebook posts under uncertainty. In: 2021 International Conference on Information and Communication Technology for Sustainable Development (ICICT4SD), pp. 389–394. IEEE (2021)
20. Nisha, S.S., Sathik, M.M., Meeral, M.N.: Application, algorithm, tools directly related to deep learning. In: Handbook of Deep Learning in Biomedical Engineering, pp. 61–84. Elsevier (2021)
21. Rahaman, S., Hossain, M.S.: A belief rule based clinical decision support system to assess suspicion of heart failure from signs, symptoms and risk factors. In: 2013 International Conference on Informatics, Electronics and Vision (ICIEV), pp. 1–6. IEEE (2013)
22. Rahaman, S., Hossain, M.S.: A belief rule based (BRB) system to assess asthma suspicion. In: 16th International Conference on Computer and Information Technology, pp. 432–437. IEEE (2014)
23. Rahaman, S., Islam, M.M., Hossain, M.S.: A belief rule based clinical decision support system framework. In: 2014 17th International Conference on Computer and Information Technology (ICCIT), pp. 165–169. IEEE (2014)
24. Ul Islam, R., Andersson, K., Hossain, M.S.: A web based belief rule based expert system to predict flood. In: Proceedings of the 17th International Conference on Information Integration and Web-Based Applications & Services, pp. 1–8 (2015)
25. Vincent, P., Larochelle, H., Bengio, Y., Manzagol, P.A.: Extracting and composing robust features with denoising autoencoders. In: Proceedings of the 25th International Conference on Machine Learning, pp. 1096–1103 (2008)
26. Yang, J.B., Liu, J., Wang, J., Sii, H.S., Wang, H.W.: Belief rule-base inference methodology using the evidential reasoning approach-RIMER. IEEE Trans. Syst. Man Cybern.-Part A: Syst. Hum. **36**(2), 266–285 (2006)
27. Yang, J.B., Liu, J., Xu, D.L., Wang, J., Wang, H.: Optimization models for training belief-rule-based systems. IEEE Trans. Syst. Man Cybern.-Part A: Syst. Hum. **37**(4), 569–585 (2007)

Glaucoma Detection Using Inception Convolutional Neural Network V3

Tasnim Afroze[1] , Shumia Akther[1] ,
Mohammed Armanuzzaman Chowdhury[2] , Emam Hossain[1] ,
Mohammad Shahadat Hossain[2(✉)] , and Karl Andersson[3]

[1] Department of Computer Science and Engineering, Port City International
University, Chattogram 4202, Bangladesh
emam.hossain@portcity.edu.bd
[2] Department of Computer Science and Engineering, University of Chittagong,
Chattogram 4331, Bangladesh
hossain_ms@cu.ac.bd
[3] Pervasive and Mobile Computing Laboratory, Luleå University of Technology,
Skellefteå, Sweden
karl.andersson@ltu.se

Abstract. Glaucoma detection is an important research area in intelligent system and it plays an important role to medical field. Glaucoma can give rise to an irreversible blindness due to lack of proper diagnosis. Doctors need to perform many tests to diagnosis this threatening disease. It requires a lot of time and expense. Sometime affected people may not have any vision loss, at the early stage of glaucoma. For detecting glaucoma, we have built a model to lessen the time and cost. Our work introduces a CNN based Inception V3 model. We used total 6072 images. Among this image 2336 were glaucomatous and 3736 were normal fundus image. For training our model we took 5460 images and for testing we took 612 images. After that we obtained an accuracy of 0.8529 and a value of 0.9387 for AUC. For comparison, we used DenseNet121 and ResNet50 algorithm and got an accuracy of 0.8153 and 0.7761 respectively.

Keywords: Glaucoma detection · CNN · Inception V3

1 Introduction

Glaucoma is a complicated disease that damages optical nerve and causes irreversible blindness due to lack of proper diagnosis. This "sneak thief of sight" can affect anyone at any age. Even newborn babies can be affected. According to doctors, it grows in such a manner that patient does not experience any complication. By 2040, the number of glaucoma affected people likely to increase 111.8 million [2]. Glaucoma causes vision loss and blindness due to damage of optic nerve. Our optic nerve provides visual sensation to our brain from both eyes. We know, eyes continuously make aqueous humor and it fills the front part of eyes. If

M. Mahmud et al. (Eds.): AII 2021, CCIS 1435, pp. 17–28, 2021.
https://doi.org/10.1007/978-3-030-82269-9_2

the drainage channels of aqueous humor are blocked, the IOP (Intraocular pressure) increases and optic nerve may become permanently damaged. There are five major types of glaucoma: Open angle glaucoma, Angle Closure Glaucoma, Congenital Glaucoma, Normal Tension Glaucoma and Secondary Glaucoma. For glaucoma diagnosis, ophthalmologist need to perform a comprehensive examination of eye, including Tonometry, Gonioscopy, Ophthalmoscopy, Nerve fiber analysis and Perimetry. These diagnosis procedures are expensive and also time consuming. So, to cope with this great ocular problem, a CNN architecture will be approached for glaucoma detection.

Glaucoma is one of the most dangerous causes of blindness. Sometimes patient have no symptoms and the vision may remain 6/6 till late stage. Actually, there are no specific symptoms during early stage. Some patient may never have increased Intra-ocular pressure. Besides some patient with high Intra-ocular pressure may not diagnose glaucoma, which is called ocular hyper tension. Early detection of glaucoma associated with immediate treatment that has been shown to prevent major problems.

Vision loss caused by glaucoma is not reversible with treatment, even surgery cannot help to recover it. In USA, after cardiac attack and cancer, blindness is the third formidable health complication. Only the better awareness could prevent permanent visual disability. In this era of artificial intelligence, automated health care system has the capability to identify diseases within a short period. In order to serve the medical community, deep learning algorithm will help to detect glaucoma. Work flow for diagnosis glaucoma will be faster than the regular one. So affected people will get proper treatment during first stage of glaucoma. However, glaucoma is preventable if it is diagnosed early and effective treatment is provided. That is what motivated us to conduct this thesis.

2   Problem Statement

Eyes are important sensory organs that provides sight. Some parts of eyes are: cornea, sclera, choroid, iris, pupil, lens, ciliary muscle, suspensory ligament, conjunctiva, anterior chamber (between cornea and iris), posterior chamber (between iris and lens), macula, vitreous humour, aqueous humour, hyaloid canal, retina, optic nerve, optic disc, blood vessels, fovea.

Glaucoma is referred as an eye disease that damage optic nerve and cause vision loss. Optica nerve carries information that we can see through eye to brain. Optic nerve head is called optic disc, it connects retina and optic nerve. The center of optic disc is called optic cup. When the optic cup enlarges and occupy more area of optical disc then the cup to disc ratio (CDR) increases. When the cup to disc ratio is greater than normal range, the patient's eye is suspected as glaucomatous eye. Doctors need to perform many tests such as: Ophthalmic Test, Tonometry, Ophthalmoscopy, Perimetry, Pachymetry, Gonioscopy. After getting results from different test, doctor have to decide whether it is a glaucomatous eye or not. Careful evolution is important to detect glaucoma and there is a high chance of not getting accurate result due to lack of skill. This work proposes an efficient method for detecting glaucoma which will lessen time and costs [25] at the same time in order to facilitate ophthalmologists and optometrists.

⇒ An automated system for glaucoma diagnosis.
⇒ Applied augmentation technique for getting varied images.
⇒ Used large amount of image data.
⇒ Collected images from different available data sets.
⇒ Compared with other popular CNN methods.

3   Literature Review

O. J. Afolabi et al. [5] introduced a redesigned U-Net model named U-Net Lite and XGB (extreme gradient boost) algorithm. From RIM ONE V3 and DRISTI-GS the extreme gradient boost algorithm achieved an accuracy of 88.6 and an AUC-ROC value of 93.6. Chaudhary P. K, and Pachori R. B. [10] has proposed the order zero and order one 2D-FBSE-EWT (two dimensional Fourier-Bessel series expansion based empirical wavelet transform) methods at quarter, half and full frequency scales which are used for disintegrating fundus image into consequential sub-images. Then from obtained sub-images, proposed method 1: a conventional ML based method and proposed method 2: an ensemble ResNet50 based method, are studied for detection. In this paper [23], S Pathan et al. proposed image processing methods are used to define an automated framework for Computer Aided Diagnosis (CAD) of glaucoma. Here pre-processing algorithm includes the identification and exclusion of blood vessels for effective OD and OC segmentation. The use of a decision tree classifier and a circle finder approach helped in robust OD segmentation. The proposed OC segmentation method aims to enhance the OC region by creating a new channel due to reduced variability between the pixels of OD and OC. The obtained threshold value for the segmentation algorithms is not limited to a single dataset. Feature extraction requires domain knowledge of glaucoma, such as the CDR and NRR area, as well as statistical color and texture features. The classifiers used for classification are SVM, ANN, and AdaBoost classifier ensemble with dynamic selection methods for identifying fundus images whether it is affected or not. A ten-fold cross validation is also performed for the ensemble of AdaBoost classifiers with dynamic selection methods, SVM, and ANN. In this paper, Mufti Mahmud et al. [20] stated that overnight advances in hardware based technologies during the previous many years have opened up additional opportunities for life researchers to assemble multimodal data in different applications, for example, omics, clinical imaging, bioimaging and (cerebrum/body)- machine interfaces which have created novel freedoms for advancement of devoted information escalated AI strategies. Specifically, recent research in reinforcement learning, deep learning, and their combination promise to advance the future of AI. Mufti Mahmud et al.discussed about different CNN architectures [19] and also stated that diverse biological data from various application domains is multi-modal, multidimensional, and complex in nature. The author included that "Currently, a massive amount of such data is publicly available". The availability of these data came with a significant challenge in analyzing and recognizing patterns in them, which necessitated the use of sophisticated machine learning [21] tools. In paper [28] Saxena et al. proposed an architecture that differentiates between the patterns for glaucoma and non-glaucoma using of the CNN. The total work was evaluated within six layers. Authors used ROI extraction, dropout, data-augmentation for preprocessing of data. For the experiments, authors used SCES and ORIGA data set. They got .822 and .882 values for the ORIGA and SCES data set respectively. In paper [22] Palakvangsa-Na-Ayudhya et al. proposed an automated system using Mask Regional - Convolutional Neural Network [32]. It is an advancement of Faster R-CNN by joining a branch for predicting segmented masks on each ROI along with the existing branch for classify an object and bounding box regression. This automatic screening system calculates CDR. They used four datasets: Drishti GS1 and RIMONE (r1, r2, r3). They used four datasets individually and also in a combined manner. They got values for 50 epochs of Individual dataset: (RIM One r3 0.66, Drishti-GS1 0.73, RIM One r1 0.74, RIM One r2 0.78) and for 100 epochs (RIM One r3 0.68, Drishti-GS1 0.75, RIM One r1 0.75, RIM One r2 0.85). With the computational time of 8 h, 4 h and 2 h they obtained 0.68(400 epoch), 0.71(200 epoch), 0.64(100 epoch) respectively for combined dataset. Then they set up the epochs to 200 with the 10-fold cross validation and achieved accuracy of 0.78. Pinos-Velez et al. [24] diagnosed glaucoma by the using of ISNT rule. In a normal eye CDR ratio is below 0.3. ISNT rule was used for measure the width of retinal rim. Juneja, M et al. proposed [17] an approach based on deep learning [18] which is disc cup segmentation glaucoma network (DC-GNet). This segmentation network extracts the CDR, DDLS and ISNT feature from fundus images. The input images to the CNN model were cropped to 512–512 pixels and resized to 256–256 pixels. This network has 28 layers: pooling layers, drop out layers, 2D convolutional layers and up sampling layers. An accuracy of 0.937 (Dristi dataset) and 0.996 (RIM One dataset) were achieved from segmentation of disc. And from cup segmentation technique they got an accuracy of 0.900 (Dristi dataset) and 0.978 (RIM One dataset). Debasree Sarkar and Soumen Das [27] proposed a method which used media filter for noise reduction. Thresholding is applied to extract to OD (optic disc) and OC (optic cup). By using RIM-ONE data set they got an accuracy of 97.58. A. Serener and S. Serte proposed a system [29] detects early and advanced glaucoma automatically. They applied ResNet50 and GoogLeNet algorithm and got an accuracy of 79 and 83 respectively.

4   Method

According to Fig. 1, After collecting fundus images, divided into two set: training and testing images. We have trained our model after applying augmentation techniques. During the training time we took 600 images for validating our model from training images. Then evaluated it using test images.

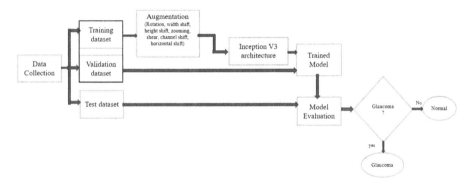

Fig. 1. System architecture.

4.1   Data Collection

For this work, we have collected images from ACRIMA dataset [1], LAG dataset [3] and Glaucoma Data set and combined them.

Table 1. Dataset details.

Training	5460 images	2036 glaucomatous fundus 3424 normal fundus
Test	612 images	300 glaucomatous fundus 312 normal fundus
Total	6072 images	Total 2336 glaucomatous fundus Total 3736 normal fundus

4.2   Data Augmentation

Data augmentation is a process which helps to increase the diversity of data for training a model without gathering new data. It acts as a regularizer. It enhance the performance of the model [14]. It helps to avoid over-fitting problem. Neural network treats augmented images as distinct images. The deep learning neural network library of Keras provides the facility of data augmentation. We augmented our data using ImageDataGenerator class. We applied rotation, width shift, height shift, zooming, sheer, channel shift and horizontal shift. After applying the augmentation [30] technique more image data were generated. We used data augmentation technique [12] only for our training dataset. And for evaluating our model we used original images rather than augmented images. Shifting of an image means moving all pixels in one direction. Two types of shift can be done width shift and height shift. Shifting helps us to change the position of an object. Flipping of an image means reversing the columns or rows of pixels in case of horizontal or vertical flip respectively. It is similar to rotating an object left to right or up to down. Rotation is done by rotating an image clockwise or

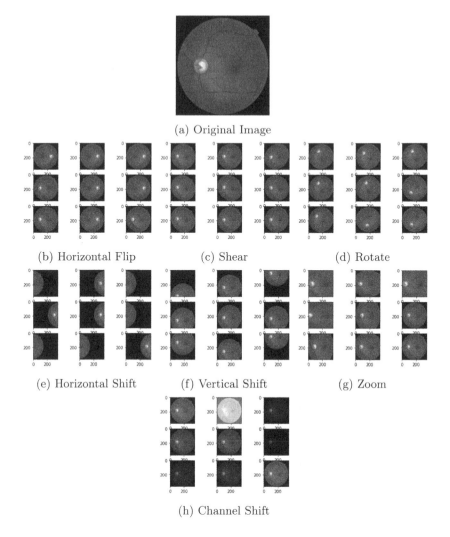

(a) Original Image

(b) Horizontal Flip   (c) Shear   (d) Rotate

(e) Horizontal Shift   (f) Vertical Shift   (g) Zoom

(h) Channel Shift

Fig. 2. Augmented Images

anticlockwise within 0 to 360°. In zooming technique, images are either zooms in or zooms out. Value less than 1 used to zoom in and greater than 1 zooms outs an image and value equals to 1 does not have any effect. Shearing of an image means shifting a specific part of the image like a parallelogram. In shear one axis remains fixed. In channel shift, RGB channel values are shifted randomly.

Figure 2 shows an original fundus image and images after applying flipping, shearing, rotating, shifting, zooming and channel shifting on the original image.

4.3   Inception V3

Inception V3 [31] is a CNN pre trained model [9]. It is computationally more efficient and focuses on using less computational power. It is a multi-level feature extractor. Inception V3 model is a collection of symmetric and asymmetric building blocks. It includes convolution, max pooling, average pooling, dropouts, concats and fully connected layers. By using Softmax, loss is computed. A schematic diagram is given below: [16]. We have collected images according to Table 1, then applied augmentation technique [7] according to Sect. 4.2 for getting varied fundus images. We trained Inception V3 model using augmented training dataset. Our model has total 312 layers: 1 input layer, 94 Cov2d layer, 94 batch normalization layer, 94 activation layer, 11 mixed layer, 8 average pooling layer, 4 max pooling layers, 2 concatenate layer, 3 global average pooling layer, 1 dense layer. We evaluated our model using test fundus images. Finally, our model will able to detect fundus images whether it is normal or glaucomatous.

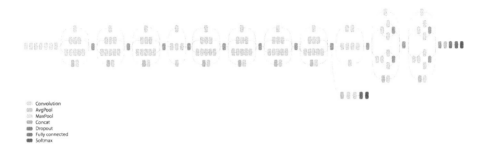

Fig. 3. Schematic diagram of Inception V3

5   Results

5.1   Evaluation Criteria

There are different performance [13] matrices for evaluating a model. In this work we utilize Confusion matrix, Accuracy, Precision, Recall, Specificity, F1 score to evaluate the performance. Confusion matrix gives a clear idea of values like True Positives, False Positives, True Negatives and False Negative.

- True Negative (TN): When the actual value was negative and predicted negative.
- True Positive (TP): When the actual value was positive and predicted positive.
- False Negative (FN): When the actual value was positive but predicted negative.

– False Positive (FP): When the actual value was negative but predicted positive.

$$Accuracy = (TP + TN)/(TP + TN + FP + FN) \qquad (1)$$

$$Specificity = TN/(TN + FP) \qquad (2)$$

$$Recall = TP/(TP + FN) \qquad (3)$$

$$Precision = TP/(TP + FP) \qquad (4)$$

$$F1 = 2TP/(2TP + FP + FN) \qquad (5)$$

5.2   Comparison of Different Types of CNN Model

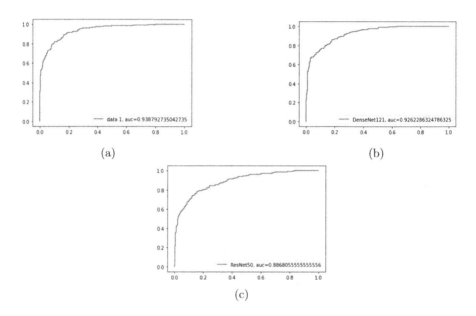

(a)   (b)

(c)

Fig. 4. AUC Curve (a) Inception V3 (b) Densenet121 (c) Resnet50

Area under curve given in Fig. 4 measures the capability of a classifier to separate between classes. Higher the value of AUC better the classifier and its performance. AUC range value lies between 0 to 1. It is an important evaluation criterion. We can notice that Fig. 3(a) has the higher AUC value for Inception v3 which is 0.9387.

From Table 2 and Fig. 5, we can notice that due to uneven class distribution, precision value (normal class) and recall value (glaucoma class) of DenseNet121 has highest value than other two models. We know F1 score is called the weighted

Table 2. Performance of various models.

Model	Test accuracy	Class name	Precision	Recall	F1 score
Inception V3	0.8529	Glaucoma	0.86	0.85	0.85
		Normal	0.85	0.86	0.86
DenseNet 121	0.8153	Glaucoma	0.74	0.96	0.84
		Normal	0.95	0.68	0.79
ResNet50	0.7761	Glaucoma	0.83	0.68	0.75
		Normal	0.74	0.87	0.80

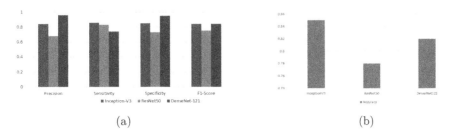

(a)   (b)

Fig. 5. Comparison between Inception-V3, ResNet50 DenseNet121.

average of precision and recall. So, for coping with this uneven class we should consider F1 score rather than precision and recall value. According to Table 2, Fig. 4, Fig. 5 we can say Inception V3 model has highest test accuracy, AUC value and F1 score. So Inception V3 is the best classifier for this problem.

6   Conclusion

Glaucoma is complication that is associated with the damage of optic nerve and causes permanent blindness. This approach to medical image processing technology [26] will enlarge the application of detecting glaucoma. This thesis work will lead to the computer-generated result to improve the clinician's judgment standard of glaucoma detection. This model can detect more normal fundus images than glaucomatous image due to higher number of normal fundus images in dataset. We got less accuracy than other previous work as we took a huge amount of data than other. Besides our dataset is a collection of different publicly available dataset.

Though optic disc is the brightest part of the fundus, we did not use multi-level segmentation [4] technique. Also, our target classes were not equally distributed with positive and negative samples.

In future we will train this model using good quality images and for coping with data imbalance issue we will introduce resampling technique to our model. We have a plan to build different integrated models to improve the detection of glaucoma. For the integration, we will use different algorithms and techniques along with Inception V3 like CNN, RNN, LSTM [11], deep learning [6], belief rule base [8,15], etc. Besides we plan to extend our study of convolutional neural network to multiple ocular diseases detection like cataract, retinal detachment, diabetic retinopathy.

References

1. figshare. https://rb.gy/vkuly5. Accessed 21 Apr 2021
2. World Glaucoma Association. https://www.glaucomapatients.org/basic/statistics/. Accessed 21 Apr 2021
3. Kaggle. https://www.kaggle.com/sreeharims/glaucoma-dataset. Accessed 21 Apr 2021
4. Abedin, M.Z., Nath, A.C., Dhar, P., Deb, K., Hossain, M.S.: License plate recognition system based on contour properties and deep learning model. In: 2017 IEEE Region 10 Humanitarian Technology Conference (R10-HTC), pp. 590–593. IEEE (2017)
5. Afolabi, O.J., Mabuza-Hocquet, G.P., Nelwamondo, F.V., Paul, B.S.: The use of U-Net lite and extreme gradient boost (XGB) for glaucoma detection. IEEE Access 9, 47411–47424 (2021). https://doi.org/10.1109/ACCESS.2021.3068204
6. Ahmed, T.U., Hossain, M.S., Alam, M.J., Andersson, K.: An integrated CNN-RNN framework to assess road crack. In: 2019 22nd International Conference on Computer and Information Technology (ICCIT), pp. 1–6. IEEE (2019)
7. Ahmed, T.U., Hossain, S., Hossain, M.S., ul Islam, R., Andersson, K.: Facial expression recognition using convolutional neural network with data augmentation. In: 2019 Joint 8th International Conference on Informatics, Electronics & Vision (ICIEV) and 2019 3rd International Conference on Imaging, Vision & Pattern Recognition (icIVPR), pp. 336–341. IEEE (2019)
8. Ahmed, T.U., Jamil, M.N., Hossain, M.S., Andersson, K., Hossain, M.S.: An integrated real-time deep learning and belief rule base intelligent system to assess facial expression under uncertainty. In: 2020 Joint 9th International Conference on Informatics, Electronics & Vision (ICIEV) and 2020 4th International Conference on Imaging, Vision & Pattern Recognition (icIVPR), pp. 1–6. IEEE (2020)
9. Basnin, N., Nahar, L., Hossain, M.S.: An integrated CNN-LSTM model for micro hand gesture recognition. In: Vasant, P., Zelinka, I., Weber, G.-W. (eds.) ICO 2020. AISC, vol. 1324, pp. 379–392. Springer, Cham (2021). https://doi.org/10.1007/978-3-030-68154-8_35
10. Chaudhary, P.K., Pachori, R.B.: Automatic diagnosis of glaucoma using two-dimensional Fourier-Bessel series expansion based empirical wavelet transform. Biomed. Signal Process. Control 64, 102237 (2021)
11. Chowdhury, R.R., Hossain, M.S., Hossain, S., Andersson, K.: Analyzing sentiment of movie reviews in bangla by applying machine learning techniques. In: 2019 International Conference on Bangla Speech and Language Processing (ICBSLP), pp. 1–6. IEEE (2019)
12. Chowdhury, R.R., Hossain, M.S., ul Islam, R., Andersson, K., Hossain, S.: Bangla handwritten character recognition using convolutional neural network with data augmentation. In: 2019 Joint 8th International Conference on Informatics, Electronics & Vision (ICIEV) and 2019 3rd International Conference on Imaging, Vision & Pattern Recognition (icIVPR), pp. 318–323. IEEE (2019)

13. Hossain, E., Shariff, M.A.U., Hossain, M.S., Andersson, K.: A novel deep learning approach to predict air quality index. In: Kaiser, M.S., Bandyopadhyay, A., Mahmud, M., Ray, K. (eds.) Proceedings of International Conference on Trends in Computational and Cognitive Engineering. AISC, vol. 1309, pp. 367–381. Springer, Singapore (2021). https://doi.org/10.1007/978-981-33-4673-4_29
14. Islam, M.Z., Hossain, M.S., ul Islam, R., Andersson, K.: Static hand gesture recognition using convolutional neural network with data augmentation. In: 2019 Joint 8th International Conference on Informatics, Electronics & Vision (ICIEV) and 2019 3rd International Conference on Imaging, Vision & Pattern Recognition (icIVPR), pp. 324–329. IEEE (2019)
15. Islam, R.U., Hossain, M.S., Andersson, K.: A deep learning inspired belief rule-based expert system. IEEE Access 8, 190637–190651 (2020)
16. Jon Shlens, S.R.S.: https://ai.googleblog.com/2016/03/train-your-own-image-classifier-with.html. Accessed 21 Apr 2021
17. Juneja, M., Thakur, S., Wani, A., Uniyal, A., Thakur, N., Jindal, P.: DC-Gnet for detection of glaucoma in retinal fundus imaging. Mach. Vis. Appl. 31, 1–14 (2020). https://doi.org/10.1007/s00138-020-01085-2
18. Kabir, S., Islam, R.U., Hossain, M.S., Andersson, K.: An integrated approach of belief rule base and deep learning to predict air pollution. Sensors 20(7), 1956 (2020)
19. Mahmud, M., Kaiser, M.S., McGinnity, T.M., Hussain, A.: Deep learning in mining biological data. Cogn. Comput. 13(1), 1–33 (2020). https://doi.org/10.1007/s12559-020-09773-x
20. Mahmud, M., Kaiser, M.S., Hussain, A., Vassanelli, S.: Applications of deep learning and reinforcement learning to biological data. IEEE Trans. Neural Netw. Learn. Syst. 29(6), 2063–2079 (2018). https://doi.org/10.1109/TNNLS.2018.2790388
21. Nahar, N., Hossain, M.S., Andersson, K.: A machine learning based fall detection for elderly people with neurodegenerative disorders. In: Mahmud, M., Vassanelli, S., Kaiser, M.S., Zhong, N. (eds.) BI 2020. LNCS (LNAI), vol. 12241, pp. 194–203. Springer, Cham (2020). https://doi.org/10.1007/978-3-030-59277-6_18
22. Palakvangsa-Na-Ayudhya, S., Sapthamrong, T., Sunthornwutthikrai, K., Sakiyalak, D.: Glaucoviz: assisting system for early glaucoma detection using mask R-CNN. In: 2020 17th International Conference on Electrical Engineering/Electronics, Computer, Telecommunications and Information Technology (ECTI-CON), pp. 364–367. IEEE (2020)
23. Pathan, S., Kumar, P., Pai, R.M., Bhandary, S.V.: Automated segmentation and classification of retinal features for glaucoma diagnosis. Biomed. Signal Process. Control 63, 102244 (2021)
24. Pinos-Velez, E., Flores-Rivera, M., Ipanque-Alama, W., Herrera-Alvarez, D., Chacon, C., Serpa-Andrade, L.: Implementation of support tools for the presumptive diagnosis of glaucoma through identification and processing of medical images of the human eye. In: 2018 IEEE International Systems Engineering Symposium (ISSE), pp. 1–5. IEEE (2018)
25. Rahaman, S., Hossain, M.S.: A belief rule based clinical decision support system to assess suspicion of heart failure from signs, symptoms and risk factors. In: 2013 International Conference on Informatics, Electronics and Vision (ICIEV), pp. 1–6. IEEE (2013)
26. Rezaoana, N., Hossain, M.S., Andersson, K.: Detection and classification of skin cancer by using a parallel CNN model. In: 2020 IEEE International Women in Engineering (WIE) Conference on Electrical and Computer Engineering (WIECON-ECE), pp. 380–386. IEEE (2020)

27. Sarkar, D., Das, S.: Automated glaucoma detection of medical image using biogeography based optimization. In: Bhattacharya, I., Chakrabarti, S., Reehal, H.S., Lakshminarayanan, V. (eds.) Advances in Optical Science and Engineering. SPP, vol. 194, pp. 381–388. Springer, Singapore (2017). https://doi.org/10.1007/978-981-10-3908-9_46

28. Saxena, A., Vyas, A., Parashar, L., Singh, U.: A glaucoma detection using convolutional neural network. In: 2020 International Conference on Electronics and Sustainable Communication Systems (ICESC), pp. 815–820. IEEE (2020)

29. Serener, A., Serte, S.: Transfer learning for early and advanced glaucoma detection with convolutional neural networks. In: 2019 Medical Technologies Congress (TIPTEKNO), pp. 1–4. IEEE (2019)

30. Shorten, C., Khoshgoftaar, T.M.: A survey on image data augmentation for deep learning. J. Big Data 6(1), 1–48 (2019)

31. Szegedy, C., Vanhoucke, V., Ioffe, S., Shlens, J., Wojna, Z.: Rethinking the inception architecture for computer vision. In: Proceedings of the IEEE Conference on Computer Vision and Pattern Recognition (CVPR) (2016)

32. Zisad, S.N., Hossain, M.S., Andersson, K.: Speech emotion recognition in neurological disorders using convolutional neural network. In: Mahmud, M., Vassanelli, S., Kaiser, M.S., Zhong, N. (eds.) BI 2020. LNCS (LNAI), vol. 12241, pp. 287–296. Springer, Cham (2020). https://doi.org/10.1007/978-3-030-59277-6_26

*i*ConDet: An Intelligent Portable Healthcare App for the Detection of Conjunctivitis

Prateeti Mukherjee[1] , Ishita Bhattacharyya[1], Meghma Mullick[1] ,
Rahul Kumar[1] , Nilanjana Dutta Roy[1(✉)] , and Mufti Mahmud[2,3(✉)]

[1] Department of Computer Science and Engineering,
Institute of Engineering and Management, Kolkata, India
nilanjana.duttaroy@iemcal.com
[2] Department of Computer Science, Nottingham Trent University,
Clifton, Nottingham NG11 8NS, UK
mufti.mahmud@ntu.ac.uk
[3] Medical Technologies Innovation Facilities, Nottingham Trent University,
Clifton, Nottingham NG11 8NS, UK

Abstract. Conjunctivitis is a common ocular disease characterized by infection or swelling in the outer membrane of human eye. This contagious ocular disease could be controlled and well treated by medicines depending upon it's category. To realize the connection between Conjunctivitis and other viral diseases, even for COVID-19, timely detection plays an important role. In this study, we have designed a mobile healthcare application (*i*ConDet) through which initial level of Conjunctivitis detection is possible. Deep learning techniques have been used upon the Conjunctivitis dataset prepared by us in support of the claim and to achieve the desired accuracy of 84%.

Keywords: Conjunctivitis · Mobile application · Deep learning · Transfer learning · Machine learning

1 Introduction

Conjunctiva is the thin clear outer layer of human eye which projects it from many aspects. Inflammation on it which causes irritation, itching, swelling and red eyes, is commonly termed as Conjunctivitis or pink eye. Viral and bacterial infections are the root causes of this highly contagious ocular disease. Red eyes with gritty sensations may last for 3 to 5 days with watery discharge for viral infections which may be treated with eye drops. Another category of it is the bacterial infection with thick, yellow-green discharge which may crust the eyes, can be treated with antibiotics. Some seasonal trends have been observed for the occurrence of the disease. However, it may be seen throughout the year. The

---

P. Mukherjee, I. Bhattacharyya and M. Mullick—Contributed equally.

© Springer Nature Switzerland AG 2021
M. Mahmud et al. (Eds.): AII 2021, CCIS 1435, pp. 29–42, 2021.
https://doi.org/10.1007/978-3-030-82269-9_3

disease is a common one and can easily be treated with some available medicines. During this COVID-19 pandemic, the occurrence of the pink eye or the Conjunctivitis has been observed in some positive cases [4]. So, we have taken an initiative to focus on the detection of Conjunctivitis by applying machine learning techniques. The presence of the pink eye will be detected through a mobile and a web based application designed specifically for this purpose. This study has been done as a preliminary preventive measure from the deadly COVID-19 disease. The speciality of this work is the development of a healthcare mobile and web application (iConDet). To make the Conjunctivitis detection process easy and accessible during this pandemic situation, iConDet comes as a useful solution. This Android application is able to adjust and perform necessary pre-processing of the eye images after capturing it through the mobile camera. It's sole responsibility is to send the eye images to the background for further processing and to display the result back to the screen, refer Fig. 3. The preliminary development of the application is successful in performing a binary classification using deep learning algorithms. Presently, it can differentiate between healthy eyes and the infected eyes (Fig. 4) captured by mobile camera. Nevertheless, the severity level classification of Conjunctivitis, along with the connection with other diseases, will be handled in future in the advanced version of iConDet. However, the challenge was to find the working Conjunctivitis dataset as a scarcity of it has been observed. So, We prepared our own dataset to train the model accordingly and to achieve the goal. We have collected data from google and from few of our acquainted eye specialists and thus, have been able to get around 150 images to help us frame a basic dataset. The data is labelled in a binary system where we have two types of data, the healthy eye and the infected eye.

The main contribution of the work can be summarised as follows:

– Creation of a new dataset with images of healthy and infected eyes.
– Labelling the newly created dataset and prepare it to be used with machine learning models.
– Development of a new mobile application suitable for Andriod devices.
– Generate a pretrained machine learning model suitable for the classification of input images to appropriate classes.

The organization of the rest of the paper is as follows: Sect. 2 covers the literature review. The complete methodology has been defined in Sect. 3. Results and discussions are shown in Sect. 4 and Sect. 5 draws the final conclusion.

2   Related Work

A doctor can often determine whether a virus, bacterium, or allergen is causing the conjunctivitis (pink eye) based on patient history, symptoms, and an examination of the eye. Conjunctivitis always involves eye redness or swelling, but it also has other symptoms that can vary depending on the cause. These symptoms can help a healthcare professional diagnose the cause of conjunctivitis. However, it can sometimes be difficult to make a firm diagnosis because some symptoms are the same no matter the cause. It can also sometimes be difficult to determine the cause without doing laboratory testing. However, nowadays data driven approach is used for the detection of conjunctivitis and other eye diseases using Machine learning and Deep learning techniques.

For an automated, fast and cost-effective diagnosis of conjunctivitis by the physicians, digital image processing (DIP) technique has been used [4]. To diagnose conjunctivitis, the vascularization and intensity of redness in pink eyes have been measured after segmenting the region of infection from the corneal images. This method detects eye infections and isolates potentially contagious patients to an accuracy of 93%. This high accuracy rate was achieved by isolating the sclera region using the automated GrabCut method that identifies the seed region from the image itself. A group of researchers used pre-processing for specified eye disease images which is followed by feature extraction and classification [8]. The image is classified as cataract disease, conjunctivitis disease and normal eye using minimum distance classifier. The authors composed an automated image processing technique that can identify conjunctivitis infected eye from a normal eye and classify it according to its type (bacterial, viral or allergic). Some statistical and texture features were used, followed by PCA for extraction of discriminatory features and then classified using supervised learning method such as multi-class SVM and KNN. The intensity of the infected eyes were also calculated using the significant red plane. Plotconfusion was used to calculate the accuracy and a high accuracy was achieved using this method. This method is efficient and cost-effective [14].

Another group of researchers [1] have proposed a novel approach to provide an automated eye disease recognition system using visually observable symptoms. They have applied digital image processing techniques and machine learning techniques such as deep convolution neural network (DCNN) and support vector machine (SVM) and the principal component analysis and t-distributed stochastic neighbor embedding methods for better feature selection. The proposed system automatically divides the facial components from the frontal facial image and extracts the eye part. The proposed method analyzes and classifies seven eye diseases including cataracts, trachoma, conjunctivitis, corneal ulcer, ectropion, periorbital cellulitis, and Bitot's spot of vitamin A deficiency. From the experimental results, it is seen that the DCNN model outperforms SVM models. The average accuracy rate of DCNN model is 98.79% with sensitivity of 97% and specificity of 99%.

Some researchers [13] carried out the work based on computer-aided diagnosis (CAD) where deep learning algorithm is applied for processing, image segmentation, and classification. Fuzzy technique was used for effective image segmentation. Data augmentation technique has been used for solving the fitting problem. Another group of researchers proposed an algorithm [11] that segregates between cataract, conjunctivitis and normal eye. The proposed approach consider the features of an optical eye image such as the big ring area, small ring area of the lens, the eye ellipse and the intensity of the affected area for computation. It takes the image of an eye as input and tells if it is normal or has any diseases. All the algorithms discussed in this context are implemented using OpenCV library.

To make the ocular detection process easy and portable, some researchers have developed a mobile and an web based application [12]. They claim to detect Cataract and Conjunctivitis through the application using image processing and deep learning techniques. They have used image preprocessing techniques and segmentation, followed by training a CNN model with a dataset of 150 images and with an accuracy of 83.3%. However, it is hard to get good accuracy in their mobile application as proper distance from the camera and image adjustment can not be maintained every time.

Various applications of Deep Learning, Reinforcement Learning, and deep reinforcement learning techniques in biological data mining, have been explored in [7]. It also addresses the open issues in challenging research areas and suggests a perspective on future development of the topic.

Analysing patterns in data from diverse biological domains using deep learning has been proposed by another research team [6]. It investigates the different Deep Learning architectures' applications to these data. Then an exploration of available open access data sources pertaining to the three data types i.e. images, signals and sequences along with popular open-source Deep Learning tools applicable to these data.The tools are also compared on the basis of qualitative, quantitative, and benchmarking perspectives.

Another work provides an overview of Convolutional Neural Network, the most widely used Deep Learning technique and its application to segment different regions of the human brain from Magnetic Resonance Imaging [2]. A quantitative analysis of the reviewed techniques is provided with a rich discussion on their performance.

Some researchers proposed a deep learning model which performs a critical examination and comparison of performances of the existing deep learning (DL)-based methods to detect neurological disorders [9]. They have especially focused on Alzheimer's disease, Parkinson's disease and schizophrenia-from MRI data acquired by using different modalities like functional and structural MRI. This comparative performance analysis of various Deep Learning architectures across different disorders and imaging modes suggests that the Convolutional Neural Network outperforms other methods in detecting neurological disorders.

3   Methodology

3.1   Proposed Pipeline

The overall architecture comprises of the following:

- The end-user clicks a photograph of the concerned individual's eye and uploads the image to the *i*ConDet application.
- The image is transferred to a bucket storage unit with policies that grant access rights to an external server, wherein the computations shall be performed.

- The image is retrieved from the aforementioned bucket and is subjected to various transformations as part of image pre-processing methodologies.
- It is then supplied to the Machine Learning Model that comprises of pre-trained CNNs, further fine-tuned on the target domain.
- Finally, the Model outputs the result of binary classification, indicative of either healthy or infected eye. This diagnosis is supplied to the application and displayed to the end-user (Fig. 1).

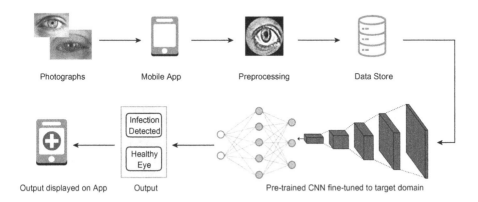

Fig. 1. Block diagram of the *i*ConDet pHealth app's detection pipeline.

3.2 Image Pre-processing

Considering the small size of the dataset, we aim to reduce the possibility of over-fitting, wherever possible. In terms of Image pre-processing, this implies careful selection of relevant features. Further, it also useful to extend the dataset with synthetic samples.

To address the former, we note that when cameras of varying aspect ratios are used to obtain images, certain images have areas that do not contain information relevant for prediction, such as structures surrounding the eye, iris patterns, etc. However, the sizes of such areas are seldom uniform. To address this, we employ a cropping function that performs pixel intensity-based marking. Image segmentation is then performed using colour spaces, wherein, upper and lower masks are identified for varying hues of red, and a full masking is done to obtain a rough segmentation. Furthermore, a mask of the image to be created by selecting rows and columns in which all pixels exceed the intensity threshold, aiding the removal of vertical or horizontal rectangular areas that do not contain pertinent information. Another area of concern is the shape of the eye, that is dependant on image parameters. Since the size and shape of structures are important cues in ocular disease identification, it is crucial to standardize these shapes. To facilitate this, we develop another function that performs a circular crop around the image centre.

In order to generate synthetic samples, we perform the following operations during training:

- Flip randomly selected samples horizontally
- Flip randomly selected samples vertically
- Rotate randomly selected samples in the range $[-360°, +360°]$

Given that there exists a soft guarantee that minor perturbations, such as the ones listed above, do not affect the classification label, this technique of data augmentation works well in reducing the chances of over-fitting.

3.3   Machine Learning Model

The small size of the data set discourages end-to-end training of deep learning models, since a greater number of parameters than samples would lead to poor performance.

This motivates the use of Transfer Learning; a popular approach in Deep Learning research for task adaptation and learning in low data regimes. To perform transfer learning, we use an EfficientNet pre-trained on the ImageNet dataset and freeze all but the last few layers (i.e. do not perform gradient updates on them) and train only the final layers of the model for our specific data set. We choose an ImageNet-trained model as our substrate because of the size and diversity of the data, with 1 billion samples and 10,000 categories. The volume and variety of the ImageNet data set enables the intermediate layers of the pre-trained EfficientNet to capture rich and highly discriminative image features, which can then be fine-tuned to suit our needs, using a smaller sub-network comprising of the final layers.

The modeling pipeline primarily comprises of the following stages:

- **Pre-training:** Since the data set is formed of a limited number of images, we first pre-train the model
- **Fine-tuning:** The fine-tuning is performed on the target data set. Cross-validation technique is used and modeling decisions are made based on the performance of out-of-fold predictions.

Pre-training. Transfer learning is adopted to avoid training a complex neural architecture from scratch, which, given the limited number of samples, is an infeasible task. Further, transfer learning also reduces the possibility of over-fitting, given that the technique itself serves the purpose of data extension. The fundamental idea behind Transfer Learning is to pre-train a model on a different data, called the source domain, and fine-tune it on a relevant data set, called the target domain.

While the ImageNet database is a suitable candidate for source data set, images are substantially different from the ocular images we wish to classify.

Therefore, in addition to the weights supplied during initialization, the ImageNet is required to learn from the target domain in order to transfer knowledge of image patterns.

We adopt the following pipeline:

- Initialize weights from a CNN trained on ImageNet
- Train on a larger data set to identify ocular structures
- Fine-tune on the target data set

In this work, we employ a CNN model with the EfficientNet architecture. This choice is motivated by the State-of-the-Art accuracy attained by EfficientNet on the ImageNet Database, with a 84.4% top-1 accuracy. The model is computationally efficient and a promising candidate for common image classification via transfer learning tasks.

It encompasses eight architecture variants (B0 to B7) that differ in the model complexity and default image size. The superior performance of the EfficientNet v2 is attributed to MBConv layers, which are essentially inverted Residual blocks found in standard ResNets. The structure is illustrated in Fig. 2.

Fig. 2. The EfficientNet architecture. Modified from [3].

Fine-Tuning. The target data set serves as the validation sample, since it is representative of the images we expect to see in the future. For each iteration, the model is instantiated with the same architecture as a prior section. The weights obtained from the pre-trained model are now frozen on all network layers, except the last, fully-connected layer, wherein, they are fine-tuned.

3.4 Mobile App Development

The *i*ConDet application is designed and developed on Android Studio. The user interface, as shown in Fig. 3, are designed using XML. It uses Firebase for its backend processes and to store the data. The primary functionalities of this application is to capture the image of the user's eye from their android device and then uploading it to the Firebase at backend for showing the result to the user (in this case whether the user has conjunctivitis or not). To preserve user privacy each user is required to create an account before the application can be accessed. It is also secure since it asks for the user permission for camera access before the initial start-up. The backend is built and connected to the app for displaying the test results. The test results depend on the binary signal received by the application from the backend database. The backend uses the model (see Sect. 3.3) to find out whether the user has conjunctivitis or not.

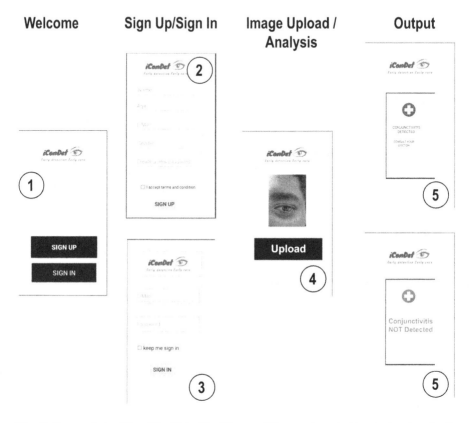

Fig. 3. Screenshot of the *i*ConDet pHealth app. The numbers in the circles denote the sequence of execution.

3.5 Evaluation Metrics

Since the model functions as a binary classifier, binary cross-entropy is a good choice of loss function. The sigmoid and negative log-likelihood loss are combined and applied to the output of the last network layer. The loss function determines the loss of an example by computing the following average:

$$\text{Loss} = -\frac{1}{\substack{\text{output} \\ \text{size}}} \sum_{i=1}^{\substack{\text{output} \\ \text{size}}} y_i \cdot \log \hat{y}_i + (1 - y_i) \cdot \log (1 - \hat{y}_i)$$

where $\hat{y}_i$ represents the i-th scalar value in the model output, y_i is the corresponding target value, and output size is the number of scalar values in the model output.

Furthermore, since there exists class imbalance in the data, we use Cohen's Kappa as an evaluation metric, since it is known to be more robust to sampling imbalances than ordinary classification accuracy. The metric is an indicator of the degree by which the concerned classifier model outperforms a classifier that simply guesses at random in accordance to the frequency of each class. It is defined as follows:

$$\kappa = \frac{p_o - p_e}{1 - p_e} = 1 - \frac{1 - p_o}{1 - p_e},$$

where p_o is the observed agreement, and p_e is the expected agreement.

Cohen's Kappa is always ≤ 1. The statistic and their corresponding strength of agreement according the widely accepted scheme provided by Landis and Koch [5] is listed in Table 1.

Table 1. Cohen's Kappa statistic and corresponding Strength of Agreement

Cohen's Kappa statistic (κ)	Strength of agreement
<0.00	Poor
0.00–0.20	Slight
0.20–0.40	Fair
0.41–0.60	Moderate
0.61–0.80	Substantial
0.81–1.00	Almost perfect

4 Results and Discussion

4.1 Dataset Creation

Due to the unavailability of labelled conjunctivitis datasets, we decided to build our own dataset for this work. We started collecting images of human eyes infected with Conjunctivitis, both bacterial and viral, from the internet. We also received some pinkeye images of patients from a known eye clinic. Once this was done, we started to collect healthy human eye images from the internet. This way we were able to collect around 150 images. The images collected were divided and kept into two separate folders, named as infected eye and healthy eye.

Since the data was collected from different sources, there was much variance in the data. We therefore cropped the images and removed the unnecessary areas of or near the eye. With this, a certain level of uniformity was achieved in the data, focus being mainly on the white part of the eye. Next, we performed manual labelling of the data as there wasn't sufficient data in hand for tool based labelling. Finally, we have a dataset where images are divided in a binary classification, the labels being *infectedeye* and *healthyeye*. Few samples of the healthy and infected eyes are shown in Fig. 4.

4.2   Experimentation

The experiments were performed on a local machine running on Ubuntu 18.04 Operating System, with 4.15.0 Kernel version and Intel(R) Core(TM) i7-7700HQ CPU @ 2.80 GHz. The scripts for the same were written using PyTorch [10]. The Adam Optimizer was used with the parameters listed in Table 2.

Table 2. Optimizer Parameters

Parameter	Value
Learning rate	0.001
Momentum Parameter	0.9
Gradient RMS	
Propagation	0.99

As mentioned in Sect. 3.2, the input images were pre-processed to obtain transformed images suitable to be provided to the model to train. The images before and after the processing are illustrated in Fig. 5. The transformations present clear structural differences between the ocular structures of the two sample types.

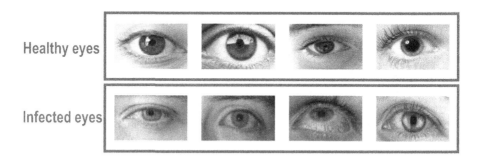

Fig. 4. Sample images from the dataset.

Original Image

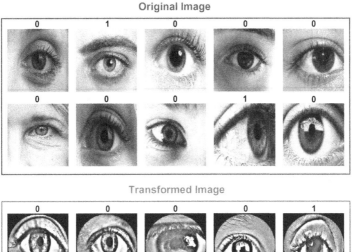

Transformed Image

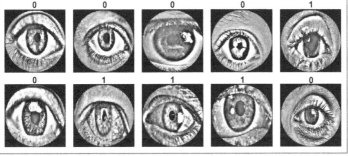

Fig. 5. Training samples before and after transformations. Labels 0 and 1 represent healthy and infected eyes, respectively. The top two rows show the original samples while the bottom two rows show the transformed samples.

A learning rate scheduler is employed to decrease the learning rate by a factor of 0.5 after every 5 epochs. This scheme facilitates smaller changes to the network weights upon reaching closer to the optimum.

4.3   Validation

Post each training epoch, the model is validated on the target data set. The class scores obtained from the last fully connected layer is exploited to predict the image class with the highest score. The accuracy scores and Cohen's kappa values are tracked throughout the process.

Termination Condition. Should κ stabilise for 5 consecutive epochs, we conclude the training process and save model weights for the epoch associated with the highest validation kappa. Early stopping is employed to further reduce the possibility of over-fitting. The κ scores for 15 epochs is represented in Fig. 6.

The best κ of 0.62 is reported at epoch 7, and stabilizes at approximately the same value beyond epoch 10. According to the schema described in Table 1, κ

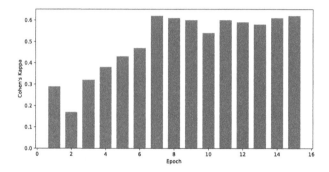

Fig. 6. The Cohen's Kappa obtained in different epochs. Epoch 7 indicates the maximum score.

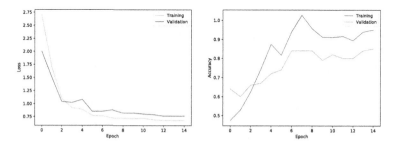

Fig. 7. The training and validation loss (a) and accuracy (b) of the model.

beyond 0.61 represents substantial strength of agreement. Therefore, despite the constraints introduced by data scarcity in the context of conjunctivitis infections, the model performs well. The corresponding best accuracy is 84%, reported at epoch 7. Given the substantial strength of agreement inferred from κ, an accuracy within the 80–90% range is expected. The trend is represented in Fig. 6.

The training and validation losses are tracked throughout the process, and the curves are reported in Fig. 7. The training loss stabilizes around 0.7, while the validation loss stabilizes at around 0.8, and the generalization gap is maintained beyond epoch 2. Therefore, despite the data scarcity, the trends suggest a good fit. The proposed model is comparable with some existing works which has been shown in Table 3.

Table 3. A comparative study has been shown with existing models

Models	Parameter	Accuracy
[3]	Digital image processing	93%
[1]	DCNN	98.79%
[8]	CNN	83.3%
Proposed model	Deep neural net	84%

5   Conclusion and Future Work

This work presents a mobile healthcare application (*i*ConDet) through which initial level of Conjunctivitis detection is possible. Deep learning techniques have been used upon the Conjunctivitis dataset prepared by us in support of the claim and to achieve the desired accuracy of 84%. This android based application is successful in performing a binary classification using deep learning algorithms at it's preliminary level. Presently, it can differentiate between healthy eyes and the infected eyes captured by mobile camera. Nevertheless, the severity detection of Conjunctivitis, along with the connection with COVID-19 will be handled in future in the advanced version of *i*ConDet. The link to the github repository is attached here: https://github.com/brai-acslab/icondet.

References

1. Akram, A., Debnath, R.: An automated eye disease recognition system from visual content of facial images using machine learning techniques. Turk. J. Electr. Eng. Comput. Sci. **28**(2), 917–932 (2020)
2. Ali, H.M., Kaiser, M.S., Mahmud, M.: Application of convolutional neural network in segmenting brain regions from MRI data. In: Liang, P., Goel, V., Shan, C. (eds.) BI 2019. LNCS, vol. 11976, pp. 136–146. Springer, Heidelberg (2019). https://doi.org/10.1007/978-3-030-37078-7_14
3. GoogleAI: Efficientnet: Improving accuracy and efficiency through autoML and model scaling. https://ai.googleblog.com/2019/05/efficientnet-improving-accuracy-and.html
4. Gunay, M., Goceri, E., Danisman, T.: Automated detection of adenoviral conjunctivitis disease from facial images using machine learning. In: 2015 IEEE 14th International Conference on Machine Learning and Applications (ICMLA), pp. 1204–1209. IEEE (2015)
5. Landis, J.R., Koch, G.G.: The measurement of observer agreement for categorical data. Biometrics **33**(1), 159–174 (1977). http://www.jstor.org/stable/2529310
6. Mahmud, M., Kaiser, M.S., McGinnity, T.M., Hussain, A.: Deep learning in mining biological data. Cogn. Comput. **13**(1), 1–33 (2021)
7. Mahmud, M., Kaiser, M.S., Hussain, A., Vassanelli, S.: Applications of deep learning and reinforcement learning to biological data. IEEE Trans. Neural Netw. Learn. Syst. **29**(6), 2063–2079 (2018). https://doi.org/10.1109/TNNLS.2018.2790388
8. Manchalwar, M., Warhade, K.: Detection of cataract and conjunctivitis disease using histogram of oriented gradient. Int. J. Eng. Technol. (IJET) (2017)
9. Noor, M.B.T., Zenia, N.Z., Kaiser, M.S., Al Mamun, S., Mahmud, M.: Application of deep learning in detecting neurological disorders from magnetic resonance images: a survey on the detection of Alzheimer's disease, Parkinson's disease and schizophrenia. Brain Inf. **7**(1), 1–21 (2020)
10. Paszke, A., et al.: PyTorch: an imperative style, high-performance deep learning library. In: Wallach, H., Larochelle, H., Beygelzimer, A., Alché-Buc, F.d., Fox, E., Garnett, R. (eds.) Advances in Neural Information Processing Systems, vol. 32, pp. 1–12. Curran Associates, Inc. (2019). https://proceedings.neurips.cc/paper/2019/file/bdbca288fee7f92f2bfa9f7012727740-Paper.pdf

11. Rahman, H., Ahmed, N., Hussain, I.: Comparison of data aggregation techniques in internet of things (iot). In: 2016 International Conference on Wireless Communications, Signal Processing and Networking (WiSPNET), pp. 1296–1300. IEEE (2016)
12. Soysa, A., De Silva, D.: A mobile base application for cataract and conjunctivitis detection. In: Proceedings of ICACT-2020, pp. 76–78 (2020)
13. Sundararajan, S.K., et al.: Detection of conjunctivitis with deep learning algorithm in medical image processing. In: 2019 Third International Conference on I-SMAC (IoT in Social, Mobile, Analytics and Cloud) (I-SMAC), pp. 714–717. IEEE (2019)
14. Tamuli, J., Jain, A., Dhan, A.V., Bhan, A., Dutta, M.K.: An image processing based method to identify and grade conjunctivitis infected eye according to its types and intensity. In: 2015 Eighth International Conference on Contemporary Computing (IC3), pp. 88–92. IEEE (2015)

Selecting Lung Cancer Patients from UK Primary Care Data: A Longitudinal Study of Feature Trends

Abeer Alzubaidi[1], Jaspreet Kaur[6], Mufti Mahmud[1,3,4(✉)],
David J. Brown[1,3,4], Jun He[1], Graham Ball[5], David R. Baldwin[2,6],
Emma O'Dowd[2,6], and Richard B. Hubbard[6]

[1] Department of Computer Science, Nottingham Trent University,
Clifton Lane, Nottingham NG11 8NS, UK
{abeer.alzubaidi,mufti.mahmud,david.brown,jun.he}@ntu.ac.uk
[2] Department of Respiratory Medicine, Nottingham University Hospitals NHS Trust,
Nottingham City Hospital, Nottingham NG5 1PB, UK
Richard.Hubbard@nottingham.ac.uk
[3] Computing and Informatics Research Centre, Nottingham Trent University,
Clifton Lane, Nottingham NG11 8NS, UK
[4] Medical Technologies Innovation Facility, Nottingham Trent University,
Clifton Lane, Nottingham NG11 8NS, UK
[5] School of Science and Technology, Nottingham Trent University, Clifton Lane,
Nottingham NG11 8NS, UK
graham.ball@ntu.ac.uk
[6] Division of Epidemiology and Public Health, University of Nottingham,
Nottingham NG5 1PB, UK
{Jaspreet.Kaur1,David.Baldwin,Emma.O'Dowd}@nottingham.ac.uk

Abstract. A high proportion of lung cancer cases are detected at a late cancer stage when they present with symptoms to general practitioners (GP). Early diagnosis is a challenge because many symptoms are also common in other diseases. Therefore, this study aims to assess UK primary care data of patients one, two and three years prior to lung cancer diagnosis to capture trends in clinical features of patients with the goal of early diagnosis and thus potentially curative treatment. This longitudinal study utilises data from the Clinical Practice Research Datalink (CPRD) with linked data from the National Cancer Registration and Analysis Service (NCRAS). A comprehensive list of Read codes is created to select features of interest to establish if a patient has experienced a certain medical condition or not. The comparison of the relative frequencies of the identified predictors associated with cases and controls reveals the importance of the following groups of features: 'Cough Wheeze' and 'Bronchitis unspecified', 'Dyspnoea' and 'Upper Respiratory Infection', which are frequent events for lung cancer cases, where a high proportion of cases were also identified using 'Haemoptysis' and 'Peripheral vascular disease'.

Keywords: Lung cancer · Cough · Bronchitis unspecified ·
Dyspnoea · Upper respiratory infection · Machine learning

M. Mahmud et al. (Eds.): AII 2021, CCIS 1435, pp. 43–59, 2021.
https://doi.org/10.1007/978-3-030-82269-9_4

1   Introduction

Lung cancer is the third most diagnosed cancer and the leading cause of cancer mortality in the United Kingdom (UK) and worldwide [3]. It is estimated that by 2030, lung cancer will be the third-highest cause of death in high-income countries and the fifth-highest cause in middle-income countries [13]. Detecting lung cancer at an early stage remains a major challenge for clinicians, where most of the lung cancer cases are undetectable until an advanced stage. The detection of lung cancer at a late stage of disease progression reduces the chance of disease cure where the disease becomes rapidly fatal, dropping the 5-year survival rate drastically to 10%. Recognition of lung cancer at an early stage can result in better prognosis with a 5-year survival rate, and thus the UK National Health Service (NHS) long-term plan is to boost cancer care[1].

In the UK, the general practitioners (GPs) play a major role in the detection and management of lung cancer, where a significant percentage of lung cancer cases are detected symptomatically when patients present to the GP with cancer alarm symptoms [14]. However, these symptoms are also quite common in other conditions, posing a challenge for healthcare professionals to determine high-risk symptomatic patients eligible for further analysis and the targeting of screening to people at a high enough risk of lung cancer to benefit, from the other individuals who will not. Currently, the identification of a high-risk target population for lung cancer screening is gaining importance due to evidence that illustrates the ability of Low-Dose Computed Tomography (LDCT) to reduce mortality. The results from NLST [20] and other pilot trials [1,4,6,8,17,19,21] show that lung cancer screening with LDCT can save lives and reduce death from lung cancer by 20% or more in high risk smokers.

GPs record primary care and referral information of patients in Electronic Medical Records (EMRs), where some GPs contribute their EMRs structured data in an anonymised form to data warehouses such as the Clinical Practice Research Datalink (CPRD). Therefore, the CPRD primary care database can be considered a rich source of health data, including demographic information, symptoms, diagnoses, tests, therapies, immunisation and referrals to secondary care. The EMRs records of the CPRD database offer great potential for researchers when conducting epidemiological studies that can address important questions of interest in healthcare. The EMRs of patients collected by GPs can provide a very valuable resource of information: many subjects screened in the past were at relatively low risk and benefited little, and costs were high. To be clinically and cost effective, LDCT screening needs to be offered to people at a high enough risk of lung cancer to benefit.

In this study, we aim to assess UK primary care data of patients one, two and three years prior to lung cancer diagnosis to capture trends in clinical features with the goal of early diagnosis and to identify those at high enough risk to benefit. This longitudinal study uses data from the Clinical Practice Research Datalink (CPRD) with linked data from the National Cancer Registration and

---

[1] www.england.nhs.uk/cancer/strategy/.

Analysis Service (NCRAS). The features were identified for patients with an incident diagnosis of lung cancer in cohorts within the study period (01/01/2000-31/12/2015). A comprehensive code list of features was created by our lung cancer clinician partners. This study is reliant on Read Codes to establish if a patient has experienced a certain medical symptom or condition or not, and the unstructured text data were inaccessible in this dataset.

2   Methods

2.1   Study Design and Population

CPRD is an ongoing primary care database of coded anonymised information about patients from GPs, including demographics, symptoms, diagnoses, drug prescriptions, immunisation, investigation and test results. Linkages enable follow-up of patients beyond the primary care setting. Data are recorded by GP staff using a hierarchical clinical classification system, called Read codes. Each Read code represents a health-related concept, which is also represented by a Read term (i.e., the plain language description described in the medical dictionary). More details about the CPRD "GOLD" dataset that is drawn from the EMRs software Vision can be found in [5,18]. Approval for use of data for this project was granted by the CPRD Independent Scientific Advisory Committee (ISAC) (Protocol numbers 18_223 and 20_014R). The study is a longitudinal case-control study in which data collected within the CPRD are used to compare features of interest between cases (i.e., individuals who later received a diagnosis of lung cancer) and controls (i.e., individuals with no lung cancer record). The initial extraction population from the CPRD GOLD database comprises all cases eligible for data linkage to the NCRAS cancer registry database. Patients are selected from the CPRD database and included in the study according to the following criteria:

1. Patients with lung cancer (cases) are identified by the presence of one or more lung cancer diagnostic codes occurring within the study period (01/01/2000-31/12/2015) and the date of the first lung cancer code was considered as the "index date". Patients who had a record of lung cancer (within 01/01/1990-31/12/2015) prior to their index date were excluded. The index date is defined as the date of the first ever record of a lung cancer diagnosis within follow up for the cases and a matched index date for the controls. The start of follow-up is defined as the latest of the patient registration date, the practice Up-to-standard (UTS) date and 01/01/2000. The end of follow-up will be defined as the earliest of the patient transfer out date, the practice last collection date, the CPRD GOLD death date and 31/12/2015. Furthermore, patients who are eligible for linkage to Hospital Episode Statistics (HES), National Cancer Registration and Analysis Service (NCRAS), ONS Death registration and patient level deprivation data are only included. Lung cancer cases were 40 years or older at the index date and had the event within their UTS follow-up. All patients within the CPRD Gold dataset matching these criteria were

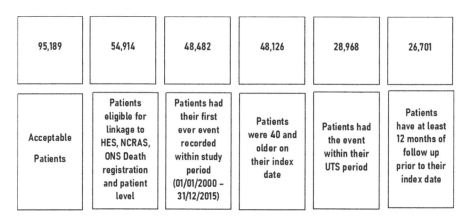

95,189	54,914	48,482	48,126	28,968	26,701
Acceptable Patients	Patients eligible for linkage to HES, NCRAS, ONS Death registration and patient level	Patients had their first ever event recorded within study period (01/01/2000 – 31/12/2015)	Patients were 40 and older on their index date	Patients had the event within their UTS period	Patients have at least 12 months of follow up prior to their index date

Fig. 1. Sample selection.

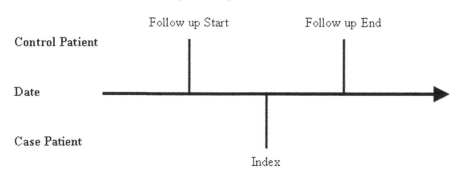

Fig. 2. Index date matching - CPRD.

extracted. 26,701 cases have at least 12 months of follow up prior to their index date, as explained in Fig. 1.

2. Control participants matched cases based on general practice, sex, and year of birth (within ±5 years), and had no lung cancer code anywhere in their patient record (either in CPRD GOLD or in the Cancer Registry). We also ensured that controls had at least 12 months of follow up prior to the index date of their matched case. CPRD used Index date Matching. In this algorithm, the case patient has a specified index date that must fall between the follow-up start and follow-up end dates of the control patient. This can be seen in Fig. 2. The start of follow up for the controls will be amended to ensure they have 12 months UTS follow up prior to the index date of their matched case.

In the final dataset, 26,701 cases were identified in the cancer registry data and CPRD GOLD. Up to 10 matching controls will be provided for each case. Once eligible patients are identified, the entire available coded records for cases and controls are extracted from the data files, as illustrated in Table 1. The data files are: Patients (i.e., 1 file), Consultation (i.e., 8 files), Clinical (i.e., 8 files),

(a)

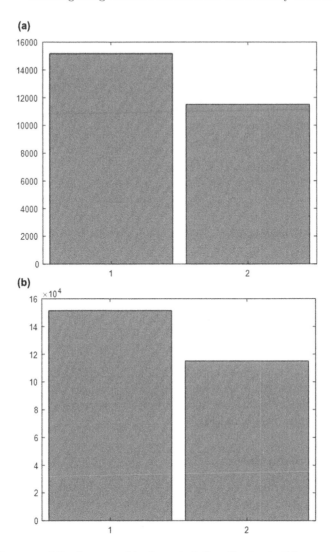

(b)

Fig. 3. Histogram of the demographic characteristics, Gender in this case, of cases (a) and controls (b). '1' denotes Male and '2' denotes Female.

Additional clinical (i.e., 2 files), Referral (i.e., 1 file), Immunisation (i.e., 1 file), Test (i.e., 10 files), and Therapy (i.e., 28 files).

2.2 Demographic Characteristics of Cases and Controls

A total of 26,701 patients and 267,010 matched controls meeting the inclusion criteria were included in the analyses. Removing the missing values from the matched controls data (i.e., 388 (0.15%)) resulted in a dataset of 26,701 patient

Table 1. Extraction of cases and controls from the data files.

File	Case records	Control records	Features
Patients	26,701	266,622	20
Consultation	10,086,803	119,305,071	7
Clinical	7,269,231	85,078,817	10
Additional Clinical	1,723,668	23,255,903	10
Referral	291,496	3,184,693	13
Immunisation	226,184	3,184,987	15
Test	6,429,816	87,653,498	16
Therapy	11,758,125	144,725,387	13

Table 2. Demographic characteristics of cases and controls (Gender).

Characteristics	Cases		Control	
	Counts	%	Counts	%
Male	15,182	56.86	151,458	56.81
Female	11,519	43.14	115,164	43.19

samples and 266,622 matched controls. Gender characteristics of both lung cancer patients and controls are shown in Table 2. Lung cancer patients and matched controls have similar age and sex distributions, as expected given the matching process, as shown in Fig. 3 and Fig. 4.

2.3   Features of Interest

Since EMRs data are recorded as Read codes, the associated data analysis relies mainly on generating code-lists to define features of interest. A code list can be defined as a collection of codes that describe certain medical conditions which can be used by researchers to investigate patient EMRs. Our code list comprises of 1,468 codes based on 17 groups of features, which are: Any Pulmonary Tuberculosis (i.e., 208 codes), Pulmonary Tuberculosis (i.e., 83 codes), Cough Wheeze (i.e., 48 codes), Pneumonia (i.e., 168 codes), Haemoptysis (i.e., 12 codes), Emphysema (i.e., 26 codes), Hypertension (i.e., 74 codes), Acute Myocardial Infarction (i.e., 65 codes), Bronchitis Unspecified (i.e., 95 codes), Dyspnoea (i.e., 65 codes), Cystic fibrosis (i.e., 17 codes), Upper Respiratory Infection (i.e., 310 codes), Idiopathic (i.e., 17 codes), Chronic Kidney Disease (i.e., 147 codes), Acute Nephritis With Lesions (i.e., 7 codes), Peripheral Vascular Disease (i.e., 90 codes), and Congestive Heart Failure (i.e., 34 codes). Read codes are utilised to select those groups of features for lung cancer reported in both cases and controls. This means that patients were identified as having experienced Dyspnoea (for instance) if they had a consultation with a Read code corresponding to that symptom. The identified list of Read codes is utilised to extract lung cancer cases and controls from the created data files (see Table 1). In this study, the relative frequencies of the identified predictors are assessed and compared between the records of cases and controls based on a set of clinical descriptions called medical codes (medcode) found in the clinical, referral, and test files, as explained in Table 3.

Table 4 explains the relative frequencies of the identified features between the clinical records of cases and controls. The group of features 'Cough Wheeze', which comprise 48 medcodes seems to be more frequent in the clinical records of

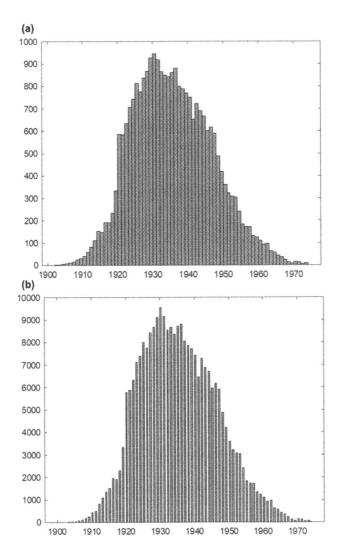

Fig. 4. Histogram for the demographic characteristics, Year of Birth here, of cases (a) and controls (b).

Table 3. Extraction of cases and controls based on the identified list of Read codes.

File	No. of case records	%	No. of control records	%
Clinical	277,076	3.81%	2,282,364	2.68%
Referral	8,041	2.76%	46,633	1.46%
Test	95,993	1.49%	1,603,901	1.83%

cases (i.e., 1.03%), compared with the controls (i.e., 0.74%) and also in comparison to other features. Furthermore, the group feature 'Bronchitis Unspecified' can be considered as a frequent event for lung cancer cases (i.e., 1.01%) compared with controls (i.e., 0.60%), and also in comparison to other subsets of features. The percentage of patients with 'Dyspnoea' as well as 'Upper Respiratory Infection' seems to be higher in the clinical records of cases (0.46%, 0.52%) compared with the clinical records of controls (0.27%, 0.34%), respectively. Furthermore, a bag of codes model is presented in Fig. 5 for cases and controls to show the frequency of codes in each cohort of clinical records. The medcode '92' (equivalent to the Read code (171..00) that represents the 'Cough' symptom) constitutes 14% of the clinical records for both groups of samples, whereas the medcode '68' (which corresponds to the medical concept of 'Chest infection' with Read code (H06z011)) constitutes 10% of the clinical records of cases and 9% of the corresponding records of controls. Moreover, the medcodes '2581' (which represents the feature 'Chest infection NOS' with Read code (H06z000)) comprises 7% of the clinical records of cases compared with 5% of the records in the control group. Medcodes '1273', and '799' ('C/O - cough' and 'Essential hypertension') are also frequent events in the clinical records of both groups of samples, as illustrated in Fig. 5.

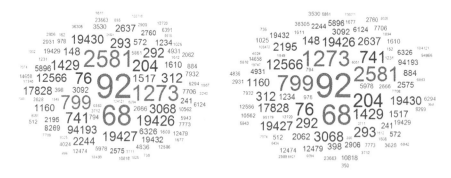

Fig. 5. Bag of codes models of the selected clinical records, where the left model represents the clinical records of cases and the right model represents the clinical records of controls.

Table 5 shows the comparison of relative frequencies of the identified predictors between the referral records of cases and controls. As we have seen in the

Table 4. Number and proportion of patients with each group of features and for each cohort in the clinical file.

Group	Codes no	Cases		Controls	
		Counts	Proportion	Counts	Proportion
Any Pulmonary Tuberculosis	208	741	0.01%	6218	0.01%
Pulmonary Tuberculosis	83	321	0.00%	2584	0.00%
Cough Wheeze	48	75000	1.03%	631269	0.74%
Pneumonia	168	4952	0.07%	27943	0.03%
Haemoptysis	12	5197	0.07%	11114	0.01%
Emphysema	26	1366	0.02%	4266	0.01%
Hypertension	74	34524	0.47%	440076	0.52%
Acute Myocardial Infarction	65	5129	0.07%	47374	0.06%
Bronchitis Unspecified	95	73637	1.01%	513700	0.60%
Dyspnoea	65	33760	0.46%	231316	0.27%
Cystic fibrosis	17	19	0.00%	179	0.00%
Upper Respiratory Infection	310	37925	0.52%	287519	0.34%
Idiopathic	17	671	0.01%	3285	0.00%
Chronic Kidney Disease	147	6490	0.09%	109613	0.13%
Acute Nephritis With Lesions	7	3	0.00%	63	0.00%
Peripheral Vascular Disease	90	7009	0.10%	40911	0.05%
Congestive Heart Failure	34	4123	0.06%	46842	0.06%

clinical file in Table 4, the percentage of patients with 'Cough Wheeze' features is higher in the referral records of lung cancer patients (i.e., 0.60%) compared to the controls (i.e., 0.30%) and in comparison to other lung cancer symptoms. Moreover, of 291,496 cases, 0.30% had 'Haemoptysis' in their referral records in comparison to (i.e., 0.06%) controls out of 3,184,693 records in the referral file. The group of features 'Bronchitis Unspecified' seems to be more frequent in the referral records of lung cancer cases (i.e., 0.33%) compared with control samples (i.e., 0.16%). The proportions of patients with 'Dyspnoea' and 'Upper Respiratory Infection' are higher in the referral records of cases (i.e., 0.55%, 0.32%) compared with the negative samples in the control group (i.e., 0.33%, 0.12%) respectively. The group of features 'Peripheral vascular disease' is more frequent in the referral records of cases (0.32%) compared to controls (0.15%) and in comparison to other groups of features. Furthermore, a bag of codes model is presented in Fig. 6 for cases and controls to show the frequency of codes in each cohort of referral records. The medcode '92' (equivalent to Read code (171..00) representing the 'Cough' symptom) constitutes 14% of the referral records of cases and 12% of the referral records of controls, highlighting the importance of this symptom. 'Shortness of breath' - (741/(R060800)) is slightly higher in the referral records of controls (10%) than cases (9%). Referring patients to the respiratory physician - (i.e., 10874/(ZL5A500)) is higher for cases (7%) than controls (5%) in the referral file. 'Intermittent claudication' (1517/(G73z000)) constitutes

7% of the referral records of cases compared to 4% of the referral records of controls. Moreover, the 'Haemoptysis' symptom (2244/(R063.00)), comprises 7% of the referral records of cases in comparison to 3% of the corresponding records of controls.

Table 5. Number and proportion of patients with each feature group and for each cohort in the Referral file

Feature group	Codes no	Cases		Control	
		Count	Proportion	Count	Proportion
Any Pulmonary Tuberculosis	208	18	0.01%	132	0.00%
Pulmonary Tuberculosis	83	10	0.00%	48	0.00%
Cough Wheeze	48	1735	0.60%	9707	0.30%
Pneumonia	168	169	0.06%	724	0.02%
Haemoptysis	12	867	0.30%	1977	0.06%
Emphysema	26	31	0.01%	116	0.00%
Hypertension	74	309	0.11%	3878	0.12%
Acute Myocardial Infarction	65	209	0.07%	1537	0.05%
Bronchitis Unspecified	95	954	0.33%	4985	0.16%
Dyspnoea	65	1605	0.55%	10644	0.33%
Cystic fibrosis	17	0	0.00%	6	0.00%
Upper Respiratory Infection	310	930	0.32%	3930	0.12%
Idiopathic	17	44	0.02%	176	0.01%
Chronic Kidney Disease	147	121	0.04%	2018	0.06%
Acute Nephritis With Lesions	7	0	0.00%	0	0.00%
Peripheral Vascular Disease	90	921	0.32%	4908	0.15%
Congestive Heart Failure	34	219	0.08%	2468	0.08%

In the Test file, the group of features 'Chronic Kidney Disease' seems to be a frequent event for both groups of samples, where its relative frequency for controls is slightly higher than cases. A bag of codes model is also created for the test records of cases and controls to show the relative frequencies of the features between these groups of samples. The 'GFR calculated abbreviated MDRD' (medcode '23250' and Read code '451E.00') comprises 80% of the test records of lung cancer cases and 81% of the test records of controls, as shown in Fig. 7. As a result, the total number of EMRs extracted from clinical, referral, and test files for cases is 1,105,653 compared to 12,620,203 EMRs for control samples, resulting in a dataset of 13,725,856 samples (Table 6).

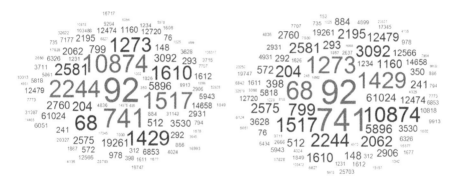

Fig. 6. Bag of codes models of the selected referral records, where the left model represents the referral records of cases and the right model represents the referral records of controls.

Table 6. Number and proportion of patients with each feature group and for each cohort in the Test file

Feature group	Codes no	Cases		Control	
		Count	Proportion	Count	Proportion
Any Pulmonary Tuberculosis	208	3	0.00%	18	0.00%
Pulmonary Tuberculosis	83	0	0.00%	1	0.00%
Cough Wheeze	48	6	0.00%	57	0.00%
Pneumonia	168	14	0.00%	73	0.00%
Haemoptysis	12	1	0.00%	27	0.00%
Emphysema	26	0	0.00%	1	0.00%
Hypertension	74	25	0.00%	234	0.00%
Acute Myocardial Infarction	65	0	0.00%	10	0.00%
Bronchitis Unspecified	95	1	0.00%	25	0.00%
Dyspnoea	65	5	0.00%	24	0.00%
Cystic fibrosis	17	0	0.00%	0	0.00%
Upper Respiratory Infection	310	3146	0.05%	24808	0.03%
Idiopathic	17	0	0.00%	0	0.00%
Chronic Kidney Disease	147	92,792	1.44%	1578628	1.80%
Acute Nephritis With Lesions	7	0	0.00%	0	0.00%
Peripheral Vascular Disease	90	1	0.00%	1	0.00%
Congestive Heart Failure	34	0	0.00%	2	0.00%

3 Data Analysis

As mentioned previously, the created dataset contains 13,725,856 samples, where the majority are the control samples (i.e., 12,620,203 (91.94%)) and the minority are the lung cancer cases (i.e., 1,105,653 (8.06%)), as shown in Fig. 8 (a). Training a machine learning classification model using a dataset that suffers from an imbalanced class distribution such as this poses a tough challenge for learning

Fig. 7. Bag of codes models of the selected test records, where the left model represents the test records of cases and the right model represents the referral test of controls.

algorithms in terms of capturing something meaningful from the minority samples. The issue of imbalanced class distribution simply refers to the challenge that occurs when the number of samples that represent the class of interest is much lower than the other classes, which can be considered a common problem in real-world data. In situations like this, the classifiers are more likely to be biased towards the majority class causing a high-level of miss-classification rate of the minority class as shown in Fig. 9 (b), where the percentage of lung cancer cases that were incorrectly classified is 95.9% compared to 99.8% correctly classified controls. However, if we attempt to quantify the predictive performance of the classification model using the well-known accuracy metric, the outcome is 92.1%, as shown in Fig. 9 (a). Therefore, adopting reliable evaluation measurements, as illustrated in Fig. 9 (b) demonstrates the consequences of feeding the learning models with imbalanced class data.

In our research problem, the dataset can be considered highly imbalanced class data, where the majority are the controls (i.e., 91.94%), due to the fact that we have 10 matched controls for each lung cancer patient defined based on the matching process of age, gender, and GPs, as discussed in Sect. 2. Due to the advent of artificial intelligence based methods in analysing clinical data [2,7,10,15,16], several methods have been proposed in the literature for tackling imbalanced class issues, including oversampling, undersampling, and hybrid approaches, which integrate oversampling and undersampling techniques [9,11,12]. For the work presented in this paper, a particular form of an undersampling technique was utilised and performed for creating several data samplings from the original dataset, rather than simply eliminating some of the samples from the majority class and losing some potentially very useful information. This undersampling technique has the potential to address the issues caused by imbalanced class data, in which we have one matching control at each file. As a result, we will have 10 matching case-control files. The matching case-control files are: Matching-file1 (i.e., 26700 samples), Matching-file2 (i.e., 26699 samples), Matching-file3 (i.e., 26695 samples), Matching-file4 (i.e., 26693 samples), Matching-file5 (i.e., 26689 samples), Matching-file6 (i.e., 26677 samples), Matching-file7 (i.e., 26663 samples), Matching-file8 (i.e., 26637 samples),

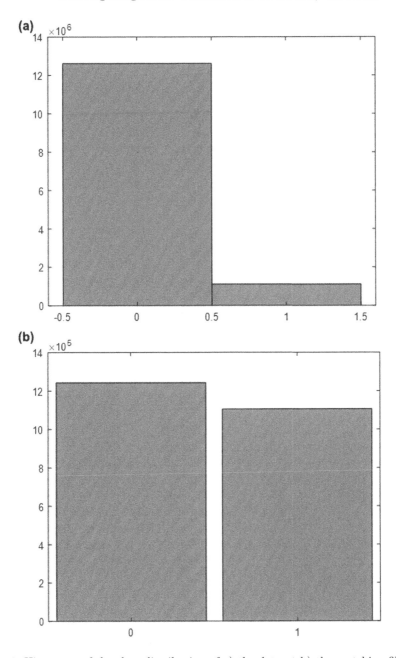

Fig. 8. Histogram of the class distribution of a) the dataset b) the matching file1.

Matching-file9 (i.e., 26610 samples), Matching-file9 (i.e., 26559 samples). The difference in the number of samples across Matching-files is due to having 388 missing values distributed in the matching files as follows respectively: (1, 2,

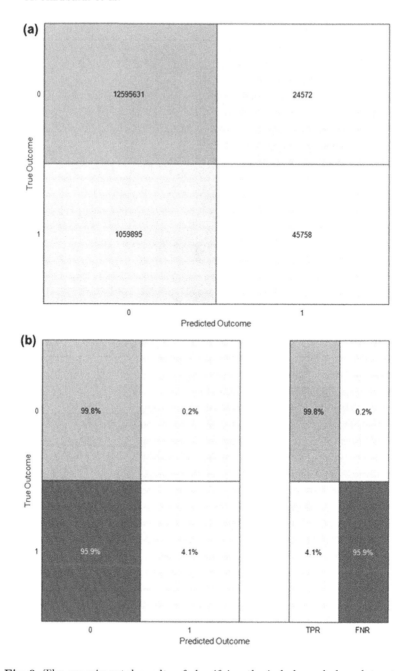

Fig. 9. The experimental results of classifying the imbalanced class dataset.

6, 8, 12, 24, 38, 64, 91, 142). For instance, selecting the first data sampling (Matching-file1 for performing the classification task), resulted in a more realis-

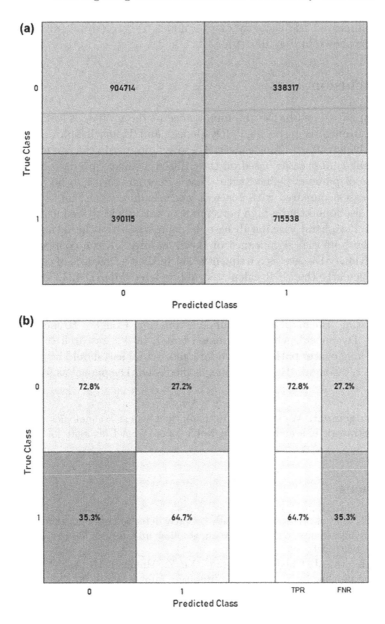

Fig. 10. The experimental results of classifying the balanced class dataset.

tic and reliable accuracy (69%), as was quantified in Fig. 10 - (a). Furthermore, detecting the underlying structure of the data has improved drastically due to having enough representative examples for each class, leading to a dramatic improvement in the True Positive rate (TP), from (4.1%) (to 64.7%), which in turn has improved the capacity of the model to correctly classifying positive patients, as shown in Fig. 10 - (b).

4   Conclusion

In this paper, we emphasise the importance of the groups of features: 'Cough Wheeze', 'Bronchitis unspecified', 'Dyspnoea', and 'Upper Respiratory Infection' for the early detection of lung cancer. These symptoms are the commonest symptoms of lung cancer cases based on the utilised medical care dataset, where the percentage of patients defined with those symptoms seems to be higher in the EMRs of cases compared with controls, and also in comparison to other symptoms. We also found that a high percentage of patients identified using 'Haemoptysis' and 'Peripheral vascular disease' in comparison to other symptoms, highlighting the potential significance of those features. In the context of testing, 'Chronic Kidney Disease' is a frequent event in the test records of cases and controls, particularly the GFR calculated abbreviated MDRD (23250/(451E.00)), which constitutes around 80% of the test EMRs of both groups of samples. Currently, in the medical domain, it has been shown that there are still trends in overestimating 'Haemoptysis' and underestimating 'Cough', 'Bronchitis unspecified' and 'Dyspnoea', which are demonstrated in our research to be frequent events for lung cancer patients. Therefore, more emphasis should be placed on the symptoms of 'Cough', 'Bronchitis unspecified' and 'Dyspnoea' as for 'Haemoptysis'.

Acknowledgement. We would like to thank the Medical Technologies and Advanced Materials Strategic Research Theme at Nottingham Trent University for financial support.

References

1. Becker, N., et al.: Randomized study on early detection of lung cancer with MSCT in Germany: results of the first 3 years of follow-up after randomization. J. Thorac. Oncol. **10**(6), 890–896 (2015)
2. Chen, L., Yan, J., Chen, J., Sheng, Y., Xu, Z., Mahmud, M.: An event based topic learning pipeline for neuroimaging literature mining. Brain Inf. **7**(1), 1–14 (2020). https://doi.org/10.1186/s40708-020-00121-1
3. Ferlay, J., et al.: Cancer incidence and mortality patterns in Europe: estimates for 40 countries in 2012. Eur. J. Cancer **49**(6), 1374–1403 (2013)
4. Field, J.K., et al.: The UK lung cancer screening trial: a pilot randomised controlled trial of low-dose computed tomography screening for the early detection of lung cancer. Health Technol. Assess. (Winchester, England) **20**(40), 1 (2016)
5. Herrett, E., et al.: Data resource profile: clinical practice research datalink (CPRD). Int. J. Epidemiol. **44**(3), 827–836 (2015)
6. Infante, M., et al.: Long-term follow-up results of the DANTE trial, a randomized study of lung cancer screening with spiral computed tomography. Am. J. Respir. Crit. Care Med. **191**(10), 1166–1175 (2015)

7. Kaiser, M.S., et al.: iWorksafe: towards healthy workplaces during COVID-19 with an intelligent phealth app for industrial settings. IEEE Access **9**, 13814–13828 (2021)

8. van Klaveren, R.J., et al.: Management of lung nodules detected by volume CT scanning. New England J. Med. **361**(23), 2221–2229 (2009)

9. López, V., Fernández, A., García, S., Palade, V., Herrera, F.: An insight into classification with imbalanced data: empirical results and current trends on using data intrinsic characteristics. Inf. Sci. **250**, 113–141 (2013)

10. Mahmud, M., Kaiser, M.S.: Machine learning in fighting pandemics: a COVID-19 case study. In: Santosh, K.C., Joshi, A. (eds.) COVID-19: Prediction, Decision-Making, and its Impacts. LNDECT, vol. 60, pp. 77–81. Springer, Singapore (2021). https://doi.org/10.1007/978-981-15-9682-7_9

11. Mahmud, M., Kaiser, M.S., McGinnity, T.M., Hussain, A.: Deep learning in mining biological data. Cogn. Comput. **13**(1), 1–33 (2020). https://doi.org/10.1007/s12559-020-09773-x

12. Mahmud, M., Kaiser, M.S., Hussain, A., Vassanelli, S.: Applications of deep learning and reinforcement learning to biological data. IEEE Trans. Neural Netw. Learn. Syst. **29**(6), 2063–2079 (2018)

13. Mathers, C.D., Loncar, D.: Projections of global mortality and burden of disease from 2002 to 2030. PLoS Med. **3**(11), 1 (2006)

14. McDonald, L., et al.: Suspected cancer symptoms and blood test results in primary care before a diagnosis of lung cancer: a case-control study. Future Oncol. **15**(33), 3755–3762 (2019)

15. Nahian, M.J.A., et al.: Towards an accelerometer-based elderly fall detection system using cross-disciplinary time series features. IEEE Access **9**, 39413–39431 (2021)

16. Noor, M.B.T., et al.: Application of deep learning in detecting neurological disorders from magnetic resonance images: a survey on the detection of Alzheimer's disease, Parkinson's disease and schizophrenia. Brain Inf. **7**(1), 1–21 (2020)

17. Paci, E., et al.: Mortality, survival and incidence rates in the ITALUNG randomised lung cancer screening trial. Thorax **72**(9), 825–831 (2017)

18. Padmanabhan, S.: Cprd gold data specification (2015). https://www.ed.ac.uk/files/atoms/files/cprd_gold_full_data_specification.pdf

19. Sverzellati, N., et al.: Low-dose computed tomography for lung cancer screening: comparison of performance between annual and biennial screen. Eur. Radiol. **26**(11), 3821–3829 (2016). https://doi.org/10.1007/s00330-016-4228-3

20. Team, N.L.S.T.R.: Reduced lung-cancer mortality with low-dose computed tomographic screening. New Engl. J. Med. **365**(5), 395–409 (2011)

21. Wille, M.M., et al.: Results of the randomized Danish lung cancer screening trial with focus on high-risk profiling. Am. J. Respir. Crit. Care Med. **193**(5), 542–551 (2016)

Extending Upon a Transfer Learning Approach for Brain Tumour Segmentation

Jiachenn Choong[(✉)] and Nazia Hameed

University of Nottingham, Nottingham NG7 2RD, UK
`hfyjc3@nottingham.ac.uk`

Abstract. The incidence of gliomas has been on the rise and are the most common malignant brain tumours diagnosed upon medical appointments. A common approach to identify and diagnose brain tumours is to use Magnetic Resonance Imaging (MRI) to pinpoint tumour regions. However, manual segmentation of brain tumours is highly time-consuming and challenging due to the multimodal structure of MRI scans coupled with the task of delineating boundaries of different brain tissues. As such, there is a need for automated and accurate segmentation techniques in the medical domain to reduce both time and task complexity. Various Deep Learning techniques such as Convolutional Neural Networks (CNN) and Fully Connected Networks (FCN) have been introduced to address this challenge with promising segmentation results on various datasets. FCNs such as U-Net in recent literature achieve state-of-the-art performance on segmentation tasks and have been adapted to tackle various domains. In this paper, we propose an improved extension upon an existing transfer learning method on the Brain Tumour Segmentation (BraTS) 2020 dataset and achieved marginally better results compared to the original approach.

Keywords: Semantic segmentation · Transfer learning · Brain tumour

1   Introduction

A tumour is an abnormal growth of cells that exist in a certain region of the body. Based on the above definition, brain tumours are mainly situated in the brain or central nervous system (CNS). The World Health Organization (WHO) has provided a classification of tumours [1] according to a grading system which ranges from Grade I to Grade IV, in increasing order of proliferative potential, indicating the potential rate and activity of the cells multiplying. Gliomas are brain tumours that arise from glial cells which are the supporting cells of the brain and spinal cord [2] can be separated into 2 main grades depending on their proliferative potential, namely low-grade gliomas (LGG) and high-grade gliomas (HGG). LGGs are benign tumours that are slow growing and have low potential to metastasize. HGGs, also known as glioblastoma multiforme [3] are

M. Mahmud et al. (Eds.): AII 2021, CCIS 1435, pp. 60–69, 2021.
https://doi.org/10.1007/978-3-030-82269-9_5

malignant tumours that have aggressive growth rates and have high potential to metastasize.

Cancer Research UK estimates that there are 12,100 new brain, central nervous system (CNS) and intracranial tumours that were diagnosed from the years 2015 to 2017. Cancer Research UK [4] also states that brain, CNS and intracranial tumours are the 8th most common cancer in the UK in the year of 2017, with the median age range of prognosis being 40–44 years old in females, and 35–39 years old in males. According to Cancer Research UK, the survival rates of patients which have brain tumours are dependent on the type of tumour and age, but generally 40% of patients survive their cancer for 1 year or more, with more than 10% of patients surviving their cancer for 5 years or more [4] with survival rates of patients being dependent on various factors such as age, tumour behaviour, patient's reaction towards treatment and tumour markers present in the body. In addition, recent research [5] has shown that the incidence of glioblastoma multiforme has increased by six times its original value between the years 2008 and 2017. Glioblastoma multiforme is also the leading type of brain tumour that occurs most frequently in adults [3] compared to other types of brain tumours.

As such, the early and accurate segmentation of brain tumours play an important role in the overall survival chance and treatment options of patients that are diagnosed with brain tumours. Various non-invasive imaging techniques such as MRI and Computed Tomography (CT) scans [6] are utilised to produce detailed images of the brain that are used to detect the presence of brain tumours in a patient. Manual segmentation of brain tumours from 3D volumetric imagery produced by MRI or CT scans are a time-consuming and intensive task [6,7] as the operator has to perform segmentations slice by slice for a great number of slices to extract the boundaries of the target structure.

2 Background and Related Work

Before the rise of deep learning techniques in the medical imaging and computer vision domain, more traditional approaches were used to segment brain tumours from medical scans produced by MRI or CT procedures. Based on our understanding, traditional approaches can be classified as non-learning approaches which do not involve machine learning techniques that use some form of learning to find features and patterns in the image to segment the tumour. One such approach is by using thresholding that provides a straightforward technique by classifying pixels according to their intensity values to a certain defined threshold. Thresholding methods can be further split into two types [8], global and local thresholding. Global thresholding is used when an image has only two classes of interest and can be split distinctively using only a single threshold. If the image has more than two classes of interest, local thresholding will be a better choice. Global thresholding in brain tumour segmentation has been used [9] for the segmentation of enhancing tumour sections from T1-weighted images. By applying an intensity threshold to a manually selected region of interest in combination with a Sobel edge filter, the resulting image which highlights edge probability is used to determine the class of border pixels with respect to the edge probabilities. However, this technique has certain drawbacks [8] as it does not take into account pixels of hyper-intense signals that represent normal brain structures in T1-weighted images.

Another traditional approach to medical image segmentation is region-based approaches. Region growing is one such approach with the goal of extracting a region of the image based off some predefined homogeneity criteria [10]. In short, region growing requires a seed point which is manually determined, it then extracts neighbouring pixels that meet the homogeneity criteria and merges them into a region. The region will "grow" until the homogeneity criteria is not fulfilled. Related region growing approaches in brain tumour segmentation include [11] where two different kinds of homogeneity criteria were used in a modified region growing technique. The criteria of "intensity" and "orientation" were used as the homogeneity criteria. Pixels are chosen if both criteria are met, where the "intensity" criteria refer to a pixel-wise intensity value that must be over a certain threshold. The "orientation" criteria is a novelty in the region growing approach by calculating the difference in gradient of neighbouring pixels, and including the neighbouring pixel if it is below a certain threshold.

Despite the vast availability of traditional segmentation techniques, semi-autonomous techniques require manual intervention from human operators. Without proper domain expertise, these techniques could produce unfavourable results. However, autonomous techniques such as deep learning in the medical imaging and computer vision domain were quickly emerging, spurred by the success of the CNN architecture on the ImageNet dataset [12]. Despite that, due to the costly and time-intensive process of preparing labelled medical data, this proposed a challenge as to the practicality of deep learning in the medical imaging domain. Several approaches to confront the problem were proposed, such as transfer learning approaches to speed up the convergence and increase the accuracy of CNNs by transferring the knowledge gained [13] from learning from a non-medical domain, to a different but related domain. The study showed that the knowledge gained from the non-medical domain was able to be transferred to the medical domain by the process of fine-tuning and more training.

Following that, Fully Convolutional Networks (FCN) for semantic segmentation by [14] were introduced in 2014 which proposed a novel architecture that replaces the fully connected (Dense) layers in CNNs with convolutional layers that allows for variable size input as compared to nonconvolutional nets which accept fixed size input such as the architecture proposed by [15]. FCNs also introduce skip connections which concatenates output of lower layers to higher layers which in turn retain the global structure in predictions, leading to less loss of detail during the final predictions. The research adapted popular classification networks such as AlexNet [12], VGGNet [16] and GoogleNet [17] and transformed them into their convolutional counterparts, which achieved state-of-the-art accuracy on the PASCAL VOC 2011 dataset.The rise of FCN led to the development of U-Net [18], being one of the key contributors to the field of semantic segmentation. Despite its original intention being the segmentation of neuronal structures, U-Net has been shown to be applicable to various other imaging domains, and has been adapted for the segmentation of various objects with examples such as the pancreas [19], coral reefs [20], and even audio signals from human voices [21].

Despite the popularity of FCNs in recent years for brain tumour segmentation tasks, Wang et al. proposed a novel CNN architecture to tackle this task. The authors proposed a cascading CNN architecture [22] used in conjunction with anisotropic convolutions and by fusing the output of the cascade of CNNs in three orthogonal views to allow a more accurate and robust segmentation prediction. The authors approach the challenge in a hierarchical structure, using an individual CNN to create a bounding box of one class of tumour region, then feeding the output into the next CNN to create another bounding box of the next tumour region to create a binary segmentation problem. Anisotropic convolutions were introduced to reduce memory consumption by introducing a smaller receptive field with the trade off being that the network loses some global feature information. In addition, residual connections [23] are used in the inter-slice layers by adding the input of the block to the output, further encouraging the learning of residual functions from the input. Predictions were made by fusing the segmentation results from axial, sagittal, and coronal views. The authors managed to introduce an architecture that produces competitive accuracy scores and more efficient at test time compared to the more common FCN approaches.

An interesting submission during the BraTS 2018 challenge was the work performed by Andriy Myronenko utilizing an asymmetrical encoder-decoder based CNN architecture [24] with the encoder being the larger part and the decoder the smaller part. The larger encoder is responsible for extracting feature maps from the image while the smaller decoder is responsible to reconstruct the segmentation mask produced. The authors introduce additional branch to the endpoint of the encoder section which induces regularization to the architecture by using skip connections to transfer lower level features to higher levels of abstraction [25]. The author does not perform image augmentation as a pre-processing step, rather performing image augmentation at test time. The final submission by the author was an ensemble of 10 models which eventually took first place in the BraTS2018 challenge.

Kamnitas et al. constructed an architecture [26] with the goal of producing a more reliable and objective deep learning model which can generalize to various types of medical databases and robust to failures of individual components. The architecture was termed the Ensemble of Multiple Models and Architectures (EMMA). The authors construct an ensemble of models based on popular and well performing architectures in the medical imaging space which include two DeepMedic [27] models, 3 FCNs [14] and two 3D U-Net architectures [18]. Slight modifications were performed on all 3 architectures to adapt to this ensemble, such as doubling the number of feature maps in the DeepMedic at each layer, changing skip connections to be a summation of signals instead of a concatenation in U-Net and other changes. All models were trained individually and for predictions, their confidence maps for each class are created by calculating for each voxel, the class that it belongs to. EMMA assigns the voxel to a class with the highest confidence. This approach won the authors first place at the BraTS2017 segmentation challenge.

Jonas et al. proposed a transfer learning approach [28] which utilizes the ResNet34 encoder. The author extended upon AlbuNet [29] proposed by A. Shvets et al. The authors dropped the T1 modality from a the BraTS2020 dataset to match the 3-channel input of ResNe34. For the evaluation of the model, Jonas et.al used the validation set of the BraTS2020 challenge, in addition to using a private dataset obtained from a Syrian-Lebanese hospital that is situated in Brazil. The research shows that their model outperforms AlbuNet2D and a introduces a more robust training process with speedier convergence compared to models without pretraining.

Yixin et al. also contributed to the segmentation task of BraTS 2020, proposing a novel architecture to tackle the challenge. Yixin et.al proposed [30] a "Modality-Pairing Network" architecture. The authors split modalities into two groups,(T1, T1ce) and (T2, FLAIR) respectively for a dual-branch network that uses the 3D U-Net. The first branch uses the FLAIR and T2 modalities to extract the features of the whole tumour, with the second branch using the T1 and T1ce modalities to learn other feature representations of the tumour. Both branches are densely connected to learn the complementary information effectively. Another unique point of the paper was the usage of an ensemble of models to provide the segmentation labels of the highest priority, by averaging the sigmoid predictions of each trained single model and selecting the label with highest priority. The authors managed to win second place for the segmentation task at the BraTS 2020 challenge with their approach.

In the paper published by Fabian et al., [31] the authors have previously developed an automated framework named nnU-Net [32] for 3D biomedical image segmentation.The authors employed nnU-Net to the BraTS 2020 segmentation challenge with BraTS-specific optimizations to better score on the challenge. Such optimizations include a region-based training approach, splitting the entire tumour region into 3 subregions based off the BraTS labelling structure, which consists of "edema", "non-enhancing tumour and necrosis" and "enhancing tumour". Each subregion is then optimized independently by changing the objective function and optimization to all three tumour subregions instead of individually optimizing each subregion. The authors increased the probability of augmentations that may happen to their data sample which artificially increases the number of data points by applying changes to the original data points, thus increasing the generalizability of the model. Lastly, the authors developed an internal BraTS-like ranking system to more realistically gauge the models produced against the BraTS segmentation benchmarks, using the evaluation metrics of BraTS to decide on the ensemble of models to use for the competition. Based on all these efforts, the team achieved first place in the BraTS 2020 segmentation challenge and has proven that nnU-Net is generalizable across various medical imaging domains and provide state-of-the-art segmentation accuracy.

In our work, we extend upon the work by Jonas et al., we aim to fill in the gaps in the research by extending AlbuNet3D to accept all 4 input modalities. We believe that by discarding the T1 modality, some valuable knowledge and feature representations are lost. We also experiment with a different noise injection owing to research that justifies the distribution of signal intensities in MRI images when exposed to noise. We utilise a combination of these techniques and report our results.

3   Methodology

3.1   BraTS2020 Dataset

The publicly released BraTS2020 dataset consists of multimodal MRI scans of glioblastomas (HGG) and lower grade gliomas (LGG) which contains 369 training entries with ground truths and 125 validation entries without ground truths.The ground truth consists of the annotation of 3 different tumour regions, namely enhancing tumour (ET) with label 4, peritumoral edema (ED) with label 2 and the non-enhancing tumour core (NCT/NET) with label 1.

3.2   Extending the Input Channels

The original AlbuNet3D only utilised a 3-channel input due to the original nature of the ResNet34 encoder. T1ce, T2 and FLAIR modalities were in use for the original paper by Jonas et al. In our project, we explore the possibility of extending the original encoder to a 4-channel input. We replace the initial 2D convolutional layer in the ResNet34 encoder with another 2D convolutional layer, that contains 4 input channels. Next, we initialize the weights of the extra convolutional layer with the pretrained weights of the first convolutional layer. The reasoning behind our actions is to recover the knowledge representation from pretrained weights instead of a random initialization of weights which might not carry any pretrained knowledge, therefore reducing the effectiveness of the original transfer learning approach.

3.3   Pre-processing and Data Augmentation Policies

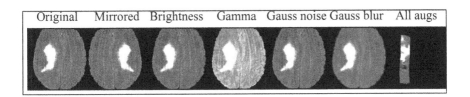

Fig. 1. Comparison between original image and transformations at slice 20 using a red heatmap plot, with all transformations applied on the last image.

All modalities undergo a Z-score normalization and are cropped to their non-zero regions to reduce subsequent computational time and memory usage. Various data augmentations are applied to all modalities such as spatial and geometric transforms by rotation, random cropping, elastic deformation, and mirroring along axes at 10% probability. Colour space transforms are then applied with 15% probability by increasing the pixel brightness multiplicatively, followed by a gamma transformation which introduces gamma correction as an augmentation. Lastly, we introduce Rician noise injection as our data augmentation technique instead of the regular Gaussian noise injection based on research [33] that intensity of MRI signals in the presence of noise follow a Rician distribution. We also experiment by doubling the probabilities of all data augmentations and transforms.

3.4   Training and Hyperparameters

Our optimizer of choice is the Adam optimizer with a learning rate of 1e−3. We use a minibatch size of 100 and a batch size of 12. Training was performed on all 369 training entries for 50 epochs. Our loss function is the Multiple Dice Loss [32] represented by Eq. 1:

$$L(X,Y) = -\frac{2}{K} \sum_{k \in K} \frac{\sum_i |X_k \cap Y_k|_i}{\sum_i |X_k|_i + \sum_i |Y_k|_i}, i \in I, k \in K \tag{1}$$

where K represents the number of classes, X and Y represent predictions by the model and ground truth segmentations respectively.

4   Results and Discussion

Table 1. Dice score and Hausdorff distance of our experiments over 5 runs on test data

Model	Dice score			Hausdorff distance (95%)		
	ET	**WT**	**TC**	**ET**	**WT**	**TC**
Baseline	0.7154	0.8799	0.7683	31.5239	6.2105	16.8746
Baseline + DA	0.6954	0.8715	0.7680	39.0705	6.7112	9.1945
4C	0.6978	0.8777	0.7285	33.6261	7.3111	22.1818
4C + DA	0.694	0.8618	0.7429	29.5483	6.7094	18.7031
4C + RN	0.7010	0.8724	0.7359	33.9554	7.3399	20.3901
4C + WI	0.7020	0.8762	0.7747	33.3952	6.494	15.4334
4C + WI + RN	0.7186	0.8736	0.7730	32.1839	6.7790	15.2054

As seen from Table 1, our approach by extending the input to 4 modalities (4C) with weight initialization (WI), using Rician Noise (RN) as the preferred noise injection yielded a marginal increase in accuracy on the Enhancing Tumour

Table 2. Standard deviation of dice scores of our experiments over 5 runs on test data

Model	Standard deviation (dice)		
	ET	**WT**	**TC**
Baseline	0.2969	0.0887	0.2527
Baseline + DA	0.2972	0.1039	0.2544
4C	0.3011	0.0894	0.2897
4C + DA	0.2929	0.1092	0.2672
4C + RN	0.2946	0.1022	0.2728
4C + WI	0.3007	0.0908	0.2285
4C + WI + RN	0.2870	0.0945	0.2473

(ET) and Tumour Core (TC) classes. From Table 2, we also notice that the standard deviation of both classes mentioned shrinks marginally, signifying that the model is more robust towards outliers. However, without weight initialization, the 4-modality approach performs slightly poorly compared to 4C + WI + RN. We hypothesize that the weight initialization using existing pretrained weights helped to stabilize the training process and provide a more robust model due to the existing knowledge and features from the pretrained weights. Without pretrained weights, the new convolutional layer for the fourth modality is just initialized with random weights that might not provide any sort of learnt representations and knowledge to the model.

Aggressive data augmentation policies (denoted by DA) often resulted in a degradation of segmentation performance. By increasing the probability of all augmentations, more images in the training set are transformed and augmented. However, these aggressive augmentations did not provide any boost in accuracy, possibly due to the model losing its ability to generalize because the augmented samples could not reflect the possible deformities in actual MRI images. It is possible that a combination of different augmentations could be used to achieve a more robust model.

5   Conclusion

We show that our results outperform the original AlbuNet3D marginally by extending the input to four channels to accept all modalities of the BraTS dataset. In order to further improve on the accuracy of our extension, further work should focus on the initialization of weights when extending the pretrained ResNet34 encoder of AlbuNet3D or to extend the approach to other pretrained encoders that may perhaps provide a greater accuracy boost. It is crucial that this line of research may continue to develop adaptive methods that may process inputs of variable modalities in the future.

In conclusion, we have achieved the original aim and objectives of the project, which is to extend upon the gaps in literature to propose an improved algorithm which can provide enhanced segmentation accuracy. Further work should focus on the adaptive initialization of weights at the start of training when extending the input channels of a pretrained network to further stabilise the training process and achieve higher segmentation accuracy.

References

1. Louis, D.N., Ohgaki, H., Wiestler, O.D., et al.: The 2007 who classiwcation of tumours of the central nervous system. Acta Neuropathol **114**, 97–109 (2007). https://doi.org/10.1007/s00401-007-0243-4
2. Astrocytoma and glioblastoma (gbm) – brain and spinal cord tumours – cancer research UK. Accessed 05 Apr 2021
3. High grade glioma – the royal marsden nhs foundation trust. Accessed 16 Dec 2020
4. Survival – brain and spinal cord tumours – cancer research UK. Accessed 21 Oct 2020
5. Grech, N., Dalli, T., Mizzi, S., Meilak, L., Calleja, N., Zrinzo, A.: Rising incidence of glioblastoma multiforme in a well-defined population. Cureus, **12**(5)
6. Despotović, I., Goossens, B., Philips, W.: Mri segmentation of the human brain: challenges, methods, and applications. Comput. Math. Methods Med. **2015**
7. Angulakshmi M., Priya, G.: Automated brain tumour segmentation techniques- a review. Int. J. Imaging Syst. Technol., **27**(1), 66–77
8. Gordillo, N., Montseny, E.,Sobrevilla, P.: State of the art survey on mri brain tumor segmentation. Magn. Reson. Imaging, **31**8), 1426–1438
9. Gibbs, P., Buckley, D., Blackband, S., Horsman, A.: Tumour volume determination from mr images by morphological segmentation. Phys. Med. Biol., **41**(11), 2437–2446
10. Pham, D., Xu, C., Prince, J.: A survey of current methods in medical image segmentation
11. Kavitha, A., Chellamuthu, C., Rupa, K.: An efficient approach for brain tumour detection based on modified region growing and neural network in mri images. In: 2012 International Conference on Computing, Electronics and Electrical Technologies, ICCEET 2012, pp. 1087–1095 (2012)
12. Krizhevsky, A., Sutskever, I., Hinton, G.: Imagenet classification with deep convolutional neural networks. Accessed 05 Apr 2021
13. Bar, Y., Diamant, I., Wolf, L., Lieberman, S., Konen, E., Greenspan, H.: Chest pathology detection using deep learning with non-medical training. In: Proceedings - International Symposium on Biomedical Imaging, vol. 2015, pp. 294–297
14. Long, J., Shelhamer, E., Darrell, T.: Fully convolutional networks for semantic segmentation
15. Le, Q.: Building high-level features using large scale unsupervised learning. In: ICASSP, IEEE International Conference on Acoustics, Speech and Signal Processing - Proceedings, pp. 8595–8598. Accessed 03 May 2021
16. Simonyan, K., Zisserman, A.: Very deep convolutional networks for large-scale image recognition. Sep. Accessed 03 May 2021
17. Szegedy, C.: Going deeper with convolutions. In: Proceedings of the IEEE Computer Society Conference on Computer Vision and Pattern Recognition, vol. 07, pp. 1–9, 12 June 2015

18. Ronneberger, O., Fischer, P., Brox, T.: U-net: convolutional networks for biomedical image segmentation. In: Lecture Notes in Computer Science (including subseries Lecture Notes in Artificial Intelligence and Lecture Notes in Bioinformatics, vol. 9351, pp. 234–241

19. Oktay, O.: Attention u-net: learning where to look for the pancreas. arXiv, Apr 2018. Accessed 05 Apr 2021

20. Mizuno, K.: An efficient coral survey method based on a large-scale 3-d structure model obtained by speedy sea scanner and u-net segmentation. Sci. Rep, **10**(1), 12416

21. Jansson, A., Humphrey, E., Montecchio, N., Bittner, R., Kumar, A., Weyde, T.: Singing voice separation with deep u-net convolutional networks. Accessed 03 May 2021

22. Wang, G., Li, W., Ourselin, S., Vercauteren, T.: Automatic brain tumor segmentation using cascaded anisotropic convolutional neural networks: In: Lecture Notes in Computer Science, vol. 10670 LNCS of including Subser. Lecture Notes in Computer Science Lecture Notes Bioinformatics, pp. 178–190

23. He, K., Zhang, X., Ren, S., Sun, J.: Deep residual learning for image recognition. In: Proceedings of the IEEE Computer Society Conference on Computer Vision and Pattern Recognition, **2016**, pp. 770–778

24. Myronenko, A.: 3d mri brain tumor segmentation using autoencoder regularization. In: Lecture Notes in Computer Science (including Subseries Lecture Notes in Artificial Intelligence Lecture Notes Bioinformatics, vol. 11384 LNCS, pp. 311–320, Accessed 03 May 2021

25. Kukačka, J., Golkov, V., Cremers, D.: Regularization for deep learning: a taxonomy. arXiv

26. Kamnitsas, K.: Ensembles of multiple models and architectures for robust brain tumour segmentation. Lecture Notes in Computer Science (including Subseries Lecture Notes in Artificial Intelligence Lecture Notes Bioinformatics, vol. 10670 LNCS, pp. 450–462. Accessed 03 May 2021

27. Kamnitsas, K.: Deepmedic for brain tumor segmentation. In: Lecture Notes in Computer Science (including Subseries Lecture Notes in Artificial Intelligence and Lecture Notes in Bioinformatics), vol. 10154 LNCS, pp. 138–149

28. Wacker, J., Ladeira, M., Nascimento, J.: Transfer learning for brain tumor segmentation. arXiv

29. Shvets, A., Iglovikov, V., Rakhlin, A., Kalinin, A.: Angiodysplasia detection and localization using deep convolutional neural networks. In: Proceedings - 17th IEEE International Conference on Machine Learning and Applications ICMLA 2018, pp. 612–617 (2018)

30. Wang, Y.: Modality-pairing learning for brain tumor segmentation. Accessed: 10 Dec

31. Isensee, F., Jaeger, P., Full, P., Vollmuth, P., Maier-Hein, K.: Nnu-net for brain tumor segmentation. Accessed 10 Dec

32. Isensee, F., Kickingereder, P., Wick, W., Bendszus, M., Maier-Hein, K.: Brain tumor segmentation and radiomics survival prediction: contribution to the brats 2017 challenge. In: Lecture Notes in Computer Science (including Subseries Lecture Notes in Artificial Intelligence Lecture Notes Bioinformatics, vol. 10670 LNCS, pp. 287–297 (2017)

33. Gudbjartsson H., Patz, S.: The rician distribution of noisy mri data. Magn. Reson. Med. **34**(6), 910–914

Automatic Seizure Prediction Based on Cross-Feature Fusion Stream Convolutional Neural Network

Yue Wang$^{(\boxtimes)}$, Yu Wang, and Yan Piao

School of Electronic and Information Engineering, Electronic and Communication Engineering Major, Changchun University of Science and Technology, Changchun, Jilin, China

Abstract. Seizure is a common nervous system disease, currently about 1% of the world's population suffer from seizure. EEG signals are the main tools for predicting seizures. Methods to accurately predict seizures would help reduce helplessness and uncertainty. In this paper, we designed a convolutional neural networks (CNNs) based on cross-feature fusion stream for seizure prediction using seizure datasets from Boston Children's Hospital. The EEG data collected in time domain, frequency domain and time frequency domain were fused with the algorithm to classify the preictal and interictal so as to predict seizure. Experimental results show that the cross-feature fusion stream CNN model achieves 97% accuracy on the CHB-MIT dataset.

Keywords: Seizure prediction · EEG · Cross-feature fusion stream convolutional neural networks · CNN

1 Introduction

Seizure, a chronic disease characterized by the occurrence of spontaneous seizures, affects 1% of the world's population [1]. EEG signals reflect the spontaneous, continuous and rhythmic activities of brain neurons, and have long been studied for seizure detection [2]. However, the manual analysis of EEG signals is a relatively subjective process, which has many shortcomings such as high cost, low efficiency and large error. Therefore, it is very necessary to develop an automatic seizure prediction model.

In recent years, deep learning has been widely used in the field of image processing due to its advantage of automatic extraction of image features. CNN is a multi-layer neural network model, which is inspired by the neurobiology of the visual cortex and consists of the convolutional layer and the full connective layer [3]. CNN has been successfully applied in auxiliary diagnosis of a variety of diseases. Havaei used CNN to segment brain tumors from magnetic resonance imaging (MRI), and Hosseini used CNN to diagnose Alzheimer's disease from magnetic resonance imaging [4]. CNN's strong learning ability can not only provide high accuracy for seizure prediction, but also greatly reduce the workload of physicians. In this study, cross-feature fusion stream CNN was used to study seizure prediction. Compared with the traditional seizure prediction model,

© Springer Nature Switzerland AG 2021
M. Mahmud et al. (Eds.): AII 2021, CCIS 1435, pp. 70–76, 2021.
https://doi.org/10.1007/978-3-030-82269-9_6

the model used in this study mainly has two points: 1. The cross-feature fusion stream CNN was used to fuse the characteristics in the time domain, frequency domain and time-frequency domain of the EEG signals. 2. A cross-patient seizure prediction model was realize.

2   Experimental Data

In this study, the open source seizure EEG dataset (abbreviated as CHB-MIT) from Boston Children's Hospital was adopted [5]. A total of 24 scalp EEG signals from pediatric seizure patients (Nos. 1 to 24 respectively) were recorded in the CHB-MIT dataset, with a total duration of over 900 h, and a total of 170 seizure signals were collected. EEG signals were collected from 23 patients with refractory seizure, including 18 girls and 5 boys, with a mean age of 9.56 years for the girls and 11.1 years for the boys. Case 1 and Case 21 were the same patient, and the dataset recorded EEG signals from the patient at 11 and 13 years of age.

Here we consider interictal as at least two hours after the end of the seizure and between two hours before the next seizure [6].In the data set, for seizures that were less than 30 min apart from the previous seizure, we treated them as one seizure and the previous seizure as the beginning of the episode. In order to extract interictal data, there should be a time interval of at least 5 h between consecutive seizures.Previous research results have shown that there are great differences between EEG signals in preictal and interictal [7], so seizure prediction can be further regarded as the detection of preictal and interictal signals. The division of EEG signal states is shown in Fig. 1. A total of 969 h of EEG and 163 seizures were captured using 23 electrodes at a 256 Hz sampling rate. According to this classification criteria, we selected 14 examples from the data set for research. The number of seizures of the patients we selected is shown in Table 1.

Table 1. The number of seizures in patients used in this study

Subjects	Chb01	Chb02	Chb04	Chb05	Chb06	Chb07	Chb08
Seizure (number)	2	2	2	3	3	2	2
Subjects	Chb09	Chb10	Chb14	Chb18	Chb19	Chb20	Chb21
Seizure (number)	2	2	2	2	1	1	1

3   Method

3.1   Denoising

The energy of EEG signals is relatively weak, and it is easily affected by various internal and external factors, resulting in some artefacts. In this study, the first type of artifact is removed by wavelet denoising and the second type of artifact is removed by band-stop filter.

Wavelet denoising is a time-frequency denoising method based on wavelet transform (CWT) [8]. The essence of wavelet threshold denoising is the process of suppressing the useless part of the signal and enhancing the useful part. The wavelet denoising process is shown in Fig. 2.

In addition to various artifacts, the CHB-MIT dataset also has power frequency interference of 60Hz. Therefore, in this study, the frequency range of 57–63 Hz and 117–123 Hz components are used by a band-stop filter, which can conveniently and effectively remove power frequency interference and power line noise.

3.2 Feature Extraction

In order to be balanced between access to each patient's interictal and preictal of EEG data, this study adopts the sliding window algorithm on brain electrical signal processing, including the size of the sliding window for 30s, sliding step for 10s. In order to reduce network computation, we extracted features from lead 6 of lead 23. These six leads were evenly distributed in the hemisphere of scalp, respectively, FP1-F7, FP2-F8, P7-O1, P8-O2, FZ-CZ and CZ-PZ.

3.2.1 Time-Frequency Feature Extraction

In this study, we converted the EEG signals into a two-dimensional matrix similar to the image format through short-time Fourier transform (STFT). STFT is often used in time-frequency analysis. For STFT, the signal $x(u)$ is prefiltered before and after time t, and the Fourier transform is calculated for each time t.

$$STFT(t,f) = \int_{-\infty}^{+\infty} x(\tau)h(\tau - t)e^{-if\tau}d\tau \tag{1}$$

Where $h(t)$ is a short time window. STFT suffers from tradeoff between its window length and its frequency resolution.

3.2.2 Feature Extraction in Frequency Domain

Fast Fourier Transform (FFT) is a fast algorithm of the discrete Fourier transform, which can transform a signal into the frequency domain and extract the spectrum of a signal. Therefore, in order to use the frequency domain features, we use the spectrogram of the EEG signal as one of the features.

3.2.3 Time Domain Characteristics

The time domain characteristic of the signal is to judge the characteristic basis of seizure by analyzing the time domain waveform, period and rhythm waveform of the EEG signal. Therefore, we input the 5S EEG data of 6 leads into the cross-feature fusion stream CNN for the extraction of time-domain features.

3.3 Cross-Feature Fusion Stream Convolutional Neural Network

Two-stream convolutional neural networks are divided into spatial stream networks and time stream networks [9]. Inspired by the double-stream convolutional neural network,

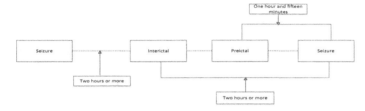

Fig. 1. Classification of EEG states

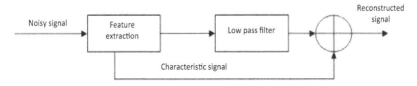

Fig. 2. Wavelet denoising flow chart

a novel cross-feature fusion stream CNN is designed in this study, which integrates the time-domain, frequency-domain and time-frequency domain features of EEG signals. The specific framework is shown in the Fig. 3. Input 1, input 2 and input 3 are respectively the time-frequency diagram of the EEG signal with lead 6 for 30s, the spectral diagram of the EEG signal with lead 6 for 30s, and the one-dimensional EEG signal with lead 6 for 5s.Where input 1 and input 2 contain three identical convolution blocks, each of which consists of a batch normalization layer, a convolution layer with a corrected linear unit (RELU) activation function, and a maximum pool layer. The size of the three convolutional layers is $16 \times 5 \times 5$ cores, and the step size is 2, $32 \times 3 \times 3$ cores, and the step size is 1, $64 \times 3 \times 3$ cores, and the size of the pooling layer in the convolutional block is 2×2.For input 3, one-dimensional convolution is used to process the two convolution layers with sizes of 5×1 and 3×1 respectively and step sizes of 2, and the two pooling layers with sizes of 2×1 and step sizes of 2 respectively. Finally, they will be stretched into eigenvectors and spliced together at the aggregation layer. In view of the need to extract features of different proportions in the fusion network, the model is not easy to overfit. In addition, each stream can make its own predictions, making learning more flexible and helping to improve accuracy. In this study, we designed a shared architecture to fuse relevant information from the time domain, frequency domain, and time-frequency domains to make better decisions than if the time-frequency domain was used alone. In the output layer, a 1×2816 full connection layer is added to connect the multimodal features to a joint representation for calculating fusion as the final goal. This fused representation provides additional regularization and can aid in generalization. Then, the model parameters.

Are optimized by applying stochastic gradient descent to the global loss, which is defined as:

$$y = \frac{\exp(\theta_k x)}{\sum_{j=1}^{m} \exp(\theta_k x)} \tag{2}$$

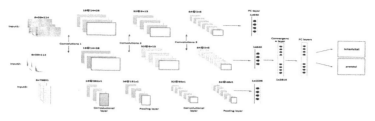

Fig. 3. Cross-feature fusion stream convolutional neural network

Where y_k is the output probability, θ_k is the weight parameter and x is the input neuron. In order to realize the cross-patient seizure prediction method, we used the scrambled characteristic data of Chb01 to Chb14 in Table 1 as the training set (80%), and the scrambled characteristic data of Chb18 to Chb21 in Table 1 as the test set (10%) and verification set (10%). Here we abbreviate the training set, validation set and test set as TS, VS and ts respectively. The number of training sets, test sets, and verification sets is shown in Table 2. We performed 10 cross-validations to optimize the neural network. We trained 200 model parameters of epochs with Adam Optimizer, and epoch was defined as a single training iteration for all batches propagated forward and backward. During the training period, the initial learning rate was set to 0.001 and attenuation was once every 5 epochs.

Table 2. Seizure data sets

Data set	Preictal	Interictal	Total
TS	596	540	1136
VS	69	63	132
ts	73	69	142
Total	738	672	1410

4   Result

Accuracy, precision and recall were calculated to quantitatively evaluate the results, so as to comprehensively investigate the performance of the proposed network architecture. The formula is as follows:

$$Accuracy = \frac{TP + TN}{TP + TN + FP + FN} \tag{3}$$

$$Precision = \frac{TP}{TP + FP} \tag{4}$$

$$Recall = \frac{TP}{TP + FN} \tag{5}$$

True positive (TP) represents the number of positive images detected correctly, also known as sensitivity; True Negative (TN) represents the number of negative images detected correctly, also known as specificity. False positive (FP) refers to the number of false positive tests, also known as misdiagnosis rate; False negative (FN) refers to the number of samples that were misclassified as negative, also known as missed diagnosis rate.

In order to verify the improvement of the classification performance of the cross-feature fusion stream model, we compared the results of the cross-feature fusion stream model with the results of the single-stream system, and the accuracy is shown in Table 2. Here we abbreviate the time domain, frequency domain, and time-frequency domain as TD, FD, and TFD, and abbreviate the cross-feature fusion stream convolutional neural network as CFS-CNN. The results showed that, compared with single-stream fusion, cross-feature fusion fusion could more accurately detect the preictal and interictal of seizure, so as toachieve accurate seizure prediction.

Table 3. Confusion matrix of seizure dataset

Actual category	Forecast category	
	Interictal	Preictal
Interictal	129	3
Preictal	5	137

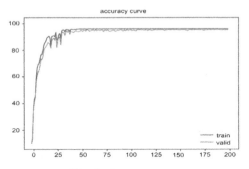

Fig. 4. Accuracy curve

Table 4. Results of fusion stream and sub-stream data sets

Data set	Accuracy	Precision	Recall
TD	0.832	0.855	0.843
FD	0.881	0.861	0.860
TFD	0.930	0.931	0.927
CFS-CNN	0.970	0.978	0.964

5   Conclusion

In order to improve the classification performance of the fusion stream convolutional neural network model, we compared the results of the sub-stream and the fusion stream system, and the correct rate is shown in Table 4. Table 3 is the confusion matrix of the network, and Fig. 4 is the accuracy curve. Especially the fusion stream can achieve the best performance. The results show that, compared with sub-streams, the fusion stream network can more accurately predict whether seizures occur, thereby significantly improving the performance and robustness of the model.

References

1. Hosseini, M.-P., Pompili, D., Elisevich, K., Soltanian-Zadeh, H.: Optimized deep learning for EEG big data and seizure prediction BCI via Internet of Things. IEEE Trans. Big Data **3**(4), 392–404 (2017). https://doi.org/10.1109/TBDATA.2017.2769670
2. Cao, J., Zhu, J., Hu, W., et al.: Epileptic signal classification with deep EEG features by stacked CNNs. IEEE Trans. Cogn. Dev. Syst. (99), 1–1 (2019)
3. Mahmud, M., Kaiser, M.S., Hussain, A., et al.: Applications of deep learning and reinforcement learning to biological data. IEEE Trans. Neural Networks Learn. Syst. **29**(6), 2063–2079 (2017)
4. Mahmud, M., Kaiser, M.S., Mcginnity, T.M., et al.: Deep learning in mining biological data. Cogn. Comput. 13(10) (2021)
5. Ramakrishnan, S., Murugavel, A.S.M.: Epileptic seizure detection using fuzzy-rules-based sub-band specific features and layered multi-class SVM. Pattern Anal. Appl. **22**, 1161–1176 (2018)
6. Truong, N.D., Nguyen, A.D., Kuhlmann, L., et al.: Convolutional neural networks for seizure prediction using intracranial and scalp electroencephalogram. Neural Networks (2018). S0893608018301485
7. Weinand, M.E., Philip Carter, L., El-Saadany, W.F., Sioutos, P.J., Labiner, D.M., Oommen, K.J.: Cerebral blood flow and temporal lobe epileptogenicity. J. Neurosurg. **86**(2), 226–232 (1997). https://doi.org/10.3171/jns.1997.86.2.0226
8. Gopinath, R.A., Burrus, C.S.: Efficient computation of the wavelet transforms. In: International Conference on Acoustics. IEEE (1990)
9. Li, X., Ding, M., Piurica, A.: deep feature fusion via two-stream convolutional neural network for hyperspectral image classification. IEEE Trans. Geosci. Remote Sens. **58**(4), 2615–2629 (2020)

Application of AI and Informatics in Healthcare

Anomaly Detection in Invasively Recorded Neuronal Signals Using Deep Neural Network: Effect of Sampling Frequency

Marcos Fabietti[1] , Mufti Mahmud[1,2,3(✉)] , and Ahmad Lotfi[1]

[1] Department of Computer Science, Nottingham Trent University, Clifton Lane, Clifton, Nottingham NG11 8NS, UK
[2] Medical Technologies Innovation Facility, Nottingham Trent University, Clifton Lane, Clifton, Nottingham NG11 8NS, UK
mufti.mahmud@ntu.ac.uk
[3] Computing and Informatics Research Center, Nottingham Trent University, Nottingham NG11 8NS, UK

Abstract. Abnormality detection has advanced in recent years with the help of machine learning, in particular with deep learning models, which can predict accurately across many types of signals and applications. In the case of neuronal signals, abnormalities can present themselves as artefacts or manifestations of neurological diseases. Among the diverse neuronal pathologies, we chose to look at the detection of seizures, as they manifest as a brief anomaly in contrast to normal brain activity in the majority portion of the data during a prolonged recording. Epileptic patients benefit from portable systems, which are dependant on efficient energy consumption, and the sampling frequency of the signal is of vital importance element to its battery lifespan. In this article, the impact of the sampling rate on a deep learning-based multi-class classification model is explored via the use of an open-source seizure dataset.

Keywords: ECoG · iEEG · Seizure · Brain signals · Data acquisition · Anomaly detection

1 Introduction

Anomaly detection is the process of identifying outliers in data from a pattern considered as "normal". The process of defining what is "normal" and "anomaly" can be data driven, where characteristics of each one are not defined a priory by a specialist of the domain, but instead measured in the sampled population. In the current age of Big Data, where the amount, complexity and dimensionality of data available to be collected and studied are significant, computational methods provide useful tools to handle it in an efficient manner [31].

Among the diverse range of methods, machine learning (ML) techniques stand out due to their known performance as classifiers and predictors. These techniques has been applied in a variety of tasks including biological data

M. Mahmud et al. (Eds.): AII 2021, CCIS 1435, pp. 79–91, 2021.
https://doi.org/10.1007/978-3-030-82269-9_7

mining [25,26], image analysis [1], financial forecasting [30], anomaly detection [41,42], disease detection [27,29], COVID-19 detection [4,10,18], natural language processing [32,40], assay detection [37]. Among them, deep neural networks stand out, which are composed of multiple layers of neurons for processing of non-linear information and were inspired by how the human brain works. There are different architectures which have been developed for specific tasks, for example one-dimensional convolutional neural networks (1D-CNN) is an adaptation for time sequences of a model originally intended for images due to their capacity to perform both as the feature extractor and classifier.

Neuronal signals, in general, reflect neuronal network activity and provide information about brain functions. In their case, abnormalities can present themselves as artefacts or manifestations of neurological diseases. Among the diverse neuronal pathologies, we selected to research the detection of seizures due to the fact that they manifest as a brief anomaly in contrast to normal brain activity in the majority portion of the data during a prolonged recording. The gold standard for evaluating neuronal activity in epilepsy patients is electrocorticography (ECoG), which is commonly used for pre-surgical preparation to direct surgical resection of the lesion and epileptogenic region. ECoG signals are obtained with electrodes placed in the epidural or subdural layers of the brain, making it an invasive procedure, but it bypasses the distortions produced by the skull and intermediate tissue. The first location has a spatial resolution of 1.4 mm, while the second one of 1.25 mm [34].

Defining which acquisition technology to employ or how to configure it is not a trivial decision, as the sampling rate with which ECoG signals are acquired has a direct impact on the subsequent processes. For off-line analysis, if we consider the acquisition of ECoG with a typical 64 multi-channel system, a sampling rate of 5 kHz, and registering each value as a double (8 bytes), it would only take 7 min of recording to generate 1 gigabyte of data. For online analysis, the energy consumption of the analogue-to-digital converter and the wireless data transmitter scale with the bit length of the data [11,24]. This means the longer the digitised or transmitted sequence is, the shorter the battery life of the device will be.

Despite the memory and energy benefits of having a reduced signal resolution, there is an expected impact on the performance of a classifier, which authors in the literature have explored. Gliske et al. [16] delved into the impact sampling rate of ECoG has on high frequency oscillation detection, which are biomarkers for epilepsy, carried out by a non-ML method. After their analysis, they recommended a sampling rate and an anti-aliasing filter of at least 2 kHz 500 Hz, respectively, to detect the oscillations. On a similar topic, but for the electroencephalography signals (EEG), Kheller et al. [20] looked into how seizure detection by a support vector machine (SVM) performed when down-sampled from 256 64 Hz. Results show that it did not significantly impact the model's performance. However, the classifier was fed 38 handcrafted features instead of the raw signal. In addition, exploration of the bit-width was carried out for 16, 12 and 8 bits, where a significant performance drop compared to the full double precision was only observed with 8 bits. In a similar fashion, Chiang et al. [8] examined the reduction of transmitted data by wireless EEG seizure detection systems via the use of data reduction techniques. They chose an SVM model for classification and compared the energy consumed by transmitting the whole signal, a compressed signal and three handcrafted features. By sending the latter, the battery life was increased fourteen-fold while maintaining a 95% seizure detection rate.

To the best of our knowledge, there is no study that explores how the performance of a machine-learning based classification model trained with raw segments of ECoG signal varies based on the sampling rate of the examples. The goal of this article is to explore this topic, not the benchmarking of the model's performance or surveying the literature comparing different methodologies. For the latter, we direct the reader to the work of Rasheed et al. [33], an up to date review of state-of-the-art machine learning techniques for predicting epileptic seizures. The remainder of the article is divided into Sect. 2 where we explore the available open datasets and choose one for our analysis, the methodology is explained and the machine learning model described. This is followed by Sect. 3 where results are obtained and subsequently discussed. Finally, Sect. 4 is where conclusions are drawn.

2   Methodology

We have compiled the available open-access seizure ECoG datasets in Table 1. The sampling rate among them varies 256 Hz up to 5 kHz, and for our analysis we choose the one with the highest rate as to have more range to compare. The chosen dataset (highlighted in the table) is composed of ECoG recordings obtained from patients who were undergoing evaluation for epilepsy surgery belonging to two hospitals [28] . Raw data was filtered in the bandwidth of 2 kHz, and downsampled to 5 kHz. The recordings were manually classified into physiological, pathological, line noise and non-cerebral artefact classes (illustrated in Fig. 1), and then segmented into three-second length sequences.

Table 1. Available open-access seizure ECoG datasets

Reference	Host	Sampling rate	Channels	Subject
[15]	CRCNS	2 kHz	Multi	Human
[38]	Kaggle	0.5 to 5 kHz	Multi	Human
		0.4 kHz		Dog
[28]	**Kaggle**	**5 kHz**	**Single**	**Human**
[7]	SWEC-ETHZ	0.5 or 1 kHz	Multi	Human
[22]	Epilepsy Ecosystem	400 Hz	Multi	Human
[23]	Open neuro	1 kHz	Multi	Human
[6]	Open neuro	0.25, 0.5,1 or 2 KHz	Multi	Human

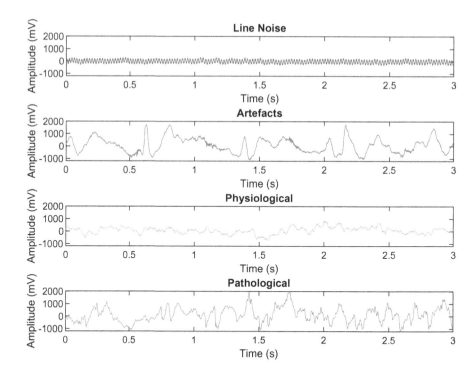

Fig. 1. Examples of the four classes in the dataset.

These sequences are time series, as they are a series of data points ordered in time. Different neural network architectures have been successfully used for their classification, such as multi layer perceptron [13], long short term memory networks [12] and convolutional neural networks [14]. A variation of the latter known as 1D-CNN was chosen for this article, which are able to extract information from areas of the signal, leading to more robust features and thus achieve better performances.

Convolutional neural networks were inspired on the biological structure of the animal visual cortex, and have the ability to learn filters which extract the patterns specific to their data. While many variations of it exist, with different sizes, order, depths and layers, they are mainly formed by five layers: convolutional (1), pooling (2), dropout (3), fully connected (4) and classification (5). The first layer is composed of of filter which slide over the input to produce a feature map. For every filter, a different feature map is generated, which captures local dependencies. Therefore, the bigger the amount of filters a network has, the more features are extracted from the input. As the network deepens, these layers extract higher level features as it considers the cumulative effect of many features in the previous layers. The function of the second layer is to decrease the dimensionality of each function map, which preserves the most relevant details by maintaining the maximum or average value of a given input group. In addition, it causes the network to become invariant to the transformation of inputs, such as distortion, translation and rotation, as well as reducing the over-fitting. The third layer reduces interdependent learning amongst the neurons, as it is is an approach to regularisation in neural networks. This is caused by turning off neurons with a probability of 1-p so that a reduced network is left, so the network is forced to learn more robust features. The fourth layer, 'fully connected', integrates non-linearly the high level features extracted up to that point via combinations, and feed them to the last layer. Finally, the fifth listed layer has n neurons, equal to the number of classes the examples will be classified as with a normalised probability score obtained via a soft-max function.

We have implemented a one dimension adaptation of AlexNet [21], achieved by flattening one dimension of the filters and pooling layers. The components of this network are described Table 2, where all 12 layers are listed. The convolutional layer's filters size are expressed inside brackets, multiplied by the quantity and succeeded by the stride (s) and the same notation is used for the pooling window's sizes and stride. The input size, number rectified linear unit in the fully connected layers and soft max units in the classification layer are within brackets as well. As the sequences are of smaller dimensionality than the images it was designed for, the amount of filters was reduced as well to multiples of 16.

Table 2. Architecture of the 1D-CNN model

Architecture	Component
Layer 1	Input
Layer 2	Convolution 1 [1,11] × 32, s = 1
Layer 3	Max pooling 1 [1,3], s = 2
Layer 4	Convolution 2 [1,5] × 64, s = 1
Layer 5	Max pooling2 [1,3], s = 2
Layer 6	Convolution 3 [1,3] × 128, s = 1
Layer 7	Convolution 4 [1,3] × 128, s = 1
Layer 8	Convolution 5 [1,3] × 128, s = 1
Layer 9	Max pooling 3 [1,3], s = 2
Layer 10	Fully connected [1024]
Layer 11	Fully connected [512]
Layer 12	Classification [4]

In order to avoid bias in training, due to fact that the datasets belonging to each hospital present a different amount of examples of each class, examples from both hospitals were randomly drawn to match the number of the one with least examples. This resulted in a total of 97,132 examples which were afterwards split into training (70%), validation (15%) and testing (15%) sets. Classification models were built for the different sampling rates of 5, 2, 1, 0.5 and 0.25 kHz, due to the fact that they are the ones that were mostly used by the various epilepsy datasets shown in Table 1. This allows us to showcase the difference in a model's performance trained with half of the previous sampling frequency in each iteration. The down-sampling was carried out with the matlab function *resample*, which applies an FIR anti-aliasing low-pass filter to the signal and compensates for the delay introduced by the filter. Subsequently, the signals were z-score normalised, as to have mean 0 and standard deviation equal to 1. The raw signal segments were used as an input to the 1D-CNN, but as it is expected to be a 3-channel image, each set was reshaped to a 4D vector: 1 × sequence length × 1 × number of sequences, where the sequence length is the sampling rate × 3 s. Finally, the models were trained with the Adam optimisation algorithm, with an initial learning rate of 0.001, momentum of 0.9 and a batch size of 512. A summary of the proposed workflow in the form of a functional block diagram is presented in Fig. 2.

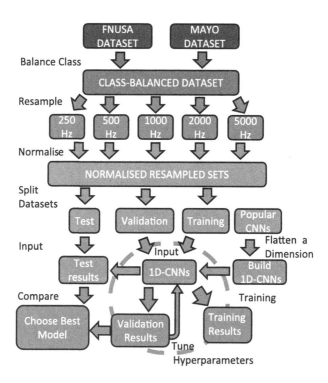

Fig. 2. Functional block diagram of the workflow.

3   Results and Discussion

The performance of the validation sets during training is shown in Fig. 3. The learning curves are similar among models, and the achieved final accuracies and losses are as well. For a closer analysis, the obtained results are summarised in Table 3, where the first column indicates the sampling rate, the second and third column the achieved accuracy of the test and validation set, and the fourth and fifth row the respective loss. The network has been able to successfully learn, as shown by the close performance between the training and validation sets. A **2.7%** difference between the performance of the highest rate and the lowest one is not significant in the obtained accuracy range. For further analysis, we proceed to observe the performance on the test set.

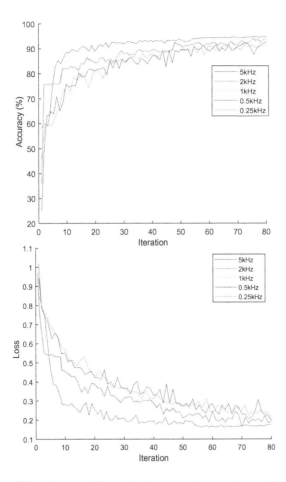

Fig. 3. Accuracy (%) and loss of the validation sets during the training process for the models of different sampling frequencies.

The performance over the test set is displayed in the form of confusion matrices in Fig. 4. The rows refer to the class predicted by the 1D-CNN (Output Class), and the columns refer to the true class (Target Class). Correctly classified segments are located in the diagonal cells (green coloured), and incorrectly classified ones in the off-diagonal cells (red coloured). In each cell it indicates both the amount of segments (in bold) and relative percentage to the overall number of segments. The precision and false discovery rate are displayed in the column on the far right, while the true positive rate and false negative rate are displayed at the bottom row. Lastly, the total accuracy is indicated at the bottom right cell.

The sensitivity of the line noise class remains consistently high (>99%) throughout every model, due to the distinct periodical waveform and low amplitude. The detection of artefacts is on the 92% range from 5 kHz to 500 Hz, but drop significantly 250 Hz, where there is a bigger miss-classification of it as pathological signals. This can be attributed to the abnormal waveform, higher amplitude and high frequency components. Identifying physiological signals correctly becomes more challenging to the model as the sampling rate is lowered, as it classifies it as artefactual more frequently. Finally, the correct classification of pathological (i.e. seizure) segments varies only a 1.5% from the highest sampling rate to the lowest, where the most common incorrect categorisation is with the physiological class.

Table 3. Training and validation results for different sampling frequencies.

Sampling frequency (kHz)	Train accuracy	Validation accuracy	Train loss	Val loss
5	0.9785	0.9471	0.0577	0.1753
2	0.9609	0.9382	0.1035	0.1967
1	0.9375	0.9304	0.1938	0.1967
0.5	0.9082	0.9283	0.2522	0.1995
0.25	0.9078	0.9198	0.2329	0.2143

Overall, The sampling rate does not seem to have a major impact on the classification model's performance. The optimal value for our dataset would be the **250 Hz**, given the trade off between sensitivity of **92.5%** and low sampling rate. The network size and results are comparable to Seizure-Net [17], an on-chip implementation of a CNN which achieved a 92.2% mean sensitivity of seizure detection of ECoG at a frequency of 256 Hz, consuming only 802 μW for a detection per second. This show the plausibility of deploying these models to a portable device, which can further be reduced 7 to 8 times by reducing the bit-size of the weights, as shown by [39].

The benefits of a reduced sampling rate are less storage consumption, smaller machine learning models and less energy consumption in portable systems. To

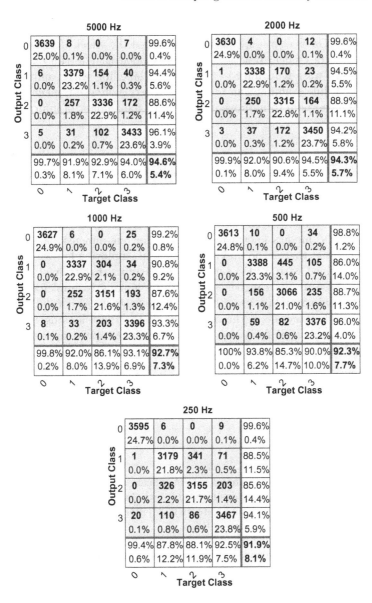

Fig. 4. Test set results for different sampling rates, for the classes: line noise (0), artefacts (1), physiological (2) and pathological (3).

this end, there has been development of techniques to compress ECoG signals which allow for faster off-line recovery and higher reconstruction quality [2,3, 5,19,35,36]. Overall, a lot of progress is being made to address the issues of machine learning models in portable systems.

If we were to contrast the capacity of these models to humans, we can look at the work of Davis et al. [9], whom investigated the effect of increased ECoG sampling rates in clinical practice. They concluded that for an expert human observer, there wasn't an improvement of the labelling with sampling rate of over 100 Hz. While a human can't compete in terms of speed, machine learning models still have room to improve in regards to the amount of information they require.

4   Conclusion

We set out to study the impact of the sampling rate of an invasive neural recording on the classification of abnormal signals by a deep learning model. After comparing the available open data, we selected the highest rate and used it to train a 1D-CNN, models known to work well for one-dimensional signals. Our findings show that there is no major difference in employing low sampling rates, as a model trained with 5 kHz performs similarly to that trained with twenty times less. These results can be used by those looking to implement portable ML systems in abnormality detection of neuronal signals, as it will have a major impact on the battery life of the device. Similarly, those looking to do an off-line analysis can benefit from the smaller file size to speed up computational time when doing resource-consuming tasks such as wavelet graphs and network connectivity studies. In the future we will expand on this topic with other invasively recorded neural signals, such as local field potentials and neural spike trains, where we expect to have similar findings and subsequently implement ML models in an on-chip system for health monitoring.

References

1. Ali, H.M., Kaiser, M.S., Mahmud, M.: Application of convolutional neural network in segmenting brain regions from mri data. In: Liang, P., Goel, V., Shan, C. (eds.) Brain Informatics. Lecture Notes in Computer Science, pp. 136–146. Springer International Publishing, Cham (2019)
2. Aprile, C., et al.: Learning-based near-optimal area-power trade-offs in hardware design for neural signal acquisition. In: 2016 International Great Lakes Symposium on VLSI (GLSVLSI), pp. 433–438. Ieee (2016)
3. Aprile, C., et al.: Adaptive learning-based compressive sampling for low-power wireless implants. IEEE Trans. Circ. Syst. I Regul. Pap. **65**(11), 3929–3941 (2018)
4. Aradhya, M.V.N., et al.: One shot cluster based approach for the detection of COVID–19 from Chest X–Ray images. Cogn. Comput. 1–9 (2021). https://doi.org/10.1007/s12559-020-09774-w
5. Baldassarre, L., Aprile, C., Shoaran, M., Leblebici, Y., Cevher, V.: Structured sampling and recovery of ieeg signals. In: 2015 IEEE 6th International Workshop on Computational Advances in Multi-Sensor Adaptive Processing (CAMSAP), pp. 269–272. IEEE (2015)
6. van Blooijs, D., Demuru, M., Zweiphenning, W., Leijten, F., Zijlmans, M.: Dataset clinical epilepsy ieeg to bids - respect longterm ieeg (2020). https://doi.org/10.18112/openneuro.ds003399.v1.0.1

7. Burrello, A., Cavigelli, L., Schindler, K., Benini, L., Rahimi, A.: Laelaps: an energy-efficient seizure detection algorithm from long-term human ieeg recordings without false alarms (2019). https://doi.org/10.3929/ETHZ-B-000307983

8. Chiang, J., Ward, R.K.: Energy-efficient data reduction techniques for wireless seizure detection systems. Sensors **14**(2), 2036–2051 (2014)

9. Davis, K.A., et al.: The effect of increased intracranial EEG sampling rates in clinical practice. Clin. Neurophysiol. **129**(2), 360–367 (2018)

10. Dey, N., Rajinikanth, V., Fong, S.J., Kaiser, M.S., Mahmud, M.: Social group optimization–assisted Kapur's entropy and morphological segmentation for automated detection of COVID-19 infection from computed tomography images. Cogn. Comput. **12**(5), 1011–1023 (2020). https://doi.org/10.1007/s12559-020-09751-3

11. Dlugosz, R., Iniewski, K.: Ultra low power current-mode algorithmic analog-to-digital converter implemented in 0.18/spl mu/m cmos technology for wireless sensor network. In: Proceedings of the International Conference Mixed Design of Integrated Circuits and System, 2006. MIXDES 2006, pp. 401–406. IEEE (2006)

12. Fabietti, M., et al.: Artifact detection in chronically recorded local field potentials using long-short term memory neural network. In: 2020 IEEE 14th International Conference on Application of Information and Communication Technologies (AICT), pp. 1–6 (2020). https://doi.org/10.1109/AICT50176.2020.9368638

13. Fabietti, M., et al.: Neural network-based artifact detection in local field potentials recorded from chronically implanted neural probes. In: Proceedings of the International Joint Conference on Neural Networks, pp. 1–8 (2020)

14. Fabietti, M., et al.: Adaptation of convolutional neural networks for multi-channel artifact detection in chronically recorded local field potentials. In: 2020 IEEE Symposium Series on Computational Intelligence (SSCI), pp. 1607–1613. IEEE (2020)

15. Fedele, T., et al.: High frequency oscillations detected in the intracranial EEG of epilepsy patients during interictal sleep, patients electrode location and outcome of epilepsy surgery (2017). https://doi.org/10.6080/K06Q1VD5

16. Gliske, S.V., Irwin, Z.T., Chestek, C., Stacey, W.C.: Effect of sampling rate and filter settings on high frequency oscillation detections. Clin. Neurophysiol. **127**(9), 3042–3050 (2016)

17. Heller, S., et al.: Hardware implementation of a performance and energy-optimized convolutional neural network for seizure detection. In: 2018 40th Annual International Conference of the IEEE Engineering in Medicine and Biology Society (EMBC), pp. 2268–2271. IEEE (2018)

18. Kaiser, M.S., et al.: iWorksafe: towards healthy workplaces during COVID-19 with an intelligent Phealth app for industrial settings. IEEE Access 9, 13814–13828 (2021)

19. Kamboh, A.M., Oweiss, K.G., Mason, A.J.: Resource constrained VLSI architecture for implantable neural data compression systems. In: 2009 IEEE International Symposium on Circuits and Systems, pp. 1481–1484. IEEE (2009)

20. Kelleher, D., Faul, S., Temko, A., Marnane, W.: On the effect of reduced sampling rate and bitwidth on seizure detection. In: 2009 IEEE International Symposium on Intelligent Signal Processing, pp. 153–156. IEEE (2009)

21. Krizhevsky, A., Sutskever, I., Hinton, G.E.: Imagenet classification with deep convolutional neural networks. In: Advances in neural information processing systems, pp. 1097–1105 (2012)

22. Kuhlmann, L., et al.: Epilepsyecosystem. org: crowd-sourcing reproducible seizure prediction with long-term human intracranial EEG. Brain **141**(9), 2619–2630 (2018)

23. Li, A., et al.: epilepsy-iEEG-multicenter-dataset (2020). https://doi.org/10.18112/openneuro.ds003029.v1.0.2
24. Liu, X., Wu, J.: A method for energy balance and data transmission optimal routing in wireless sensor networks. Sensors **19**(13), 3017 (2019)
25. Mahmud, M., Kaiser, M.S., McGinnity, T.M., Hussain, A.: Deep learning in mining biological data. Cogn. Comput. **13**(1), 1–33 (2020). https://doi.org/10.1007/s12559-020-09773-x
26. Mahmud, M., Kaiser, M.S., Hussain, A., Vassanelli, S.: Applications of deep learning and reinforcement learning to biological data. IEEE Trans. Neural Netw. Learn. Syst. **29**(6), 2063–2079 (2018). https://doi.org/10.1109/TNNLS.2018.2790388
27. Miah, Y., Prima, C.N.E., Seema, S.J., Mahmud, M., Shamim Kaiser, M.: Performance comparison of machine learning techniques in identifying dementia from open access clinical datasets. In: Saeed, F., Al-Hadhrami, T., Mohammed, F., Mohammed, E. (eds.) Advances on Smart and Soft Computing. AISC, vol. 1188, pp. 79–89. Springer, Singapore (2021). https://doi.org/10.1007/978-981-15-6048-4_8
28. Nejedly, P.: Multicenter intracranial eeg dataset (2019). https://www.kaggle.com/nejedlypetr/multicenter-intracranial-eeg-dataset. Accessed 14 Mar 2021
29. Noor, M.B.T., Zenia, N.Z., Kaiser, M.S., Mahmud, M., Al Mamun, S.: Detecting neurodegenerative disease from MRI: a brief review on a deep learning perspective. In: Liang, P., Goel, V., Shan, C. (eds.) Brain Informatics. Lecture Notes in Computer Science, pp. 115–125. Springer International Publishing, Cham (2019). https://doi.org/10.1007/978-3-030-37078-7_12
30. Orojo, O., Tepper, J., McGinnity, T., Mahmud, M.: A multi-recurrent network for crude oil price prediction. In: Proceedings of the Symposium Series on Computational Intelligence, pp. 2940–2945, December 2019. https://doi.org/10.1109/SSCI44817.2019.9002841
31. Pang, G., Shen, C., Cao, L., Hengel, A.V.D.: Deep learning for anomaly detection: a review. arXiv preprint arXiv:2007.02500 (2020)
32. Rabby, G., Azad, S., Mahmud, M., Zamli, K.Z., Rahman, M.M.: TeKET: a tree-based unsupervised keyphrase extraction technique. Cogn. Comput. **12**(4), 811–833 (2020). https://doi.org/10.1007/s12559-019-09706-3
33. Rasheed, K., et al.: Machine learning for predicting epileptic seizuresusing EEG signals: a review. IEEE Reviews in Biomedical Engineering (2020)
34. Schalk, G., Leuthardt, E.C.: Brain-computer interfaces using electrocorticographic signals. IEEE Rev. Biomed. Eng. **4**, 140–154 (2011)
35. Shoaran, M., Kamal, M.H., Pollo, C., Vandergheynst, P., Schmid, A.: Compact low-power cortical recording architecture for compressive multichannel data acquisition. IEEE Trans. Biomed. Circ. Syst. **8**(6), 857–870 (2014)
36. Shrivastwa, R.R., Pudi, V., Chattopadhyay, A.: An FPGA-based brain computer interfacing using compressive sensing and machine learning. In: 2018 IEEE Computer Society Annual Symposium on VLSI (ISVLSI), pp. 726–731. IEEE (2018)
37. Tania, M.H., et al.: Assay type detection using advanced machine learning algorithms. In: Proceedings of the Software, Knowledge, Information Management and Applications, pp. 1–8 (2019)
38. Temko, A., Sarkar, A., Lightbody, G.: Detection of seizures in intracranial EEG: UPenn and mayo clinic's seizure detection challenge. In: Proceedings of the Engineering in Medicine and Biology Society, pp. 6582–6585 (2015). https://www.kaggle.com/c/seizure-detection. Accessed 14 June 2020
39. Truong, N.D., et al.: Integer convolutional neural network for seizure detection. IEEE J. Emerg. Sel. Top. Circuit. Syst. **8**(4), 849–857 (2018)

40. Watkins, J., Fabietti, M., Mahmud, M.: Sense: a student performance quantifier using sentiment analysis. In: Proceedings of the International Joint Conference on Neural Networks, pp. 1–6 (2020)
41. Yahaya, S.W., Lotfi, A., Mahmud, M.: A consensus novelty detection ensembleapproach for anomaly detection in activities of daily living. Appl. Soft Comput. **83**, 105613 (2019)
42. Yahaya, S.W., Lotfi, A., Mahmud, M., Machado, P., Kubota, N.: Gesture recognition intermediary robot for abnormality detection in human activities. In: Proceedings of the Symposium Series on Computational Intelligence, pp. 1415–1421, December 2019. https://doi.org/10.1109/SSCI44817.2019.9003121

Classification of First Trimester Ultrasound Images Using Deep Convolutional Neural Network

Rishi Singh[1] , Mufti Mahmud[1,2,3](✉) , and Luis Yovera[4]

[1] Department of Computer Science, Nottingham Trent University, Clifton,
Nottingham NG11 8NS, UK
mufti.mahmud@ntu.ac.uk

[2] Medical Technologies Innovation Facility, Nottingham Trent University, Clifton,
Nottingham NG11 8NS, UK

[3] Computing and Informatics Research Center, Nottingham Trent University,
Clifton, Nottingham NG11 8NS, UK

[4] Kypros Nicholaides Fetal Medicine Centre, Southend University Hospital,
Westcliff-on-Sea, Essex SS0 0RY, UK

Abstract. Fetal ultrasound imaging is commonly used in correctly identifying fetal anatomical structures. This is particularly important in the first-trimester to diagnose any possible fetal malformations. However, inter-observer variation in identifying the correct image can lead to misdiagnosis of fetal growth and hence to aid the sonographers machine learning techniques, such as deep learning, have been increasingly used. This work describes the use of ResNet50, a pretrained deep convolutional neural network model, in classifying $11 - 13^{+6}$ weeks Crown to Rump Length (CRL) fetal ultrasound images into correct and incorrect categories. The presented model adopted a skip connection approach to create a deeper network with hyperparameters which were tuned for the task. This article discusses how to distinguish Crown to Rump Length (CRL) fetal ultrasound images into correct and incorrect categories using ResNet50. The presented model used a skip link approach to construct a deeper network with task-specific hyperparameters. The model was applied to a real data set of 900 CRL images, 450 of which were right and 450 of which were incorrect, and it was able to identify the images with an accuracy of 87% on the preparation, validation, and test data sets. This model can be used by the sonographers to identify correct images for CRL measurements and hence help avoid incorrect dating of pregnancies by reducing the inter-observer variation. This can also be used to train sonographers in performing first-trimester scans.

Keywords: Convolutional neural network · Machine learning · Fetal ultrasound imaging · Crown to rump length · Deep learning · Medical imaging

1 Introduction

Machine learning (ML) has emerged, in recent years, as an essential tool in the field of medical imaging. With advances in medical imaging, new imaging modal-

M. Mahmud et al. (Eds.): AII 2021, CCIS 1435, pp. 92–105, 2021.
https://doi.org/10.1007/978-3-030-82269-9_8

ities and methodologies, as well as new machine learning algorithms, are being increasingly used in medical imaging [48]. Pregnancy dating is a keystone in high-quality pregnancy care, as it will not only determine the gestational age and the estimated due date but also will establish the periods of time in which different screening or diagnostic tests need to be performed, such as first-trimester screening for chromosomal abnormalities. The importance of CRL becomes even greater if one takes into consideration the fact that up to 30% of women attending an antenatal clinic have uncertain or unreliable menstrual dates [34]. Benefits of correct dating pregnancy include reducing the number of pregnancies classified as preterm [7] and the incidence of post-term delivery and its resultant complications such as stillbirths [49], as well as the reduction in the number of unnecessary obstetric interventions [9].

ML has shown its promise as an effective tool to analyse data from diverse application domains. Various ML based methods, including deep learning, have been successfully applied to fields such as: anomaly detection [12–15,52,53], biological data analysis [26,27,29], cyber security [16,30] disease detection [4,46] [3,6,11,20,31,35,36,42], elderly people management [1,2,32], language processing [40,51], etc. In particular, application of Convolutional Neural Network (CNN) based methods have been successfully applied to medical image analysis including: diagnosis of fetal brain malformations [33], organ segmentation [43] segmentation of fetal heart [39] and breast tumour detection [50].

First-trimester ultrasound is the most accurate method to estimate the gestational age of the fetus that will better inform obstetrical monitoring and management. The most accurate parameter to establish or confirm gestational ages is the ultrasound evaluation of the fetus in the first trimester ($\leq 13^{+6}$ weeks) is based on the measurement of the CRL, which has an accuracy of ±5–7 d [37]. However, pregnancy dating requires accurate manual CRL measurements by the operator, which means that the quality of the measurement is user-dependent. Manual measurements are time-consuming with typical examination times of more than 15 min. In addition, visual estimation of CRL is prone to inter-observer errors affecting the clinical value of obtained results [38]. Moreover, the quality of the image obtained cannot be assessed during the examination and poor-quality views will result in inaccurate measurements of the CRL.

Kagan et al. [19] reported that in 95% of the cases the differences between two CRL measurements were roughly within ±5 mm or 2.5 d of gestation. Even such a small under- or overestimation of CRL may have a major impact on patient-specific risks, resulting in substantial under- or overestimation of those risks.

The aim of this study is to develop a computerised model, supervised machine learning based, for the classification of fetal ultrasound images taken at a 11–13^{+6}-week scan into correct and incorrect categories quantifying the quality of the image and preparing the image for the sonographer to measure the CRL of the fetal ultrasound. The study uses a novel transfer learning approach using the ResNet50 architecture to perform a binary classification.

Image analysis of ultrasound images using artificial intelligence techniques such as CNN has been conducted in the past, providing successful results in respective fields of medicine. This research aims to reduce inter-observer variation when dating pregnancies at $11-13^{+6}$ weeks using CNN. The research proposed can be a key contribution to the combined field of machine learning and fetal medicine as being one of the first projects to explore the classification of the correctness of $11-13^{+6}$ weeks CRL images using real world data.

In the rest of this paper, Sect. 2 reviews the literature, Sect. 3 describes the proposed method, Sect. 4 reports the results and the discussion, and Sect. 5 concludes the paper along with some possible future research directions.

2   Related Works

The use of CNN in routine fetal ultrasounds has been restricted to the fetal brain, heart and placenta [5]. This novel study involves the use of transfer learning and a ResNet50 architecture to classify $11-13^{+6}$-week fetal ultrasound scan images.

Various Deep Learning methods, have been successfully applied to different fields which can be seen by the work of Mahmud et al. [28] who investigates the use of different Deep Learning architectures in mining biological data. The work of Mufti et al. illustrates different underlying theories in Deep Learning along with presenting open source deep learning tools. This works highlights the pros and cons of tools that can be used for the development of the CNN model being developed. A specific tool to highlight from this work is the use Keras and its rich documentation. Other work in regards to ML has been conducted in fields regarding biological data and the recent COVID-19 pandemic [20,29].

CNN can be described as a popular method for the classification of images due to the evolution of several CNN architectures such as AlexNet, GoogLeNet, and ResNet [44]. This can be supported by the work of Ye et al. [54] implementing a deep convolutional neural network for a fetal head plane identification. In this study a group of classification networks have been compiled and applied for the identification of fetal anatomical landmarks using various residual networks such as ResNet50. The results of the study show a high precision and recall of 89.67% and 89.61% respectively. This implies the popular architectures chosen for this study are highly accurate for this domain.

A variety of research has been conducted related to deep learning methods in respects to medical image analysis. Lundervold et al. [25] created an overview of the application of deep learning methods explaining how deep learning models can be applied to MRI scans from segmenting images in predicting diseases. Lundervold's research consists of three main aims: providing a brief introduction to deep learning, the application of deep learning to MRI scans and providing a foundation point for other researchers interested in the field. From Lundervold et al.'s research a familiarisation of the building blocks of CNN has been formed as Lundervold discusses convolutional layers, activation layers and pooling along with a brief description of several CNN architectures such as AlexNet, GoogLeNet and more.

Liu et al. [24] proposed the integration of S-Mask R-CNN to enable the diagnosis of prostate cancer and successfully outlining the region of the prostate in an ultrasound. Using the integrated S-Mask and regional-CNN the experimental results Lui et al. observed proves the proposed method can accurately detect a prostate in an ultrasound image and the proposed method has a higher accuracy than the detection and diagnosis of a doctor. The use of deep learning has shown huge potential in the image analysis of ultrasound images. Lui et al. discusses and summarises the application of deep learning models on ultrasound images using image analysis tools such as classification, detection and segmentation. Specifying the different aspects where ultrasounds are used in medicine for example in the detection of tumours, fetus and organs. Lui et al., discusses the theoretical knowledge behind convolution neural networks and states the development of classical convolutional neural networks which explains the increasing popularity and practicability.

Additional research using CNN and ultrasound images can be seen by Burgos-Artizzu et al. [8] evaluating deep CNN when automatically classifying the maternal fetal ultrasound planes. Burgos-Artizzu et al. records DenseNet-169 as the best performing net with a 93.6% average class accuracy. A comparison between the DenseNet-169 and a human, suggests the performance of the CNN can be seen by perfect results of two out of the six classes Burgos-Artizzu et al. had investigated. The work of Deepika et al. [10] also looks into the use of CNN in ultrasound images. Deepika et al. uses a U-Net framework which is able to diagnose fetal anomaly in ultrasounds by segmenting the abdominal region and implementing a CNN to extract hidden features from the images. This framework by can be seen out performing other CNN approaches such as the work of Kim et al. [22].

3 Proposed Method

The proposed method applies a transfer learning approach which is used to train CNN architectures to classify (11–13^{+6} weeks) fetal ultrasound scan images into correct or incorrect images. The proposed pipeline is shown in Fig. 1. Due to the small number of ultrasound images, a transfer learning approach has been adopted, to classify these images is more practical as traditional CNN architectures requires a large data set of images [18]. Before creating a new architecture it is useful to check the implementation of pre-existing models on the new data set of fetal ultrasound scan images. In this method, we have used a pretrained ResNet50 architecture which has previously achieved state of the art performance when classifying images on a the ImageNet dataset. The rationale in behind using a pretrained ResNet50 architecture has been conceived because of its performance and ability to use binary classification to classify correct and incorrect fetal ultrasound scan images. The ResNet50 model was chosen due to its accuracy and the vast applications in medical transfer learning applications [23,41]. This has also been illustrated by the work of Zhang et al. [55] as the ResNet50 architecture outperformed other state of the art architectures in the direct estimation of fetal head circumferences from ultrasound images. The residual network mitigates the vanishing gradient problem by incorporating a skip layer connection into the architecture allowing the gradient to flow through alternative paths.

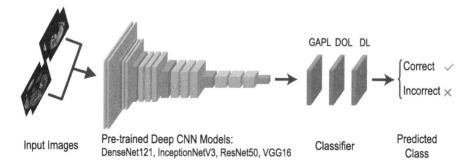

Fig. 1. Analysis pipeline detailing the various stages of the process. GAPL: Global Average Pooling layer, DOL: Dropout Layer and DL: Dense Layer.

A residual network is made up of residual blocks which consist of a large number of layers that can be denoted as l. Suppose we take two activation layers from the network and denote the first activation layer as a^l, which is then applied to a linear operator (weight layer). this application can be represented by $z^{l+1} = a^l.W^{l+1} + b^{l+1}$ which represents the multiplication of the activation layer by the weight matrix (W^{l+1}) and the addition of a bias vector (B^l). After this a ReLU layer is applied which can be represented by $(a^{l+1} = g(z^{l+1}))$ followed by the application of another linear operator and ReLU layer. The final output we get after following the path of the two activation layers can be represented by $a^{l+2} = g(z^{l+2})$. This mathematical formulation represents the flow of information from a^l to a^{l+2}. However in a residual net, the first activation layer is fast forwarded and added before the non linearity is applied which is known as the skip layer allowing information to go much deeper into the neural network. Instead of the final output being $a^{l+2} = g(z^{l+2})$ due to the skip layer we get the final output as $a^{l+2} = g(z^{l+2} + a^l)$.

3.1   Network Construction

The proposed method uses a transfer learning approach where pretrained models such as DenseNet121, InceptionV3, ResNet50 and VGG16 are trained to classify fetal ultrasound images into correct and incorrect categories. Before the model can be trained the data set is augmented with a 0.2 rotation and horizontal fit to avoid the possibility of over-fitting [45]. The images are preprocessed depending on the architecture they are going to be implemented in. In this case the ResNet50 architecture requires images of a size of 224 X 224. For this step the tensorflow preprocess input has been used which is different for each architecture and the images are re-scaled depending on the architecture. The base model is then initialised and the convolution base is frozen as this prevents weights from updating during training. After the base model is initialised, a global average 2D pooling layer is added to act as a classification head by converting the features of the image to a single vector. Finally, a dense layer is added to the model, to convert features into a single prediction and the model is then compiled. When images are ran through the model the classification of an image is returned in logits which can be denoted in mathematical terms as "logit$(p) = \log(\frac{p}{p-1})$". From this the logit values are passed through the sigmoid activation function which is able to convert these values into a 0 or 1 representing incorrect and correct categories. The sigmoid function is best used in a binary classification as they are able to convert the logit values into values in between 0 and 1 which can be denoted by $\sigma(x) = (\frac{1}{1-e^{-x}})$. Values that fall in between 0 and 0.5 can be represented as 0 and values between 0.5 and 1 can be represented as 1.

3.2 Experimentation

CRL Data. This is a cross sectional study that was conducted at Kypros Nicolaides Fetal Medicine Centre in Southend University Hospital between November 2020 and February 2021. This study was approved by the local research and ethics committee of Mid and South Essex NHS Foundation Trust Hospitals. All images were strictly anonymized and exported for off-line processing. Static CRL images were selected with measurements between 45 and 84mm ($11–13^{+6}$ weeks). All scans were performed by trained sonographers holding the appropriate certification provided by the Fetal Medicine Foundation. They had undergone rigorous training in CRL measurement and submitted images as part of quality control. The clinical fellows obtained 900 images from patients with singleton pregnancies. No personal or medical data was saved or used for this research purposes.

For developing and training the machine learning model images were separated in "correct" and "incorrect" categories. For quality assessment sonographers subjectively evaluated each picture based on [21]:

- Magnification: Fetus should fill more than two-thirds of image.
- Mid-sagittal section: Midline facial profile, fetal spine and rump should all be visible in one complete image.
- Position: Fetus should be in a neutral position.
- Clear borders: Crown and rump should both be clearly visible.
- Horizontal orientation: Fetus should be horizontal with line connecting crown and rump positioned between 75 degrees and 105 degrees to the ultrasound beam.

Quality assessment of the CRL images was performed by two trained operators who did not take part in the model development. The images were exported into a JPEG format and then were split into a training and validation set. The data set was split into 80% training and 20% validation thus a total of 720 images

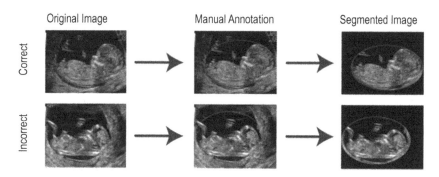

Fig. 2. Segmentation process of $11 - 13^{+6}$ weeks ultrasound images.

were used in training and 180 images were used in validation. In order to perform the most optimal classification of these images the data set was balanced with the same number of images in both the correct and incorrect categories respectively.

The original CRL images were examined and oval shapes were drawn ontop of the image of the fetus manually in both categories (correct and incorrect). Image segmentation was then carried out on the annotated images, removing areas of the original images that are not required during the classification of these images allowed the reduction in the noise of the images hence improving the accuracy [17].

3.3   Parameter Selection

The parameters were selected after a number of models were run which included: varying the number of epochs, batch size, dropout and learning rate. The most optimal parameters were used for this model from analysing the computational time taken to run the models and if the results displayed any overfitting or underfitting of data. The models were run on a number of different set of epochs such 25, 50 and 100. By varying the number epochs we found that the model worked optimally on on 50 epochs and provided an adequate accuracy and computational time taken to run the model. Using 100 epochs increased the computational time significantly and did not vary the accuracy.

- Epochs: 50
- Dropout: 0.2
- Batch size: 32
- Loss function: Keras Binary Crossentropy
- Optimizer: Adam
- Learning Rate: 0.002

4   Results and Discussion

4.1   Model Performance

Using the parameters stated above, the pretrained ResNet50 architecture was compared to three other CNN architectures. ResNet50 provided the best set of results which can be seen by the learning curves provided in Fig. 3A and Fig. 3B. From this set of results,it can be demonstrated that when the ResNet50 was trained on the $11-13^{+6}$ weeks ultrasound image data set post segmentation, the training accuracy of 87% and a validation accuracy of 87% was achieved at the end of 50 epochs with a batch size of 32 and learning rate of 0.002. This demonstrates that the models training data has an accuracy of 87% to classify correct and incorrect images. This is similar for the validation data set which includes images that the model was not been exposed to before. The reason for such a high accuracy of a new data set which may still hold some inconsistencies can be attributed due to the unique skip layer found in the ResNet50 architecture allowing information to flow deeper into the neural network.

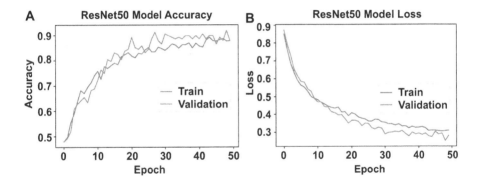

Fig. 3. Training accuracy (A) and loss (B) of the ResNet50 Model.

A batch of images from the validation set was split from the original set to be tested after the model was trained. An accuracy of 84% was noted as model predicted the classification of the images that had been separated. This can be seen by the confusion matrix displayed in Fig. 4. Due to the limited data set, 32 images were used to test the model and provide an overview of the behaviour of the model. On analysis of the confusion matrix we can demonstrate that a out of the total 32 images 27 were classified correctly and 5 images were misclassified. A total of 5 incorrect images were inappropriately classified as correct, and hence giving a false positive rate of 27%. However, this maybe due to the inflexibility of the criteria of a correct image. The classification report shown in Table 1 supports the false postive rate stated above and displays the precison and recall of the model. Increasing the flexibility of the criteria for the classification of correct images does not lead to a significant clinical impact and hence in future models the false positive rate can be reduced [47]. The objective of this research was to prepare a model that could help sonographers in training to identify correct and incorrect images so they can measure an accurate CRL when dating pregnancies.

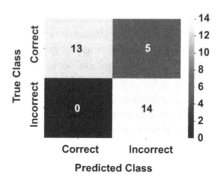

Fig. 4. Confusion matrix of the proposed method

Table 1. Classification Report of testing model

	Precision	Recall	F1-score	Support
Good	1	0.72	0.84	18
Bad	0	1	0.85	14
Accuracy	–	–	0.84	32
Macro avg	0.87	0.86	0.84	32
Weighted avg	0.88	0.84	0.84	32

The classification report shown in Table 1 supports the false postive rate stated above and displays the precison and recall of the model. The report shows the performance of the ResNet50 model on a batch of 32 images that were split from the validation set. The classification report shows 100% classification of incorrect images that is supported by the confusion matrix in Fig. 4.

4.2   Comparison of Model Performance

The ResNet50 model proposed, was also compared against three other popular Convolutional Neural Network architectures which have been stated in 2. These architectures were implemented in the same pipeline as shown in Fig. 1 and the training, validation accuracies and loss were noted for comparison. As demonstrated in Table 2 the residual architecture performs better than the other architectures implemented in the pipeline using the same parameters. This is supported by the adequate computational time taken to run the architecture and providing the best training and validation accuracies without any overfitting or underfitting of data.

Table 2. Accuracy comparisons with other state of the art architectures

Architecture	TA	VA	TL	VL	TTT
DenseNet121	0.7792	0.7973	0.4308	0.4715	130 min
InceptionNetV3	0.8333	0.7056	0.3890	0.4898	36 min
VGG16	0.7726	0.7778	0.4845	0.5283	206 min
ResNet50	0.8708	0.8778	0.3014	0.3787	65 min

Legend – **TA**: Training Accuracy; **VA**: Validation Accuracy; **TL**: Training Loss; **VL**: Validation Loss; **TTT**: Training Time Taken

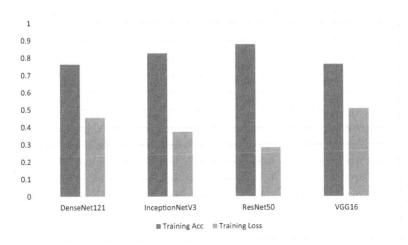

Fig. 5. Experimental Average of Training Accuracy & Loss (Legend – **TA**: Training Accuracy; **TL**: Training Loss)

An in-depth comparison of the training accuracy's and loss of the state of the art architectures can be seen in the results illustrated in Fig. 5. The results illustrated in Fig. 5 represent the average values of the training accuracy and training loss calculated after five experiments had been carried out. For each state of the art architecture implemented the architectures were deployed five times and the training accuracy and loss was noted. From the average of these results the consistency of the models can be denoted and results gathered support the results shown in Table 2. The ResNet50 architecture displayed an average training accuracy of 0.8775 which was the highest compared to the other architectures implemented and provided the lowest average training loss value.

5   Conclusion and Future Work

In this study, we have demonstrated the ResNet50 architecture using a transfer learning approach was able to perform a binary classification of $11 - 13^{+6}$ weeks fetal ultrasound images of CRL measurements into correct and incorrect categories with an accuracy of 87%. The classification of images, into correct and incorrect categories can help sonographers measure an accurate CRL and provide an accurate gestational age. The pretrained ResNet50 architecture was chosen to accurately classify images into correct and incorrect categories. The unique characteristic of this architecture to employ multiple skip layers and allow the network to be simplified helps in solving the vanishing gradient problem. The architecture was fitted to a unique segmented data set of $11 - 13^{+6}$ week fetal ultrasound images and suitable parameters were chosen to provide a good performance and appropriate computational time taken to run the model. Furthermore, this model was then compared to three state of the art architectures that were also entered into the proposed pipeline. From the comparison, we can conclude that the ResNet50 architecture provided the best results out of the four architectures chosen. The implemented model can be adopted onto other binary classification problems using the transfer learning approach however the results may differ depending on the data set of the classification problem. The accuracy of this model can be improved by increasing the number of epochs and increasing the depth of the data set with the use of more computational power which can then be adopted on to other different binary classification problems associated with fetal ultrasound imaging. In the future, this classification software would need to be developed and integrated with hardware components to be used in real-time classification of correct and incorrect ultrasound images.

Acknowledgements. Data used in the preparation of this article were obtained from the Fetal Medicine Centre at Southend University Hospital.

References

1. Al Nahian, M.J., et al.: Towards artificial intelligence driven emotion aware fall monitoring framework suitable for elderly people with neurological disorder. In: Proceedings of the Brain Informatics, pp. 275–286 (2020)
2. Al Nahian, M.J., et al.: Towards an accelerometer-based elderly fall detection system using cross-disciplinary time series features. IEEE Access **9**, 39413–39431 (2021)
3. Ali, H.M., Kaiser, M.S., Mahmud, M.: Application of convolutional neural network in segmenting brain regions from MRI data. In: Proceedings of the Brain Informatics, pp. 136–146 (2019)

4. Aradhya, V.M., Mahmud, M., Agarwal, B., Kaiser, M.: One shot cluster based approach for the detection of covid-19 from chest x-ray images. Cogn. Comput. 1–9 (2021). https://doi.org/10.1007/s12559-020-09774-w
5. Bandeira Diniz, P., Yin, Y., Collins, S.: Deep learning strategies for ultrasound in pregnancy. Eur. Med. J. **6**(1) 73–80 (2020)
6. Bhapkar, H.R., Mahalle, P.N., Shinde, G.R., Mahmud, M.: Rough sets in COVID-19 to predict symptomatic cases. In: Santosh, K.C., Joshi, A. (eds.) COVID-19: Prediction, Decision-Making, and its Impacts. LNDECT, vol. 60, pp. 57–68. Springer, Singapore (2021). https://doi.org/10.1007/978-981-15-9682-7_7
7. Blondel, B., Morin, I., Platt, R.W., Kramer, M.S., Usher, R., Bréart, G.: Algorithms for combining menstrual and ultrasound estimates of gestational age: consequences for rates of preterm and postterm birth. BJOG Int. J. Obstet. Gynaecol. **109**(6), 718–720 (2002)
8. Burgos-Artizzu, X.P., et al.: Evaluation of deep convolutional neural networks for automatic classification of common maternal fetal ultrasound planes. Sci. Rep. **10**(1), 1–12 (2020)
9. Caughey, A.B., Nicholson, J.M., Washington, A.E.: First-vs second-trimester ultrasound: the effect on pregnancy dating and perinatal outcomes. Am. J. Obstet. Gynecol. **198**(6), 703 (2008)
10. Deepika, P., Suresh, R., Pabitha, P.: Defending against child death: deep learning-based diagnosis method for abnormal identification of fetus ultrasound images. Comput. Intell. **37**(1), 128–154 (2021)
11. Dey, N., Rajinikanth, V., Fong, S., Kaiser, M., Mahmud, M.: Social-group-optimization assisted Kapur's entropy and morphological segmentation for automated detection of covid-19 infection from computed tomography images. Cogn. Comput. **12**(5), 1011–1023 (2020)
12. Fabietti, M., Mahmud, M., Lotfi, A.: Machine learning in analysing invasively recorded neuronal signals: available open access data sources. In: Proceedings of the Brain Informatics, pp. 151–162 (2020)
13. Fabietti, M., Mahmud, M., et al.: Neural network-based artifact detection in local field potentials recorded from chronically implanted neural probes. In: Proceedings of the IJCNN, pp. 1–8 (2020)
14. Fabietti, M., et al.: Adaptation of convolutional neural networks for multi-channel artifact detection in chronically recorded local field potentials. In: Proceedings of the SSCI, pp. 1607–1613 (2020)
15. Fabietti, M., et al.: Artifact detection in chronically recorded local field potentials using long-short term memory neural network. In: Proceedings of the AICT, pp. 1–6 (2020)
16. Farhin, F., Kaiser, M.S., Mahmud, M.: Secured smart healthcare system: blockchain and bayesian inference based approach. In: Proceedings of the TCCE, pp. 455–465 (2021)
17. Jamal, I., Akram, M.U., Tariq, A.: Retinal image preprocessing: background and noise segmentation. Telkomnika **10**(3), 537–544 (2012)
18. Jokandan, A.S., et al.: An uncertainty-aware transfer learning-based framework for covid-19 diagnosis (2020)
19. Kagan, K.O., Hoopmann, M., Baker, A., Huebner, M., Abele, H., Wright, D.: Impact of bias in crown-rump length measurement at first-trimester screening for trisomy 21. Ultrasound Obstet. Gynecol. **40**(2), 135–139 (2012)
20. Kaiser, M., et al.: iworksafe: towards healthy workplaces during covid-19 with an intelligent phealth app for industrial settings. IEEE Access **9**, 13814–13828 (2021)

21. Kalish, R.B., et al.: First-and second-trimester ultrasound assessment of gestational age. Am. J. Obstet. Gynecol. **191**(3), 975–978 (2004)
22. Kim, B., Kim, K.C., Park, Y., Kwon, J.Y., Jang, J., Seo, J.K.:Machine-learning-based automatic identification of fetal abdominal circumference from ultrasound images. Physiol. Meas. **39**(10), 105007 (2018)
23. LeCun, Y., Bengio, Y., Hinton, G.: Deep learning. Nature **521**(7553), 436–444 (2015)
24. Liu, Z., Yang, C., Huang, J., Liu, S., Zhuo, Y., Lu, X.: Deep learning framework based on integration of s-mask R-CNN and inception-v3 for ultrasound image-aided diagnosis of prostate cancer. Future Gener. Comput. Syst. **114**, 358–367 (2020)
25. Lundervold, A.S., Lundervold, A.: An overview of deep learning in medical imaging focusing on MRI. Z. Med. Phys. **29**(2), 102–127 (2019)
26. Mahmud, M., Kaiser, M.S.: Machine learning in fighting pandemics: a COVID-19 case study. In: Santosh, K.C., Joshi, A. (eds.) COVID-19: Prediction, Decision-Making, and its Impacts. LNDECT, vol. 60, pp. 77–81. Springer, Singapore (2021). https://doi.org/10.1007/978-981-15-9682-7_9
27. Mahmud, M., Kaiser, M.S., McGinnity, T.M., Hussain, A.: Deep learning in mining biological data. Cogn. Comput. **13**(1), 1–33 (2020)
28. Mahmud, M., Kaiser, M.S., McGinnity, T.M., Hussain, A.: Deep learning in mining biological data. Cogn. Comput. **13**(1), 1–33 (2021)
29. Mahmud, M., Kaiser, M.S., Hussain, A., Vassanelli, S.: Applications of deep learning and reinforcement learning to biological data. IEEE Trans. Neural Netw. Learn. Syst. **29**(6), 2063–2079 (2018)
30. Mahmud, M., et al.: A brain-inspired trust management model to assure security in a cloud based iot framework for neuroscience applications. Cogn. Comput. **10**(5), 864–873 (2018)
31. Miah, Y., Prima, C.N.E., Seema, S.J., Mahmud, M., Kaiser, M.S.: Performance comparison of machine learning techniques in identifying dementia from open access clinical datasets. In: Proceedings of the ICACIn, pp. 79–89 (2021)
32. Nahiduzzaman, M., et al.: Machine learning based early fall detection for elderly people with neurological disorder using multimodal data fusion. In: Proceedings of the Brain Informatics, pp. 204–214 (2020)
33. Namburete, A.I., Xie, W., Yaqub, M., Zisserman, A., Noble, J.A.: Fully-automated alignment of 3d fetal brain ultrasound to a canonical reference space using multi-task learning. Med. Image Anal. **46**, 1–14 (2018)
34. Napolitano, R., et al.: Pregnancy dating by fetal crown-rump length: a systematic review of charts. BJOG Int. J. Obstet. Gynaecol. **121**(5), 556–565 (2014)
35. Noor, M.B.T., Zenia, N.Z., et al.: Application of deep learning in detecting neurological disorders from magnetic resonance images: a survey on the detection of alzheimer's disease, parkinson's disease and schizophrenia. Brain Informatics **7**(1), 1–21 (2020)
36. Noor, M.B.T., et al.: Detecting Neurodegenerative Disease from MRI: A Brief Review on a Deep Learning Perspective. In: Proceedings of the Brain Informatics, pp. 115–125 (2019)
37. Committee on Obstetric Practice, American Institute of Ultrasound in Medicine, & Society for Maternal-Fetal Medicine, et al.: Committee opinion no 700: methods for estimating the due date. Obstet. Gynecol. **129**(5), e150–e154 (2017)
38. Pashaj, S., Merz, E., Petrela, E.: Automated ultrasonographic measurement of basic fetal growth parameters. Ultraschall in der Medizin Eur. J. Ultrasound **34**(02), 137–144 (2013)

39. Philip, M.E., Sowmya, A., Avnet, H., Ferreira, A., Stevenson, G., Welsh, A.: Convolutional neural networks for automated fetal cardiac assessment using 4d b-mode ultrasound. In: 2019 IEEE 16th International Symposium on Biomedical Imaging (ISBI 2019), pp. 824–828. IEEE (2019)
40. Rabby, G., et al.: TeKET: a tree-based unsupervised keyphrase extraction technique. Cogn. Comput. **12**(4), 811–833 (2020). https://doi.org/10.1007/s12559-019-09706-3
41. Raghu, M., Zhang, C., Kleinberg, J., Bengio, S.: Transfusion: understanding transfer learning for medical imaging (2019)
42. Ruiz, J., Mahmud, M., Modasshir, M., Kaiser, M.S., et al.: 3d densenet ensemble in 4-way classification of alzheimer's disease. In: Proceedings of the Brain Informatics, pp. 85–96 (2020)
43. Sahiner, B., et al.: Deep learning in medical imaging and radiation therapy. Med. Phys. **46**(1), e1–e36 (2019)
44. Sharma, N., Jain, V., Mishra, A.: An analysis of convolutional neural networks for image classification. Procedia Comput. Sci. **132**, 377–384 (2018)
45. Simard, P.Y., Steinkraus, D., Platt, J.C., et al.: Best practices for convolutional neural networks applied to visual document analysis. In: Icdar, vol. 3. Citeseer (2003)
46. Singh, A.K., Kumar, A., Mahmud, M., Kaiser, M.S., Kishore, A.: Covid-19 infection detection from chest x-ray images using hybrid social group optimization and support vector classifier. Cogn. Comput. 1–13 (2021)
47. Souka, A.P., Pilalis, A., Papastefanou, I., Salamalekis, G., Kassanos, D.: Reproducibility study of crown-rump length and biparietal diameter measurements in the first trimester. Prenat. Diagn. **32**(12), 1158–1165 (2012)
48. Suk, H.I., Liu, M., Yan, P., Lian, C.: Machine Learning in Medical Imaging: 10th International Workshop, MLMI 2019, Held in Conjunction with MICCAI 2019, Shenzhen, China, October 13, 2019, Proceedings, vol. 11861. Springer Nature (2019)
49. Taipale, P., Hiilesmaa, V.: Predicting delivery date by ultrasound and last menstrual period in early gestation. Obstet. Gynecol. **97**(2), 189–194 (2001)
50. Wang, Z., Yu, G., Kang, Y., Zhao, Y., Qu, Q.: Breast tumor detection in digital mammography based on extreme learning machine. Neurocomputing **128**, 175–184 (2014)
51. Watkins, J., Fabietti, M., Mahmud, M.: Sense: a student performance quantifier using sentiment analysis. In: Proceedings of the IJCNN, pp. 1–6 (2020)
52. Yahaya, S.W., Lotfi, A., Mahmud, M.: Detecting anomaly and its sources in activities of daily living. SN Comput. Sci. **2**(1), 1–18 (2021)
53. Yahaya, S.W., Lotfi, A., Mahmud, M.: Towards a data-driven adaptive anomaly detection system for human activity. Pattern Recognit. Lett. **145**, 200–207 (2021)
54. Ye, J., et al.: A deep convolutional neural network based hybrid framework for fetal head standard plane identification. Authorea Preprints (2020)
55. Zhang, J., Petitjean, C., Lopez, P., Ainouz, S.: Direct estimation of fetal head circumference from ultrasound images based on regression CNN. In: Medical Imaging with Deep Learning, pp. 914–922. PMLR (2020)

Method to Enhance Classification of Skin Cancer Using Back Propagated Artificial Neural Network

V. Nyemeesha[1] and B. Mohammed Ismail[2(✉)]

[1] Department of Computer Science and Engineering, Koneru Lakshmaiah Education Foundation, Vaddeswaram, A.P., India
[2] Department of Information Technology, Kannur University Campus, Mangattuparamba, Kannur, Kerala, India

Abstract. Skin cancer is one of the kinds of cancer that leads to millions of deaths of human beings. Early identification and appropriate medications for new harmful skin malignancy cases are fundamental to guarantee a low death rate as the survival rate. Most of the related works are focusing on machine learning-based algorithms, but they provide the maximum accuracy of and specificity. In the preprocessing stage, sharpening filter and smoothening filters are used to remove the noise along with enhancement operations. Then Otsu's segmentation used for efficient detection of the region of skin cancer. Finally, to achieve the maximum accuracy for classification back-propagated based artificial neural network (BP-ANN) developed for the categorization of skin cancer with the spatially gray level dependency matrix (SGLD) features. The suggested research work can be effectively used for the organization of various Benign and Melanoma skin cancers.

Keywords: Back-propagattion · Artificial neural network · Spatially gray level dependency matrix · Support vector matrix

1 Introduction

In recent days, skin cancer becomes the most affected disease among different types of cancers, and it is divided as benign and malignant. In these two types, melanoma is recognized as deadliest one while comparing with the non-melanoma skin cancers. It is a known fact that melanoma affects more people a year by year wise and early treatment is important for the survival of the patients. Inspection of malignant melanoma needs well-experienced dermatologists. These people use a computer-assisted system early detection of melanoma. In deep learning various procedure prototypes were used for the diagnosis of a skin cancer diagnosis. Many research papers have utilized image preprocessing for the identification of melanoma at the initial times, which leads to effective treatment. In [1, 22], authors have utilized image preprocessing for the identification of melanoma at the initial times, which leads to effective treatment. Recently, new activities in

© Springer Nature Switzerland AG 2021
M. Mahmud et al. (Eds.): AII 2021, CCIS 1435, pp. 106–122, 2021.
https://doi.org/10.1007/978-3-030-82269-9_9

the improvement of CNN have allowed computers and beat dermatologists in skin cancer identification activities.

The remainder of the broadside is structured in Literature survey conducted for paper is covered in Sect. 2. Section 3 covers the suggested melanoma detection method while Sect. 4 describes the environment in which experiments were conducted. Finally, Sect. 5 has remarks that conclude the outcomes and draw inferences from the presented research work.

2   Literature Survey

In recent years artificial intelligence has gained popularity in research for their abilities to predict patterns. They have been applied to many different fields including disease detection [10,30,35,36,43] and classification [9,12,26,45], elderly care [20,21] and fall detection [4,5,33], anomaly detection [7,13,48,49], biological data mining [32,34], cyber security [28], earthquake prediction [2,3], financial prediction [37], safeguarding workers in workplaces [22], text analytics [39,46], and urban planning [23]. Related work about skin image processing and their multiple applications using different kinds of methods and approaches. It also describes different approaches used in the skin cancer identification methodology which is used to detect tuberculosis utilizing technical and medical approaches. Through the elaborate survey is the motivation for the present suggested work.

2.1   Filter and Adaptive Histogram Technique

The adaptive histogram equalization technique used for preprocessing operation. In this work use novel classification and segmentation of skin lesions [34]. The main purpose through this work is a skin cancer identification system with a minimum error by selecting the proper approach in every stage. The standard digital camera is used for capturing the skin lesion image is shows the high screening process of lesion images. The combination of an analytical method and segmentation method aims to enhance these two approaches to create an interface for assist dermatologists in the diagnostic process [32]. The initial step in this work, a series of preprocessing is executed to unwanted structures and removes noise from the given image. Then, an automatic segmentation method traces the skin lesion. Send step is feature extraction is done by using ABCD rule which used to calculate the Total Dermoscopy score.

2.2   Gaussian Method

The segmentation processing of Magnetic Resonance Images (MRI) by utilizing the Unsupervised Neural Network Algorithm (UNNA) [1]. Here considering two different kinds of problems: such as the trained network takes a long time to obtain the Desired Output. Another one that has obtained results from the training process is not correct which contains a lot of noise as a result of the training process. Thus, in this work employed the2D Discrete Wavelet Transform (DWT) learned Patterns for denoise operation (noise removal or reduction) by processing entire the outcomes from the activity of the segmentation of MRI. The UNNA like Kohonen Network considering the outcome image and the trained process is findings of the given original images. The quality of the image by utilizing the de-noising and resolution concepts such as wiener filter, median filter, average filter, discrete wavelet transform, and the dual tree-based complex wavelet transform approach.

The different preprocessing methods for detecting the lesions and micro-calcification from the mammogram image [29]. These preprocessing methods eliminate the unwanted noise present in the input image which is implemented in the MATLAB tool. Then the accuracy of the preprocessing methods has been validated using 30 different mammogram image and the efficiency is examined using the peak signal to noise ratio.

Enhancing the quality of the images by applying the filtering and resolution methods such as median, average, and wavelet filters [14]. These filters estimate the neighboring pixel value for efficiently estimating the new brightness values. Also, these filters maintain the quality of the edge and contour information. Then the performance of the system is analyzed using the peak to signal ratio metrics. These resolution based preprocessing methods improves the quality also enhance the classification accuracy efficiently.

2.3   Segmentation Techniques

Melanoma is a sort of dangerous skin disease; it can be diagnosed only in its early stage but using the normal conventional dermatological approach is a difficult one. An image processing approach by using an efficient segmentation algorithm named a radial search method to obtain the truth of the lesion region in dermoscopy skin images [16]. DL – especially its different architectures – has contributed and been utilized in the mining of biological data pertaining to those three types, a meta-analysis has been performed and the resulting resources have been critically analysed. Focusing on the use of DL to analyse patterns in data from diverse biological domains, this work investigates different DL architectures' applications to these data.

The melanoma skin cancer by using the Otsu thresholding which is used to segments the lesion from the whole image [40]. Further segmentation is done by using a Boundary tracing algorithm. After removing the features from the lesion, the classification process is done by using the Stolz algorithm stage.

The skin-tone regions with the help of edge detection and color spaces in green red channels [14]. The prominent feature of the face is extracted by using wavelet approximations. The experimental results obtained the enhanced False Acceptance Rates (FAR) over either utilizing a grayscale image for segmentation and which algorithm not using any kinds of edge detection.

2.4   Artificial Neural Network Based Techniques

The ANN-based Classification methodology utilizing Artificial Intelligence and Image processing approach for early diagnosis [14]. In this work dermoscopy image of skin cancer is taken for analysis using Computer-Aided Classification, and it is considered different kinds of image enhancement and pre-processing. The 2D Wavelet transform is a well-known Feature Extraction approach is used in this work. These features are feed into as input as in ANN Classifier. It classifies the given data set into non-cancerous or cancerous.

The automatic cancer detection process by utilizing the effective image segmentation process [42]. Before segmenting the image, the noise present in the image should be eliminated by converting the RGB images into the Grayscale image. Then the region growing method has been applied to the noise removed image which combining a similar gradient value based on the image intensity constraints. From the segmented image the affected region related features are calculated which is fed into the supervisor classifier to analyze cancer effectively.

The tumor region by utilizing the fuzzy c means based support vector machine [31]. Initially, the MRI image neighboring pixel value has been analyzed and the input is labeled by using the Fuzzy C - Means method. From the input vectors, the membership function is applied and the affected region is efficiently segmented by using the support vector machine. Then the suggested FCM with Support Vector Machine based segmentation methods has been analyzed using the quadratic kernel function and the non-linearity approach. Thus the suggested method enhances the segmentation process which used to achieve the enhanced results while classifying the segmented region. Finally, the performance of the system is compared with the silhouette method, fuzzy entropy, fuzzy partition coefficient methods.

2.5   Different Feature Extraction Methods

The different feature extraction methods for identifying cancer were elaborated [17]. The author examined skin cancer detection using the computer-aided diagnosis process. The biopsy method is known as the Conventional diagnosis method is used for the skin cancer detection process. In this work utilize a neural network (NN) system as promising modalities for the skin cancer detection process. This work involves different stages of detection which contain a collection of Dermoscopic images, feature extraction utilizing GLCM and classification utilizing ANN, segmenting the images utilizing Maximum Entropy Threshold, filtering the images for removing noises and hairs, It classifies the given data set into the non-cancerous or cancerous image. Cancerous images are classified as non-melanoma and melanoma skin cancer. The identifying techniques utilize Artificial Intelligence and Image processing methods in this paper were projected [11]. The dermoscopy image is taken and then the different pre-processing operation is done for image enhancement and noise removal. After that, the image is fed into the segmentation process utilizing Thresholding.

In this working diagnosis the psoriasis skin disease [44]. This suggested system gives promising results in terms of finding the generalization face. Extracting the shearlet features from the ultrasound cancer image for detecting the normal and abnormal tissues in the affected part. The shearlet transform analyzes the image and the texture metrics are analyzed in the high dimensional way. The extracted features are classified by applying the different classifiers such as the support vector machine, ad boost technique. The extracted features are compared with the different feature extraction techniques such as the contourlet, curvelet, and GLCM approach. The performance of the suggested system is analyzed using the experimental results in terms of accuracy, sensitivity, specificity, predictive values.

2.6   Feature Selection Techniques

Automatic detection of cancer by selecting the optimal feature set from the various Features [47]. During the feature selection process, the features are ranked and the best features are selected using the wrapper approach. Then the selected features are fed into the nearest neighbor classifiers which classify cancer into the benign and malignant. Thus, the suggested system efficiently effectively classifies the tumors.

Analyzing the various feature selection methods such as information gain, gain ratio, best-first search algorithm, chi-square test, recursive feature elimination processes, and the random forest approach [16]. These features select the optimal features from the set features such as the texture, shape, color, and other spectral features. The selected features reduce the dimensionality of the feature set which is fed into the different machine classifiers for identifying the normal and abnormal tissues. Thus, the optimal features ensure efficient results with minimum time complexity.

2.7   Machine Learning Techniques

In this work use the soft computing techniques for analyzing the skin lesion image [41]. Here differentiate the melanoma skin lesions is done by using ABCD and this approach is also done the preprocessing operation and finally, the optimization is done by soft computing operation. The author shows better accuracy in terms of diagnosing melanoma. An intelligent automated approach for identifying the different sorts of skin lesions utilizing machine learning procedures.

Initially, local information is getting over the Local Binary Pattern (LBP) on various kinds of scales, and GLCM at different angles has been mined as a kind of texture feature. Typically, these features are robust because of scale rotation invariant property of GLCM features and invariant property of LBP. The Global information of altered color channels has been integrated through four various moments mined in six different color spaces. Thus, a merged hybrid texture color and local as global features have been recommended to categorize the nonmelanoma and melanoma. The SVM has been utilized as a classifier to classify non-melanoma and melanoma.

The mined feature parameters are utilized to categorize the image as Melanoma cancer lesion and Normal skin. The automatic skin detection process after an initial camera calibration and basically, the test individuals are taken from the human sampling [18]. A scaling is implemented on the work data, before employing the distance that confirms better results than preceding works. In this work use the TSL color space and also successfully utilized, where undesired effects are minimized, and the Gaussian model shows the better skin distribution process considering other color spaces. Additionally, utilizing an initial filter, generally, huge parts of effortlessly distinct non-skin pixels, are eradicated from further processing. Grouping and analyzing the resulting features from the discriminator progresses the ratio of precise detection and minimize the small nonskin region existent in a common complex image including interracial descent persons, Caucasian, background, African, and Asiatic. Also, this approach is not limited to grouping, size, or orientation candidates.

The skin disease utilizing skin image texture analysis and by comparing the test image to reference images or defined images [15]. The matching of reference and test images compared that get the skin diseases percentage in the obtained skin texture image. The classification detection process by extracting only the specified features such as shape, intensity, and histogram values. The captured images are processed by applying the gamma correction process. The extracted methods are categorized into support vector machine which classifies into the malignant and benign. The performance of the system is analyzed using the different feature extraction methods.

2.8   Digital Image Utilizing Technique

The image processing approaches such as a fuzzy inference system and a Neural Network (NN) system were utilized in this work as promising modalities for the detection of various sorts of skin cancer [8]. Extracting the shearlet features from the ultrasound cancer image for detecting the normal and abnormal tissues in the affected part. The Shearlet transform analyzes the image and the texture metrics are analyzed in the high dimensional way. The extracted features are classified by applying the different classifiers such as the support vector machine technique.

The extracted features are compared with the different feature extraction techniques such as the contourlet, curvelet, and GLCM approach. The performance of the suggested system is analyzed using the experimental results in terms of accuracy, sensitivity, specificity, predictive values. Hierarchal Neural Network gets 90.67% while utilizing the neuro-fuzzy system is get 91.26% and NN sensitivity is 95% and specificity is 88% [38]. At the same time, the skin diagnosis system using the neuro-fuzzy system is getting 89% of specificity and 98% sensitivity.

The optical spectroscopy and a multi-spectral classification scheme utilizing SVM to assistance dermatologists in the diagnosis of malign, benign, and normal skin lesions [19]. Initially, in this works show effective classification with 94.9% of skin 45 lesions from normal skin in 48 patients depends on the 436 features. The various classifiers involved in the cancer recognition process which is explained as follows. There are several classification techniques like Bayesian Classifiers, Hidden Markov Model, Support Vector Machine, Self-Organization Map, Fuzzy based Approach, and Neural Networks are used to analyze the different type of cancer. The traditional telemedicine across the world and this study focus on modeling a designing a system and here initially collate past Pigmented Skin Lesion (ELM) in aiding diagnosis. In this work use Pigmented Skin Lesion (PSL) and analysis the images related to skin cancer. In this work also use the computational intelligence methods to examine, classify, and process the given image library. Here texture and morphological features from the given image are extracted. These results are shown in mobile data acquisition devices which in turn specify the benign (non-threatening) or malignancy (life-threatening) status of the imaged PSL. This forms the fundamental for upcoming automated classification process in term of skin lesions in skin cancer patients.

2.9 Data Mining Techniques

The data mining concepts, and their different methods are available in the literature on medical data mining [38]. In this work mainly emphasize on the data mining application on skin diseases. A classification has been offered depends on the various kinds of data mining approaches. The effectiveness of the numerous data mining procedures is highlighted. Usually, association mining is suitable for mining rules. It has been utilized particularly in cancer diagnosis. A classification is a robust approach to medical mining. This work summarized the various kinds of classification and their using process in dermatology. It is one of the most significant approaches for the diagnosis of erythematous-squamous diseases. The computer vision-based diagnosis system which discussed some clinical diagnosis approach which is being combined with the tool for detecting a different type of lesion process. In the epidermis area, finding the Melanocytes in the epidermis is a significant process and a difficult process also. Experimental evaluation based on 40 different histopathological images it comprises 341 is Melanocytes.

A novel approach for skin cancer analysis and detection from cancer effected images [41]. The image enhancement and denoising process by using Wavelet Transformation and the Asymmetry, Border irregularity, Color, Diameter (ACBD) rules are used for histogram analysis. Finally, the classification process is done by using the Fuzzy inference system. The pixel color is used for determining the final decision of 48 skin cancer type, the decision may be two stages like a malignant stage and begin the stage of skin cancer. A computer vision-based skin image Diagnosis system and Initially, in this work skin, the lesion segmentation process is done. After those vital steps are to mine the pattern and feature analysis processes to create a diagnosis of the skin cancer affected area. This work provides an idea to process the classification, detection, and segmentation of skin cancer and the skin cancer affected area utilizing a hybrid image processing approach.

The k-means algorithm, watershed method, and the difference in strength methods [27]. Initially, the image has been segmented into the different regions by using the k-means clustering approach. From the segmented regions, the intensity value is calculated for each region, and the effective boundary and edge information is obtained by the difference strength method. Finally, the watershed algorithm is applied to each edge to analyze the broken lines in the entire image. From the region, the tumors have been segmented efficiently.

An intelligent automated approach for identifying the different sorts of skin lesions utilizing machine learning procedures [27]. Initially, local information is getting over the Local Binary Pattern (LBP) on various kinds of scales, and GLCM at different angles has been mined as a kind of texture feature. Typically, these features are robust because of scale rotation invariant property of GLCM features and invariant property of LBP. The Global information of altered color channels has been integrated through four various moments mined in six different color spaces. Thus a merged hybrid texture color and local as global features have been recommended along with SVM to categorize the non-melanoma and melanoma.

3   Proposed Method

This research work majorly focusing on the identification of skin cancers such as Malignant – Melanoma, Malignant - Basal Cell Carcinoma, Malignant - Basal Cell Carcinoma, Benign - Melanocytic Nevi, Benign - Melanocytic Nevi, Benign - Seborrheic Keratoses and Benign – Acrochordon. The detailed operation of skin cancer detection and classification approach is presented in Fig. 1.

3.1   Database Training and Testing

The database is trained from the collected images of "International Skin Imaging Collaboration (ISIC)" The dataset consisted of 1000 benign and 1000 malignant images of melanoma. All the images are trained using the BP-ANN network model with SGLD features. And random unknown test sample is applied to the system for detection and classification, respectively.

3.2   Preprocessing

The query image is obtained through the image acquisition phase, includes background data and noise. Pre-processing is mandatory to remove irrelevant information noises,labels, tape and artifacts, and the pectoral muscle from the skin image. Contrast limited adaptive histogram equalization CLAHE is also performed on the skin lesion to get the enhanced image in the spatial domain. Histogram equalization works on the whole image and enhances the contrast of the image, whereas adaptive histogram equalization divides the whole image and works on the small regions called tiles. Each tile is typically 8×8 pixels, and within each tile histogram is equalized, thus enhancing the edges of the lesion. Contrast limiting is applied to limit the contrast below the specific limit to limit the noise (Table 1).

Table 1. Comparison of various machine learning-based methods applied to skin cancer detection.

Ref.	Type	Features	Method	Advantages	Challenges
[34]	Melanoma	Texture	K-NN	This method has effectively segmented the image with high accuracy	Due to texture features Asymmetry property was not fulfilled and results in inaccurate classification
[22]	Dermal cell images	Global	CNN	This method was effectively utilized to classify the dermal cells but not useful for radiologists	The Global features are majorly focused on entire image properties; thus, the background image properties affect the classification accuracy
[1]	Melanoma	Entropy controlled NCA	CNN	The multi-layer deep learning CNN architecture gives the maximum specificity	Due to neighborhood component analysis, the homogeneity and color properties will not be covered for classification
[47]	Benign, Malignant	Color	CNN	The hybrid multilayer neural network model can effectively improve the quantitative metrics	Only the color-based features are not enough to classify cancer, it also needs the asymmetry, border and texture features
[24]	Melanoma	HOG, SURF, COLOUR	Cubic SVM	The detection of cancer region extracted effectively, and multiple features are extracted	The cubic SVM is failed to classify the benign type of skin cancers and sensitivity related issues are raised
[18]	Benign, Malignant	Deep learning Features	DCNN	The multi-layer deep learning CNN architecture gives the maximum specificity	The computational complexity is much high and takes more time to extract deep learning features

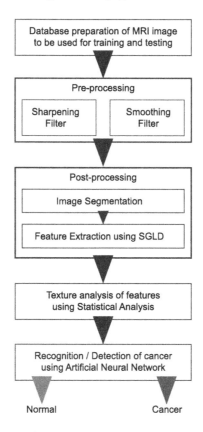

Fig. 1. Pipeline for skin cancer detection and classification.

3.3 Image Segmentation

After the preprocessing stage, segmentation of lesion was done to get the transparent portion of the affected area of skin. The Ostu's technique is utilized to the image to segment the skin lesion area based on thresholding [6]. In the Ostus algorithm, Segmentation is the initial process of this work, at the cluster centers, cost junction must be minimized which varies concerning memberships of inputs.

3.4 Feature Extraction

In this various feature can be extracted through the skin lesion to categorize various given lesions. We extracted some of the prominent features which help us in distinguishing the skin lesions, those are statistical and texture features [25]. SGLD is a statistical technique of scrutinizing textures considering the spatial connection of image pixels. The texture of mage gets characterized by SGLD functions through computations of how often pairs of pixels with explicit values and in a particular spatial connection are present in the image.

SGLD matrix can be created, and then statistical texture features are extracted from the SGLD matrix. SGLD shows how different combinations of pixel brightness values which are also known as grey levels are present in the image. It defines the probability of a particular grey level is present in the surrounding area of other grey levels. In the following formulas, let a, b be several rows and columns of matrix respectively, $S_{a,b}$ the probability value recorded for the cell (a, b), and the number of gray levels in the image be 'N'. Then several textural features (including mean, variance, standard deviation, skewness, kurtosis, contrast, correlation, dissimilarity, homogeneity, angular second movement, and energy) can be extracted from these matrices.

3.5   Texture Analysis of Features

Feature of Lesion. According to previous work on skin lesion feature extraction, computing the variance and mean of various color channels would assist in classifying the melanoma from non-melanoma images. Hence on segmenting the skin lesion image, the binary image is converted into a red, green, and blue (RGB) scale, Hue, Saturation Value (HSV), and grayscale [19]. Thus, computing the mean, variance, histograms, and non-zero bins of skin lesions in different color spaces.

Border Feature of Lesion. The border feature of the lesion is essential as melanoma has a highly irregular border as compared to the normal skin lesions. Border features can be computed by using the solidity, convex area, entropy, and convexity features.

- Solidity: It is defined as the area of the image divided by the area of its convex hull, and it is used to quantify the size and the cavities in an object boundary.
- Entropy: It is defined as the randomness of the texture of the skin lesion.
- Convex Area: It is defined as the area of the skin lesion.

3.6   Classifications of Cancer

The BP-ANN architecture has eight layers with weights. It contains the sequence of three alternating convolutional 2D layers and the MaxPooling 2D layer and three fully connected layers. The first convolutional 2D layer of the net takes in $224 \times 224 \times 3$ pixels skin lesion images and applies 96 11×11 filters at stride 4 pixels, followed by a ReLU activation layer and cross channel normalization layer. The second layer (MaxPooling) contains 3×3 filters applied at stride 2 pixels and zero paddings. Next convolutional 2D layer applies 5 256×256 pixel filters at stride 4 pixels, followed by max pooling 2D layer which contains 3×3 pixels filters applied at stride 2 pixels and zero paddings [18]. The third convolutional 2D layer of the net takes applies 384 3×3 filters at stride 1 pixel and one padding. The last dense layer of the BP-ANN contains three fully connected layers with ReLU activation and a 50% dropout to give 60 million parameters.

4   Results

4.1   Evaluation Metrics

For valuation of classification outcomes, we utilized three qualitative metrics such as specificity, accuracy and sensitivity. The accuracy can be defined as out of certain random test cases, how many outcomes give the perfect classification output. The sensitivity is defined as individual classification accuracy, how much the method is sensitive towards the malignant and benign cancers. And specificity is defined as the how much accurately the location of cancer is recognized.

- Accuracy $= \frac{TP+TN}{TP+FP+TN+FN}$
- Specificity $= \frac{TN}{TN+FP}$
- Sensitivity $= \frac{TP}{TP+FN}$

where TP conveys the amount of test cases properly recognized as malignant, FP conveys the amount of test cases improperly recognized as malignant, TN conveys the amount of test cases properly recognized as benign and FN is conveys the amount of test cases improperly recognized as benign.

4.2   Performance Comparison

In this work, three diagnosis methods are utilized such as benign skin lesion, suspicion, and melanoma. The experimental work uses 40 images comprising suspicious melanoma skin cancer. From the experimental results in this work obtain 92% classification accuracy reflects its viability. It has implemented the morphological operations for the removal of hair. The foreground is removed in the first phase using Opening operation whereas, in the second phase, the closing operation removes the background. The morphological operation has given the hair removed image that helped in further processing. Finally, Edges are detected by using Prewitt edge detection and Sobel edge detection techniques. The morphological operation gives better Peak Signal to Noise Ratio and Mean Square Error values, Prewitt edge detection is better than Sobel edge detection based on the PSNR value.

The proposed method was compared with the existing ones and as shown in Table 2, the proposed method outperformed the existing one published in the literature. The proposed method outperformed KNN [24], SVM [41], MK-SVM [18] and LSTM [38]. The superiority of the prpposed method has been clear in terms of the accuracy (97.91%), specificity (98.41%) and sensitivity (98.14%).

Also, the method was compared with techniques such as soft colour morphology [44], morphological inpainting [47], flow-guided [17] and convolutional neural network (CNN) [42]. It can be seen in Fig. 2 that the proposed method outperforms these techniques in terms of peak signal-to-noise ratio (PSNR), Structural Similarity Index (SSIM) and mean-square error (MSE).

Table 2. Comparison of performance with existing methods.

Method	Accuracy (in %)	Specificity (in %)	Sensitivity (in %)
KNN [24]	81.62	84.80	80.81
SVM [41]	75.19	72.54	78.20
MK-SVM [18]	79.90	80.08	79.72
LSTM [38]	86.02	85.02	81.02
Proposed	**97.91**	**98.41**	**98.14**

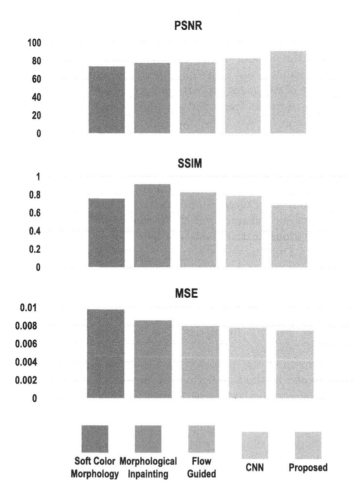

Fig. 2. Performance comparison in terms of PSNR, SSIM and MSE among popular methods and the proposed methods.

5   Conclusion

Finally, this article concludes the following challenges presented in the various literatures. By using the standard filters in preprocessing stage, they were effectively removed the noise from the images. But they are failed to remove the hair artifacts from the dermoscopy images. This results in effective segmentation. As the Melanoma is a life threatens skin cancer, it should be segmented very precisely with exact localization of borders. But conventional approaches failed to detect the cancer region accurately. The feature extraction should be done very accurately for proper classification. The state of art approaches focusing on only few categories of features but not all the types of features. The training of either deep learning or machine learning model should be done with variety of skin cancer types. But, the conventional methods failed to provide the maximum accuracy for various types of cancer. For this purpose a multi layer and error resilient back propagation based artificial network will be effectively used.

To solve this challenges, this suggests a computational methodology for the detection & classification of skin cancer from dermoscopy images using a deep learning-based approach. Here, sharpening and smoothing filters are utilized for preprocessing, which eliminates any unwanted noise elements or artifacts innovated while imaging acquisition. These filtering methods can effectively removes the hair from the skin images. Then otsu's segmentation is employed for ROI extraction and detection of cancerous cells with the accurate borders. Then the SGLD matrix method was developed for the extraction of all kind of statistical and texture features from segmented images respectively.

References

1. Akram, T., et al.: A multilevel features selection framework for skin lesion classification. Hum. Centric Comput. Inf. Sci. **10**(1), 1–26 (2020). https://doi.org/10.1186/s13673-020-00216-y
2. Al Banna, M.H., et al.: Attention-based bi-directional long-short term memory network for earthquake prediction. IEEE Access **9**, 56589–56603 (2021)
3. Al Banna, M.H., et al.: Application of artificial intelligence in predicting earthquakes: state-of-the-art and future challenges. IEEE Access **8**, 192880–192923 (2020)
4. Al Nahian, M.J., et al.: Towards artificial intelligence driven emotion aware fall monitoring framework suitable for elderly people with neurological disorder. In: Proceedings of the Brain Informatics, pp. 275–286 (2020)
5. Al Nahian, M.J., et al.: Towards an accelerometer-based elderly fall detection system using cross-disciplinary time series features. IEEE Access **9**, 39413–39431 (2021)
6. Alam, M., Tahernezhadi, M., Vege, H.K., Rajesh, P., et al.: A machine learning classification technique for predicting prostate cancer. In: 2020 IEEE International Conference on Electro Information Technology (EIT), pp. 228–232. IEEE (2020)
7. Ali, H.M., Kaiser, M.S., Mahmud, M.: Application of convolutional neural network in segmenting brain regions from MRI data. In: Proceedings of the Brain Informatics, pp. 136–146 (2019)

8. Amin, J., Sharif, A., Gul, N., Anjum, M.A., Nisar, M.W., Azam, F., Bukhari, S.A.C.: Integrated design of deep features fusion for localization and classification of skin cancer. Pattern Recognit. Lett. **131**, 63–70 (2020)
9. Aradhya, V.M., Mahmud, M., Agarwal, B., Kaiser, M.: One shot cluster based approach for the detection of covid-19 from chest x-ray images. Cogn. Comput. 1–9 (2021). https://doi.org/10.1007/s12559-020-09774-w
10. Bhapkar, H.R., Mahalle, P.N., Shinde, G.R., Mahmud, M.: Rough sets in COVID-19 to predict symptomatic cases. In: Santosh, K.C., Joshi, A. (eds.) COVID-19: Prediction, Decision-Making, and its Impacts. LNDECT, vol. 60, pp. 57–68. Springer, Singapore (2021). https://doi.org/10.1007/978-981-15-9682-7_7
11. Dascalu, A., David, E.: Skin cancer detection by deep learning and sound analysis algorithms: a prospective clinical study of an elementary dermoscope. EBioMedicine **43**, 107–113 (2019)
12. Dey, N., Rajinikanth, V., Fong, S., Kaiser, M., Mahmud, M.: Social-group-optimization assisted kapur's entropy and morphological segmentation for automated detection of covid-19 infection from computed tomography images. Cogn. Comput. **12**(5), 1011–1023 (2020)
13. Fabietti, M., Mahmud, M., et al.: Neural network-based artifact detection in local field potentials recorded from chronically implanted neural probes. In: Proceedings of the IJCNN, pp. 1–8 (2020)
14. Gaonkar, R., Singh, K., Prashanth, G., Kuppili, V.: Lesion analysis towards melanoma detection using soft computing techniques. Clin. Epidemiol. Global Health **8**(2), 501–508 (2020)
15. Han, S.S., et al.: Keratinocytic skin cancer detection on the face using region-based convolutional neural network. JAMA Dermatol. **156**(1), 29–37 (2020)
16. Hekler, A., et al.: Superior skin cancer classification by the combination of human and artificial intelligence. Eur. J. Cancer **120**, 114–121 (2019)
17. Hosny, K.M., Kassem, M.A., Foaud, M.M.: Skin cancer classification using deep learning and transfer learning. In: 2018 9th Cairo International Biomedical Engineering Conference (CIBEC), pp. 90–93. IEEE (2018)
18. Ismail, B.M., Basha, S.M., Reddy, B.E.: Improved fractal image compression using range block size. In: 2015 IEEE International Conference on Computer Graphics, Vision and Information Security (CGVIS), pp. 284–289. IEEE (2015)
19. Ismail, B.M., Reddy, T.B., Reddy, B.E.: Spiral architecture based hybrid fractal image compression. In: 2016 International Conference on Electrical, Electronics, Communication, Computer and Optimization Techniques (ICEECCOT), pp. 21–26. IEEE (2016)
20. Jesmin, S., Kaiser, M.S., Mahmud, M.: Towards artificial intelligence driven stress monitoring for mental wellbeing tracking during covid-19. In: Proceedings of the WI-IAT 2021, pp. 1–6 (2021)
21. Jesmin, S., Kaiser, M.S., Mahmud, M.: Artificial and internet of healthcare things based Alzheimer care during COVID 19. In: Mahmud, M., Vassanelli, S., Kaiser, M.S., Zhong, N. (eds.) BI 2020. LNCS (LNAI), vol. 12241, pp. 263–274. Springer, Cham (2020). https://doi.org/10.1007/978-3-030-59277-6_24
22. Kadampur, M.A., Al Riyaee, S.: Skin cancer detection: applying a deep learning based model driven architecture in the cloud for classifying dermal cell images. Inform. Med. Unlocked **18**, 100282 (2020)
23. Kaiser, M.S., et al.: Advances in crowd analysis for urban applications through urban event detection. IEEE Trans. Intell. Transp. Syst. **19**(10), 3092–3112 (2018)

24. Khamparia, A., Singh, P.K., Rani, P., Samanta, D., Khanna, A., Bhushan, B.: An internet of health things-driven deep learning framework for detection and classification of skin cancer using transfer learning. Transactions on Emerging Telecommunications Technologies, p. e3963 (2020)
25. Lakshmi, K.N., Reddy, Y.K., Kireeti, M., Swathi, T., Ismail, M.: Design and implementation of student chat bot using aiml and lsa. Int. J. Innov. Technol. Explor. Eng. **8**(6), 1742–1746 (2019)
26. Mahmud, M., Kaiser, M.S.: Machine learning in fighting pandemics: a COVID-19 case study. In: Santosh, K., Joshi, A. (eds.) COVID-19: Prediction, Decision-Making, and its Impacts. Lecture Notes on Data Engineering and Communications Technologies, vol. 60, pp. 77–81. Springer, Singapore (2021). https://doi.org/10. 1007/978-981-15-9682-7_9
27. Mahmud, M., Kaiser, M.S., Hussain, A., Vassanelli, S.: Applications of deep learning and reinforcement learning to biological data. IEEE Trans. Neural Netw. Learn. Syst. **29**(6), 2063–2079 (2018)
28. Mahmud, M., et al.: A brain-inspired trust management model to assure security in a cloud based IoT framework for neuroscience applications. Cogn. Comput. **10**(5), 864–873 (2018)
29. Marka, A., Carter, J.B., Toto, E., Hassanpour, S.: Automated detection of non-melanoma skin cancer using digital images: a systematic review. BMC Med. Imaging **19**(1), 1–12 (2019)
30. Miah, Y., Prima, C.N.E., Seema, S.J., Mahmud, M., Kaiser, M.S.: Performance comparison of machine learning techniques in identifying dementia from open access clinical datasets. In: Proceedings of the ICACIn, pp. 79–89 (2021)
31. Moqadam, S.M., Grewal, P.K., Haeri, Z., Ingledew, P.A., Kohli, K., Golnaraghi, F.: Cancer detection based on electrical impedance spectroscopy: a clinical study. J. Electr. Bioimpedance **9**(1), 17–23 (2018)
32. Munir, K., Elahi, H., Ayub, A., Frezza, F., Rizzi, A.: Cancer diagnosis using deep learning: a bibliographic review. Cancers **11**(9), 1235 (2019)
33. Nahiduzzaman, M., et al.: Machine learning based early fall detection for elderly people with neurological disorder using multimodal data fusion. In: Proceedings of the Brain Informatics, pp. 204–214 (2020)
34. Nasiri, S., Helsper, J., Jung, M., Fathi, M.: Depict melanoma deep-class: a deep convolutional neural networks approach to classify skin lesion images. BMC Bioinformatics **21**(2), 1–13 (2020)
35. Noor, M.B.T., Zenia, N.Z., et al.: Application of deep learning in detecting neurological disorders from magnetic resonance images: a survey on the detection of Alzheimer's disease, Parkinson's disease and schizophrenia. Brain informatics **7**(1), 1–21 (2020)
36. Noor, M.B.T., et al.: Detecting neurodegenerative disease from MRI: a brief review on a deep learning perspective. In: Proceedings of the Brain Informatics, pp. 115–125 (2019)
37. Orojo, O., Tepper, J., McGinnity, T., Mahmud, M.: A Multi-recurrent Network for Crude Oil Price Prediction. In: Proceedings of the 2019 IEEE Symposium Series on Computational Intelligence (SSCI), pp. 2940–2945 (December 2019). https:// doi.org/10.1109/SSCI44817.2019.9002841
38. Pacheco, A.G., Krohling, R.A.: The impact of patient clinical information on automated skin cancer detection. Computer. Biol. Med. **116**, 103545 (2020)
39. Rabby, G., et al.: TeKET: a tree-based unsupervised keyphrase extraction technique. Cogn. Comput. **12**(4), 811–833 (2020). https://doi.org/10.1007/s12559-019-09706-3

40. Rajasekhar, K., Babu, T.R.: Skin lesion classification using convolution neural networks. Indian J. Public Health Res. Dev. **10**(12), 118–123 (2019)
41. Rehman, A., Khan, M.A., Mehmood, Z., Saba, T., Sardaraz, M., Rashid, M.: Microscopic melanoma detection and classification: a framework of pixel-based fusion and multilevel features reduction. Microscopy Res. Tech. **83**(4), 410–423 (2020)
42. Roslin, S.E., et al.: Classification of melanoma from dermoscopic data using machine learning techniques. Multimedia Tools Appl. **79**(5), 3713–3728 (2020)
43. Ruiz, J., Mahmud, M., Modasshir, M., Kaiser, M.S., et al.: 3d densenet ensemble in 4-way classification of Alzheimer's disease. In: Proceedings of the Brain Informatics, pp. 85–96 (2020)
44. Shahane, R., Ismail, M., Prabhu, C.: A survey on deep learning techniques for prognosis and diagnosis of cancer from microarray gene expression data. J. Comput. Theor. Nanoscience **16**(12), 5078–5088 (2019)
45. Singh, A.K., Kumar, A., Mahmud, M., Kaiser, M.S., Kishore, A.: Covid-19 infection detection from chest x-ray images using hybrid social group optimization and support vector classifier. Cogn. Comput. 1–13 (2021). https://doi.org/10.1007/s12559-021-09848-3
46. Watkins, J., Fabietti, M., Mahmud, M.: Sense: a student performance quantifier using sentiment analysis. In: Proceedings of the IJCNN, pp. 1–6 (2020)
47. Wibowo, A., Hartanto, C.A., Wirawan, P.W.: Android skin cancer detection and classification based on mobilenet v2 model. Int. J. Adv. Intell. Inform. **6**(2), 135–148 (2020)
48. Yahaya, S.W., Lotfi, A., Mahmud, M.: A consensus novelty detection ensembleapproach for anomaly detection in activities of daily living. Appl. SoftComput. **83**, 105613 (2019)
49. Yahaya, S.W., Lotfi, A., Mahmud, M.: Towards a data-driven adaptive anomaly detection system for human activity. Pattern Recognit. Lett. **145**, 200–207 (2021)

Knowledge Discovery from Tumor Volume Using Adaptive Neuro Fuzzy Inference System Rules

V. V. Gomathi[1]([✉]), S. Karthikeyan[2], and R. Madhu Sairam[3]

[1] KG College of Arts and Science, Coimbatore, India
[2] University of Technology and Applied Sciences, Suhar, Sultanate of Oman
`karthikeyan.soh@cas.edu.om`
[3] Kovai Medical Center and Hospital (KMCH), Coimbatore, India

Abstract. The primary difficult in medical fields is the mining of understandable information from medical analysis data. The growing of medical data has made labour-intensive analysis, a tiresome job and sometimes not possible by medical experts. Many unknown and hypothetically valuable associations are not be recognized by the expert. The massive development of images necessitates a programmed manner to excerpt valuable information. The data mining or Knowledge Discovery Databases is main promising approach to solve this problem. Fruitful and interesting information can be mined and the discovered information can be used in the associated domain to improve the working level and to increase the feature of decision making through data mining. A significant task in knowledge discovery is to mine intelligible classification rules from the data. These rules are mainly informative for medical issues which are tremendously useful especially in the application of medical diagnosis. Automatic extraction of hidden information from images is a challenging task. The field of automated diagnostic systems performs an important part in the present technological revolution of computerized fully automated trend of living. The main aim of this research work is to extract tumor stage information. In this research, presents a method for extricating phases of cancer via Adaptive Neuro-Fuzzy Inference System (ANFIS), it has been given a more precise result than other methods. ANFIS is exhibited as a diagnostic tool to aid medical experts in the identification of tumor stages.

Keywords: Medical data analysis · ANFIS · Fuzzy system · Fuzzy logic · Image analysis · Tumor detection

1 Introduction

Automatic diagnostic systems are a significant use for study of database and pattern recognition. It aims at supporting doctors in marking diagnostic decisions [25]. This system is mainly used to diagnose the variety of cancers. The

© Springer Nature Switzerland AG 2021
M. Mahmud et al. (Eds.): AII 2021, CCIS 1435, pp. 123–135, 2021.
https://doi.org/10.1007/978-3-030-82269-9_10

cancer is second major cause for death in the world, because of this fact, and is expected to move top level to cause of death in few years [1]. The classification of medical images is very essential in the medical field and it is important for therapy preparation, identifying deformity, quantifies tissue volume to check tumor progress, analyses anatomical structure. Manual classification of Computed Tomography images is a challenging and cumbersome task and highly possible to make an error due to inter-observer variability. The classification results are highly substandard which leads to erroneous results. Thus, an automatic or classification approach is highly desirable as it decreases the complexity on the human work. Rule-based approach or Adaptive Neuro-Fuzzy Inference System (ANFIS) has been employed in a variety of applications, such as disease detection, data fusion [14], information security, trust management [2,19] etc. throughout the last decade. ANFIS is one of the extensively used neuro-fuzzy systems [13,16]. In this research work, the neuro-fuzzy based approach called ANFIS is applied for tumor recognition and classification.

2   Literature Review

The underlying objective of this research is to discover interesting knowledge from Computer Tomography (CT) images to give effective radiotherapy. This literature review presents some works that are needed to accomplish the objective of this research.

Hosseini et al. emphasized ANFIS as classifier and it overcomes the problems of fuzzy systems and neural networks [8]. Roy et al. explored an improved classifier with ANFIS for brain tumor tissue characterization. They have used Harvard benchmark dataset and obtained 98.25% accuracy for both contrast and non-contrast images [21]. Deshmukh et al. exhibits a computerized identification approach for the MRI image with the help of neuro fuzzy logic [4]. The substantial iteration time and the precision level are attained to be around 50–60% upgraded in identification compared to the existent neuro classifier. Mishra et al. presented ANFIS and ANN in identifying the tumor cells in the brain [18]. Sharma and Mukherji presented an image segmentation technique for locating brain tumor. GLCM is used for feature extraction in their proposed work. Fuzzy rules and membership functions are defined to increase the accuracy using hybrid Genetic algorithm and based on certain features. An adaptive network integrates the benefits of both fuzzy and neural network for segmenting brain tumor from MRI images [23]. Selvapandian and Manivannan proposed fusion based brain Tumor detection and Segmentation using ANFIS Classification by using BRATS open data set [22]. Fathima Zahira M et al. proposed novel segmentation and classification methodology using ANFIS for efficient classification [26]. Mahmud et al. discussed the broad investigation on the application of various learning techniques in biological data mining and also presented various open source tools and specified pros and cons [15,17]. Kaiser et al. exhibits fuzzy neural Network based COVID-19 for self-screening and identify employee admissibility to be present at the workplace. They proposed iWorkSafe that can help in confirming social distancing parameter with the scores which are replicating the fitness of the employees [13].

3   Tumor Stage Identification

Staging designates the sternness of an individual's cancer growth depends on the dimensions of the main tumor and depends on cancer has spread in the body. It is very essential because of the below points:

- Staging aids the physician to make the strategy and decide the appropriate therapy.
- The stage of the cancer can be used in recognizing a person's diagnosis.
- The identification of cancer stage is significant in recognizing clinical trials that will be an appropriate therapy choice of any patient.

Automatic investigative systems are mainly used as a major application for analysis of database entities and pattern recognition, which are aiming at helping medical experts in marking investigative assessments [25]. Automated diagnosis is mainly used to recognize the cancer types. The classification of medical images is becoming progressively more significant in the medical domain since it is vital for therapy preparation and identifying anomaly, quantify tissue volume to perceive tumor progress, study anatomical structure. Manual classification of Computed Tomography images is a challenging task and it is also takes more time. Hence, an automatic diagnostic method is required as it shrinks the hitches on the manual process. ANFIS is one of the extensively used neuro-fuzzy systems. In this research work, the neuro-fuzzy based approach specifically ANFIS is applied for tumor recognition and classification.

4   Adaptive Neuro-Fuzzy Inference System (ANFIS) for Tumor Stage Classification

ANFIS is the most popular techniques which has been applied frequently in recent years and is an amalgamation of two predictive analytics methods: Neural Network (NN) and Fuzzy Inference System (FIS) proposed by Jang et al. [10]. The aim of ANFIS is to incorporate the finest advantages of fuzzy systems and neural networks. The benefit of fuzzy set is the depiction of preceding facts into a set of constraints to decrease the utilization of search space. It is a hybrid intelligent system which combines the least squares and the back propagation gradient descent method of Sugeno type fuzzy inference systems (FIS). The classification precision of ANFIS is relatively greater than the fuzzy and neural classifiers. The conjunction time period of ANFIS is better compared to neural and the fuzzy classifier [7]. ANFIS is mainly used to optimize the parameters of fuzzy systems and replaces the manual process.

Some benefits of ANFIS are:

- Mainly is used in segment an image to improve the fuzzy if-then rules.
- It does not necessitate manual intervention.
- It increases many membership functions.
- The reason for using ANFIS is to give more accurate classification. Only minimal difference is present between different stages. So ANFIS is used for precise tumor classification.

4.1   Architecture of ANFIS

An ANFIS modify parameters and structural design of FIS implements neural learning rules. The FIS can be categorized into three types. In this research work, type 3 architecture called Takagi and Sugeno's fuzzy if- then rules and triangular membership function are used that is illustrated in Fig. 1. The object degree represents the membership value between the range of 0 and 1, which indicates the fuzzy set. The fuzzy set matches between input value and its membership values with interrelated membership function.

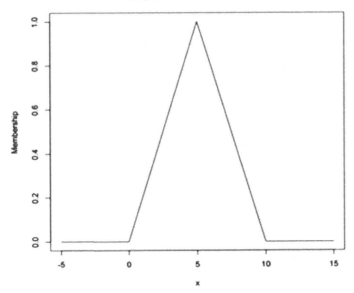

Fig. 1. Illustration of the triangular membership function.

ANFIS uses two sets of arguments: a set of premise arguments and a set of consequent arguments for membership function and rules. Two fuzzy if-then rules are used to design the ANFIS architecture.

$$R_1 : \text{If } p \text{ is } A_1 \text{ and } q \text{ is } B_1, \text{ then } f_1 = l_1 p + m_1 q + n_1$$
$$R_2 : \text{If } q \text{ is } A_2 \text{ and } q \text{ is } B_2, \text{ then } f_2 = l_2 p + m_2 q + n_2$$

where p and q are the inputs, The fuzzy sets are represented as A_i and B_i, f_i are specified by the fuzzy rule within the fuzzy region, remaining parameters such as l_i, m_i and n_i are the parameters of design which are used during the training process.

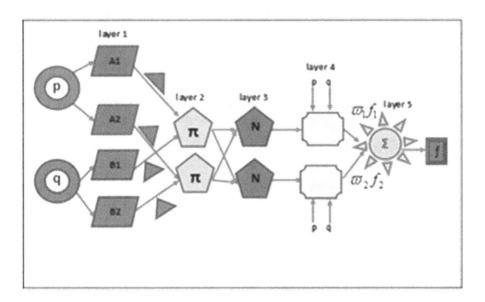

Fig. 2. Structure of the ANFIS Layers.

These two rules are used in the ANFIS architecture i.e., is shown in Fig. 2, the symbol circle is denoted for a stable node, and the flexible node is represented by square symbol. This ANFIS consists of a five layer architecture as below:

Layer 1: The layer 1 node represents the flexible nodes:

$$O_{1,i} = \mu_{A_i}(p); i = 1, 2$$
$$O_{1,i} = \mu_{B_i-2}(q); i = 3, 4$$

where $\mu_{A_i}(p)$, $\mu_{B_i-2}(q)$ represents fuzzy membership function [9,11]. The triangular membership functions are given by using three parameters such a, b and c:

$$\text{triangle}(x; a, b, c) = \begin{cases} 0, & x \leq a. \\ \frac{x-a}{b-a}, & a \leq x \leq b. \\ \frac{c-x}{c-b}, & b \leq x \leq c. \\ 0, & c \leq x. \end{cases}$$

The another expression for the previous equation is specified by:

$$f(x; a, b, c) = \max\left(\min\left(\frac{x-a}{b-a}, \frac{c-x}{c-b}\right), 0\right)$$

Layer 2: This layer represent nodes are fixed. They are labeled with π. The layer 2 output is represented as below and called as firing strengths of the rules:

$$O_{2,i} = w_i = \mu_{Ai}(p)\mu_{Bi}(q) \text{ for } i = 1, 2$$

Layer 3: The nodes are representing normalization part of the layer 2 [20]. The outputs are called as normalized firing strengths and are denoted as:

$$O_{3,i} = \overline{w_i} = \frac{w_i}{w_i + w_2} \text{ for } i = 1, 2$$

Layer 4: It contains adaptive nodes. The outputs of this layer are:

$$O_{4,i} = \overline{w_i}f_i = overlinew_i(l_ip + m_iq + n_i) \text{ for } i = 1, 2$$

Layer 5: The label $\sum$ represents the single fixed node. It sums up all input signals. The output of this part is:

$$O_{5,i} = \sum_i \overline{w_i}f_i = \frac{\sum_i W_i f_i}{\sum_i W_i}$$

It is inspected that the layer1 have three changeable parameters a_i, b_i, c_i also called as premise parameters, are associated with the input membership functions. There are also three modifiable parameters or consequent parameters l_i, m_i, n_i, concerning to the first order polynomial on the layer4. Hence, an adaptive network is formulated which are matches to a type-3 fuzzy inference system [10, 24].

The structure of ANFIS consists of two input node and ten output node. The two input represent the height and width calculated from each lung tumor slices of image. The triangular membership function is implemented. The output of the ten rules is condensed into one single output, representing the Lung cancer stage for a particular patient. The set of premise parameters and consequent parameters are most significant feature in ANFIS architecture. The parameters which change the range of the membership function are called the premise parameter. The parameters which conclude the output based on the condition is called consequent parameter. Two nonlinear parameters and ten linear parameters are used in the proposed ANFIS architecture. Height and width are the premise parameter and between stage1a to stage3 are the consequent parameters. The fuzzy if-then rules are followed to make the input in the ANFIS architecture [12].

5   NCCN Guidelines Version 2.0 Staging Nom-Small Cell Lung Cancer

Lung cancer is the leading reason of cancer demise in the world wide, and the delay in identification is a fundamental obstacle to improving lung cancer outcomes. 1.59 million deaths occur worldwide due to lung cancer. The patient survival rate can be increase in a substantial manner if early stage identification of lung cancer. The males are affected more in Lung cancer than females in 5:1 ratio [3].

6   The Tumor, Node, and Metastasized Staging System

Staging helps to choose what our suggested therapy plan may be. Staging means finding out:

- tumor location.
- its size.
- if and how much the lung cancer has spread.

The stage of a cancer will calculate the spreading level in the human body. The International Association of the Study of Lung Cancer (IASLC) [5,6] was modified the International staging system. The accurate identification of the stages of cancer is very important to select the appropriate treatment.

The TNM staging system is used to narrate the development and extent of Non-Small Cell Lung Cancer (NSCLC).

- **T** represents the tumor size and it affected places.
- **N** narrates the spreading of cancer in lymph nodes. These nodes are group of immune cells in the human body.
- **M** indicates the percentage of cancer has spreads out in the organs of body.

6.1   Prediction of Stages in Lung Cancer

The stage grouping is framed based on the T, N and M values to prepare the entire stages. Sometime the stages are divided into two stages named as A and B. Recognize the cancers using these stages, which have a related outlook, treated on a same approach.

- **Stage I:** The cancer is identified in the lungs, not extended to any nearby places such as lymph nodes.
- **Stage II:** The cancer is spreads out in both lung and lymph nodes.
- **Stage III:** This stage is advanced stage. The cancer is located in the lung and in the lymph nodes in the middle of the chest. The stage III has two subtypes:
  - **Stage IIIA** represents the affected lymph nodes, which are available on the same side of the cancer affected chest.

Table 1. Descriptor, T and M Categories, and Stage Grouping (NCCN Clinical Practice Guidelines in Oncology, 2012)

T/M Descriptor	T/M	N0	N1	N2	N3
T1 (less than or equal to 2 cm)	T1a	1A	IIA	IIIA	IIIB
T1 (>2–3 cm)	T1b	1A	IIA	IIIA	IIIB
T2 (less than or equal to 5 cm)	T2a	IB	IIA	IIIA	IIIB
T2 (>5–7 cm)	T2b	IIA	IIB	IIIA	IIIB
T2 (>7 cm)	T3	IIB	IIIA	IIIA	IIIB
T3 invasion	T3	IIB	IIIA	IIIA	IIIB
T4 same lobe nodules	T3	IIB	IIIA	IIIA	IIIB
T4 (extension)	T4	IIIA	IIIA	IIIB	IIIB
M1 (ipsilateral lung)	T4	IIIA	IIIA	IIIB	IIIB
T4 (pleural effusion)	M1a	IV	IV	IV	IV
M1 (Contralateral lung)	M1a	IV	IV	IV	IV
M1 (distant)	M1b	IV	IV	IV	IV

- **Stage IIIB** denoted the infected lymph nodes. These nodes are now situated on the opposite side of the chest.
- **Stage IV:** In this stage, the cancer has spread to both lungs or to another part of the body. The NCCN Clinical Practice Guidelines for lung tumour is narrated in Table 1.

7   ANFIS Rules

The model of fuzzy if-then rules is outlined for the cancer stage classification is represented as below.

if biopsy==p && stage_1a_height==1 && stage_1b_height == 0 && stage_2a_height==0 && stage_2b_height == 0 && stage_3_height ==0 then tumor_height_stage = 1;

if biopsy==p && stage_1a_height==0 && stage_1b_height == 1 && stage_2a_height==0 && stage_2b_height == 0 && stage_3_height ==0 then tumor_height_stage = 2;

if biopsy==p && stage_1a_height==0 && stage_1b_height == 0 && stage_2a_height==1 && stage_2b_height == 0 && stage_3_height ==0 then tumor_height_stage = 3;

if biopsy==p && stage_1a_height==0 && stage_1b_height == 0 && stage_2a_height==0 && stage_2b_height == 1 && stage_3_height ==0 then tumor_height_stage = 4;

if biopsy==p && stage_1a_height==0 && stage_1b_height == 0 && stage_2a_height==0 && stage_2b_height == 0 && stage_3_height ==1 then tumor_height_stage = 5;

if biopsy==p && stage_1a_width==1 && stage_1b_width == 0 && stage_2a_width==0 && stage_2b_width == 0 && stage_3_width ==0 then tumor_width_stage = 1;

if biopsy==p && stage_1a_width==0 && stage_1b_width == 1 && stage_2a_width==0 && stage_2b_width == 0 && stage_3_width ==0 then tumor_width_stage = 2;

if biopsy==p && stage_1a_width==0 && stage_1b_width == 0 && stage_2a_width==1 && stage_2b_width == 0 && stage_3_width ==0 then tumor_width_stage = 3;

if biopsy==p && stage_1a_width==0 && stage_1b_width == 0 && stage_2a_width==0 && stage_2b_width == 1 && stage_3_width ==0 then tumor_width_stage = 4;

if biopsy==p && stage_1a_width==0 && stage_1b_width == 0 && stage_2a_width==0 && stage_2b_width == 0 && stage_3_width ==1 then tumor_width_stage = 5;

8   Experimental Results and Discussions

An automatic detection of lung cancer stage from multiple slices of CT images is presented based on ANFIS rules. The experimental result demonstrates lung tumor slices in the whole slice of the patient. Six patients who had previously undergone CT scans for the treatment of lung cancer were selected for this study. GTVs, CTVs, PTVs were contoured manually on all tumors by the radiation oncologist. Here the patient id 002 tumor slices only presented.

8.1   Patient Id: 002 – Slice No 63-74

The patient id 002 consists of 103 slices. The tumor present in this patient is between slice no 63 and 74 out of 103 slices.

In Fig. 4, the red color indicates GTV. It is a primary tumor volume. Pink color indicates CTV. The CTV is represented the margin either fixed or variable length surround the GTV. Yellow color indicates PTV. PTV denotes the CTV plus a fixed or variable margin.

In this research, only the Stage classification for lung tumor is considered. Because esophagus and rectum staging is not based on size at all. It is entirely on the depth of invasion of tumor. So size parameter cannot co-relate with staging. So the stage is not identified for esophagus and rectum tumor. In addition to the tumor volumes, a biopsy report is also used as supporting information for this research. But the aim of the research is to identify the tumor and its stage before performing the biopsy.

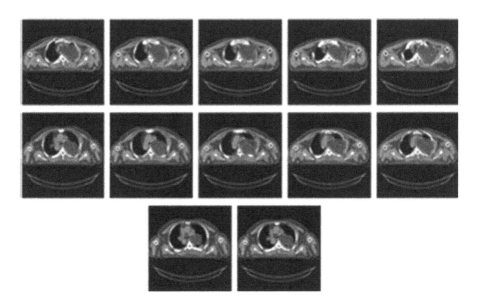

Fig. 3. Illustration of the slice by slice Contours of GTV, CTV and PTV have been identified on this CT slice no 63 to 74 for a Lung tumor patient.

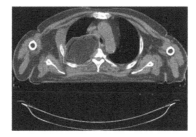

Fig. 4. Illustrate the Contours of GTV, CTV and PTV have been identified on the CT slice for a Lung Tumor (Slice no. 68).

The two important parameter height and width is used to identify the stage. The tumor height and width is calculated based on the number of pixels for each row and column. Each pixel value consists of 0.1. Each pixel value is calculated for every row and column in tumor contouring. So the size of the tumor is based on height and width. According to Table 1 the stages are classified as stage 1A, stage 1B, stage IIA, stage IIB and stage III. In this research, primary tumor stage is found. The other lymph nodes such as N0, N1, N2 and N3 are not considered. Based on the size of the tumor, we classify the stages of the tumor. Size of the tumor is calculated in cm unit. Height and width is calculated for all tumor slices. The average of all tumor slices is taken for the size of the GTV. In this research work, the lung tumor stage classification for the patient id 002, 005, 006, 008, 013, 014 is represented.

The patient id 002 consists of 103 slices. The tumor slice is present from slice no 63 to 74 out of 103 slices i.e. shown in Fig. 3. The height and width of GTV is calculated for every slice. The maximum, minimum and average value is taken to identify the stage. The tumor height is 11 cm and width is 10 cm for patient ID 002. The average is 10.5 cm. According to Table 1, this value exceeds greater than 7cm. It indicates that the stage is T3, i.e., Stage III. The nodes are not considered in this research. Similarly the other lung tumor patient width and height value is shown in Table 2. This table number 2 represents the results obtained by the proposed method and also verified with radiation oncologist result. The proposed method gives very close result in patient id 005,006,013,014 and exactly same in patient id 002 and 008. The primary tumor (T) result is the same for all patients.

Table 2. Comparison of Lung Tumor Stage Classification by the Radiation Oncologist and by proposed method with ANFIS

Patient ID	Tumor Stage Diagnosed by the radiation oncologist			Tumor Stage Identified by proposed method with ANFIS		
	Tumor Height (GTV)	Tumor Width (GTV)	Tumor Stage	Tumor Height (GTV)	Tumor Width (GTV)	Tumor Stage
002	11	10	T3N1 - Stage IIIA	11	10	T3- Stage III
005	8	9	T3N0 - Stage IIB	6	7	T3- Stage III
006	12	11	T3N2/T4 - Stage IIIA or Stage IIIB	7	7	T3- Stage III
008	7	5	T3N2 - Stage IIIA	7	5	T3- Stage III
013	11	8	T3N2 - Stage IIIA	7	5	T3- Stage III
014	4	5	T2N2 - Stage IIIA	3	4	T2A- Stage IIA

9   Conclusion

The medical diagnosis data is huge and more complicated. The mining of understandable knowledge in this data is the difficult task in medical domain. In this research presents the knowledge discovery process from tumor volume (GTV) for cancer stage identification using ANFIS rules. The proposed system yielded good results and can be used in diagnosis of cancer in an efficient way. The primary Lung tumor detection has been discussed using classification accuracy. From the study it has been found that the accuracy of the proposed methods with ANFIS is 98%, which means that this system can help the radiologists and radio oncologist to increase their diagnostic confidence. The tumor stage result demonstrates that this research is valuable to improve the diagnosis and reduce the number of unnecessary biopsies. The system can be used as an intelligent tool by radiologists and radio oncologists to help them make more reliable diagnosis.

References

1. Abarghouei, A.A., Ghanizadeh, A., Sinaie, S., Shamsuddin, S.M.: A survey of pattern recognition applications in cancer diagnosis. In: 2009 International Conference of Soft Computing and Pattern Recognition, pp. 448–453. IEEE (2009)
2. Arifeen, M.M., Rahman, M.M., Taher, K.A., Islam, M.M., Kaiser, M.S., et al.: ANFIS based trust management model to enhance location privacy in underwater wireless sensor networks. In: 2019 International Conference on Electrical, Computer and Communication Engineering (ECCE), pp. 1–6. IEEE (2019)
3. Chute, J.P., Chen, T., Feigal, E., Simon, R., Johnson, B.E.: Twenty years of phase III trials for patients with extensive-stage small-cell lung cancer: perceptible progress. J. Clin. Oncol. **17**(6), 1794 (1999)
4. Deshmukh, R., Khule, R.: Brain tumor detection using artificial neural network fuzzy inference system (ANFIS). Int. J. Comput. Appl. Technol. Res. **3**(3), 150–154 (2014)
5. Detterbeck, F.C., Boffa, D.J., Tanoue, L.T.: The new lung cancer staging system. Chest **136**(1), 260–271 (2009)
6. Goldstraw, P., et al.: The IASLC lung cancer staging project: proposals for the revision of the TNM stage groupings in the forthcoming (seventh) edition of the TNM classification of malignant tumours. J. Thorac. Oncol. **2**(8), 706–714 (2007)
7. Hemanth, D.J., Vijila, C.K.S., Anitha, J.: Application of neuro-fuzzy model for MR brain tumor image classification. Int. J. Biomed. Soft Comput. Hum. Sci. Official J. Biomed. Fuzzy Syst. Assoc. **16**(1), 95–102 (2011)
8. Hosseini, M.S., Zekri, M.: Review of medical image classification using the adaptive neuro-fuzzy inference system. J. Med. Signals Sens. **2**(1), 49 (2012)
9. Iqbal, M.A., Zahin, A., Islam, Z.S., Kaiser, M.S.: Neuro-fuzzy based adaptive traffic flow control system. In: 2012 International Conference on Communications, Devices and Intelligent Systems (CODIS), pp. 349–352. IEEE (2012)
10. Jang, J.S.: ANFIS: adaptive-network-based fuzzy inference system. IEEE Trans. Syst. Man Cybern. **23**(3), 665–685 (1993)
11. Kaiser, M.S., Adachi, F., Khan, I., Ahmed, K.M.: Fuzzy logic based relay search algorithm for cooperative systems. In: 2009 First International Communication Systems and Networks and Workshops, pp. 1–7. IEEE (2009)

12. Kaiser, M.S., Chowdhury, Z.I., Al Mamun, S., Hussain, A., Mahmud, M.: A neuro-fuzzy control system based on feature extraction of surface electromyogram signal for solar-powered wheelchair. Cogn. Comput. **8**(5), 946–954 (2016)
13. Kaiser, M.S., et al.: iWorksafe: towards healthy workplaces during Covid-19 with an intelligent pHealth app for industrial settings. IEEE Access **9**, 13814–13828 (2021)
14. Kaiser, M.S., et al.: Advances in crowd analysis for urban applications through urban event detection. IEEE Trans. Intell. Transp. Syst. **19**(10), 3092–3112 (2017)
15. Mahmud, M., Kaiser, M.S., Hussain, A.: Deep learning in mining biological data. arXiv:2003.00108 [cs, q-bio, stat], pp. 1–36, February 2020
16. Mahmud, M., et al.: A brain-inspired trust management model to assure security in a cloud based IoT framework for neuroscience applications. Cogn. Comput. **10**(5), 864–873 (2018)
17. Mahmud, M., Kaiser, M.S., Hussain, A., Vassanelli, S.: Applications of deep learning and reinforcement learning to biological data. IEEE Trans. Neural Netw. Learn. Syst. **29**(6), 2063–2079 (2018). https://doi.org/10.1109/TNNLS.2018.2790388
18. Mishra, S., Prakash, M., Hafsa, A., Anchana, G.: ANFIS to detect brain tumor using MRI. Int. J. Eng. Technol. **7**(3), 209–214 (2018)
19. Rahman, S., Ahmed, M., Kaiser, M.S.: ANFIS based cyber physical attack detection system. In: 2016 5th International Conference on Informatics, Electronics and Vision (ICIEV), pp. 944–948. IEEE (2016)
20. Rahman, S., Al Mamun, S., Ahmed, M.U., Kaiser, M.S.: PHY/MAC layer attack detection system using neuro-fuzzy algorithm for IoT network. In: 2016 International Conference on Electrical, Electronics, and Optimization Techniques (ICEEOT), pp. 2531–2536. IEEE (2016)
21. Roy, S., Sadhu, S., Bandyopadhyay, S.K., Bhattacharyya, D., Kim, T.H.: Brain tumor classification using adaptive neuro-fuzzy inference system from MRI. Int. J. Bio-Sci. Bio-Technol. **8**(3), 203–218 (2016)
22. Selvapandian, A., Manivannan, K.: Fusion based glioma brain tumor detection and segmentation using ANFIS classification. Comput. Methods Programs Biomed. **166**, 33–38 (2018)
23. Sharma, M., Mukharjee, S.: Brain tumor segmentation using genetic algorithm and artificial neural network fuzzy inference system (ANFIS). In: Meghanathan, N., Nagamalai, D., Chaki, N. (eds.) Advances in Computing and Information Technology. AISC, vol. 177, pp. 329–339. Springer, Heidelberg (2013). https://doi.org/10.1007/978-3-642-31552-7_35
24. Sumi, A.I., Zohora, M.F., Mahjabeen, M., Faria, T.J., Mahmud, M., Kaiser, M.S.: *f*ASSERT: a fuzzy assistive system for children with autism using Internet of Things. In: Wang, S., et al. (eds.) BI 2018. LNCS (LNAI), vol. 11309, pp. 403–412. Springer, Cham (2018). https://doi.org/10.1007/978-3-030-05587-5_38
25. Übeyli, E.D.: Adaptive neuro-fuzzy inference systems for automatic detection of breast cancer. J. Med. Syst. **33**(5), 353–358 (2009)
26. Zahira, M.F., Sathik, M.M.: A novel classification of MRI brain images using ANFIS and 3D reconstruction. Int. J. Eng. Adv. Technol. **9**(1), 5434–5440 (2019)

Key Techniques and Challenges
for Processing of Heart Sound Signals

Sheikh Hussain Shaikh Salleh[1]🆔, Fuad M. Noman[2], Ting Chee-Ming[2]🆔,
Syed Rasul Bin G. Syed Hamid[3], Siti Hadrina Bt Sheikh Hussain[1],
M. A. Jalil[4]🆔, A. L. Ahmad Zubaidi[5], Kavikumar Jacob[6]🆔, Kanad Ray[7]🆔,
M. Shamim Kaiser[8]([✉]), and Jalil Ali[9]🆔

[1] HealUltra PLT, 020 Jalan Pulai 18, Taman Pulai Utama,
81300 Skudai, Johore, Malaysia
[2] School of Information Technology, Monash University Malaysia,
47500 Bandar Sunway, Selangor, Malaysia
[3] Department of Cardiothoracic Surgery, Hospital Sultanah Aminah,
80100 Johor Bahru, Johor, Malaysia
[4] Department of Physics, Faculty of Science, Universiti Teknologi Malaysia,
81310 Skudai, Johor, Malaysia
[5] Faculty of Medicine, Universiti Sultan Zainal Abidin, Medical Campus,
20400 Kuala Terengganu, Terengganu, Malaysia
[6] Faculty of Applied Sciences and Technology, Universiti Tun Hussein Onn Malaysia,
Parit Raja, Malaysia
[7] Amity School of Applied Sciences, Amity University, Jaipur 303001,
Rajasthan, India
[8] Institute of Information Technology, Jahangirnagar University, Savar,
Dhaka 1342, Bangladesh
mskaiser@juniv.edu
[9] Asia Metropolitan University, 6, Jalan Lembah, Bandar Baru Seri Alam,
81750 Masai, Johor, Malaysia

Abstract. Recently, new advances and emerging technologies in health-care and medicine have been growing rapidly, allowing for automatic disease diagnosis. Healthcare technology advances entail monitoring devices and processing signals. Advanced signal processing and analytical techniques were effectively implemented in numerous research domains. Thus, adopting such methods for biomedical signal processing is an essential study field. The signal processing techniques are explicitly applied to heart sound (called phonocardiogram or PCG) signals as part of biomedical signals for heart health monitoring in this paper. The automatic detection of life-threatening cardiac arrhythmias has been a subject of interest for many decades. However, the computer-based PCG segmentation and classification methods are still not an end-to-end task; the process involves several tasks and challenges to overcome. The conducted evaluation scheme of the classifier also has a significant impact on the reliability of the proposed method. Our main contributions are twofold. First, we provided a systematic overview of various methods that can be employed in real applications for heart sound abnormalities. Second, we indicated potential future research opportunities. PCG segmentation

© Springer Nature Switzerland AG 2021
M. Mahmud et al. (Eds.): AII 2021, CCIS 1435, pp. 136–149, 2021.
https://doi.org/10.1007/978-3-030-82269-9_11

is critical, and arguably the hardest stage in PCG processing. Basically, basic heart sounds can be identified by detecting the offset R-peak and T-wave in the ECG signal. Unfortunately, utilizing the ECG signal as a reference to the PCG segment is not always an easy operation because: it requires synchronous recording of ECG and PCG signals; precise identification of T-wave offset is often difficult; and ECG-PCG temporal alignment is not always consistent. Using machine learning methods in PCG segmentation involves multiple types and many features retrieved in both univariate or multivariate formats. This leads to selecting the best PCG-segmentation performance feature sets. PCG segmentation approaches that use featureless methods based on powerful statistical models have the potential to solve the problem of feature extraction and minimize the total computational cost of the segmentation approach.

Keywords: Cardiovascular diseases · Machine learning · Bio-signal · PCG · Classifier · Segmentation

1   Introduction

Cardiovascular diseases (CVDs) remain the top leading cause of death worldwide. According to the latest world health organization (WHO) statistics, 17.7 million people die annually from CVDs, approximately 31% of all deaths worldwide. WHO had forecasted that by 2030, almost 23.6 mil-lion people would die from CVDs, mainly from heart disease and stroke [40]. In 2016, WHO and partners launched a new initiative aiming to reduce the global threat of cardiovascular disease, including heart attack and stroke. One of the three main packages aimed by this global initiative is the reduction of heart attacks and strokes can be made through equitable and cost-effective healthcare technical tools. Eventually, for most heart disease cases, the existing approach may come up with a more complex and expensive solution because the patient has already been in a high degree of danger. The heartbeats are generated as a result of systematic electromechanical activity within the heart muscle. Two signals are produced as a representation of the heart's electromechanical activity (see Fig. 1). Electrocardiogram (ECG) is a measure of the heart's electrical activity, whereas a phonocardiogram (PCG) is used to represent the mechanical activity of the heart valves.

Both ECG and PCG are non-invasive tests that play important roles in heart abnormality detection; however, diagnosis based on ECG signal or PCG signal alone cannot detect all cases of heart symptoms. In other words, the ECG signal is assumed to be a more efficient diagnosis tool than PCG. There are heart defects that cannot be detected using ECG but can be detected with PCG; mainly the problems are related to heart valves and heart murmurs. Moreover, PCG could reveal some heart abnormalities before they can be manifested on the ECG graph.

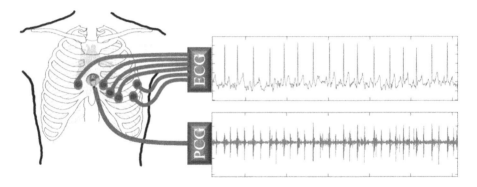

Fig. 1. Example of a single lead ECG recording and single-channel heart sound (PCG) signal. Both signals are recorded using Meditron Welch Allyn digital stethoscope.

2 Background

Throughout this paper, the electrical and mechanical activities are the primary research subjects. Accordingly, a brief review of the heart anatomy and physiology is introduced in this section.

2.1 The Heart Muscle Structure

The cardiovascular system (CVS) consists of the heart, which acts like the blood hub in the human body, and the blood vessels network that distributes the blood to the body organs. The heart is the main station of the CVS, where an exchange of oxygenated (from lungs) and deoxygenated (from body organs) blood happens and redistributed in a cell-to-cell basis in the human body [14]. The four chambers of heart are built from special cells called the cardiomyocytes. Besides the cardiomyocyte cells, the heart also has some unique cells named the cardiac pacemaker cells, which act as an electrical supply for the heart to keep beating.

2.2 Basic Components of PCG

The normal heart contracts periodically, making an average of 70 beats per minute. Each beat is a full cardiac cycle and a result of a series of contractions in different parts of the heart muscle. The human ear translates the two major sounds of the heart as "lub dub" sounds, where the lub sound is the first sound that is caused by the opening and closure of tricuspidmitral valves. On the other hand, the dub sound is a result of the opening and closure of pulmonary-aortic valves. In between these two sounds, the heart normally remains silent or produces a very low sound.

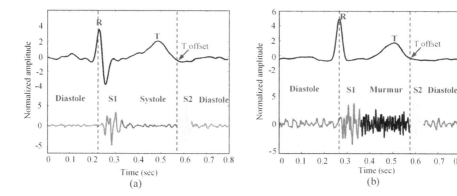

Fig. 2. The heart electromechanical activity in the form of ECG and heart sound (PCG) signals. Show-ing the fundamental heart sound (PCG) components along with the reference ECG graph. (a) Shows an example of normal heartbeat (record a0068 from [9]), (b) shows an example of abnormal heartbeat (record a0002 from [21]).

Figure 2, shows examples of normal and abnormal PCG heart-beats, respectively. A single cardiac cycle is divided into two phases, diastole and systole. The diastole is the period of time when the blood flows from the atria to ventricles; in this case, ventricles are in relaxing mode (not contracting). The systole represents the period of time in which the ventricles contract pushing the blood into the aorta and pulmonary artery. Between these two intervals, the two major sounds of heart (lub-dub), formally known as S1 and S2 sounds, occur. One of the main concerns of the researchers working in this area is to understand the abnormalities of the heart valves in cases where the backflow and the effect of the forward blood movement in the heart cycle stages.

3   PCG Preprocessing

The PCG is an acoustic signal, and it is more likely to be contaminated with various types of surrounding noises, especially in clinical environments. A normal heartbeat contains two fundamental heart sounds, S1 sound and S2 sounds separated by silent intervals. These silent intervals are called systole interval (the interval from the end of S1 to the beginning of S2 sound) and diastole interval (the interval from the end of S2 to the beginning of subsequent S1 sound). For abnormal heartbeats, additional sounds (called murmurs) are manifested in the silent intervals, in which the type of murmur is always referred to as a systolic or diastolic murmur.

During the early stages, the low amplitude murmur sound could be easily buried in noise. The presence of noise will increase the possibility of false alarms occurring in automatic diagnostic systems. Furthermore, PCG may show some innocent murmurs, which leads the primary care physicians and expert cardiologists to misdiagnose the heart status using a simple stethoscope. False alarms must be avoided in any automatic processing of PCG signals. Two possibilities may occur to the patient under test with false alarms. The healthy patient is sent for an echo-cardiogram that is costly and not easy to reach at any time. The pathological patient is sent home without medication or treatment [11].

4   PCG Segmentation

The identification of fundamental components of PCG signals is an essential step towards the automatic analysis of heart sounds. The process involves the localization of the main heart sounds, S1 and S2 sound, followed by boundary detection of these sounds. The segmentation allows the automatic analysis method to explore the intra-beat segments (S1, systole, S2, and diastole) characteristics which could be used for abnormality detection and heart disease diagnosis. Several approached of PCG segmentation have been reported in the literature, which can be grouped into four categories, for example, but not limited to; (1) envelope-based methods, (2) decomposition methods, (3) time-frequency methods, (4) machine learning-based methods. Category (1) and (4) may share a similar methodology; for example, the machine learning approach was built based on envelope features. Some of the recent PCG segmentation will be briefly discussed in this section.

4.1   Envelope-Based Methods

PCG segmentation using the popular envelope-based approach is addressed. The Shannon and Hilbert procedures are two examples of energy envelope-based approaches that are extensively employed. With regard to accuracy of PCG classification, both systems offer advantages and limitations. It is generally difficult for the Shannon type to capture the nuances of PCG signals, but the Hilbert type has many burrs and is unsmooth. As a result, segmentation is a difficult process to complete in the PCG study. Identification of the cardiac cycle is the most critical stage in PCG signal analysis. During a cardiac cycle, the heart produces four different heart sounds. It is the initial (S1) and second (S2) heart sounds that can be heard that are the most basic. With PCG segmentation, the goal is to detect as accurately as possible the positions of S1 and S2, which will allow for the estimation of the cardiac cycle to be performed. The ECG is used by the majority of segmentation algorithms. The ECG and PCG signals are not available at the same time, which is a disappointment. If you use the envelope-based methodology, you compute the energy enveloped by applying the S-transform on the PCG signal, and you can choose between the Shannon or Hilbert types. It is possible that others will employ the empirical wavelet transform for this segmentation as well. As a result, using the energy enveloped model, it is possible to predict the cardiac cycle.

4.2   Decomposition-Based Segmentation Methods

PCG signals are usually segmented based on their time-domain characteristics. Tang et al. [37] proposed a dynamic clustering-based method for segmenting heart sounds. In this method, the short-term cycle frequency spectrum was used to compute the instantaneous cycle frequency (ICF); the ICF was then used to segment the PCG signal into cardiac cycles (heartbeats). These cardiac cycles were then decomposed into 38 time-frequency atoms using Gaussian modulation model. Then compute the weighted density function using Gaussian density kernel estimation to emphasize S1 and S2 sounds in the time-frequency domain. The second-order derivative of the density function was employed to find the peaks (hills) to create dynamic clusters for the involved atoms. Finally, some frequency, timing, and energy constraints were applied for locating the atoms that represent S1 and S2 sounds; other thresholds and level-set method were used to find the boundaries of S1 and S2 sounds. The method was evaluated on a self-collected database containing only 565 cycles in total. Figure 3 shows Example of PCG signal with viola integral envelop. The data was collected using iStethoscope iPhone application.

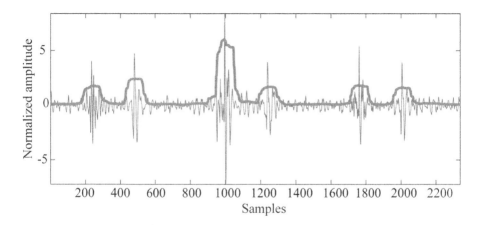

Fig. 3. Example of PCG signal with viola integral envelop. The data was collected using iStethoscope iPhone application.

4.3   Time-Frequency

Time-frequency representation methods also provide some contributions in the direction of heart sounds (PCG) segmentations. Gavrovska et al. [13] presented the use of Wigner-Ville distribution (WVD) for time-frequency representation of PCG signals. Two features (criteria) involved recognizing S1 and S2 viz, the maximum (peak) of the envelope with the detected margins and the duration between current and next candidate sound. Finally, k-mean clustering with city block distance was used to classify the candidate sounds into three classes, S1, S2, and others.

4.4   Probabilistic Models and Machine Learning-Based Methods

Probabilistic and Machine Learning (ML) methods can learn the underlying characteristics of the PCG components; hence, building discrimi-native models that can be used in segmentation, clustering, or classification purposes. Schmidt et al. [34] proposed a breakthrough application of duration-dependent HMM (called DHMM, also known as, hidden semi-Markov model (HSMM)) on PCG segmentation. In standard Markov models, each PCG component is referred to as a state. Some probabilistic rules control the jump from one state to another regardless of the duration of time a particular state remains unchanged. This may lead to rapid jumps between states, hence misdetection of PCG components. Schmidt et al. addressed this problem using labeled S1 and S2 sounds databases; a rough average estimation of the heart sounds duration was found from this database. In the DHMM training phase, multivariate features were extracted from PCG signals including, homomorphic envelogram, STFT energy of band 25–50 Hz, 50–100 Hz and 100–150 Hz.

Springer et al. [36] made extensive attempts and other researches to further improve the performance of HMM for PCG segmentation. Authors investigated the use of different types of features from PCG signals, including Hilbert envelope, DWT-based envelope, and short-time PSD envelope. The procedure is similar to the one using HSMM, except instead of using Gaussian distributions, the emission probabilities of the HMM were derived using SVM. The method was evaluated and compared with [34] on the normal and pathologic database. The performance showed an improvement of 2% when using the modified HSMM. In contrast, the features are not showing a significant improvement in the performance.

5   PCG Feature Extraction

Feature extraction is a fundamental step in PCG signal processing which is carried out to convert the raw data to some distinctive parametric representation. This parametric representation, called a feature, was then used for further analysis and processing [20]. Several methods and approaches are presented in the literature for feature extraction aim to achieve effective PCG classification performance. There is no feature set that can be said to be an optimal representation of the PCG signal diverse characteristics. The review was only conducted on a sample of methods in the literature over the past few years, and it is obvious the wide options of feature extraction methods from PCG signals. However, the MFCC and wavelet transform-based features are the most widely used for HS classifications, and the results presented recently in the literature have demonstrated their effectiveness. Another recently proposed PCG deep feature extraction method [43] is also worth to be further explored and investigated on their effectiveness with more real noisy PCG data, especially pathological PCG data. Some methods may result in a huge number of extracted features, which is impractical and may lead to classification overfitting. Therefore, feature selection or reduction approaches are utilized to solve this issue, some of the previously proposed methods are also reviewed in the following sub-sections. The feature extraction methods from PCG signals can be categorized into four domains: time domain, frequency domain, time-frequency domain, and a mixture of domains. Most of the methods required to perform PCG segmentation prior to the feature extraction process, in which features are extracted from specific intervals within the cardiac cycle or globally from the whole cardiac cycle. A cardiac cycle represents the complete heart mechanical activity in a single heart-beat which consists of S1, S2, and other sounds like S3, S4, and murmurs.

6 Classification Models and Performance Evaluation

Automated PCG analysis has been widely studied during the past few decades. The typical methods for PCG classification can be grouped into six categories: (1) SVM-based classification; (2) Artificial Neural Net-work-based classification; (3) Statistical Tests-based classification; (4) Deep Learning-based classification; (5) Ensemble of classifiers; (6) others including probabilistic and clustering methods. Building on previous review articles, which can be found in [8, 21, 25] some of the reported studies which involve using a considerable database are discussed briefly in the following sub-sections.

6.1 SVM-Based Classifiers

SVM is the acronynm for a single-layer nonlinear network. It first trans-forms the data into higher-dimensional space using some specialized kernel transformation functions. Then it uses the distance metric to create a boundary between the data groups in which this distance is simultaneously maximized. SVM has been widely used for PCG signal classification and is a well-studied machine learning approach. It has been provided through well-tested libraries and toolboxes, i.e. library of support vector machine (LibSVM) and MATLAB. In addition to linear classification, the SVM has the ability to handle a large number of features by efficiently performing a non-linear classification using what is known as the kernel functions, implicitly mapping their inputs 2D features space into high-dimensional feature spaces enabling accurate classes discrimination. How-ever, SVM has various types of kernel functions, each of which uses some hyperparameters. The kernel function and hyperparameters have to be carefully selected and tuned to achieve the best classification performance.

It is worth to note that, there are three publicly open sources of PCG database; (1) Michigan Heart Sound and Murmur database (MHSDB) was provided by the University of Michigan Health System. MHSDB includes only 23 PCG recordings with a total of 1496.8 s duration. (2) PASCAL challenge database, a total of 832 recordings with varying lengths, between 1 s and 30 s. (3) Physionet CinC challenge 2016 database, contains a total of 3,126 PCG recordings, lasting from 5 s to 120 s. The Physionet CinC is the current largest open source database, which includes clean and very noisy, normal and pathologic, children and adults' recordings. The database comprises of normal and abnormal classes with some PCG recordings labeled as "unsure" which has low-quality heart sounds.

6.2   Artificial-Based Neural Network Based Classifiers

In recent years Machine Learning (ML) techniques have emerged for their notable predictive abilities in a number of fields such as anomaly detection [5,12,41,42], biological data mining [23,25], cyber security [24], disease detection [7,26,29,30, 33] and classification [6,10,22,35], earthquake prediction [1,2], elderly care [16, 17], elderly fall detection [3,4,27], financial prediction [31], safeguarding workers in workplaces [19], text analytics [32,39], and urban planning [18]. Out of these number of different methods, the artificial neural network technology has been widely adopted for PCG classification. An example is a recurrent neural network (RNN). The RNN is a multilayer neural network in which the output of some or all layers do not only depend on the current input but also the previous output is looped back and reused as extra input. RNNs can be configured in two designs namely, fully connected or partially connected.

6.3   Statistical Tests-Based Classification

There are 2 types of statistical tests-based classifiers, namely the Hidden Markov Model (HMM) and the Gaussian Mixture Model (GMM).

6.4   HMM-Based Classifiers

HMM are the time-averaged signal recorded during each measurement of the heart and is assumed to be representative of some hidden state. This hidden is not directly observed, is assumed to undergo a Markovian process that is governed by statistical models.

6.5   GMM-Based Classifiers

Gaussian Mixture Model is a probabilistic model. The database consisting of abnormalities is assumed to be generated by the Gaussian processes inside the heart having arbitrary stochastic distribution. The classification technique is based on the ECG signal extraction using specific algorithm.

GMM classifier is a basic supervised method which has the ability to auto-matically cluster the data into a limited set of overlapped clusters. In training, two Gaussian mixtures were used to represent the normal and diseased datasets. The Gaussian parameters (mean, covariance, weights) were estimated iteratively using an expectation maximization algorithm. In testing, the same feature vector from the test ECG heartbeats was used to find the fitted Gaussian parameters, the likelihood was calculated and com-pared with the already built GMM mod-els. The main limitation of GMM based methods is that the number of mixture models must be determined manually, which forces the GMM to cluster the data into a limited number of clusters, which is highly dependent on the correlation of the input data.

6.6   Deep-Learning-Based Classifiers

Over the last few years, deep learning was getting more attention due to its ability to learn and perform classification tasks from raw data directly. Re-cent studies showed that deep learning methods were achieving results that were not possible before, sometimes surpassing human-level performance. PCG classification approach is based on the convolutional neural network (CNN). A CNN is employed as a feature extractor, and features extracted by the CNN are input into a heart-sound classification SVM. Time-frequency features are put into a CNN model to classify normal and abnormal cardiac sounds. Deep-learning architecture has a sequential mode employing a linear layer stack, namely one input layer, and numerous dense layer. Layers' aim is to transform data. PCG segmentation is performed using fixed-length segments with one step from each recording. For each segment, a PSD-based spectrogram was recovered using STFT, and the spectrogram was regarded as the CNN model feature input. The proposed CNN structure consisted of five-layers: input, convolutional with max-pooling, two fully connected layers and output layer. The Physionet training database was first transformed to an overlapped (5-second) PSD spectrograms; the CNN treated these spectrograms as images in the input layer. The CNN model was then trained with stochastic gradient descent using an optimizer, while the output layer contained a single neuron with sigmoid activation function. The system was designed to classify each 5-second segment whether it belongs to a normal or abnormal class.

Ensemble of Classifiers. Homsi et al. [15] used a nesting of three ensemble classifiers: Random Forests (RF), Logit-Boost (LB), and a cost-sensitive classifier (CSC). Each recording in the Physionet database was first segmented by identifying the fundamental heart sounds (S1, systole, S2, and diastole). A total of 131 features were then extracted from time, frequency, wavelet, and statistical domains. The study investigated the tuning of different parameters involved in meta-classifier in an attempt to improve the overall classification accuracy. 10-fold stratified cross-validation was used to partition the Physionet database into train-test sets to evaluate the proposed classification approach. The method achieved a MAcc score of 88.4% on 10-fold test-ing set and MAcc of 84.48% on Physionet hidden test set.

Vernekar et al. [38] proposed a PCG classification method using a weighted ensemble of four XGBoost (extreme gradient boosting) and four ANN classifiers. The Physionet heart sound database was used in this study, ignoring the recordings labeled as noisy. The rest were split into 2615 recordings for training and 296 for validation. The annotations for four heart sound components (S1, systole, S2, diastole), for each heartbeat, were then obtained using Springer's HSMM segmentation algorithm [36]. A total of 108 features were extracted from the time domain, frequency domain, and Markov chain analysis. However, feature importance analysis selected only 36 features to train the classifiers. The proposed method achieved MAcc score of 81.75% on the validation set and MAcc of 77.2% on Physionet hidden test set.

7   Future Work

ECG and PCG are two easy-to-use non-invasive tools for monitoring heart electromechanical activity. Despite the amount of research proposed in the literature, the performance of automatic diagnosis of heart disease is still not satisfying to be implemented in clinical systems. However, the current methodologies could be used in primary healthcare units or at home as the first screening tool and diagnosis tool. This will provide great assistance to help physicians to perform a correct and final diagnosis. The ECG and PCG signals analysis are not end-to-end processing but usually ensembles various methods for each processing step. In general, the state of the art on techniques oriented to the use of neural networks and deep learning should look into for example, classification methods through the use of networks with low computational complexity without domain transformation and with or without feature extraction.

Deep learning methods besides showing promising results also has its disadvantages such as there are numerous parameters of the deep learning model, with a large amount of data to be optimized which can lead to a long execution time and a large training data set required. Moreover, the deep learning modelling needs higher configuration of the computer with powerful CPU and GPU for calculation; hence the model is unsuitable for home computers and microcomputers. Existing deep learning research using only ECG data from multiple perspectives and highlights the present challenges and problems to identify potential future research directions. There are too many different learning architectures that has been used in areas such as disease detection/classification, annotation/localization, sleep staging, bio-metric human identification, and denoising. The deep learning model for disease detection is to map input ECG data to output disease targets through multiple layers of neural networks. Detection of cardiac arrhythmias (e.g., atrial flutter, supraventricular tachyarrhythmia, and ventricular trigeminy) is one of the most common tasks for deep learning models based on ECG signals. However, there are still some unresolved challenges and problems related to these deep learning methods.

Simultaneously analyzing multivariate time series from the same source provides insight into exploring the intersection of underlying dynamics in cardiovascular signals. Simultaneous PCG data recording at multiple auscultation points on the chest area with multiple sensors is more beneficial in terms of diagnostic accuracy since the results from a single HS signal can be cross-referenced with those obtained from other locations. In fact, the introduced SLDS methods in [28] were used for multivariate data analysis and modeling in the literature. Hence, these methods are assumed to provide higher performance if applied to multivariate PCG data, i.e., PCG segmentation application. This research was constrained by using univariate HS data because currently there is no existing clinically approved technology for multivariate HS data acquisition from different heart auscultation points. The recently published benchmark database (Physionet CinC challenge 2016) does not consist of a precise diagnosis of the whole large provided dataset. The accurate automatic diagnostic systems of the multi-class problem are needed, which would help cardiovascular monitoring and pre-screening.

8   Conclusion

In this paper, we provided a systematic overview on the state-of-the-art studies conducted in the last two years on new techniques for classifying cardiac pathologies using ECG/PCG and machine/deep learning techniques from the perspectives of models, data and tasks in real life applications. We found that deep learning methods can generally achieve better performance than traditional methods for ECG/PCG modeling.

References

1. Al Banna, M.H., et al.: Attention-based bi-directional long-short term memory network for earthquake prediction. IEEE Access **9**, 56589–56603 (2021)
2. Al Banna, M.H., et al.: Application of artificial intelligence in predicting earthquakes: state-of-the-art and future challenges. IEEE Access **8**, 192880–192923 (2020)
3. Al Nahian, M.J., Ghosh, T., Uddin, M.N., Islam, M.M., Mahmud, M., Kaiser, M.S.: Towards artificial intelligence driven emotion aware fall monitoring framework suitable for elderly people with neurological disorder. In: Mahmud, M., Vassanelli, S., Kaiser, M.S., Zhong, N. (eds.) BI 2020. LNCS (LNAI), vol. 12241, pp. 275–286. Springer, Cham (2020). https://doi.org/10.1007/978-3-030-59277-6_25
4. Al Nahian, M.J., et al.: Towards an accelerometer-based elderly fall detection system using cross-disciplinary time series features. IEEE Access **9**, 39413–39431 (2021). https://doi.org/10.1109/ACCESS.2021.3056441
5. Ali, H.M., Kaiser, M.S., Mahmud, M.: Application of convolutional neural network in segmenting brain regions from MRI data. In: Liang, P., Goel, V., Shan, C. (eds.) Brain Informatics. LNCS, vol. 11976, pp. 136–146. Springer, Cham (2019). https://doi.org/10.1007/978-3-030-37078-7_14
6. Aradhya, V.M., Mahmud, M., Agarwal, B., Kaiser, M.: One shot cluster based approach for the detection of Covid-19 from chest x-ray images. Cogn. Comput. 1–9 (2021). https://doi.org/10.1007/s12559-020-09774-w
7. Bhapkar, H.R., Mahalle, P.N., Shinde, G.R., Mahmud, M.: Rough sets in COVID-19 to predict symptomatic cases. In: Santosh, K.C., Joshi, A. (eds.) COVID-19: Prediction, Decision-Making, and its Impacts. LNDECT, vol. 60, pp. 57–68. Springer, Singapore (2021). https://doi.org/10.1007/978-981-15-9682-7_7
8. Clifford, G.D., et al.: Recent advances in heart sound analysis. Physiol. Meas. **38**, E10–E25 (2017)
9. Deng, S.W., Han, J.Q.: Adaptive overlapping-group sparse denoising for heart sound signals. Biomed. Signal Process. Control **40**, 49–57 (2018)
10. Dey, N., Rajinikanth, V., Fong, S., Kaiser, M., Mahmud, M.: Social-group-optimization assisted Kapur's entropy and morphological segmentation for automated detection of Covid-19 infection from computed tomography images. Cogn. Comput. **12**(5), 1011–1023 (2020)
11. Dominguez-Morales, J.P., Jimenez-Fernandez, A.F., Dominguez-Morales, M.J., Jimenez-Moreno, G.: Deep neural networks for the recognition and classification of heart murmurs using neuromorphic auditory sensors. IEEE Trans. Biomed. Circuits Syst. **12**(1), 24–34 (2017)

12. Fabietti, M., et al.: Neural network-based artifact detection in local field potentials recorded from chronically implanted neural probes. In: Proceedings of the IJCNN, pp. 1–8 (2020)
13. Gavrovska, A., Bogdanović, V., Reljin, I., Reljin, B.: Automatic heart sound detection in pediatric patients without electrocardiogram reference via pseudo-affine Wigner-Ville distribution and Haar wavelet lifting. Comput. Methods Programs Biomed. **113**(2), 515–528 (2014)
14. Hall, J.E., Hall, M.E.: Guyton and Hall Textbook of Medical Physiology e-Book. Elsevier Health Sciences (2020)
15. Homsi, M.N., et al.: Automatic heart sound recording classification using a nested set of ensemble algorithms. In: 2016 Computing in Cardiology Conference (CinC), pp. 817–820. IEEE (2016)
16. Jesmin, S., Kaiser, M.S., Mahmud, M.: Towards artificial intelligence driven stress monitoring for mental wellbeing tracking during Covid-19. In: Proceedings of WI-IAT 2020, pp. 1–6 (2021)
17. Jesmin, S., Kaiser, M.S., Mahmud, M.: Artificial and internet of healthcare things based Alzheimer care during COVID 19. In: Mahmud, M., Vassanelli, S., Kaiser, M.S., Zhong, N. (eds.) BI 2020. LNCS (LNAI), vol. 12241, pp. 263–274. Springer, Cham (2020). https://doi.org/10.1007/978-3-030-59277-6_24
18. Kaiser, M.S., et al.: Advances in crowd analysis for urban applications through urban event detection. IEEE Trans. Intell. Transp. Syst. **19**(10), 3092–3112 (2018)
19. Kaiser, M., et al.: iWorksafe: towards healthy workplaces during Covid-19 with an intelligent pHealth app for industrial settings. IEEE Access **9**, 13814–13828 (2021)
20. Leng, S., San Tan, R., Chai, K.T.C., Wang, C., Ghista, D., Zhong, L.: The electronic stethoscope. Biomed. Eng. Online **14**(1), 1–37 (2015)
21. Liu, C., et al.: An open access database for the evaluation of heart sound algorithms. Physiol. Meas. **37**(12), 2181 (2016)
22. Mahmud, M., Kaiser, M.S.: Machine learning in fighting pandemics: a COVID-19 case study. In: Santosh, K.C., Joshi, A. (eds.) COVID-19: Prediction, Decision-Making, and its Impacts. LNDECT, vol. 60, pp. 77–81. Springer, Singapore (2021). https://doi.org/10.1007/978-981-15-9682-7_9
23. Mahmud, M., Kaiser, M.S., McGinnity, T.M., Hussain, A.: Deep learning in mining biological data. Cogn. Comput. **13**(1), 1–33 (2020). https://doi.org/10.1007/s12559-020-09773-x
24. Mahmud, M., et al.: A brain-inspired trust management model to assure security in a cloud based IoT framework for neuroscience applications. Cogn. Comput. **10**(5), 864–873 (2018)
25. Mahmud, M., Kaiser, M.S., Hussain, A., Vassanelli, S.: Applications of deep learning and reinforcement learning to biological data. IEEE Trans. Neural Netw. Learn. Syst. **29**(6), 2063–2079 (2018)
26. Miah, Y., Prima, C.N.E., Seema, S.J., Mahmud, M., Shamim Kaiser, M.: Performance comparison of machine learning techniques in identifying dementia from open access clinical datasets. In: Saeed, F., Al-Hadhrami, T., Mohammed, F., Mohammed, E. (eds.) Advances on Smart and Soft Computing. AISC, vol. 1188, pp. 79–89. Springer, Singapore (2021). https://doi.org/10.1007/978-981-15-6048-4_8
27. Nahiduzzaman, Md, Tasnim, M., Newaz, N.T., Kaiser, M.S., Mahmud, M.: Machine learning based early fall detection for elderly people with neurological disorder using multimodal data fusion. In: Mahmud, M., Vassanelli, S., Kaiser, M.S., Zhong, N. (eds.) BI 2020. LNCS (LNAI), vol. 12241, pp. 204–214. Springer, Cham (2020). https://doi.org/10.1007/978-3-030-59277-6_19

28. Noman, F., et al.: A Markov-switching model approach to heart sound segmentation and classification. IEEE J. Biomed. Health Inform. **24**(3), 705–716 (2019)
29. Noor, M.B.T., Zenia, N.Z., Kaiser, M.S., Al Mamun, S., Mahmud, M.: Application of deep learning in detecting neurological disorders from magnetic resonance images: a survey on the detection of Alzheimer's disease, Parkinson's disease and schizophrenia. Brain Inform. **7**(1), 1–21 (2020)
30. Noor, M.B.T., Zenia, N.Z., Kaiser, M.S., Mahmud, M., Al Mamun, S.: Detecting neurodegenerative disease from MRI: a brief review on a deep learning perspective. In: Liang, P., Goel, V., Shan, C. (eds.) Brain Informatics. LNCS, vol. 11976, pp. 115–125. Springer, Cham (2019). https://doi.org/10.1007/978-3-030-37078-7_12
31. Orojo, O., Tepper, J., McGinnity, T.M., Mahmud, M.: A multi-recurrent network for crude oil price prediction. In: Proceedings of the IEEE SSCI, pp. 2953–2958. IEEE (2019)
32. Rabby, G., Azad, S., Mahmud, M., Zamli, K.Z., Rahman, M.M.: TeKET: a tree-based unsupervised keyphrase extraction technique. Cogn. Comput. **12**(4), 811–833 (2020)
33. Ruiz, J., Mahmud, M., Modasshir, Md., Shamim Kaiser, M., for the Alzheimer's Disease Neuroimaging Initiative, et al.: 3D DenseNet ensemble in 4-way classification of Alzheimer's disease. In: Mahmud, M., Vassanelli, S., Kaiser, M.S., Zhong, N. (eds.) BI 2020. LNCS (LNAI), vol. 12241, pp. 85–96. Springer, Cham (2020). https://doi.org/10.1007/978-3-030-59277-6_8
34. Schmidt, S.E., Holst-Hansen, C., Graff, C., Toft, E., Struijk, J.J.: Segmentation of heart sound recordings by a duration-dependent hidden Markov model. Physiol. Meas. **31**(4), 513 (2010)
35. Singh, A.K., Kumar, A., Mahmud, M., Kaiser, M.S., Kishore, A.: Covid-19 infection detection from chest X-ray images using hybrid social group optimization and support vector classifier. Cogn. Comput. 1–13 (2021). https://doi.org/10.1007/s12559-021-09848-3
36. Springer, D., Zühlke, L., Mayosi, B., Tarassenko, L., Clifford, G.: Mobile phone-based rheumatic heart disease diagnosis. In: Appropriate Healthcare Technologies for Low Resource Settings (AHT 2014), pp. 1–4. IET (2014). https://doi.org/10.1049/cp.2014.0761
37. Tang, H., Li, T., Qiu, T., Park, Y.: Segmentation of heart sounds based on dynamic clustering. Biomed. Signal Process. Control **7**(5), 509–516 (2012)
38. Vernekar, S., Nair, S., Vijaysenan, D., Ranjan, R.: A novel approach for classification of normal/abnormal phonocardiogram recordings using temporal signal analysis and machine learning. In: 2016 Computing in Cardiology Conference (CinC), pp. 1141–1144. IEEE (2016)
39. Watkins, J., Fabietti, M., Mahmud, M.: Sense: a student performance quantifier using sentiment analysis. In: Proceedings of the IJCNN, pp. 1–6 (2020)
40. WHO: Cardiovascular diseases (CVDs) (2021). https://www.who.int/news-room/fact-sheets/detail/cardiovascular-diseases-(cvds)
41. Yahaya, S.W., Lotfi, A., Mahmud, M.: A consensus novelty detection ensemble approach for anomaly detection in activities of daily living. Appl. Soft Comput. **83**, 105613 (2019)
42. Yahaya, S.W., Lotfi, A., Mahmud, M.: Towards a data-driven adaptive anomaly detection system for human activity. Pattern Recogn. Lett. **145**, 200–207 (2021)
43. Zhang, W., Han, J., Deng, S.: Heart sound classification based on scaled spectrogram and tensor decomposition. Expert Syst. Appl. **84**, 220–231 (2017)

Enhanced Signal Processing Using Modified Cyclic Shift Tree Denoising

Hadri Hussain[1], W. S. N. A. Wan Abd Aziz[1,2], Ting Chee-Ming[3],
Fuad M. Noman[3], A. L. Ahmad Zubaidi[4,5], S. B. Samdin[6], Hadrina Sh[1],
M. A. Jalil[7], Yusmeera Yusoff[8], Kavikumar Jacob[9], Kanad Ray[10],
M. Shamim Kaiser[11(✉)], Sheikh Hussain Shaikh Salleh[1], and Jalil Ali[12]

[1] HealUltra PLT, N020 Jalan Pulai 18, Taman Pulai Utama,
81300 Skudai, Johore, Malaysia
[2] Persada Digital Sdn Bhd, B-3A-40, Dataran Cascades Mitraland,
Jalan PJU 5/1, 47810 Petaling Jaya, Selangor, Malaysia
[3] Monash University Malaysia, Jalan Lagoon Selatan, Bandar Sunway,
47500 Subang Jaya, Selangor, Malaysia
[4] Universiti Sultan Zainal Abidin, Kampung Gong Badak,
21300 Kuala Terengganu, Terengganu, Malaysia
[5] Ministry of Health, Malaysia, 62000 Putrajaya, Malaysia
[6] School of Electrical and Computer Engineering, Xiamen University Malaysia,
43900 Sepang, Malaysia
[7] Physics Department, Faculty Science, Universiti Teknologi Malaysia,
81310 Johor Bahru, Malaysia
[8] Department of ORL-HNS (ENT), Putrajaya Hospital, Precinct 7,
62250 Putrajaya, Malaysia
[9] Faculty of Applied Sciences and Technology, Universiti Tun Hussein Onn Malaysia,
Parit Raja, Malaysia
[10] Amity School of Applied Sciences, Amity University,
Jaipur 303001, Rajasthan, India
[11] Institute of Information Technology, Jahangirnagar University,
Savar, Dhaka 1342, Bangladesh
mskaiser@juniv.edu
[12] Asia Metropolitan University, 6, Jalan Lembah, Bandar Baru Seri Alam,
81750 Masai, Johor, Malaysia

Abstract. The cortical pyramidal neurons in the cerebral cortex, which
are positioned perpendicularly to the brain's surface, are assumed to
be the primary source of the electroencephalogram (EEG) reading.
The EEG reading generated by the brainstem in response to auditory
impulses is known as the Auditory Brainstem Response (ABR). The
identification of wave V in ABR is now regarded as the most efficient
method for audiology testing. The ABR signal is modest in amplitude
and is lost in the background noise. The traditional approach of retriev-
ing the underlying wave V, which employs an averaging methodology,
necessitates more attempts. This results in a protracted length of screening time, which causes the subject discomfort. For the detection of wave
V, this paper uses Kalman filtering and Cyclic Shift Tree Denoising
(CSTD). In state space form, we applied Markov process modeling of

M. Mahmud et al. (Eds.): AII 2021, CCIS 1435, pp. 150–160, 2021.
https://doi.org/10.1007/978-3-030-82269-9_12

ABR dynamics. The Kalman filter, which is optimum in the mean-square sense, is used to estimate the clean ABRs. To save time and effort, discrete wavelet transform (DWT) coefficients are employed as features instead of filtering the raw ABR signal. The results show that even with a smaller number of epochs, the wave is still visible and the morphology of the ABR signal is preserved.

Keywords: Cyclic Shift Tree · Auditory Brainstem Response · Wavelet Kalman Filter · Inter-wave intervals · EEG · Wave V

1 Introduction

Genetic predisposition, [post/peri]-natal factors, intrauterine environment, all have a part in the growth of childhood hearing impairment. Due to the presence of various categorization systems, the definition of hearing loss/deficit may fluctuate. In early development, being exposed to spoken language is essential. As a result, children with undiagnosed hearing loss, including mild and unilateral deficits, may experience significant delays in speech development as well as psychological and mental behavioral disorders, which can have an impact on their social and academic skills as well as their overall development [15,18,22].

The Auditory Brainstem Response (ABR) is a regularly used tool for evaluating neonatal auditory function. This method has long been considered the gold standard for neonatal diagnostic evaluation throughout the first six months of life. However, employing repeated averaging of the trials for meaningful ABR waveform, ABR is also utilized for detecting hearing loss in adults [1]. To find the lowest level that provokes a discernible response, the electroencephalogram (EEG) ABR waveform is sampled, averaged, and waveforms are recorded for stimuli of various intensities [13,17]. Noise interferences can cause the morphology of the ABR to be distorted, affecting its accuracy. As a result, identifying the wave V can be a difficult task since noise can be emitted by equipment, circuits, or power sources. To correctly identify the presence of the ABR and differentiate it from physiologic noise, skilled clinical interpretation is required; unfortunately, subjective interpretation and the possibility of human mistake impair an objective physiologic measure [18]. For this reason, researchers like Wang et al. [23] suggested reasonable techniques to make hearing screening feasible. They suggested use a Kalman filter to adaptively extract sounds from ABR signals, reducing the number of trials required to enhance efficiency. Their work shows that with proper denoising using Kalman filter, fewer sweeps was required to obtain reliable ABR waveforms. In another related study, a wavelet based algorithm was introduced by [4] known as cyclic shift tree denoising (CSTD) method that technically gives a faster convergence on estimating the underlying ABR waveform compared to the conventional averaging methods [10,21]. The CSTD method is computationally stable and it has uncomplicated algorithm which motivates us to apply the method in this study.

2   Materials and Methods

Stimulus such as click, tonal, or chirp can be used in ABR measurements [20]. Though click stimulus is widely used in ABR measurements, however the responses obtained are not from the whole cochlea but are rather thought to originate from basal regions (2–4 kHz) [12]. Therefore, the chirp stimulus was developed. This chirp purpose is to stimulate the entire cochlea simultaneously and provide effective neural synchronisation. Studies report that, since chirp stimulus has a specific sequence from low frequency to high, larger amplitude ABR waves can be formed than with click sounds and the whole cochlea can be stimulated at the same time [6,7,11]. A chirp is a quick sweep through frequencies which is either low to high or high to low frequency. The stimulus of Audio chirp was generated using a personal computer for each participant, which simultaneously processes and records the ABR signals. By simultaneously connecting output audio to both the trigger box and the g.PAH Programmable Attenuator Headphone buffer, the triggering procedure could be completed (Guger Technologies, Austria). The trigger box receives the computer's audio signal and converts it to a square signal (trigger signal), which is utilized as a reference point for framing the EEG signal according to the provided stimulus. At the same time, the g.PAH attenuator sent the signal to the headphones such that every time the "click" played on the computer, the participant hears it. The device input power is 100–240 V with a maximum frequency of 50–60 Hz; thus, we used a bandpass filter with cutoff 100 Hz–1500 kHz for the recorded signal. Twenty chirps per second of stimulus rate were used to record the ABR signal with a sampling rate of 19.2 kHz and 24-bit resolution. Although, this sampling rate was empirically set supported by previous studies, which was found to be around 20 kHz. In this study, the intensity level of the stimulus was set in the range of 30–60 dBnHL with an increment of 10 dB. The EEG data were then recorded and averaged using sliding windows of 2000 frames. Each recorded epoch start-point is aligned with the start of the triggering signal and ends within a window of 40 ms (768 samples) for chirp and 20 ms (384 samples) for a click. The processing steps were implemented using MATLAB. Figure 1 shows the experiment setup and devices used for data collection of the ABR signals.

2.1   Wavelets Methods

The two wavelet denoising methods subjected to performance evaluation are as follows:

– Wavelet Kalman Filter (WKF)
– Cyclic Shift Tree Denoising (CSTD)

Figure 2, shows the flow of the two types wavelet based denoising methods, (a) Wavelet Kalman filter approach, (b) Cyclic Shift Tree Denoising.

A detail description of WKF method could be found in [19] while CSTD method could be found in [4]. This section only covered the process of modification. Due to the closeness in morphology between the ABR and the synthesis

Fig. 1. Hardware system setup with g-tech equipment which include gUSBamp, gPAH, trigger box and Sound Card.

wavelet, the biorthogonal 5.5 wavelets were used as proposed by [8]. The signal was split into high-pass (HP) and low-pass (LP) components, which correspond to details and approximates components, respectively, using the discrete wavelet transform (DWT). The signal was dissected to level 5, at which point the ABR's main frequencies were 200, 500, 900 Hz, respectively [8].

2.2   Wavelet Kalman Filter Approach

DWT is the digital form of continuous Wavelet transform (CWT) and can be used by setting discrete values of $s = 2^j$ and $u = n(2^j)$, where j and n are integer numbers, such that,

$$S_{2^j} f(n) = \sum_{k \in Z} h_k S_{2^{j-1}} f\left(n - 2^{j-1}k\right) \tag{1}$$

$$W_2 f(n) = \sum_{k \in Z} g_k S_{2^{j-1}} f\left(n - 2^{j-1}k\right) \tag{2}$$

where $S_{2^j} f(n)$ are the approximation coefficients (represent the low frequency sub-band), $W_{2^j} f(n)$ are the detail coefficients (represent the high frequency sub-band), j, n, $k \in Z$, Z is a set of all integer numbers. h_k and g_k are the low and high pass filters coefficients respectively. This study used wavelet coefficients for the observation model as suggested by [16] to reduce the state dimensions as shown in Fig. 2(a). The biorthogonal 5.5 wavelets were chosen as suggested in [16,24] by considering the similarity in the morphology of the ABR with the synthesis wavelet. The improved signal was then decomposed with DWT to obtain the coefficients for the Kalman filter process. Algorithm 1 summarizes

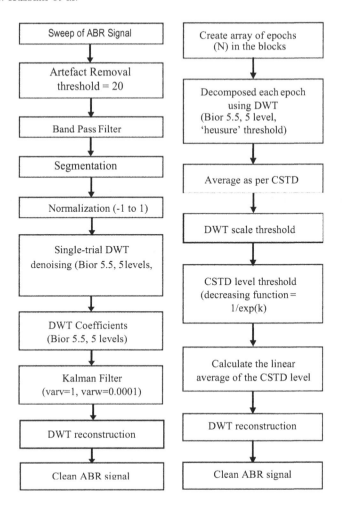

Fig. 2. Flowchart (a) Wavelet Kalman filter approach and (b) Cyclic Shift Tree Denoising.

the recursive procedure of Kalman filter where H and C are reshaping matrices. When applying Kalman filter, the ABR estimation model was assumed as a linear additive model according to [5]. From the analysis, the minimum number of epochs sufficient to detect wave V was chosen based on the experimental result. This method was introduced to overcome the high computational complexity due to the high dimensional state vector. This data fusion algorithm gives a small computational requirement, elegant recursive properties and is the optimal estimator for one-dimensional linear systems with Gaussian error statistics. They typically used for smoothing noisy data and provide the estimated parameter of interest. It is also widely used for positioning system receivers, phase locked loops in radio equipment, smoothing the output from laptop track pads and more.

2.3 Cyclic Shift Tree Denoising

The flow chart in Fig. 2(b) shows CSTD method, an array of wavelet coefficients was created by performing a DWT on each frame and arranged as a successive original frame. Proceeding with the final average created by linearly averaging all the frames and applied the scale threshold to obtain a smooth ABR signal. The array of wavelet coefficients was then denoised using CSTD, with each denoised in a distinct way. To create a sequence of total N frames, linearly average all different denoised reordering of frames to which CSTD has been performed [3,9]. Time domain samples were obtained by linearly averaging the N frames to generate one frame of wavelet coefficient and then reconstructing this average frame. This new estimation technique has a faster rate of convergence to the underlying signal than linear averaging, and it outperforms linear averaging in terms of performance [2,8]. This current technique, however, has a number of drawbacks, including the inability to apply it to a single frame of data. Other constraints include the requirement for multiple measurements of the same signal. The CSTD algorithm requires a power of two number of initial frames, with the signal being estimated being constant between frames.

Algorithm 1: Kalman filter algorithm

Result: X and P

X_0 and P_0;

while $t = 1, 2, ..., T$ **do**

    //Previous state

    X_{t-1} and P_{t-1} ;

    //Predicted state

    $X_{tp} = AX_{t-1}$;

    //Predicted process co-variance

    $P_{tp} = AP_{t-1}A' + Q$;

    //Kalman gain

    $K = \frac{P_{tp}H'}{HP_{tp}H'+R}$;

    //Measurement value

    $Y_t = CX_t + \epsilon_t$;

    //Updated state

    $X_t = X_{tp} + K(y_t - HX_{tp})$;

    //Updated process co-variance

    $P_t = (1 - KH)P_{tp}$;

end

---

3 Results and Discussion

Wave V amplitudes and latencies, for example, were recognized as crucial components. In the acceptance area of latencies, the wave V was traced whether it existed or not. The average of 2048 epochs of data from each subject were used to calculate the delay. In addition, data collection from tainted data with noise interference was examined using a new modified methodology called MCSTD, which was recommended by the researchers. Female shows earlier latencies than male and larger amplitude than male. Table 1, below shows the average latency values of 11 normal adult's subjects for chirp stimulus at 2048 sweep.

Wave V amplitudes and latencies were identified as key components. The wave V was traced in the acceptance zone of latencies, whether it exists or not. The average of 2048 epochs recorded data from each subject was used to calculate the delay. In addition, data collection from contaminated data with noise interference were analyzed using new suggested modified approach MCSTD. Female shows earlier latencies than male and larger amplitude than male. Table 1, below shows the average latency values of 11 normal adult's subjects for chirp stimulus at 2048 sweep.

Table 1. The average latency values of wave V ABR for adult subjects

Stimulus	Gender	Intensity			
		60	50	40	30
Chirp	Female	14.36	14.86	16.29	17
	Male	16.6	16.63	17.5	17.75

The inter-wave intervals for females are shorter due to the effect of negligible for a wave I and more pronounced for later waves. Females have smaller head size and less brain volume compared to male. Thus, the inter-wave latencies become shorter if the distance between the generators for each of the waves is shorter and the amplitude will be larger if the recording electrode is relatively closure to the wave generator. Figure 3, is the comparison between female's and male's signal.

3.1   Selection Minimum Number of Epochs

The signal was analyzed using averaging, KF, CSTD and MCSTD approaches. The data were recorded for four different intensity levels consist of 60, 50, 40 and 30 dBnHL. Wave V recognition between different intensity levels was related to their latency and frequency for each stimulus. Corona-Strauss et al. [5] stated that the latency value increased by decreasing the frequency content of chirps. Moreover, the latency of the responses evoked by higher intensity levels is shorter than the response evoked from a lower intensity level. Decreased the intensity level will longer the latency and smaller the amplitude.

Figure 4 (a) and (b) showed the results for the wave V detection at sweeps number of 16 and 8. When decreasing the sweep number, the signal amplitude increased. According to [16] the ABR signal amplitude is between 0.1 to 1.0 µV.

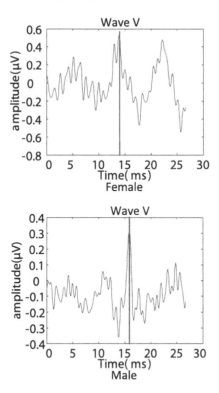

Fig. 3. ABR signal for female and male at 60 dB, 2048 sweeps.

However, ABR signal amplitude at 16 and 8 sweeps exceeded $1\,\mu$V showed by the straight red line. In addition, wave V detection failed when decreasing the sweeps number to 16 and 8. Thus, 16 and 8 sweeps are not reliable for detecting wave V. The goal of this research is to determine the minimal trial that will be fulfilled in detecting the presence of wave V and denoising the tainted signals. By comparing the results of averaged data morphology, the performance of each methodology was assessed. Each recorded signal was averaged sweep by sweep and the sweep was divided into 2048, 1024, 512, 256, 128, 64 and 32 sweeps. When the signal is averaged over 2048 epochs, all techniques provide an accurate assessment of the ABR signal. When the number of epochs is reduced, however, wave V identification differs between techniques. As a result, when compared to other approaches, MCSTD performs admirably. When decreasing the epoch's number to 16 and 8, the signal amplitude increases and exceeded $1\,\mu$V in which ABR amplitude is between 0.1 to $1.0\,\mu$V [14].

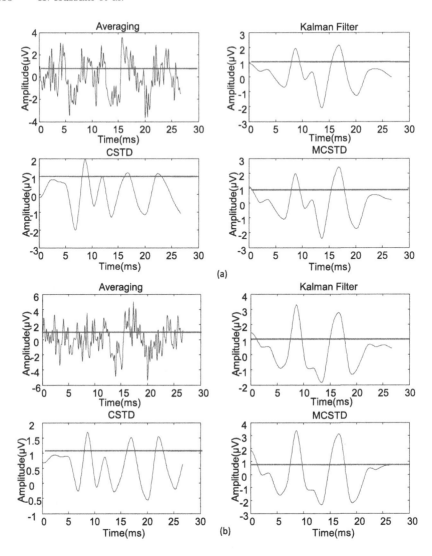

Fig. 4. ABR signal for female and male at 60 dB, 2048 sweeps.

4   Conclusion

Analyzing EEG signal is very challenging due to their high complexity, low SNR, non-linearity and non-stationary. ABR is currently the most reliable method for hearing screening, however, the noise interference from environment, equipment, and subject movement can be a difficult task for wave V detection. The aim of this study is to reduce screening time by using a better signal processing approach, reducing the sweeping number and lowering the noise interference effects. This study focused on detecting wave V in normal adults by applying

KF and CSTD. From the result, it is shown that better detection of wave V is obtained using WKF with the reduced number of epochs by considering the SNR and RMSE. Further work should be carried to see the performance based on Modified Cyclic Shift Tree Denoising.

References

1. Afsana, F., Asif-Ur-Rahman, M., Ahmed, M.R., Mahmud, M., Kaiser, M.S.: An energy conserving routing scheme for wireless body sensor nanonetwork communication. IEEE Access **6**, 9186–9200 (2018)
2. Al Nahian, M.J., et al.: Towards an accelerometer-based elderly fall detection system using cross-disciplinary time series features. IEEE Access **9**, 39413–39431 (2021)
3. Al Nahian, M.J., et al.: Social group optimized machine-learning based elderly fall detection approach using interdisciplinary time-series features. In: 2021 International Conference on Information and Communication Technology for Sustainable Development (ICICT4SD), pp. 321–325. IEEE (2021)
4. Causevic, E., Morley, R.E., Wickerhauser, M.V., Jacquin, A.E.: Fast wavelet estimation of weak biosignals. IEEE Trans. Biomed. Eng. **52**(6), 1021–1032 (2005)
5. Corona-Strauss, F.I., Schick, B., Delb, W., Strauss, D.J.: Notched-noise embedded frequency specific chirps for objective audiometry using auditory brainstem responses. Audiol. Res. **2**(1), 30–38 (2012)
6. Dau, T., Wegner, O., Mellert, V., Kollmeier, B.: Auditory brainstem responses with optimized chirp signals compensating basilar-membrane dispersion. J. Acoust. Soc. Am. **107**(3), 1530–1540 (2000)
7. Davis, M.H., et al.: Dissociating speech perception and comprehension at reduced levels of awareness. Proc. Natl. Acad. Sci. **104**(41), 16032–16037 (2007)
8. De Silva, A., Schier, M.: Evaluation of wavelet techniques in rapid extraction of ABR variations from underlying EEG. Physiol. Meas. **32**(11), 1747 (2011)
9. Dey, N., Rajinikanth, V., Fong, S., Kaiser, M., Mahmud, M.: Social-group-optimization assisted Kapur's entropy and morphological segmentation for automated detection of Covid-19 infection from computed tomography images. Cogn. Comput. **12**(5), 1011–1023 (2020)
10. Farhin, F., Kaiser, M.S., Mahmud, M.: Secured smart healthcare system: blockchain and Bayesian inference based approach. In: Kaiser, M.S., Bandyopadhyay, A., Mahmud, M., Ray, K. (eds.) Proceedings of International Conference on Trends in Computational and Cognitive Engineering. AISC, vol. 1309, pp. 455–465. Springer, Singapore (2021). https://doi.org/10.1007/978-981-33-4673-4_36
11. Freeman, W., Quiroga, R.Q.: Imaging Brain Function with EEG: Advanced Temporal and Spatial Analysis of Electroencephalographic Signals. Springer, Heidelberg (2012)
12. Gorga, M.P., Johnson, T.A., Kaminski, J.K., Beauchaine, K.L., Garner, C.A., Neely, S.T.: Using a combination of click-and toneburst-evoked auditory brainstem response measurements to estimate pure-tone thresholds. Ear Hear. **27**(1), 60 (2006)
13. Kaiser, M.S., Chowdhury, Z.I., Al Mamun, S., Hussain, A., Mahmud, M.: A neuro-fuzzy control system based on feature extraction of surface electromyogram signal for solar-powered wheelchair. Cogn. Comput. **8**(5), 946–954 (2016)

14. Maglione, J., Pincilotti, M., Acevedo, R., Bonell, C., Gentiletti, G.: Estimation of the auditory brainstem response's wave V by means of wavelet transform. In: Proceedings of the 25th Annual International Conference of the IEEE Engineering in Medicine and Biology Society (IEEE Cat. No. 03CH37439), vol. 3, pp. 2631–2634. IEEE (2003)
15. Mahmud, M., Kaiser, M.S., Hussain, A., Vassanelli, S.: Applications of deep learning and reinforcement learning to biological data. IEEE Trans. Neural Netw. Learn. Syst. **29**(6), 2063–2079 (2018)
16. Mohseni, H.R., Nazarpour, K., Wilding, E.L., Sanei, S.: The application of particle filters in single trial event-related potential estimation. Physiol. Meas. **30**(10), 1101 (2009)
17. Noor, M.B.T., Zenia, N.Z., et al.: Application of deep learning in detecting neurological disorders from magnetic resonance images: a survey on the detection of alzheimer's disease, parkinson's disease and schizophrenia. Brain Inform. **7**(1), 1–21 (2020)
18. Noor, M.B.T., Zenia, N.Z., Kaiser, M.S., Mahmud, M., Al Mamun, S.: Detecting neurodegenerative disease from MRI: a brief review on a deep learning perspective. In: Liang, P., Goel, V., Shan, C. (eds.) Brain Informatics. LNCS, vol. 11976, pp. 115–125. Springer, Cham (2019). https://doi.org/10.1007/978-3-030-37078-7_12
19. Omar, M.H.: Single trial estimation for auditory brainstem response signal analysis. Ph.D. thesis, Universiti Teknologi Malaysia (2013)
20. Purdy, S.C., Abbas, P.J.: ABR thresholds to tonebursts gated with Blackman and linear windows in adults with high-frequency sensorineural hearing loss. Ear Hear. **23**(4), 358–368 (2002)
21. Sharma, M.K., Ray, K., Yupapin, P., Kaiser, M.S., Ong, C.T., Ali, J.: Comparative analysis of different classifiers on EEG signals for predicting epileptic seizure. In: Kaiser, M.S., Bandyopadhyay, A., Mahmud, M., Ray, K. (eds.) Proceedings of International Conference on Trends in Computational and Cognitive Engineering. AISC, vol. 1309, pp. 193–204. Springer, Singapore (2021). https://doi.org/10.1007/978-981-33-4673-4_17
22. Singh, A.K., Kumar, A., Mahmud, M., Kaiser, M.S., Kishore, A.: Covid-19 infection detection from chest X-ray images using hybrid social group optimization and support vector classifier. Cogn. Comput. 1–13 (2021)
23. Wang, X., et al.: The effects of random stimulation rate on measurements of auditory brainstem response. Front. Hum. Neurosci. **14** (2020)
24. Wilson, W.: The relationship between the auditory brain-stem response and its reconstructed waveforms following discrete wavelet transformation. Clin. Neurophysiol. **115**(5), 1129–1139 (2004)

Application of AI and Informatics in Pattern Recognition

A Machine Learning Driven Android Based Mobile Application for Flower Identification

Towhidul Islam[1], Nurul Absar[1(✉)], Abzetdin Z. Adamov[2], and Mayeen Uddin Khandaker[3]

[1] Department of Computer Science and Engineering,
BGC Trust University Bangladesh, Chittagong 4301, Bangladesh
towhidul@bgctub.ac.bd
[2] Center for Data Analytics Research (CeDAR), ADA University Baku,
Baku, Azerbaijan
aadamov@ada.edu.az
[3] Centre for Applied Physics and Radiation Technologies,
School of Engineering and Technology, Sunway University,
Bandar Sunway, 47500 Selangor, Malaysia
mayeenk@sunway.edu.my

Abstract. In the field of Botany the research of flower classification scheme is an extremely significant topic. A classifier of flowers by maximum precision will also carry numerous enjoyments to human lives. However, there are tranquil a few disclaim in the identification of flower images due to the multipart conditions of flowers, the resemblance connecting the unusual flowers of species, and the variations surrounded by the similar species of flowers. The classification of flower is largely depend on the Color, shape and texture features which needs populace to choose features for classification and the accurateness is not extremely high. We were designed an Android application using machine learning techniques for flower identification. In this paper, based on Image Net model of DNN Tensor Flow Framework platform, to get better the accuracy of flower classification significantly, the Deep Neural Network (DNN) knowledge were used to retrain the flower category datasets. We were used ten category datasets. The accuracy of Image Net based MobileBetV2 model was 98.47% and proposed Deep CNN Model accuracy was 89.87% in our result. Any user can identify the flower by using our application from the flower images.

Keywords: Flower classification · Tensorflow · Keras · CNN · Feature extraction · Machine learning · MobilenetV2 · GoogLeNet

1 Introduction

Image recognition is one of the core fields in computer vision which can use the outcome for example hand writing recognition like in and fingerprint recognition

© Springer Nature Switzerland AG 2021
M. Mahmud et al. (Eds.): AII 2021, CCIS 1435, pp. 163–175, 2021.
https://doi.org/10.1007/978-3-030-82269-9_13

otherwise flush in extra significant studies for example medical researches etc., this value involving through the endeavour to facilitate must be involved for the classification method and by the amount of applications. In the cultivation of flowers, flower findings for apparent study, etc. applications of classification of flowers is used frequently.

Seed and bulb invention, flower trade, micro propagation, garden centre and preserved plants, and removal of important flowers oil comprises in the floriculture industry. Computerisation of flower classification is important in such belongings. Computerization of the categorisation of flower images is a essential job since these works are done physically and are very work comprehensive. There are more or less two millions and fifty thousand species of flowering plants as a named in the world. Categorise the plants by their flowers be able to be finished only by trained taxonomists and a lot of blooming flowers are detected in the park, backyard, wayside and various supplementary locations by skilled people also. People frequently must need flowers conduct manual or need the interrelated websites on the internet to peruse the knowledge with keywords because most of the public do not cover information concerning these flowers and in arrange to identify concerning them.

Artificial intelligence (AI) techniques in specific machine learning (ML) have been used over time to make easy classification, recognition and identification of patterns in biological data [33]. A multilayer neural network (NN) of CNN has achieved recognition in analysing image-based data [31]. In the midst of the current development of computing and superior understanding of AI different types of rule base and ML approaches have gained unrivalled awareness of the researchers in the last decade for the biological and healthcare big data mining, disease prediction and detection, text processing, disease management, and mobile health based app [25]. The main perception of deep learning (DL) is to be trained data representations through growing generalisation levels [25,31,33].

We are proposing a flower recognition approach with android application derived from image processing technique and deep convolutional neural network algorithm using Tensor Flow and Image Net in this work. People easily classify the flower image from our android device approach more accurately. We were used Google-11 and Tensorflow-5 dataset to implement of our proposed model including our local collection of flower.

2   Related Work

In recent years ML techniques have gained popularity in research for their abilities to predict patterns. They have been applied to many different fields including disease detection [12,34,39,40,44] and classification [11,17,30,47], elderly care [22,23] and fall detection [5,6,36], anomaly detection [8,18,51,52], biological data mining [31,33], cyber security [32], earthquake prediction [3,4], financial prediction [41], safeguarding workers in workplaces [25], text analytics [43,50], and urban planning [24].

Three primary contributions are discussed in [37]. Deep CNN for extracting the features and different machine learning algorithms for classifying objectives is used the categorization model to grow the performance of classifying of flower images in the first proposed model. In Second, the make use of image expansion for gaining enhanced substantiation consequences is established. KNN, Random Forest, Multi-Perceptions, and SVM are compared in last part of their research to measure the ability of the machine-learning classifiers. The author found 97.2% on oxford dataset using SVM and 98% accuracy on Oxford-17 using MLP.

Oxford 102 flowers dataset is used in [9] which containing of eight thousand one hundred eighty nine flowers images that fit in to 102 flower species. Four main steps were explained in this paper starting image augmentation, in gathering of images accustomed to settle in dataset images to generate further appropriate dataset for subsequently stage. To split the forefront from the backdrop image segmentation introduced. The accuracy rate was found 81.19% in this research.

Texture and color features used for flower classification by the author in [46]. From the segmented images, Texture and color features are extracted. GLCM method is used for Texture feature extraction and Color moment is used for color feature extraction. 95.0% accuracy of the system is found.

The authors uses a supervised model to extract flower content in [54] and [38] which consider the flower textures with graph cuts. The author in [29] used Novel Framework based Convolution Neural Network (CNN) to resolve this difficulty. They had implemented the algorithm on Oxford flower data set images from 102 species.

In [37] this author the flower sections are chosen to be individual in color (e.g., for example) and vary considerably in size, scale, and appearance developing a visual vocabulary that clearly represents different flowers (e.g., color, shape, and texture) for differentiate one flower from any more, Author can prevail over the ambiguities that be present stuck between flower sections. The results are presented in a data set of 1360 images with 17 flower species.

The [2] author used image classification using by Deep neural network (DDN) and five types of flowers that have been used the authors. They found the average result 90%. In [42] the system was developed using Python and Random Forest Classifier Method and Flower Identification used on RGB Histogram data. The Researchers found the proposed system is able to classify flower image with an average accuracy of 80.67% using 15 type of flower.

In [7] features based on color, texture, and shape on Image Classification and showed high result accuracy on oxford-17 dataset. Neural Network Based Image Processing is used for flower classification in [35]. They have proposed a method for classification of flowers based on Artificial Neural Network (ANN) classifier. GLCM and DWT of textural features is used of their proposed method. They got classification accuracy 85% more using GLCM features. The back propagation algorithm is used to train the neural network. Own dataset were created base of flowers of five classes, each one heaving ten flower images. They have got the result with MLP offers accuracy 87% with GLCM features.

ANN classifiers were studied in favor of the classification of flowers by the researcher in [20]. GLCM, DWT and Color features for instance normalized color histogram were used for textural features in their suggested model. A threshold based method is also used for flower image segmentation. A review of forty research work that make use of deep learning approaches used to different farming and food manufacture challenges performed by the authors in [26]. They study the specific agricultural harms with this research. The investigate result show that deep learning gives maximum accuracy.

A foreground background model is used in [10] where the segmentation is tested on five hundred seventy-eight flower species with two million fifty thousand images and hundred two flower species of OUFD with secure segmentation outcome. The contour matching algorithm is used getting the result in [48] which were not very encouraging of both flower and leaf images. In [13] K-means and OSTU segmentation algorithm were used. SVM and K-Nearest Neighbour (KNN) classifier is used for classifying the images to produce good results for those images.

In [28] the authors considered the transfer learning knowledge to retrain the flower category datasets based on Inception-v3 model of Tensor Flow platform which can very much increased the truthfulness of flower classification. Back propagation learning algorithm is used to trained Multilayer feed- forward networks in [21]. Color and shape features dependent segmentation model of flower is used by the authors in [13]. Training and testing were conducted on Oxford-102 flower and the findings illustrate a close to exact boundary recognition on a big set of images.

3   System Architecture

Our used system structural design of our proposed model is shown in following Fig. 1. This structural design showed that whole classification system in our model.

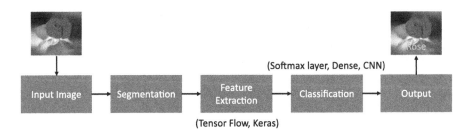

Fig. 1. System architecture in our proposed model.

4   Experimentation

4.1   Required Tools

Tensor Processing Unit (TPU). In May 2016 Google declared its TPU as an application of particular incorporated circuit that made exclusively for machine learning and tailored for TensorFlow [1]. In addition to the accessibility of the TPUs in Google Compute Engine, the 2nd generation announced in May 2017 which can deliver up to one hundred eighty teraflops of performance, and when prepared into clusters of sixty four TPUs, it is able to deliver 11.5 petaflops. The third-generation TPUs are announced by Google in May 2018 for supplying capable of four hundred twenty teraflops of execution and 128 GB HBM. Google were building TPUs easy to get to in beta on the Google Cloud Platform in February 2018.

Tensor Flow Lite. Tensor Flow Lite is a software stack exclusively for mobile expansion developed by Google in May 2017 [49]. A builder foretaste GPU inference engine for the mobile for the use of Open GL ES 3.1 Compute Shaders on Android devices and Metal Compute Shaders on iOS devices is released by Tensor Flow team in January 2019. Google introduced that their TensorFlow Lite Micro and ARM's tensor would be integration in May 2019.

Keras. Keras is an online resource documents that helps a Python interface for ANN which uses as an interface for the Tensor Flow library. Keras version 2.3 is used to support multiple backends, as well as Tensor Flow, R, Theano, Microsoft Cognitive Toolkit, and Plaid ML where the version 2.4, only TensorFlow is supported [27].

Features. Keras has various implementations of generally second-hand neural-network building. The code is generated on GitHub, and community support forums include the GitHub issues page, and a Slack channel [14].

ImageNet. An image dataset organized consistent with the WordNet hierarchy referred to ImageNet [19]. WordNet, possibly described "synonym set" or "synset" by using multiple words or word phrases. More than 100,000 synsets in WordNet are there wher 80,000+(majority) are nouns of them. Each synset provide on average 1000 images in ImageNet. ImageNet can offer tens of millions of modestly sorted images for most of the concepts in the WordNet hierarchy [45]. The need for more data the ImageNet project is encouraged by a rising response in the image and vision research field [53]. Ween vision Image Net as a valuable resource to researchers in the academic world, as well as educators around the world [15,16].

First training and testing dataset were divided from the input dataset where training and testing data were 80% and 20% respectively. We were used 11 category image data set in our research containing 4630 images where 3708 images for training set and 922images testing set. A sample of Google 11-flower dataset is shown in Fig. 2.

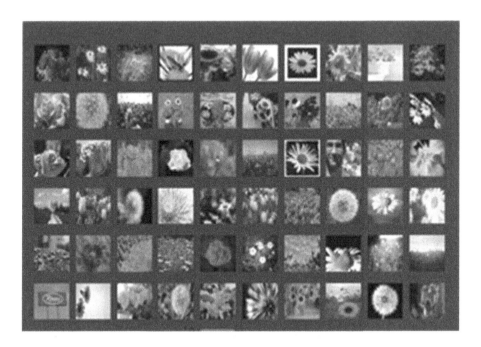

Fig. 2. Samples of 60 species of flowers in Google 11 -Flower Dataset.

We were proposed a two-step approach for the flower classification problem. The First step is designed multi stage CNN model. The model is constructed with input layer, five convolutional layers, seven rectified linear units (ReLu),

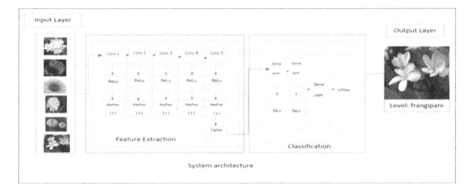

Fig. 3. The feature extraction and classification system architecture.

five stochastic pooling layers, two dense and one Soft Max output layer. The proposed CNN architecture uses five convolutional layers with same window sizes followed by an activation function, and a rectified linear unit for non-linearities. The feature extraction and classification system architecture has given in Fig. 3.

The Second Step is designed by ImageNet Model on MobileNetV2 which is shown in Table 1. In MobileNetV2, there are two types of blocks. One is residual block with stride of 1.

Table 1. ImageNet Model on MobileNetV2

Input	Operator	Output
$h \times w \times k$	1×1 conv2d, ReLU6	$h \times w \times (tk)$
$h \times w \times tk$	3×3 dwise $s = s$, ReLU6	$h/s \times w/s \times (tk)$
$h/s \times w/s \times tk$	linear 1×1 conv2d	$h/s \times w/s \times k'$

Another one is block with stride of 2 for down sizing. In both types of blocks 3 layers are there. 1×1 convolution with ReLU6 is the first layer. The second layer is the depth wise convolution. Without any non-linearity 1×1 convolution is the third layer also that is demanded that if ReLU is used over again. For all main experiments there is an extension factor t. where t = 6 for the post of Image. The internal output would get 64 × t=64 × 6 = 384 channels, if the input got 64 channels which is shown in Fig. 4.

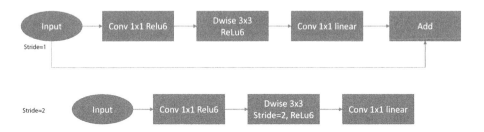

Fig. 4. Image input architecture.

5   Result and Discussion

The major purpose of our study is to properly demonstrate the flower image as of the traditional flower dataset. The suggested model of CNN was used to the

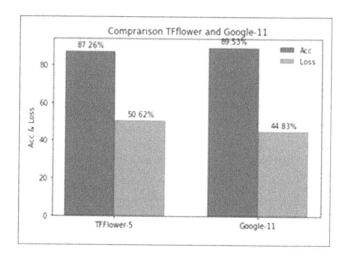

Fig. 5. Comparative results for Google-11 and Tensorflow-5 Flowers Dataset.

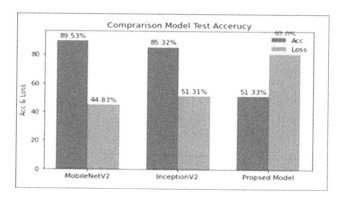

Fig. 6. Comparative results for Mobile NetV2, InceptionV2 and proposed model.

flower database for categorization. The database contains custom flower dataset were created by us in various orientations. The entire dataset were used with 10 classes. Dataset was having only flower images with reduced lighting provision. The training accuracy was 87.05%. and Image Net based MobileNetV2 model being trained Result accuracy was 98.07%. The comparative results for Google-11 and Tensorflow-5 Flowers Dataset has given in Fig. 5 and where the comparative results for Mobile NetV2, InceptionV2 and proposed model as shown in Fig. 6. Sample Output result using android application with accuracy as shown in Fig. 7.

Fig. 7. Sample Output using android application with accuracy.

6   Conclusion and Future Work

The rapid development of technology, Artificial Intelligence has been useful in many fields. An application of machine learning and two different learning forms of machine learning explained the working principle of machine learning in our proposed work. In addition, it is shown that a research of flower identification and classification to initiate the workflow of machine learning in prototype recognition. The pattern recognition and its procedure in pattern recognition were clearly explained in our study. The CNN algorithm, which is a Deep learning algorithm from the ImageNet method, was used. Future work includes using other features of the flowers in classification, for example, texture and shapes. Other method for classification can be explored to provide more accuracy. Also, the database should be improved to contain more data. The system is very easy to use, therefore, it can be implemented for other objects.

Acknowledgement. This work was supported by the Sunway University Research Grant (GRTIN-IRG-05-2021). The authors also express their gratitude to the Department of Computer Science and Engineering, BGC Trust University Bangladesh.

References

1. Abadi, M., et al.: Tensorflow: a system for large-scale machine learning. In: 12th {USENIX} Symposium on Operating Systems Design and Implementation ({OSDI} 16), pp. 265–283 (2016)

2. Abu, M.A., Indra, N.H., Abd Rahman, A.H., Sapiee, N.A., Ahmad, I.: A study on image classification based on deep learning and TensorFlow. Int. J. Eng. Res. Technol. **12**(4), 563–569 (2019)

3. Al Banna, M.H., et al.: Attention-based bi-directional long-short term memory network for earthquake prediction. IEEE Access **9**, 56589–56603 (2021)

4. Al Banna, M.H., et al.: Application of artificial intelligence in predicting earthquakes: state-of-the-art and future challenges. IEEE Access **8**, 192880–192923 (2020)

5. Al Nahian, M.J., Ghosh, T., Uddin, M.N., Islam, M.M., Mahmud, M., Kaiser, M.S.: Towards artificial intelligence driven emotion aware fall monitoring framework suitable for elderly people with neurological disorder. In: Mahmud, M., Vassanelli, S., Kaiser, M.S., Zhong, N. (eds.) BI 2020. LNCS (LNAI), vol. 12241, pp. 275–286. Springer, Cham (2020). https://doi.org/10.1007/978-3-030-59277-6_25

6. Al Nahian, M.J., et al.: Towards an accelerometer-based elderly fall detection system using cross-disciplinary time series features. IEEE Access **9**, 39413–39431 (2021). https://doi.org/10.1109/ACCESS.2021.3056441

7. Albadarneh, A., Ahmad, A.: Automated flower species detection and recognition from digital images. IJCSNS Int. J. Comput. Sci. Netw. Secur. **17**(4), 144–151 (2017)

8. Ali, H.M., Kaiser, M.S., Mahmud, M.: Application of convolutional neural network in segmenting brain regions from MRI data. In: Liang, P., Goel, V., Shan, C. (eds.) Brain Informatics. LNCS, pp. 136–146. Springer, Cham (2019). https://doi.org/10.1007/978-3-030-37078-7_14

9. Almogdady, H., Manaseer, S., Hiary, H.: A flower recognition system based on image processing and neural networks. Int. J. Sci. Technol. Res. **7**(11), 166–173 (2018)

10. Angelova, A., Zhu, S., Lin, Y.: Image segmentation for large-scale subcategory flower recognition. In: 2013 IEEE Workshop on Applications of Computer Vision (WACV), pp. 39–45. IEEE (2013)

11. Aradhya, V.M., Mahmud, M., Agarwal, B., Kaiser, M.: One shot cluster based approach for the detection of COVID-19 from chest x-ray images. Cogn. Comput. 1–9 (2021). https://doi.org/10.1007/s12559-020-09774-w

12. Bhapkar, H.R., Mahalle, P.N., Shinde, G.R., Mahmud, M.: Rough sets in COVID-19 to predict symptomatic cases. In: Santosh, K.C., Joshi, A. (eds.) COVID-19: Prediction, Decision-Making, and its Impacts. LNDECT, vol. 60, pp. 57–68. Springer, Singapore (2021). https://doi.org/10.1007/978-981-15-9682-7_7

13. Chithra, P., Bhavani, P.: A study on various image processing techniques. Int. J. Emerg. Technol. Innov. Eng. **5**(5), 316–322 (2019)

14. Chollet, F.: Xception: deep learning with depthwise separable convolutions. In: Proceedings of the IEEE Conference on Computer Vision and Pattern Recognition, pp. 1251–1258 (2017)

15. Deng, J., Dong, W., Socher, R., Li, L.J., Li, K., Fei-Fei, L.: ImageNet: a large-scale hierarchical image database. In: 2009 IEEE Conference on Computer Vision and Pattern Recognition, pp. 248–255. IEEE (2009)

16. Deng, J., Li, K., Do, M., Su, H., Fei-Fei, L.: Construction and analysis of a large scale image ontology. Vis. Sci. Soc. **186**(2) (2009)

17. Dey, N., Rajinikanth, V., Fong, S., Kaiser, M., Mahmud, M.: Social-group-optimization assisted Kapur's entropy and morphological segmentation for automated detection of COVID-19 infection from computed tomography images. Cogn. Comput. **12**(5), 1011–1023 (2020). https://doi.org/10.1007/s12559-020-09751-3

18. Fabietti, M., et al.: Neural network-based artifact detection in local field potentials recorded from chronically implanted neural probes. In: Proceedings of IJCNN, pp. 1–8 (2020)

19. Fei-Fei, L., Deng, J., Li, K.: ImageNet: constructing a large-scale image database. J. Vis. **9**(8), 1037 (2009)

20. Hiary, H., Saadeh, H., Saadeh, M., Yaqub, M.: Flower classification using deep convolutional neural networks. IET Comput. Vis. **12**(6), 855–862 (2018)

21. Hsu, T.H., Lee, C.H., Chen, L.H.: An interactive flower image recognition system. Multimed. Tools Appl. **53**(1), 53–73 (2011). https://doi.org/10.1007/s11042-010-0490-6

22. Jesmin, S., Kaiser, M.S., Mahmud, M.: Towards artificial intelligence driven stress monitoring for mental wellbeing tracking during COVID-19. In: Proceedings of WI-IAT 2020, pp. 1–6 (2021)

23. Jesmin, S., Kaiser, M.S., Mahmud, M.: Artificial and internet of healthcare things based Alzheimer care during COVID 19. In: Mahmud, M., Vassanelli, S., Kaiser, M.S., Zhong, N. (eds.) BI 2020. LNCS (LNAI), vol. 12241, pp. 263–274. Springer, Cham (2020). https://doi.org/10.1007/978-3-030-59277-6_24

24. Kaiser, M.S., et al.: Advances in crowd analysis for urban applications through urban event detection. IEEE Trans. Intell. Transp. Syst. **19**(10), 3092–3112 (2018)

25. Kaiser, M., et al.: iworksafe: towards healthy workplaces during COVID-19 with an intelligent Phealth app for industrial settings. IEEE Access **9**, 13814–13828 (2021)

26. Kamilaris, A., Prenafeta-Boldú, F.X.: Deep learning in agriculture: a survey. Comput. Electron. Agric. **147**, 70–90 (2018)

27. Ketkar, N.: Introduction to Keras. In: Deep Learning with Python, pp. 95–109. Springer, Berkeley (2017). https://doi.org/10.1007/978-1-4842-2766-4_7

28. Lakesar, A.L.: A review on flower classification using neural network classifier. Int. J. Sci. Res. **7**(5), 1644–1646 (2018)

29. Liu, Y., Tang, F., Zhou, D., Meng, Y., Dong, W.: Flower classification via convolutional neural network. In: 2016 IEEE International Conference on Functional-Structural Plant Growth Modeling, Simulation, Visualization and Applications (FSPMA), pp. 110–116. IEEE (2016)

30. Mahmud, M., Kaiser, M.S.: Machine learning in fighting pandemics: a COVID-19 case study. In: Santosh, K.C., Joshi, A. (eds.) COVID-19: Prediction, Decision-Making, and its Impacts. LNDECT, vol. 60, pp. 77–81. Springer, Singapore (2021). https://doi.org/10.1007/978-981-15-9682-7_9

31. Mahmud, M., Kaiser, M.S., McGinnity, T., Hussain, A.: Deep learning in mining biological data. Cogn. Comput. **13**(1), 1–33 (2021). https://doi.org/10.1007/s12559-020-09773-x

32. Mahmud, M.: A brain-inspired trust management model to assure security in a cloud based IoT framework for neuroscience applications. Cogn. Comput. **10**(5), 864–873 (2018). https://doi.org/10.1007/s12559-018-9543-3

33. Mahmud, M., Kaiser, M.S., Hussain, A., Vassanelli, S.: Applications of deep learning and reinforcement learning to biological data. IEEE Trans. Neural Netw. Learn. Syst. **29**(6), 2063–2079 (2018)

34. Miah, Y., Prima, C.N.E., Seema, S.J., Mahmud, M., Shamim Kaiser, M.: Performance comparison of machine learning techniques in identifying dementia from open access clinical datasets. In: Saeed, F., Al-Hadhrami, T., Mohammed, F., Mohammed, E. (eds.) Advances on Smart and Soft Computing. AISC, vol. 1188, pp. 79–89. Springer, Singapore (2021). https://doi.org/10.1007/978-981-15-6048-4_8
35. Mukane, S., Kendule, J.: Flower classification using neural network based image processing. IOSR J. Electron. Commun. Eng **7**, 80–85 (2013)
36. Nahiduzzaman, M., Tasnim, M., Newaz, N.T., Kaiser, M.S., Mahmud, M.: Machine learning based early fall detection for elderly people with neurological disorder using multimodal data fusion. In: Mahmud, M., Vassanelli, S., Kaiser, M.S., Zhong, N. (eds.) BI 2020. LNCS (LNAI), vol. 12241, pp. 204–214. Springer, Cham (2020). https://doi.org/10.1007/978-3-030-59277-6_19
37. Nilsback, M.E., Zisserman, A.: A visual vocabulary for flower classification. In: 2006 IEEE Computer Society Conference on Computer Vision and Pattern Recognition (CVPR 2006), vol. 2, pp. 1447–1454. IEEE (2006)
38. Nilsback, M.E., Zisserman, A.: Delving deeper into the whorl of flower segmentation. Image Vis. Comput. **28**(6), 1049–1062 (2010)
39. Noor, M.B.T., Zenia, N.Z., Kaiser, M.S., Al Mamun, S., Mahmud, M.: Application of deep learning in detecting neurological disorders from magnetic resonance images: a survey on the detection of Alzheimer's disease, Parkinson's disease and schizophrenia. Brain Inform. **7**(1), 1–21 (2020)
40. Noor, M.B.T., Zenia, N.Z., Kaiser, M.S., Al Mamud, M., Mamun, S.: Detecting neurodegenerative disease from MRI: a brief review on a deep learning perspective. In: Liang, P., Goel, V., Shan, C. (eds.) BI 2019. LNCS, vol. 11976, pp. 115–125. Springer, Cham (2019). https://doi.org/10.1007/978-3-030-37078-7_12
41. Orojo, O., Tepper, J., McGinnity, T.M., Mahmud, M.: A multi-recurrent network for crude oil price prediction. In: Proceedings of IEEE SSCI, pp. 2953–2958. IEEE (2019)
42. Pardee, W., Yusungnern, P., Sripian, P.: Flower identification system by image processing. In: 3rd International Conference on Creative Technology CRETECH, vol. 1, pp. 1–4 (2015)
43. Rabby, G., Azad, S., Mahmud, M., Zamli, K.Z., Rahman, M.M.: TeKET: a tree-based unsupervised keyphrase extraction technique. Cogn. Comput. **12**(4), 811–833 (2020). https://doi.org/10.1007/s12559-019-09706-3
44. Ruiz, J., Mahmud, M., Modasshir, Md., Shamim Kaiser, M.: 3D DenseNet ensemble in 4-way classification of Alzheimer's disease. In: Mahmud, M., Vassanelli, S., Kaiser, M.S., Zhong, N. (eds.) BI 2020. LNCS (LNAI), vol. 12241, pp. 85–96. Springer, Cham (2020). https://doi.org/10.1007/978-3-030-59277-6_8 Alzheimer's Disease Neuroimaging Initiative
45. Russakovsky, O., et al.: ImageNet large scale visual recognition challenge. Int. J. Comput. Vis. **115**(3), 211–252 (2015). https://doi.org/10.1007/s11263-015-0816-y
46. Shaparia, R., Patel, N., Shah, Z.: Flower classification using texture and color features. Kalpa Publ. Comput. **2**, 113–118 (2017)
47. Singh, A.K., Kumar, A., Mahmud, M., Kaiser, M.S., Kishore, A.: COVID-19 infection detection from chest x-ray images using hybrid social group optimization and support vector classifier. Cogn. Comput. 1–13 (2021). https://doi.org/10.1007/s12559-021-09848-3
48. Valliammal, N., Geethalakshmi, S.: Automatic recognition system using preferential image segmentation for leaf and flower images. Comput. Sci. Eng. **1**(4), 13 (2011)

49. Vincent, J.: Google's new machine learning framework is going to put more AI on your phone (2017). https://www.theverge.com/2017/5/17/15645908/google-ai-tensorflowlite-machine-learning-announcement-io-2017
50. Watkins, J., Fabietti, M., Mahmud, M.: Sense: a student performance quantifier using sentiment analysis. In: Proceedings of IJCNN, pp. 1–6 (2020)
51. Yahaya, S.W., Lotfi, A., Mahmud, M.: A consensus novelty detection ensemble approach for anomaly detection in activities of daily living. Appl. Soft Comput. **83**, 105613 (2019)
52. Yahaya, S.W., Lotfi, A., Mahmud, M.: Towards a data-driven adaptive anomaly detection system for human activity. Pattern Recogn. Lett. **145**, 200–207 (2021)
53. Yang, K., Qinami, K., Fei-Fei, L., Deng, J., Russakovsky, O.: Towards fairer datasets: filtering and balancing the distribution of the people subtree in the ImageNet hierarchy. In: Proceedings of the 2020 Conference on Fairness, Accountability, and Transparency, pp. 547–558 (2020)
54. Zhou, H., Zheng, J., Wei, L.: Texture aware image segmentation using graph cuts and active contours. Pattern Recogn. **46**(6), 1719–1733 (2013)

A Generative Text Summarization Model Based on Document Structure Neural Network

Haihui Huang and Maohong Zha[(✉)]

School of Software Engineering, Chongqing University of Posts and Telecommunications,
Chongqing, China
huanghh@cqupt.edu.cn

Abstract. Aiming at the low accuracy of the automatic generation of text summaries in the field of data mining, as well as the defects of the existing encoder and decoder models, this paper proposes a generative text summarization model based on the document structure neural network. The model introduces the document structure, divides the text into a word encoding layer and a sentence encoding layer, and builds a top-down hierarchical structure to avoid the back propagation error problem caused by the long input sequence in the traditional encoder and decoder model; At each level, an attention mechanism is added, and a multi-attention mechanism is proposed and introduced, which refines the granularity of the attention mechanism, thereby improving the accuracy of text summary generation. Experimental results show that, compared with the original encoder-decoder model, this model can effectively refines the granularity of the attention mechanism and significantly improve the accuracy of text summary generation.

Keywords: Data mining · Text summarization generation · Multi attention mechanism · Document structure neural network

1 Introduction

There are a lot of text data such as news and blogs on the Internet that fill our lives [1]. However, there are often redundant and useless information in these text data. Through a short summary, we can efficiently retrieve text content and mine text information. However, manually writing abstracts for each article, news, and blog requires a lot of manpower and material resources.

Natural language processing is a relatively active processing method in the field of data processing, and it is also an important step for public opinion analysis and data mining [2]. Text summarization is an important field in natural language processing, including extractive text summaries and generative text summaries. Extractive text summaries extract the most important sentences in the original text as abstracts, while generative text summaries automatically generate abstract sentences based on the content of the text. Text summaries can summarize a medium-length text in one sentence, which can greatly improve efficiency compared with manual text summaries. But its accuracy is still relatively low, especially in the capture of key words [3].

© Springer Nature Switzerland AG 2021
M. Mahmud et al. (Eds.): AII 2021, CCIS 1435, pp. 176–187, 2021.
https://doi.org/10.1007/978-3-030-82269-9_14

The traditional encoder-decoder model [4] first encodes the words of the text, then adds the attention mechanism [5] to learn the key words of the article, and then decodes the word encoding to generate a text summary. Compared with the previous rule-based and statistical-based summary generation methods, this type of method has a significant improvement in efficiency, but the granularity of its attention mechanism is relatively rough, and it cannot achieve good attention for long text learning. As a result, it is difficult to capture the key sentences and key words in a medium-length text, resulting in a large deviation in the accuracy of the generated abstract. For example, given a text [In addition, according to the "Business Insider" website, in response to Trump's above remarks, Andrew Bates, the director of rapid response of the Biden campaign team, responded: "Due to the failure of Donald Trump, China's position has become stronger in all aspects, while the US's status has declined." He said, "Trump is the weakest president in American history against China."] Humans can quickly capture the key sentence "Trump is the weakest president in the history of the United States against China." However, the text in this text is too long and the relationship between the characters involved is complex, the traditional encoder-decoder model will produce large deviations in key words and sentence capture. The reason is that although it introduces an attention mechanism, the traditional model processes the entire text sequence and uses a time-series neural network. However, for a long text vector sequence, gradient dispersion or derivative calculation deviation will still occur, resulting in deviations. Introducing the attention matrix on the basis of, will increase the error and cause the final generated summary to have a large deviation. The structure of the document has the following characteristics: sentences are composed of words, and documents are composed of sentences, which a bottom-up hierarchical structure can be constructed. Based on this, this paper proposes a generative text summarization model based on the document structure neural network (DSNN-GSM) to improve the granularity of the attention mechanism and improve the accuracy of the generative text summary.

This paper mainly studies the generation of text generative summaries. Based on the encoder-decoder model based on the attention mechanism, this paper proposes an improved model DSNN-GSM that divides the neural network model into layers. The neural network level is divided into word coding layer and sentence coding layer, which is more in line with the text structure. At each level, attention mechanism and multi-attention mechanism are added to make the attention mechanism more granular and make the model better Understand the meaning of the text. In general, the contribution of this article has the following two points:

1. The original encoder-decoder model is divided into a bottom-up model of word coding level and sentence coding level, which shortens the length of the input sequence of each processing unit, thereby alleviating the back propagation caused by the excessively long sequence Problems with large derivation errors;
2. At each level, an attention mechanism or a multi-attention mechanism is introduced to refine the attention granularity of the model, so that it can more accurately capture the key information in the article, and improve the accuracy of generating abstracts.

Next, this article will analyze specific issues. In Sect. 2 we will introduce other processing methods in this field; in Sect. 3, we will focus on the main content, which will introduce the generative text summarization model based on document structure neural network; Sect. 4 will introduce the evaluation method of the text summary and make a confirmatory comparison between the model in this article and the reference model; Sect. 5 gives the conclusion of this article; Sect. 6 is the part of the cited references.

2 Related Work

2.1 Encoder-Decoder Model Based on LSTM

Generative text summaries are mainly realized by the structure of deep neural networks. The Sequence-to-Sequence sequence proposed by the Google Brain team in 2014 opened up the fiery research on end-to-end networks in NLP. Sequence-to-Sequence is also known as Encoder-Decoder (Encoder-Decoder) architecture. Encoder and Decoder are both composed of several layers of RNN or LSTM. Encoder is responsible for encoding the original text into a vector C; Decoder is responsible for extracting information from this vector C, obtaining semantics, and generating text summaries. However, due to the problem of "long-distance dependence", when the RNN entered the word at the last time step, a large part of the data had been lost. At this time, the vector C generated by the encoder also lost a lot of information, resulting in inaccurate results. Therefore, the LSTM neural network is used, and the Attention mechanism is introduced to capture the key words in the text [6].

2.2 Gated Recurrent Unit (GRU) Neural Network

The structure diagram of GRU neural network [7] is shown in Fig. 1. GRU is a very effective variant of the LSTM network. It has a simpler structure than the LSTM network, and the effect is also very good, so it is also a very manifold network at present. Since GRU is a variant of LSTM, it can also solve the long dependency problem in RNN networks.

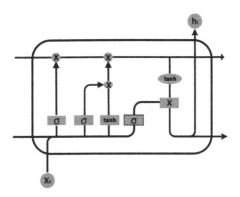

Fig. 1. Neural network structure diagram

Both LSTM and GRU introduce a gating mechanism in the recurrent neural network [8]. In a general RNN recurrent neural network, If the prediction y_t at time t depends on the input $x_t - k$ at time $t - k$, when the time interval k is relatively large, the problem of gradient disappearance or gradient explosion is prone to occur, then it is difficult for the recurrent neural network to learn such long input information. In this case, when the current forecast requires longer-term information, the problem of long-term dependence will arise. However, if all the information entered at the past moment is stored in order to learn very long information, it will cause the saturation of the stored information in the hidden state h and the loss of important information. To this end, a better solution is to introduce a gating mechanism to control the speed of information accumulation, including selectively adding new information, and selectively forgetting previously accumulated information.

There are only two gates in the GRU model, namely the update gate Z_t and the reset gate R_t The update gate Z_t is used according to formula (2.1) to control how much information the current state h_t needs to retain from the historical state h_{t-1}, and how much new information needs to be received from the candidate state h_t. The larger value of the update gate, the more state information from the previous moment is brought in.

$$Z_t = \delta(W_z x_t + U_z h(t-1) + b_Z) \tag{2.1}$$

Then calculate the hidden state h_t according to formula (2.2).

$$h_t = Z_t \odot h(t-1) + (1 - Z_t) \odot \widetilde{h}_t \tag{2.2}$$

The reset gate R_t controls whether the calculation of the candidate state $\widetilde{h}_t$ depends on the state h_{t-1} at the previous moment according to formula (2.3). In other words, it is used to control the degree of ignoring the state information at the previous moment. The smaller the value of the reset gate, the more ignorance.

$$r_t = \delta(W_r x_t + U_r h(t-1) + b_r) \tag{2.3}$$

The candidate state $\widetilde{h}_t$ at the current moment can be obtained by formula (2.4):

$$\tilde{h}^t = \tanh(W_h x_t + U_h(r_t \odot h_{t-1}) + b_h) \tag{2.4}$$

3 Generative Text Summary Model Based on Document Structure Neural Network (DSNN-GSM)

3.1 DSNN-GSM Model Structure

This paper proposes a generative text summarization model DSNN-GSM based on document structure neural network. The model architecture is shown in Fig. 2. It is divided into word embedding layer, word encoding layer, sentence encoding layer and decoding layer.

Word embedding layer is used to segment the text and convert it into a one-hot encoding, and at the same time do partition processing, and divide each sentence into a processing unit for subsequent processing.

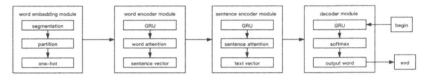

Fig. 2. DSNN-GSM model architecture

Word encoding layer uses the bidirectional GRU neural network to perform word encoding processing on the one-hot vector to obtain the word encode with high representation and add the word attention matrix to obtain the sentence vector.

Sentence encoding layer uses the bidirectional GRU neural network to perform sentence encoding processing on the sentence vector obtained above to obtain a sentence encode with high representation and add the word attention matrix to obtain a text vector.

Decoding layer decodes the obtained text vector, takes the above obtained text vector and BEGIN tag as input to the decoding module, and then performs a softmax calculation to obtain the probability of the next word to be output, and outputs the word with the highest probability. This predicted word will be used as input in the next time sequence, and the weight parameters of the neural network will be updated through the current state, and then the next word to be output will be calculated through softmax. By analogy, a complete text summary is finally generated.

3.2 Algorithm Flow Description

The hierarchical structure diagram of DSNN-GSM is shown in Fig. 3.

The DSNN-GSM algorithm process has the following 6 steps:

1. Split the text into words and perform partition processing to obtain multiple processing units. Convert each word in each processing unit into an embedded representation of a one-hot vector, record it as w_{ij}, and input it to the word-level coding layer. Where i represents the i-th sentence and j represents the j-th word in the i-th sentence.
2. Use each sentence as a processing unit and perform word encoding operations on it. Input the GRU neural network and its variants to perform word encoding processing on the one-hot vector to obtain training parameter matrix and word encoding with high representation. Among them, the training parameter matrix is an incidental product of the neural network model training process, which is used to adaptively adjust the model error.
3. Introduce a random context matrix u_w, do a softmax operation with the word encoding obtained above to obtain the word attention matrix, and then do the dot product and weight the results of the attention matrix and the hidden layer to obtain a highly representative sentence vector S_L. L represents the L-th sentence vector.
4. Input the above sentence vectors into GRU neural network for sentence coding. The sentence vector with high representation is obtained.
5. Introduce a random sentence attention matrix, encode it with the obtained sentence and do a softmax operation to generate a document vector T with high representation.
6. Pass the finally generated text vector as an initialization parameter to the decoder for decoding operation to generate a text summary.

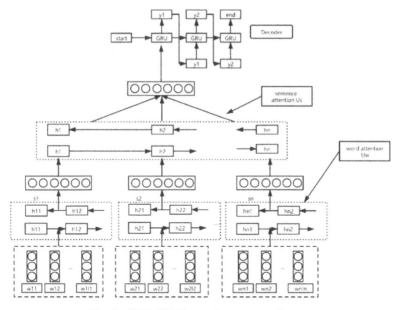

Fig. 3. SNN-GSM hierarchy structure diagram

Among them, the steps of the decoding operation in step 6 are as follows:

a. Input the text vector T as an initialization parameter to the decoder, and pass the label 'begin' as an input parameter to the initialized decoder;
b. The initialized decoder module runs time step once, and uses softmax to calculate the next word with the highest probability and output it.
c. Use the word output at the previous moment as the input at the current moment, and the neural network will adaptively update the weight of the neural network according to the error value of the back propagation process, run time stpe again, calculate the next word with the highest probability through softmax and output it.
d. Repeat the iterative process of c until the 'end' tag is decoded, then end the iterative process, and get the complete summary of the text.

The specific algorithm implementation process is described as follows:

First, word embedding layer performs word segmentation processing on the input sample data, and partitions the set of words in each sentence into a processing unit to obtain the original word sequence $(x_{11}, x_{12}, \cdots, x_{1m}, x_{21}, x_{22}, \cdots, x_{2m}, \cdots, x_{nm})$, where x_{ij} represents the jth word of the i-th sentence.

Then it is transformed into a one-hot vector $(x_{11}, x_{12}, \cdots, x_{1m}, x_{21}, x_{22}, \cdots, x_{2m}, \cdots, x_{nm})$. After that, the one-hot vector is used as the input of the word encoding module. It should be noted that each partition is processed as an independent module, that is, there is no relationship between sentences at this time, and only the relationship between words within each sentence is considered.

Adopt GRU neural network model based on time series. The feature of GRU neural network is that it has update gate and reset gate. It is a variant of long and short memory neural network. The update gate is used to control the extent to which the state information from the previous moment is brought into the current state. The larger the value of the update gate, the more state information from the previous moment is brought in; the reset gate is used to control ignoring the previous moment. The degree of status information, the smaller the reset gate value, the more ignored. Using this feature can solve the problem of gradient dispersion of long text sequences in the neural network training process. Through the two-way GRU model, the new word vector u_{ij} of each word can be mapped.

At the same time, the bidirectional GRU splices the forward and backward states, as shown in formula (3.1):

$$h = \left(h_{forward} \; h_{backward} \right) \tag{3.1}$$

Among them, h represents the state vector of the hidden layer after forward and backward propagation, $h_{forward}$ represents the state vector of the hidden layer forward propagation, and $h_{backward}$ represents the state vector of the hidden layer backward propagation.

Then, the word context matrix u_w is randomly initialized, and the attention matrix is obtained according to formula (3.2):

$$\partial_{ij} = \frac{\exp\left(u_{ij}^T u_w \right)}{\sum_L \exp\left(u_{ij}^T u_w \right)} \tag{3.2}$$

Where L represents the L-th partition.

Then, take the weighted dot product of ∂_{ij} and the hidden layer value h to obtain the sentence vector. After that, each obtained sentence vector s_i is used as the input of the sentence encoding module, and the Bidirectional GRU is used to encode the sentence, and the forward and backward state splicing $h = (h_{forward}, h_{backward})$ is obtained. Then, the sentence context matrix u_s is initialized, and the sentence attention matrix is obtained according to formula (3.3).

$$\partial_{ij} = \frac{\exp\left(u_{ij}^T u_s \right)}{\sum_s \exp\left(u_{ij}^T u_s \right)} \tag{3.3}$$

Among them, S indicates that the scope is the entire text.

Then do a weighted dot product of ∂_{ij} and the hidden layer value h to get the final text vector. The context matrix is learned through the network in the training process. Finally, the last state of the encoding process, that is, the last generated text vector, is used as the initialization parameter of the decoder to be passed to the decoder to be decoded to obtain a generative summary of the result text.

3.3 Multiple Attention Mechanism

The attention mechanism introduced by the word encoding layer and sentence encoding layer in the model is a single attention mechanism. This paper also proposes a multiple attention mechanism. Since the introduction method of the attention mechanism of the word encoding layer is the same as that of the sentence encoding layer, only the word coding layer module is taken as an example here. The multiple attention mechanism is changed to randomly initialize n context matrices u_{wk} based on the original attention mechanism, and a single attention matrix is calculated according to formula (3.4).

$$\partial_{ijk} = \frac{\exp\left(u_{ij}^T u_{wk}\right)}{\sum_L \exp\left(u_{ij}^T u_{wk}\right)} \tag{3.4}$$

Then use formula (3.5) to weight all its attention matrices to get the final attention matrix.

$$\partial = \sum_n \frac{1}{n} \frac{\exp\left(u_{ij}^T u_{wk}\right)}{\sum_L \exp\left(u_{ij}^T u_{wk}\right)} \tag{3.5}$$

Among them, $k \in (1, n)$. The selection of n depends on the number of nodes in the calculation unit, and the maximum number of nodes in the calculation unit cannot be exceeded. The best selection of n can be obtained by formula (3.6).

$$n = N_{node} * U_{use} * (1 + W/C) \tag{3.6}$$

Among them, $*$ in the equation is a multiplication operator, W/C is the ratio of idle time to computing time, N_{node} is the number of nodes, and U_{use} is the utilization rate of all nodes. That is, the higher the proportion of node idle time, the larger n can be set. The higher the proportion of node calculation time, the lower n, but the total number of n cannot exceed the total number of nodes N.

Using multiple attention matrices to replace a single attention matrix can superimpose the attention effect of a single matrix and strengthen the attention effect of attention.

4 Experiment

4.1 Text Summary Evaluation Method

Text summary evaluation methods are divided into two categories. One is internal evaluation methods, which provide reference abstracts and evaluate the quality of text abstracts on the basis of reference abstracts. It is the most commonly used text summary evaluation method in the industry. The second is an external evaluation method, which does not provide a reference abstract, and uses the document abstract to replace the original document to execute a document-related application. This paper adopts the Edmundson evaluation method [9] of the internal evaluation method, which is to objectively evaluate the text summary by comparing the overlap rate of the text summary w_{match} generated by the model and the target text summary (expert summary) w_{total}. Calculate the coincidence rate p_i of each text summary by formula (4.1).

$$p_i = \frac{w_{match}}{w_{total}} * 100\% \tag{4.1}$$

This paper then uses the ROUGE (recall-oriented understudy for gisting evaluation) index proposed by Lin et al. to compare and evaluate each model [10]. This indicator evaluates the pros and cons of the summary model based on the number of n-ary common subsequences of the generated summary in the standard summary, where R-1 and R-2 refer to 1-element and 2-element subsequences, and RL means the longest Common subsequence.

4.2 Experimental Parameter Settings

This article uses the public Chinese text abstract data set Test Data of NLPCC 2017 Task1 of the NLPCC 2017 conference organizer to conduct experiments. In the experiment, the data set is preprocessed by keras [11], word segmentation is used by hanLP, converted into one-hot vector input, and word2vec matrix is obtained using word2vec [12] to training. The output dimension of the word embedding module is set to 200, and the output dimension of the word encoding module is set to 100. The GRU hidden state vector dimension is set to 200, the activation function uses softmax [13], the batchsize is set to 64, and the learning rate is set to 0.05. Among them, the weight parameter matrix in the GRU and softmax classifiers is determined by the model itself, and the gradients of all parameters are calculated through back propagation, and the parameters are updated adaptively. At the same time, in order to prevent overfitting, this paper introduces the Dropout technology [14] and sets its parameter ratio to 0.5 to reduce the overfitting phenomenon that occurs on the training set.

4.3 Activation Function Selection Analysis

The core of the DSNN-GSM model is the activation function selection. Generally, a nonlinear function is introduced as the activation function, which can make the expressive ability of the deep neural network more powerful. This paper selects softmax function, Sigmoid function, Relu function and tanh function [15], and compares and analyzes different activation functions under the same data conditions, and finally obtains the activation function with higher summary accuracy and less time.

Figure 4 compares four different activation functions in terms of accuracy and time consumption. In terms of accuracy, the softmax activation function has the highest accuracy rate of 91.4%, the relu function is the closest to softamax, the accuracy rate reaches 84.3%, and the sigmod function has the lowest accuracy rate, only 49.0%. In terms of time, the softmax function, relu function and tanh function are relatively close, and softmax takes the least time. From the comparison results; it can be seen that the softmax function is most suitable for this model.

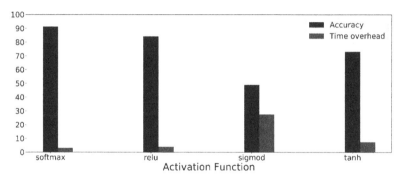

Fig. 4. Activation function analysis

4.4 Comparative Analysis of Methods

In order to prove the advantages of the proposed model, the DSNN-GSM model, BiL-STM [16] and RNN-context [17] model are used to compare the coincidence rate on the "test data of nlpcc 2017 task 1" of the nlpcc 2017 conference. The results are shown in Table 1.

Table 1. Comparison of three methods

Sample category	method	DSNN-GSM	BiLSTM	RNN-context
Training sample	Coincidence rate (%)	91.40	81.00	81.67
Test sample	Coincidence rate (%)	86.65	72.71	75.56

Experimental results show that the coincidence rate of BiLSTM under the test sample is 72.71%, and the coincidence rate of RNN-context is about 75.56%. In contrast, the overlap rate of abstracts generated by the DSNN-GSM model can reach 86.65%, which is better than the former.

Figure 5 shows the performance of DSNN-GSM, BiLSTM and RNN-context. Under the same data set, DSNN-GSM maintains a stable accuracy rate of about 91.4% after 10 rounds of training. BiLSTM maintains a stable accuracy rate after 15 rounds of training, about 81.67%. The RNN-context shows that the rate of change is unstable.

In addition, this article compares RNN-context, Cover-5 [18], DRGD [19], LEAD [20] and other various neural network models on the data set for experimental comparison of ROUGE indicators. It can be seen from the results that the DSNN-GSM model proposed in this paper has a certain degree of improvement in these three ROUGE indicators (Table 2).

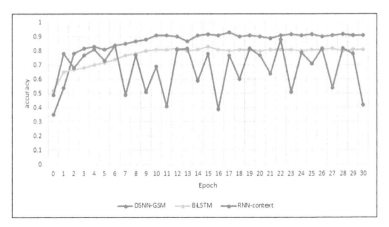

Fig. 5. Model performance comparison

Table 2. Comparison of rouge evaluation results

Methods	R-1	R-2	R-L
RNN-context	30.1	17.3	27.1
Cover-5	36.5	21.0	31.2
DRGD	37.2	24.1	34.3
LEAD	29.9	14.5	28.6
DSNN-GSM	38.9	25.8	34.8

5   Conclusion

This paper studies the traditional encoder-decoder model based on LSTM and analyzes its pros and cons: Although a long and short memory neural network is used to memorize the input content before the current input, if the input sequence is too long, it will still cause errors in the back propagation derivation; and the problem of coarse granularity of the attention mechanism. Based on the analysis of the above problems, a generative text summarization model based on the neural network of the document structure is proposed. It divides the complete text input sequence into a word encoding layer and a sentence encoding layer. Input one-hot code to Bidirectional GRU to generate word code, word code forms sentence code, sentence code generates text vector, and finally decodes. In attention, DSNN-GSM alleviates the problem of large derivative error in the back-propagation caused by long sequence; it introduces attention mechanism or multi attention mechanism in each level, which refines the attention granularity of the model, so that it can capture the key information in the article more accurately, and improve the accuracy of generating summary.

References

1. Jing, C.: Development and application of data science in the Internet plus big data Era. Civil Mil. Integr. **6**, 17–20 (2019)
2. Mahmud, M., Kaiser, M.S., McGinnity, T.M., et al.: Deep learning in mining biological data. Cogn. Comput. **13**, 1–33 (2021)
3. Mahmud, M., Kaiser, M.S., Hussain, A., Vassanelli, S.: Applications of deep learning and reinforcement learning to biological data. IEEE Trans. Neural Netw. Learn. Syst. **29**(6), 2063–2079 (2018)
4. Lin, J., Sun, X., Ma, S. and Su, Q.: Global encoding for abstractive summarization. Comput. Lang. **19**(6) 17 (2017)
5. Vaswani, A., et al.: Attention is all you need. In: 31st Conference on Neural Information Processing Systems (NIPS 2017) (2017)
6. Song, S., Huang, H., Ruan, T.: Abstractive text summarization using LSTM-CNN based deep learning. Multimedia Tools Appl. **78**(1), 857–875 (2018). https://doi.org/10.1007/s11042-018-5749-3
7. Dey, R., Salem, F.M.: Gate-Variants of Gated Recurrent Unit (GRU) Neural Networks. In: 2017 IEEE 60th International Midwest Symposium on Circuits and Systems (MWSCAS) (2017)
8. Zhang, Y., Liu, Q., Song, L.: Sentence-state LSTM for text representation (2018)
9. Edmundson, H.: New methods in automatic extracting. J. Assoc. Comput. Mach. **16**(2), 264–285 (1969)
10. Lin, C.: ROUGE: a package for automatic evaluation of summaries. In: Proceedings of the 42nd Annual Meeting of the Association for Computational Linguistics, Pennsylvania, ACL Press, pp. 74–81 (2004)
11. Gulli, A., Pal, S.: Deep Learning with Keras. Packt Publishing Ltd., Birmingham, United Kingdom (2017)
12. Rong, X.: word2vec parameter learning explained. arXiv preprint arXiv:1411.2738 (2014)
13. Hinton, G.E., Salakhutdinov, R.R.: Replicated softmax: an undirected topic model. Adv. Neural Inf. Process. Syst. **22**, 1607–1614 (2009)
14. Baldi, P., Sadowski, P.J.: Understanding dropout. Adv. Neural Inf. Process. Syst. **26**, 2814–2822 (2013)
15. Agarap, A.F.: Deep learning using rectified linear units (relu). arXiv preprint arXiv:1803.08375 (2018)
16. Wang, H.-C., Hsiao, W.-C., Chang, S.-H.: Automatic paper writing based on a RNN and the TextRank algorithm. Appl. Soft Comput. **97**, 106767 (2020). https://doi.org/10.1016/j.asoc.2020.106767
17. Sun, M.C., Hsu, S.H., Yang, M.C., Chien, J.H.: Context-aware cascade attention-based RNN for video emotion recognition. In: 2018 First Asian Conference on Affective Computing and Intelligent Interaction (ACII Asia) (2018)
18. Gong, Y., et al.: Research on text summarization model with coverage mechanism. J. Front. Comput. Sci. Technol. **13**(2), 205–213 (2019)
19. Li, P., et al.: Deep recurrent generative decoder for abstractive text summarization. In: Proceedings of the 22th Conference on Empirical Methods in Natural Language Processing, Pennsylvania, ACL Press, pp. 2091–2100 (2017)
20. Wasson, M.: Using leading text for news summaries: evaluation results and implications for commercial summarization applications. In: 36th Annual Meeting of the Association for Computational Linguistics and 17th International Conference on Computational Linguistics, vol. 2, pp. 1364–1368 (1998)

Human Gender Detection from Facial Images Using Convolution Neural Network

Tahmina Akter Sumi[1] , Mohammad Shahadat Hossain[1(✉)] ,
Raihan Ul Islam[2] , and Karl Andersson[2]

[1] Department of Computer Science and Engineering, University of Chittagong,
Chittagong, Bangladesh
hossain_ms@cu.ac.bd
[2] Pervasive and Mobile Computing Laboratory, Luleå University of Technology,
Skellefteå, Sweden
{raihan.ul.islam,karl.andersson}@ltu.se

Abstract. Human gender detection which is a part of facial recognition has received extensive attention because of it's different kind of application. Previous research works on gender detection have been accomplished based on different static body feature for example face, eyebrow, hand-shape, body-shape, finger nail etc. In this research work, we have presented human gender classification using Convolution Neural Network (CNN) from human face images as CNN has been recognised as best algorithm in the field of image classification. To implement our system, at first a pre-processing technique has been applied on each image using image processing. The pre-processed image is passed through the Convolution, RELU and Pooling layer for feature extraction. A fully connected layer and a classifier is applied in the classification part of the image. To obtain a better result, we have implemented our system using different optimizers and also have used k fold cross-validation as deep learning approach. The whole method has been evaluated on two dataset collected from Kaggle website and Nottingham Scan Database. The experimented result shows a highest accuracy which is 97.44% using Kaggle dataset and 90% accuracy using Nottingham Scan Database.

Keywords: Convolution neural network · Convolution · RELU · Pooling layer · Fully connected layer · K-fold cross-validation · Optimizers · Kaggle datset · Nottingham Scan Database

1 Introduction

Gender detection plays a significant role in modern technology. The detection of gender has many dynamic applications such as social interaction, security maintenance and surveillance, video games, human-computer interaction, criminal identification, mobile application, commercial development, monitoring application etc. It has occupied a great space in the field of facial recognition. The main

© Springer Nature Switzerland AG 2021
M. Mahmud et al. (Eds.): AII 2021, CCIS 1435, pp. 188–203, 2021.
https://doi.org/10.1007/978-3-030-82269-9_15

purpose of gender detection is to differentiate male and female based on different features of human.

In recent years, various research papers have been published regarding human gender classification using different methods. Human gender can be classified using different features such as face, eyebrow [12], hand-shape [5], body-shape [8], finger nail [32]. Among these, the majority of the gender detection research have been accomplished using face images. The feature extraction is classified into two categories [7], namely geometric based and appearance based.

In the geometric based feature extraction, different facial components or feature points are extracted which mainly represents the face geometry [11]. In the appearance based feature extraction, the features are extracted applying image filter the whole image or particular component of an image [11]. The appearance based feature extraction has an advantage over the geometric based feature extraction. In the geometric based feature extraction, only some fixed points of face image are used where in the appearance based feature extraction, information is extracted from the whole face image. The training process of classifying gender includes several methods such as Support Vector Machine (SVM), Principal Component Analysis (PCA), and Neural Networks (NN) [7]. However, in the field of image classification the Convolution Neural Network (CNN) has been proved to perform as best algorithm comparing with other machine learning algorithms [3,27]. The filters are optimized through automated learning in CNN [6,33] whereas they are hand-engineered in other traditional algorithms. This is a major advantage of CNN as it is independent of human intervention in feature extraction. Moreover, while using an algorithm with pixel vector, a lot of spatial interaction between pixels are lost. A CNN can effectively use adjacent pixel information by convolution and then uses a prediction layer at the end.

Our main purpose of this research is to detect human gender from facial images where we have used an image processing technique for appearance based feature extraction and Convolution Neural Network (CNN) for the classification of human gender. In this regard, at first we have applied an image processing technique where we have converted the face image into a two dimensional array where the values of the array indicates the pixel values of the image. After that, all the pixel values have been divided by 255 so that all the values of the array come to a range between 0 to 1. This is done to reduce the difference among the values. After this pre-processing step, a machine learning algorithm called Convolution Neural Network is applied for the classification of gender using a compact variant of VGGNet architecture on 2 dataset which are Kaggle dataset and Nottingham Scan Database. After implementation, a highest accuracy 97.44% has been gained using Kaggle dataset and 90% has been gained using Nottingham Scan Database. The significant contributions of our research are:

1. Performance comparison has been shown among different optimizers.
2. K-fold cross validation has been applied as a deep learning approach.
3. Performance comparison has been shown among different activation function.
4. Dataset has been splitted into different ratio to gain a best accuracy.

The next sections of the paper are arranged accordingly: Sect. 2 contains the previous works regarding gender classification. Section 3 describes the methodology where Convolution Neural Network is discussed broadly. Section 4 shows experimental setup where the experimental tools used in implementing our system has been stated. Section 5 is about the result and discussion and finally in Sect. 6 conclusion and future work has been discussed.

2   Literature Review

In the field of image processing and machine learning, a lot of research work has been done on human gender estimation. In this section, a brief overview of previous work on human gender estimation has been presented.

Lian HC [20] obtained an accuracy of 94.81% applying local binary pattern (LBP) and SVM with polynomial kernel on the CAS-PEAL face database. According to this method, a good accuracy can be achieved if the block size for the LBP operator is correctly selected, which is really a difficult task. Li et al. [19] performed the classification of gender utilizing only five facial features (eyes, nose, mouth, brows, forehead). One drawback of this research is that the feature extraction method they have used is affected by complex backgrounds. Saeed Mozaffari, Hamid Behravan and Rohollah Akbari [23] used geometric based feature for male female classification where they have used AR and Ethnic dataset containing 126 frontal images in each dataset. Here they have achieved 80.3% and 86.6% accuracy respectively. In [10] a texture based local binary pattern has been used for feature extraction and as classification algorithm naïve Bayes, ANN and linear SVM has been applied. They achieved 63% accuracy with only 100 face images that has been collected from Nottingham Scan database which is quite low. Sajja, T. K., Kalluri, H. K. [28] have worked on gender classification from face images using LBP, SVM and Back Propagation. In this research they have used ORL dataset which contains 400 images and Nottingham Scan database which contains 100 images. After implementation they gained 100% accuracy for ORL dataset and 71% accuracy for Nottingham Scan database respectively. The work in [24] showed a high classification accuracy of 99.30% using SUMS face database. In this work, the researchers applied 2D-DCT feature extraction, Viola and Jones face detection and the K-means nearest neighbor (KNN) algorithm as classifier. Being a compute-intensive algorithm, 2D-DCT is not suitable for real-time applications. Using principal component analysis (PCA), researchers in [30] processed the face image to reduce the dimensionality. After that, a good subset of eigenfeatures has been selected using genetic algorithm (GA). Here, they reported an average error rate of 11.30%. The main drawback of this method is that, the GA exhibits high computational complexity. Althnian et al. [4] used hand crafted and fused features for face gender recognition where they have used both SVM and CNN and gained best accuracy 86.60% using CNN which can be improved further. Serna et al. [29] worked on gender detection using VGG and ResNet where they analyzed how bias affects deep learning. They divided the images into 3 ethnic groups and also experimented on an unbiased group. Here they achieved best average accuracy 95.27% for unbiased group using VGG and 95.67% Biased group 3 using ResNet.

Deviating from only facial based gender recognition, some researchers have worked on estimating human gender from different body parts for example body shape, eyebrow, hand shape, finger nail etc. Dong, Yujie & Woodard, Damon [12] approached a new technique where they classified gender using eyebrow shape. For classification MD, LDA and SVM were used in this paper and they gained 96% and 97% accuracy for MBGC and FRGC dataset respectively. In [5] they investigated human gender from hand shape from a small dataset containing 40 images and they achieved 98% accuracy. As classification algorithm Score-level fusion and LDA have been applied here. HongáLim et al. [32] presented a novel method for gender classification using finger nail with 80 samples donated by 40 people. With the use of PCA and SVM as classification algorithm, they showed about 90% accuracy in this research.

So considering the whole literature review, it is clear that an improvement in gender classification is needed. The main disadvantages of the above gender classification research works is that, the feature extraction and the classification are performed separately. To obtain an optimum pre-processing and feature extraction design, prior knowledge is needed here. In case of CNN which is a multilayer neural network model [21, 22], it can optimize filters through automated learning where it is independent of prior knowledge which demonstrate a superior performance can be achieved using CNN.

3   Methodology

In our proposed system, we have utilized a CNN (Convolutional Neural Network) architecture. CNN which is a deep learning algorithm is capable of distinguishing images from their characteristics [1, 9, 14]. CNN is generally used for image analysis, image segmentation, image classification, medical image analysis, image and video recognition, etc. [2, 13]. In this research, at first we have applied an image processing technique as pre-processing on images to transform the raw data into an efficient and useful format. Later, the CNN architecture has been applied. Here, it has been decomposed into two parts:

- Feature Extraction
- Classification

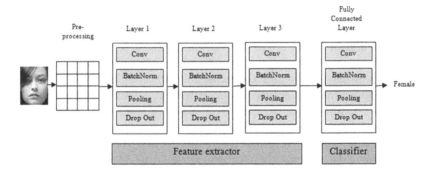

Fig. 1. Network architecture

The convolution and the pooling layers performs the feature extraction of image which actually extract information from input for decision making. Finally, fully connected layer performs as the classification part. Our basic network architecture has been illustrated in Fig. 1.

3.1   Dataset

In the field of gender estimation, there are several global datasets used in different research works. In this paper, we have used two global datasets so that we can show the comparison of the result achieved using different datasets. One of the two datasets is collected from kaggle website and the other is Nottingham Scan database.

Kaggle Dataset. The CELEBA aligned data set has been used in kaggle dataset to provide image. This dataset is of good quality and large. Here, the images are separated into 1747 female and 1747 male as training images, 100 male and 100 female as test image and 100 male, 100 female as validation images. A face cropping function using MTCNN has been applied here to crop the images so that only face images are included here. In Fig. 2 a sample of Kaggle Database have been shown.

Fig. 2. Sample of Kaggle Dataset

Nottingham Scan Database. Nottingham Scan database is comprise of 100 human faces where half of the images are of male and half images are of female. The format of images used in this database is .gif format. 438×538 pixel size image hase been used here with 256 a gray-levels. As per our requirement, the images have been converted to .jpg format from .gif format. In Fig. 3 a sample of Nottingham Scan Database have been shown.

3.2   Pre-processing

Pre-processing of image generally removes low frequency background noise, normalizes the intensification of the individual practical image, removes reflection of light to get rid of the image noise, and prepares the face image to better feature extraction. In our system, we have first resized the images into 96×96 dimension. Then We have converted the image to an array of pixel value. Each pixel value of the array is converted to float and divided by 255.0 so that all the pixel values comes to a range between 0 to 1. In Fig. 4, the whole pre-processing system has been illustrated.

Fig. 3. Sample of Nottingham Scan database

3.3   Feature Extraction

In Convolutional Neural Network (CNN), the feature extraction is performed by the Convolution and the Pooling layer. In our proposed system these layers are defined as follows:

1. The convolution layer contains 32 filters with a 3×3 kernel. Here RELU is used as the activation function followed by batch normalization.
2. The POOL layer uses a 3×3 pool size to reduce spatial dimension from 96×96 to 32×32. A dropout is used in our network architecture which disconnects nodes arbitrarily from layer to layer.
3. Next the convolution and ReLU layers are applied twice before applying another POOL layer. This operation of multiple convolutional and ReLU layers allow to learn a richer set of features. Here-

- The filter size is being increased from 32 to 64. As we go deep into the network, we will learn the filters more.
- The max pooling size is decreased from 3 × 3 to 2 × 2 so that spatial dimensions don't get reduced too quickly. Dropout is again performed at this stage.

4. Again the convolution and ReLU layers is applied twice before applying another POOL layer. The filter size is increased to 128. And 25% dropout of the nodes is executed in this step for the reduction of over fitting.

3.4   Classification

Fully Connected and RELU operation is performed and a sigmoid classifier is used for classification. Here-

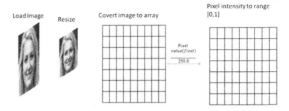

Fig. 4. Pre-processing steps

1. RELU and batch normalization with dense (1024) defines the fully connected layer where dropout is executed for the last time. This time 50% of the node is being dropped during training.
2. Finally, sigmoid function is used as classifier to return the predicted probabilities for each class label.

$$Sigmoid(x) = \frac{1}{1 + e^{-\theta^T x}}$$

In Fig. 5 the whole schematic diagram of our network architecture has been provided.

4   Experimental Setup

Our system has been implemented using python programming language. Matplotlib, keras, numpy libraries has been used for system implementation. Keras provides some built in functions such as activation functions, optimizers, layers etc. Tensorflow has also been used as the system backend. In Table 1, the experimental tools used in this system implementation has been showed.

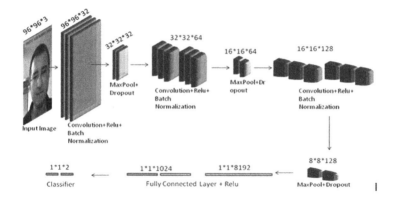

Fig. 5. A full schematic diagram of network architecture

Table 1. Experimental tools

Name	Experimental tool
Hardware	i. Microsoft Windows 8.1 pro ii. Processor Intel (R) core (TM) i3-5005U, 4 GB RAM
Software	Spyder (Python3.7)
Programming Language	Pythonn
Method implementation	i. Keras 2.2.4 ii. Tensorflow 1.15.0

5   Result and Discussion

As stated in earlier section, we have used two dataset to evaluate our model. For both dataset, we have implemented our model using different optimizers so that best accuracy can be obtained. After that we have trained our model using 5 fold cross validation as deep learning approach.

5.1   Comparison of Result Among Different Optimizers and Activation Functions

Table 2 shows the training and testing accuracy for different optimizers for both Kaggle and Nottingham Scan Database.

As we can see using Kaggle dataset, we have achieved satisfactory accuracy using Adam, Adamax, RMSprop and Adagrad optimizer which is above 90%. Using SGD and Adadelta optimizer the accuracy gained less comparing with the others. Among all of these, the best accuracy has been gained using the Adam optimizer. For Nottingham Scan Database, the Adam optimizer shows the best accuracy and also it maintains a good balance between training and testing accuracy. So, we can say that for both dataset the best accuracy is obtained using adam optimizer.

Table 2. Accuracy using different optimizers

Optimizers	Kaggle Dataset		Nottingham Scan Dataset	
	Training accuracy	Testing accuracy	Training accuracy	Testing accuracy
Adam	98%	95%	90.62%	90%
Adamax	96%	94%	78.12%	85%
RMSprop	97%	93%	93.75%	65%
Adagrad	91%	93%	87.50%	85%
SGD	84%	86%	53.12%	82.50%
Adadelta	70%	76%	40.62%	65%

Figure 6 and 7 shows Loss/Accuracy curve using Adam optimizer for Kaggle dataset and nottingham scan database respectively.

In Table 3, we have shown the accuracy acquired by splitting the dataset into different ratio. Here, the best training and testing accuracy we have achieved by splitting both dataset into 80% training and 20% testing which is 98.09% training accuracy and 95% testing accuracy for Kaggle dataset and 87.50% training accuracy and 80.50% testing accuracy for Nottingham Scan Dataset.

Table 3. Accuracy comparison of splitting dataset

Split Ratio	Kaggle Dataset		Nottingham Scan Dataset	
	Training accuracy	Testing accuracy	Training accuracy	Testing accuracy
60%–40%	96.49%	93.63%	80.77%	80%
70%–30%	96.63%	93.03%	75.67%	80%
80%–20%	98.09%	95%	87.50%	80.50%
90%–10%	93.41%	94%	80.62%	75%

Table 4 shows the result of our system implementation using different activation functions to see which activation function generates the best result. In this case we have considered the splitting ratio as 80%-20% as we achieved a satisfactory accuracy by splitting the dataset into 80% training and 20% testing. Here as we can see, the sigmoid function results the best for each dataset. Softmax function performs well for Kaggle dataset but it shows overfitting problem in Nottingham Scan Dataset. On the other hand, Relu activation function shows a poor accuracy for both dataset.

5.2   K-Fold Cross Validation

Cross validation is a re-sampling method which is used to evaluate machine learning models on a limited data sample. Here we have implemented our model

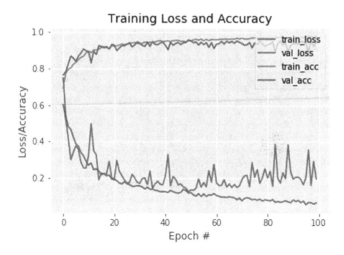

Fig. 6. The Loss vs Accuracy curve using Adam optimizer for Kaggle dataset

Table 4. Accuracy using different activation function

Activation function	Kaggle Dataset		Nottingham Scan Dataset	
	Training accuracy	Testing accuracy	Training accuracy	Testing accuracy
Sigmoid	98%	95%	90.62%	90%
Softmax	93.20%	87.98%	93.10%	60%
Relu	28.35%	26.20%	28.12%	50%

using K-fold cross validation as a deep learning approach on both Kaggle Dataset and Nottingham Scan Database. We have chosen the value of k=5 here as 5 fold cross-validation.

Table 5 shows the result of our model using 5 fold cross-validation and also the average accuracy and the best accuracy achieved after the 5 fold cross-validation. As we can see, the average accuracy and the best accuracy we have achieved are respectively 95.06% and 97.44% for Kaggle Dataset and 83.50% and 90% for Nottingham Scan Database.

In Table 6, we have shown the comparison of our proposed method with two existing method where Nottingham Scan Database have been used. Datta et al. [10] applied texture based LBP for feature extraction. Artificial Neural Network (ANN), Naïve Bayes, Linear SVM algorithms have been applied for classification. They have achieved a highest accuracy of 63% using ANN classification algorithm. In [28], the researchers used a combination of LBP and SVM where they achieved 55% accuracy and used a combination of LBP and NN where they

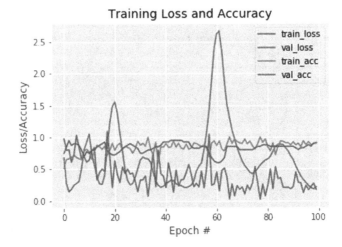

Fig. 7. The Loss vs Accuracy curve using Adam optimizer for Nottingham Scan database

Table 5. Accuracy using K-fold cross validation

Fold	Kaggle Dataset		Nottingham Scan Dataset	
	Training accuracy	Testing accuracy	Training accuracy	Testing accuracy
1	98.07%	93.92%	90.62%	90%
2	97.62%	94.28%	96.88%	82.85%
3	98.09%	97.44%	87.50%	77.50%
4	96.93%	94.28%	90.62%	85%
5	97.44%	95.42%	90%	82.50%
Average Accuracy	97.51%	95.06%	90%	83.50%
Best Accuracy	98.09%	97.44%	96.88%	90%

Table 6. Comparison of the proposed approach with existing method

Serial No	Reference	Method	Database	Accuracy
1	Datta et al. [10]	LBP+ANN	Nottingham Scan Database	63%
2	Sajja, T.K. [28]	LBP+NN	Nottingham Scan Database	71%
3	Our proposed method	CNN	Nottingham Scan Database	83.5%

achieved 71% from the Nottingham Scan database. But in our proposed method, we have got a best accuracy 90% using CNN model with 5 fold cross-validation and the average accuracy of the 5 folds is 83.50%.

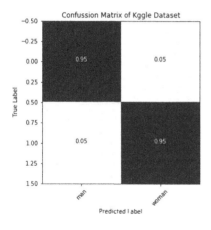 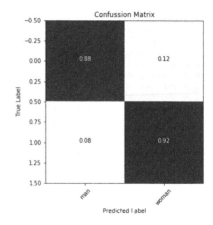

Fig. 8. Confusion matrix of 5-fold cross-validation on Kaggle dataset and Nottingham Scan Database

Figure 8 shows the confusion matrix of 5-fold cross-validation on Nottingham Scan Database and Kaggle Dataset respectively.

Figure 9 shows accuracy vs epoch curve using 5 fold cross-validation for kaggle dataset and nottingham scan database respectively. As we can see here, we have achieved a satisfactory accuracy after 100 epoch.

5.3 Performance Metrics

Researchers generally evaluate the overall performance and also the efficiency of machine learning algorithms using these factors [26]. In our model we have evaluated performance metrics to understand how well our model is performing on given dataset. In this study, the performances have been evaluated based on three criteria- Recall, Precision, F1-score. In Table 7, the comparison of the performance metrics for both datasets are shown.

Table 7. Different parameters

Performance matrices	Kaggle Dataset			Nottingham Scan Dataset		
	Man	Woman	Macro Average	Man	Woman	Macro Average
Precision	0.95	0.95	0.95	0.88	0.92	0.90
Recall	0.95	0.95	0.95	0.88	0.92	0.90
F1-score	0.95	0.95	0.95	0.88	0.92	0.90

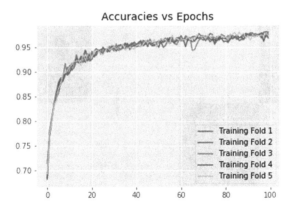

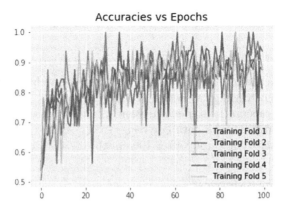

Fig. 9. The Accuracy vs Epoch curve using 5 fold for Kaggle dataset and Nottinghum scan database

6   Conclusion and Future Work

In this paper, we have used both image processing technique and machine learning algorithm for implementation and achieved a promising result for both Kaggle dataset and Nottingham Scan Database. As part of image processing, a pre-processing technique has been applied first. After pre-processing, feature extraction and classification are implemented in this system. A sigmoid function has been used as classifier in our model. Different optimizers have been used to determine which optimizer gives a better result. For assessing the effectiveness of our model, we have applied 5 fold cross-validation which has helped to evaluate our model. After analysing the result, a comparison of two previous work with our paper has also been shown where our system gives better result than them.

However, our system can be improved using different classifier for example softmax function and ReLU. A more efficient system can be built for human gender classification using Belief Rule Based Expert Systems (BRBES) [15–18, 25,31]. So in future, we will implement all these for human gender classification.

References

1. Abedin, M.Z., Nath, A.C., Dhar, P., Deb, K., Hossain, M.S.: License plate recognition system based on contour properties and deep learning model. In: 2017 IEEE Region 10 Humanitarian Technology Conference (R10-HTC), pp. 590–593. IEEE (2017)
2. Ahmed, T.U., Hossain, M.S., Alam, M.J., Andersson, K.: An integrated CNN-RNN framework to assess road crack. In: 2019 22nd International Conference on Computer and Information Technology (ICCIT), pp. 1–6. IEEE (2019)
3. Ahmed, T.U., Hossain, S., Hossain, M.S., ul Islam, R., Andersson, K.: Facial expression recognition using convolutional neural network with data augmentation. In: 2019 Joint 8th International Conference on Informatics, Electronics & Vision (ICIEV) and 2019 3rd International Conference on Imaging, Vision & Pattern Recognition (icIVPR), pp. 336–341. IEEE (2019)
4. Althnian, A., Aloboud, N., Alkharashi, N., Alduwaish, F., Alrshoud, M., Kurdi, H.: Face gender recognition in the wild: an extensive performance comparison of deep-learned, hand-crafted, and fused features with deep and traditional models. Appl. Sci. **11**(1), 89 (2021)
5. Amayeh, G., Bebis, G., Nicolescu, M.: Gender classification from hand shape. In: 2008 IEEE Computer Society Conference on Computer Vision and Pattern Recognition Workshops, pp. 1–7. IEEE (2008)
6. Basnin, N., Nahar, L., Hossain, M.S.: An integrated CNN-LSTM model for micro hand gesture recognition. In: Vasant, P., Zelinka, I., Weber, G.-W. (eds.) ICO 2020. AISC, vol. 1324, pp. 379–392. Springer, Cham (2021). https://doi.org/10.1007/978-3-030-68154-8_35
7. BenAbdelkader, C., Griffin, P.: A local region-based approach to gender classi. cation from face images. In: 2005 IEEE Computer Society Conference on Computer Vision and Pattern Recognition (CVPR'05)-Workshops, p. 52. IEEE (2005)
8. Cao, L., Dikmen, M., Fu, Y., Huang, T.S.: Gender recognition from body. In: Proceedings of the 16th ACM International Conference on Multimedia, pp. 725–728 (2008)
9. Chowdhury, R.R., Hossain, M.S., ul Islam, R., Andersson, K., Hossain, S.: Bangla handwritten character recognition using convolutional neural network with data augmentation. In: 2019 Joint 8th International Conference on Informatics, Electronics & Vision (ICIEV) and 2019 3rd International Conference on Imaging, Vision & Pattern Recognition (icIVPR), pp. 318–323. IEEE (2019)
10. Datta, S., Das, A.K.: Gender identification from facial images using local texture based features (2018)
11. Dhall, S., Sethi, P.: Geometric and appearance feature analysis for facial expression recognition. Int. J. Adv. Eng. Technol. **7**(111), 01–11 (2014)
12. Dong, Y., Woodard, D.L.: Eyebrow shape-based features for biometric recognition and gender classification: a feasibility study. In: 2011 International Joint Conference on Biometrics (IJCB), pp. 1–8. IEEE (2011)
13. Hossain, M.S., Sultana, Z., Nahar, L., Andersson, K.: An intelligent system to diagnose chikungunya under uncertainty. J. Wirel. Mobile Netw. Ubiquit. Comput. Dependable Appl. **10**(2), 37–54 (2019)
14. Islam, M.Z., Hossain, M.S., ul Islam, R., Andersson, K.: Static hand gesture recognition using convolutional neural network with data augmentation. In: 2019 Joint 8th International Conference on Informatics, Electronics & Vision (ICIEV) and 2019 3rd International Conference on Imaging, Vision & Pattern Recognition (icIVPR), pp. 324–329. IEEE (2019)

15. Islam, R.U., Hossain, M.S., Andersson, K.: A deep learning inspired belief rule-based expert system. IEEE Access **8**, 190637–190651 (2020)
16. Jamil, M.N., Hossain, M.S., ul Islam, R., Andersson, K.: A belief rule based expert system for evaluating technological innovation capability of high-tech firms under uncertainty. In: 2019 Joint 8th International Conference on Informatics, Electronics & Vision (ICIEV) and 2019 3rd International Conference on Imaging, Vision & Pattern Recognition (icIVPR), pp. 330–335. IEEE (2019)
17. Kabir, S., Islam, R.U., Hossain, M.S., Andersson, K.: An integrated approach of belief rule base and deep learning to predict air pollution. Sensors **20**(7), 1956 (2020)
18. Karim, R., Andersson, K., Hossain, M.S., Uddin, M.J., Meah, M.P.: A belief rule based expert system to assess clinical bronchopneumonia suspicion. In: 2016 Future Technologies Conference (FTC), pp. 655–660. IEEE (2016)
19. Li, B., Lian, X.C., Lu, B.L.: Gender classification by combining clothing, hair and facial component classifiers. Neurocomputing **76**(1), 18–27 (2012)
20. Lian, H.-C., Lu, B.-L.: Multi-view gender classification using local binary patterns and support vector machines. In: Wang, J., Yi, Z., Zurada, J.M., Lu, B.-L., Yin, H. (eds.) ISNN 2006. LNCS, vol. 3972, pp. 202–209. Springer, Heidelberg (2006). https://doi.org/10.1007/11760023_30
21. Mahmud, M., Kaiser, M.S., McGinnity, T.M., Hussain, A.: Deep learning in mining biological data. Cogn. Comput. **13**(1), 1–33 (2021). https://doi.org/10.1007/s12559-020-09773-x
22. Mahmud, M., Kaiser, M.S., Hussain, A., Vassanelli, S.: Applications of deep learning and reinforcement learning to biological data. IEEE Trans. Neural Netw. Learn. Syst. **29**(6), 2063–2079 (2018). https://doi.org/10.1109/TNNLS.2018.2790388
23. Mozaffari, S., Behravan, H., Akbari, R.: Gender classification using single frontal image per person: combination of appearance and geometric based features. In: 2010 20th International Conference on Pattern Recognition, pp. 1192–1195. IEEE (2010)
24. Nazir, M., Ishtiaq, M., Batool, A., Jaffar, M.A., Mirza, A.M.: Feature selection for efficient gender classification. In: Proceedings of the 11th WSEAS International Conference, pp. 70–75 (2010)
25. Rahaman, S., Hossain, M.S.: A belief rule based clinical decision support system to assess suspicion of heart failure from signs, symptoms and risk factors. In: 2013 International Conference on Informatics, Electronics and Vision (ICIEV), pp. 1–6. IEEE (2013)
26. Ramteke, S.P., Gurjar, A.A., Deshmukh, D.S.: A streamlined OCR system for handwritten Marathi text document classification and recognition using SVM-ACS algorithm. Int. J. Intell. Eng. Syst. **11**(3), 186–195 (2018)
27. Rezaoana, N., Hossain, M.S., Andersson, K.: Detection and classification of skin cancer by using a parallel CNN model. In: 2020 IEEE International Women in Engineering (WIE) Conference on Electrical and Computer Engineering (WIECON-ECE), pp. 380–386. IEEE (2020)
28. Sajja, T.K., Kalluri, H.K.: Gender classification based on face images of local binary pattern using support vector machine and back propagation neural networks. Adv. Modell. Anal. B **62**(1), 31–35 (2019)
29. Serna, I., Peña, A., Morales, A., Fierrez, J.: InsideBias: measuring bias in deep networks and application to face gender biometrics. In: 2020 25th International Conference on Pattern Recognition (ICPR), pp. 3720–3727. IEEE (2021)

30. Sun, Z., Yuan, X., Bebis, G., Louis, S.J.: Neural-network-based gender classification using genetic search for eigen-feature selection. In: Proceedings of the 2002 International Joint Conference on Neural Networks. IJCNN'02 (Cat. No. 02CH37290), vol. 3, pp. 2433–2438. IEEE (2002)
31. Uddin Ahmed, T., Jamil, M.N., Hossain, M.S., Andersson, K., Hossain, M.S.: An integrated real-time deep learning and belief rule base intelligent system to assess facial expression under uncertainty. In: 9th International Conference on Informatics, Electronics & Vision (ICIEV). IEEE Computer Society (2020)
32. Widjaja, E., Lim, G.H., An, A.: A novel method for human gender classification using Raman spectroscopy of fingernail clippings. Analyst **133**(4), 493–498 (2008)
33. Zisad, S.N., Hossain, M.S., Andersson, K.: Speech emotion recognition in neurological disorders using convolutional neural network. In: Mahmud, M., Vassanelli, S., Kaiser, M.S., Zhong, N. (eds.) BI 2020. LNCS (LNAI), vol. 12241, pp. 287–296. Springer, Cham (2020). https://doi.org/10.1007/978-3-030-59277-6_26

Few-Shot Learning for Tamil Handwritten Character Recognition Using Deep Siamese Convolutional Neural Network

Noushath Shaffi$^{(\boxtimes)}$ and Faizal Hajamohideen

University of Technology and Applied Sciences - Sohar, Sohar, Sultanate of Oman
{noushath,faizalh}.soh@cas.edu.om

Abstract. Optical Character Recognition (OCR) is at the forefront of numerous applications such as digitalization of legal and legacy documents, automatic form processing, writer identification in forensic intelligence. Most of these applications seldom have sufficient training samples in order to achieve an accuracy worthy of real-time deployments. Inspired by the demonstrated performance of Siamese Neural Networks (SNN) in various fields such as Computer vision, Natural Language Processing, Signal processing etc., in this paper, we explore the application of SNN for Tamil Handwritten character recognition. The Siamese-CNN learning is implemented using cross-entropy loss and subsequently used to validate the few-shot learning. It achieved an optimal accuracy of 83.39% for n-way-40-shot learning. Rigorous experiments were conducted all through and the results are indicative of a promising new direction for the development of efficient Indic OCR models using Siamese networks.

Keywords: Siamese network · Cross-entropy loss · Few-shot learning · One-shot learning · Indic OCR

1 Introduction

Humans exhibit supernatural power when it comes to cognitive abilities and the automated systems are striving hard only to come near to this intelligence let alone surpassing it. Conversely, there are several AI based systems that exceed human intelligence but the pitfall is that the former relies on hundreds or thousands of training images than the latter [7]. These systems despite their state-of-the-art advancements, their reliance on the enormous data for model building may lead to failure when presented with less samples [12].

One such application that demands huge data for adequate training of the model is Optical Character Recognition (OCR) – a classic application in the field of Pattern Recognition for the longest time and it has immense value for multilingual multiscript countries like India [10]. Any official document (passport application form, competitive examination forms, judicial documents) may contain the same text in at least 2 or 3 languages. Hence, OCR carries a substantial application potential for a country like India which has 22 official languages and several hundreds of regional languages [10].

© Springer Nature Switzerland AG 2021
M. Mahmud et al. (Eds.): AII 2021, CCIS 1435, pp. 204–215, 2021.
https://doi.org/10.1007/978-3-030-82269-9_16

Development of a robust Indic OCR system using advanced Deep learning algorithms need huge amounts of training samples in order to generalize well on a previously unseen set of data [12]. Such models when presented with insufficient supervised data may overfit the training samples and/or fail to build a model with good generalizability [12]. Research communities have attempted to address the low-data regime applications through the application of Generative Adversarial Network (GAN), transfer learning or through various data augmentation techniques.

However, there are several shortcomings surrounding the application of these techniques to augment the dataset. For instance, the GANs face the problem of emulating samples that are true representative of character class which may lead to biased model learning. Transfer learning too has limitations such as fine-tuning of the model for the underlying dataset [6]. These are few reasons as to why OCR for many Indic languages have not reported state-of-the-art accuracy.

There exist many Indian languages that fall into the low-data regime – either lacking data or inadequate samples to leverage well established image recognition models (such as VGG16, ResNet, etc.) for the development of robust OCR. As reported in [10], there exists only 19 systematized and comprehensive databases pertaining to 8 Indian script such as Tamil, Telugu, Bangla, Oriya, etc. India is a country with diverse culture and there have been enormous contributions in the field of technology by people belonging to different ethnicities. Hence, it becomes paramount importance to contribute in the advancement of technology concerning all ethnicities. Currently, the research literature indicates that there have been numerous works concerning only those Indian languages that have comprehensive data. Some official Indian languages such as Konkani, Manipuri, Bodo have not even reported the baseline accuracy on the performance of OCR for the respective script. This incapacitated benchmarking can mainly be attributed to the non-availability of sufficient training samples that conventional machine learning and deep learning algorithm demand.

Nevertheless, this can be circumvented by the application of a deep learning technique known as the Siamese Convolutional Neural Networks (CNN) for its ability to learn the model from a limited sample size. The Siamese CNN can effectively assist in the classification task with the constraint that the model can learn only from a single sample per class. This is known as one-shot learning. A natural extension of this concept is zero-shot or few-shot learning, in which the model can either have no sample or only few samples for learning from the target classes. Our primary focus of this paper is to see few-shot learning scenario in the development of an efficient OCR for an Indian language.

- Overall the application of Siamese CNN is still in its infancy especially in the field of development of Indic OCR. Our paper set the benchmark as a new entrant for this field and can serve as a future reference material.
- for very few Indian languages, there are many Indic scripts that lack comprehensive samples for training and testing the model. We propose deep Siamese network models that could maximally leverage from limited data for developing an efficient Indic OCR.

– Models based on Siamese are robust to class imbalance as they rely only on a few samples per class. It is of no significance even if some classes are underrepresented.

In this paper, considering Tamil language as a case study, we leverage a Siamese-CNN for N-way-K-shot learning strategy for the classification of Tamil Handwritten characters, where K can be 1 (one-shot), 0 (zero-shot) or any positive constant (few-shot). This study will pave the way for studying the efficacy of a Siamese model to maximally leverage from the limited data concerning many Indian scripts. We build a twin CNN architecture for feature extraction for subsequent similarity learning between a pair of sample characters. This model is then used to measure the similarity-score between a pair of samples to measure the relative closeness in the classification of 156 Tamil characters. The models built are evaluated using binary cross entropy loss and experiments are substantiated with appropriate analysis. The remainder of this paper is structured as follows: Sect. 2 presents the comprehensive review Siamese CNN in various domains. Sect. 3 presents the model architecture and associated implementation details. Experimental results and analysis are presented in Sect. 4. Finally, conclusion and avenues for sequel are presented in Sect. 5.

2   Literature Review

The Siamese CNN has been applied in various research domains successfully ever since it was first proposed by Tiagman et al. in 2014 [13]. In this section, we report some notable research work done in the last 5 years that employs the Siamese based machine learning model for solving various problems of computer vision and pattern recognition. In [2], a method was presented for word spotting using Siamese-CNN based on similarity between two input word images. The trained model was used to spot words of varying writing styles with vocabulary words that are not in the training set. In [1], the Siamese model was adopted in the process of offline writer identification. The probability distribution functions along with auto-derived CNN features were fed into the Siamese neural network that resulted in encouraging performance. In another work, the Siamese model was used for vehicle reidentification purposes [8]. The model was fed with vehicle shape and features extracted from the license plate where these elements were merged using distance descriptors with a sequence of dense layers. The experiments conducted resulted in an accuracy of 98.7% on a 2 h of video containing 2982 vehicles. Another work was proposed [5] based on the Siamese model for text recognition by measuring the visual similarity and thereby predicting the content of the unlabeled texts. The results demonstrated that the predicted labels sometimes outperformed human labels. Very recently in [11], Siamese Denoising Autoencoder network was proposed which can automatically remove position noise, recover the missing skeleton points and correct outliers in joint trajectories in the process of gait recognition. The Siamese mechanism to reduce between class and increase within-class variations resulted in a robust model against inaccurate skeleton estimation. Another work reported in [4] successfully employed Siamese graph convolution network (SGCN) using contrastive loss for the task of content-based image retrieval of very high resolution images. Using SGCN, a similarity function is learnt that uses region adjacency graph to better represent the semantically closer samples from dissimilar points thereby a robust CBIR performance was seen. In [3], authors have applied the Siamese framework for an object tracking process that has multiple stages:

Firstly, dynamic weighting module is introduced in the Siamese framework to predict the response maps discriminatively. Secondly a residual structure in order to form the residual dynamic weight module is introduced. Finally, a pyramid-re-detection module was included to avoid unnecessary local search. The resultant model outperformed state-of-the-art object trackers. Another object tracking method was proposed in [14] that introduced the attention module in the traditional Siamese network. A attention shake layer replaced the max pooling layer in the Siamese network which helped to enhance the expression power of Siamese without increasing the depth of the network. Empirical results exhibited good performance on multiple benchmarks. Based on this brief study of existing literature, we can conclude that:

- Siamese models have been applied successfully in various domains of pattern recognition and computer vision and hence it becomes imperative to see its performance in the field of OCR.
- Not much work has been reported in the field of document image processing, especially in the domain of OCR that makes use of a Siamese model in the recognition or clustering of the handwritten characters.
- Overall, the research adapting Siamese models for the development of efficient Indic OCR is fairly immature till-date. We believe that this work will pave the way for more such research in this field to fully exploit the benefit of much acclaimed Siamese models for the few-shot/one-shot/zero-shot learning process.

3   Methodology

We present here the overall architecture of our Siamese CNN for few-shot learning model to classify samples of Handwritten Tamil characters.

3.1   Siamese-CNN Model

The input to the Siamese CNN model are image pairs: Image-1 and Image-2 as shown in the left of Fig. 1. These two images are passed through a ConvNet encoder to transform the input images into an embedding space represented as h_1 and h_2. The dual ConvNet encoders represent the Siamese network. Although the Siamese architecture is depicted as having dual ConvNet encoders, it basically has a single ConvNet encoder that sequentially extracts features for Image-1 and Image-2. The output of ConvNet encoder is a fully connected (FC) layer

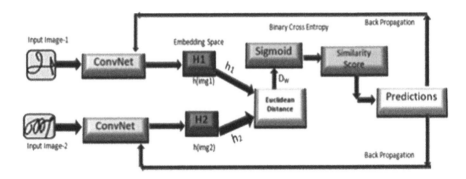

Fig. 1. The Siamese architecture

representing the embeddings. The Euclidean distance (D_w) is then computed between extracted features h_1 and h_2 and fed to a sigmoid activation function to determine the similarity between pairs of images that were input to the model.

The CNN that we used for ConvNet encoder has 2 convolutional layers, 2 pooling layers and 1 FC layer. The input layer contains 64×64 sized images. The architecture can be represented as: 64C2-MP2-64C2-MP2-48N, where nCj indicates a convolutional layer with n filters and $j \times j$ kernel, MPk refers to a max pool layers with $k \times k$ kernel and fN refers to a fully connected dense layer with 48 neurons. This way a 64×64 sized image is transformed into a 48-dimensional feature vector. Objective is to learn a similarity model that represents image pairs to have high or low similarity for pairs belonging respectively to the same or different classes. Another component of the Siamese model is the loss function which has consequential effects on the overall output produced by the model. The loss function takes Euclidean distance between h_1 and h_2 features and determines if the Siamese model made the correct decision or not. This way the weights of the model are adjusted to output optimal prediction. The objective of the model is to minimize the loss while predicted values remain as closer to true labels as possible.

3.2 Cross-entropy Loss

The cross-entropy loss is also called logarithmic loss. The predicted probability y^p through SoftMax activation will be compared with the actual values y^a and penalized accordingly.

Based on how far the difference between y^p and y^a, the cross-entropy loss will inflict a large penalty closer to 1 for large difference and small penalty closer to 0 for small difference.

As can be seen from Fig. 1 that the cross-entropy loss function will be used for adjusting the weights of the model. A perfect model built will have a cross entropy loss of 0. For binary classification as in our case (similar or dissimilar), the binary cross entropy is defined as follows:

$$L = \frac{1}{N} \left[\sum_{j=1}^{N} y^a log(P_j) - (1 - y^a)log(1 - P_j) \right] \qquad (1)$$

Where y^a is the actual value (1 or 0), P_j is the SoftMax probability of jth sample, N is the total training sample.

The Siamese CNN model has a ConvNet for feature extraction followed by a neural network for learning the similarity model. Firstly, the ConvNet encoder will be instantiated as a feature extractor. Then, Image-1 and Image-2 will be transformed to h_1 and h_2 respectively (known as embedding space) using this feature extractor. The (h_1, h_2) pair will be considered as input of the neural network model. The Euclidean distance (L2 norm) between h_1 and h_2 are computed as follows:

$$D_w = ||h1 - h2||_2 \qquad (2)$$

The Euclidean distance computed will be fed to sigmoid activation function - which will be considered as output from the neural network. Finally, the neural network model will be created with these input and output parameters. Pairwise training of the model will optimize the loss function based on these predicted output and actual ground truth values.

Finally, to check the class to which the input test image x_t belongs – we can pair images as (x_c, x_t) (where c is in range of $1, 2, 3, \cdots 156$ and t represent the class of test image x_t) and predict the class corresponding to the maximum similarity as follows:

$$c^* = argmax_c(P(x_c, x_t)) \qquad (3)$$

4   Experimental Results

In this section, we report on a series of experiments conducted to test the efficacy of Siamese architecture for the application of OCR systems. The Siamese model was used to test the efficacy of few-shot learning using the uTHCD database. The uTHCD database is a unified collection of offline and online handwritten samples collected from native Tamil speakers and it has a collection of 55000, 7870 and 28080 samples in train, validation and test sets respectively [9]. This database has approximately 600 samples in each of the 156 distinct classes of Tamil script.

The Siamese network needs positive and negative image pairs for training the similarity model. Positive pair is a pair that has samples from the same class and a negative pair has a pair of images from different classes. For every image in the training subset, we randomly pick:

- a sample from the same class for the second image (positive pair)
- a sample from a different class for the second image (negative pair)

All experiments were conducted using this database with different training subset configurations suiting the nature of the underlying test. However, for the

Fig. 2. Sample positive (P) and negative (N) pairs generated for training.

Table 1. Hyperparameter values used in the architecture

Hyperparameter	Value
Embedding Size	48
Loss function	Cross entropy
Batch size	32
Epochs	150
Activation function	ReLU and Sigmoid (last layer)
Learning rate	0.001
Batch size	64

validation set, the random draws are fixed once for all experiments to avoid validating on different datasets at each epoch.

The entire implementation was done using Tensorflow deep learning library with Keras API using Python 3.7.10 environment. The model training and evaluation was done on a GPU machine (NVIDIA GeForce MX330) running alongside an Intel i7 1.6 GHz CPU with 16 GB RAM. All models were learned with *EarlyStopping* callback in Keras to reduce overfitting.

The CNN architecture (as shown in Fig. 1) used in the Siamese model is not very deep but can extract powerful similarity features. There are several hyperparameters such as learning rate, epochs, optimizer etc. that control overall dynamics of the architecture. For the rest of the experiments, unless explicitly mentioned, the hyperparameter values are empirically fixed as shown in Table 1.

To test the effectiveness of similarity learning using the SCNN model, we conducted an experiment by considering the entire 55000 training set. For every image in the training set, we randomly created a positive pair and a negative pair resulting in a total of 110000 pairs. A corresponding label vector was generated that has either 1 or 0 to denote a positive or negative pair respectively. The pair images and corresponding label vectors were used for training the similarity using the SCNN model. Similarly, pair images were generated out of validation set (15740 pairs) and test set (56160 pairs). The Fig. 2 shows some sample positive and negative pairs.

The Siamese model used in this section resulted in a training accuracy of 90.19% with a validation accuracy of 88.04%. The plot of training and valida-tion accuracy and loss are as demonstrated in Fig. 3. It can be seen that the model converged around the 80th epoch. The model resulted in a testing accu-racy of 89.23%. It is to be noted that this experiment will result in different values for accuracy and losses depending on the image pairs randomly generated for train, test, validation sets. Hence it is important to fix the randomness of NumPy, Tensorflow and Python built-in pseudo-random generators in order to get reproducible results. Figure 4 shows similarity between random image pairs.

It can be noted that the model outputs a high and low similarity respectively for samples belonging to intra-class and inter-class image pairs. This experiment ensures that the Siamese model was successful in learning the similarity between random samples to a great extent.

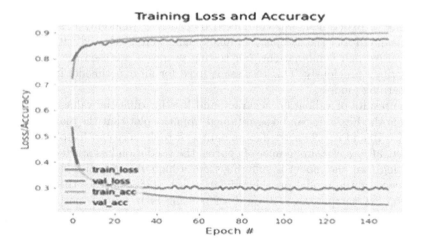

Fig. 3. Learning accuracy of Siamese architecture.

Fig. 4. Result of similarity learning for positive (top) and negative (bottom) image pairs.

The advantage of Siamese learning is in its applicability to learn a model using less, one or zero samples. This is respectively known as K-shot (few-shot), one-shot and zero-shot learning. As mentioned earlier, not all Indic scripts have adequate training samples to build a reliable OCR system. It is important to build a system that leverages maximally from the resources available to eventually reach a stage where it can be practically deployable. This is essentially investigating how well a typical Siamese based OCR performance changes with varying numbers of shots. In order to check the effectiveness of the Siamese network for this purpose, in this section, we conducted a series of experiments for few-shot learning by fixing only K number of samples from each of the 156 classes. The experiment was conducted by choosing randomly K samples from each class and for each sample, ten image pairs were generated with 5 negative and positive pair combinations. For testing purposes, we used the same subset as described previously. This test set is fixed for all experiments involving few shot learning models.

The results of validation accuracy and loss for different values of K are as shown in the Fig. 5. It can be ascertained from the plot that the Siamese models with K = 10 and K = 20 needed more data as it took more epochs to converge. In addition, after a certain number of epochs, the validation loss started to increase indicating that the model is suffering from a high-variance problem leading to divergence of the model on the validation set. This suggests that the model with too few samples (K = 10 or K = 20) using Siamese may not be adequate to develop a reliable OCR for Indic script. Rest of the models (K = 40, K = 60 and K = 80) exhibit performance that are on par with each other. Among these models, the model with K = 40 seems to be a good choice as it was able to learn sufficiently when presented with less data (40 samples per class) and there is no significant difference between results of this model with models using a higher number of samples.

Table 2 presents the optimal value of training and validation accuracy for different values of K. The testing accuracy saw an incremental improvement only when trained with rapidly increased pairs of images. The model with K = 40

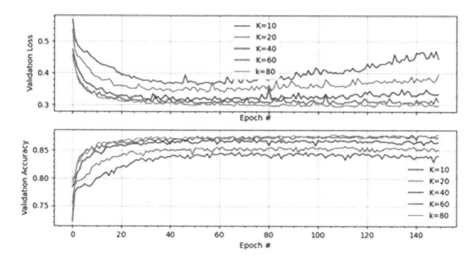

Fig. 5. The results of few-shot learning.

seems to strike a very good balance in the computational time and accuracy trade-off. Testing accuracy indicates the total number of image pairs that were correctly classified as similar or dissimilar with a threshold of 0.5. It is evident from these results that the performance metrics gradually increase with increased number of shots (varying K) as the model has access to an increased number of pairs for training.

Table 2. Result of few shot learning

Model	Number of pairs	Precision	Recall	F1-score	Validation accuracy	Test accuracy
10-shot	15600	0.8057	0.8052	0.8051	0.8396	0.8052
20-shot	31200	0.8147	0.8146	0.8146	0.8532	0.8146
40-shot	62400	0.8325	0.8323	0.8322	0.8745	0.8339
60-shot	93600	0.8404	0.8400	0.8399	0.8775	0.84001
80-shot	124800	0.8477	0.8471	0.8471	0.8881	0.8471
100-shot	156000	0.8495	0.8493	0.8493	0.8934	0.8493

5   Conclusion and Future Avenues

In this paper we have proposed the Siamese CNN for implementing few-shot learning - a mechanism that leverages a minimal number of samples to build a robust model – for the problem of Tamil OCR. We used the binary cross-entropy loss to calibrate the Siamese-CNN model. The model resulted with a test accuracy of 83.39% with 40-shot learning. Among the models we tested, the model with 40-shots (40 samples per class) achieved an optimal accuracy. The work presented in this paper can be extended in a number of ways as below which deserves further study:

- The Siamese model can be implemented using the contrastive loss function instead of just relying on the cross-entropy loss function. As this loss function is based on distance measure, it ensures semantically closer examples are embedded closer as against binary cross-entropy loss function that adjusts the weights of the model based on probability output by the model.
- Tamil script is a language where there may exist only minor inter-class variation through the presence/absence of tiny-dot, a loop, a stroke etc. This way samples from different classes look near-identical and can drastically impact the performance metrics of the Siamese model. This can be mitigated by considering 50% each of training pairs from hard and easy categories. In the hard category, for every image (base) the negative pair was formed by considering any compound characters pertaining to the same base character. An easy category is where the negative pair was composed randomly as done in all experiments in this paper. This will ensure a robust similarity model learning unlike the model that we developed only based on random samples (easy category).
- The ConvNet encoder that we utilized in the implemented Siamese model is not deep. The Siamese architecture is known to perform even better when the CNN used for feature extraction is a deep architecture. Hence, the performance can be further increased if we can fine tune the pretrained models such as VGG16, VGG19, AlexNet, ResNet etc.

The Siamese Neural network has not seen a wide-spread applicability so far in the field of Indic OCR development. We believe that the work presented in this paper would serve as a prelude for many such works based on Siamese models.

References

1. Adak, C., Marinai, S., Chaudhuri, B.B., Blumenstein, M.: Offline Bengali writer verification by PDF-CNN and Siamese net. In: 2018 13th IAPR International Workshop on Document Analysis Systems (DAS), pp. 381–386. IEEE (2018)
2. Barakat, B.K., Alasam, R., El-Sana, J.: Word spotting using convolutional Siamese network. In: 2018 13th IAPR International Workshop on Document Analysis Systems (DAS), pp. 229–234. IEEE (2018)
3. Cao, Y., Ji, H., Zhang, W., Xue, F.: Visual tracking via dynamic weighting with pyramid-redetection based Siamese networks. J. Vis. Commun. Image Represent. **65**, 102635 (2019)
4. Chaudhuri, U., Banerjee, B., Bhattacharya, A.: Siamese graph convolutional network for content based remote sensing image retrieval. Comput. Vis. Image Underst. **184**, 22–30 (2019)
5. Hosseini-Asl, E., Guha, A.: Similarity-based text recognition by deeply supervised Siamese network. arXiv preprint arXiv:1511.04397 (2015)

6. Kornblith, S., Shlens, J., Le, Q.V.: Do better imagenet models transfer better? In: Proceedings of the IEEE/CVF Conference on Computer Vision and Pattern Recognition, pp. 2661–2671 (2019)
7. Krizhevsky, A., Sutskever, I., Hinton, G.E.: ImageNet classification with deep convolutional neural networks. Adv. Neural. Inf. Process. Syst. **25**, 1097–1105 (2012)
8. de Oliveira, I.O., Fonseca, K.V., Minetto, R.: A two-stream Siamese neural network for vehicle re-identification by using non-overlapping cameras. In: 2019 IEEE International Conference on Image Processing (ICIP), pp. 669–673. IEEE (2019)
9. Shaffi, N., Hajamohideen, F.: uTHCD: a new benchmarking for Tamil handwritten OCR. arXiv preprint arXiv:2103.07676 (2021)
10. Sharma, R., Kaushik, B.: Offline recognition of handwritten Indic scripts: a state-of-the-art survey and future perspectives. Comput. Sci. Rev. **38**, 100302 (2020)
11. Sheng, W., Li, X.: Siamese denoising autoencoders for joints trajectories reconstruction and robust gait recognition. Neurocomputing **395**, 86–94 (2020)
12. Strang, G.: Linear Algebra and Learning from Data. Wellesley-Cambridge Press, Cambridge (2019)
13. Taigman, Y., Yang, M., Ranzato, M., Wolf, L.: DeepFace: closing the gap to human-level performance in face verification. In: Proceedings of the IEEE Conference on Computer Vision and Pattern Recognition, pp. 1701–1708 (2014)
14. Wang, J., Liu, W., Xing, W., Wang, L., Zhang, S.: Attention shake Siamese network with auxiliary relocation branch for visual object tracking. Neurocomputing **400**, 53–72 (2020)

A CNN Based Model for Venomous and Non-venomous Snake Classification

Nagifa Ilma Progga[1](✉)(iD), Noortaz Rezoana[1](✉)(iD),
Mohammad Shahadat Hossain[1], Raihan Ul Islam[2], and Karl Andersson[2](iD)

[1] Department of Computer Science and Engineering, University of Chittagong,
Chittagong, Bangladesh
hossain_ms@cu.ac.bd
[2] Department of Computer Science, Electrical and Space Engineering,
Luleå University of Technology, Skellefteå, Sweden
{raihan.ul.islam,karl.andersson}@ltu.se

Abstract. Snakes are curved, limbless, warm blooded reptiles of the phylum serpents. Any characteristics, including head form, body shape, physical appearance, texture of skin and eye structure, might be used to individually identify nonvenomous and venomous snakes, that are not usual among non-experts peoples. A standard machine learning methodology has also been used to create an automated categorization of species of snake dependent upon the photograph, in which the characteristics must be manually adjusted. As a result, a Deep convolutional neural network has been proposed in this paper to classify snakes into two categories: venomous and non-venomous. A set of data of 1766 snake pictures is used to implement seven Neural network with our proposed model. The amount of photographs even has been increased by utilizing various image enhancement techniques. Ultimately, the transfer learning methodology is utilized to boost the identification process accuracy even more. Five-fold cross-validating for SGD optimizer shows that the proposed model is capable of classifying the snake images with a high accuracy of 91.30%. Without Cross validation the model shows 90.50% accuracy.

Keywords: Snake · CNN · Data augmentation · Deep learning · Transfer learning · Cross validation

1 Introduction

Snakes are ectothermic, amniotic reptiles, surrounded in sepals, just like other squamates. Several snake species have skulls with a slew of joints than their reptile ancestral, allowing it to swallow predators with their extremely maneuverable jaws relatively large unlike there own heads. There are two types of snakes such as non-venomous (non-poisonous snake) and venomous (poisonous

---

N. Rezoana—equal contribution.

M. Mahmud et al. (Eds.): AII 2021, CCIS 1435, pp. 216–231, 2021.
https://doi.org/10.1007/978-3-030-82269-9_17

snake). Venomous snakes are members of the suborder Serpents and are able to develop venom that they use to attack prey, defend themselves and help digest their prey. Utilizing hollow or grooved fangs, the venom is usually released by injection, while other venomous snakes lack well-developed fangs. Non-venomous snakes, except for massive constrictor snakes such as the Green Anaconda or the Burmese Python, are generally benign to humans. Like venomous snakes, non-venomous snakes have teeth. Snake envenoming is a major, worldwide common health issue with the greatest prevalence in Southeast Asia.

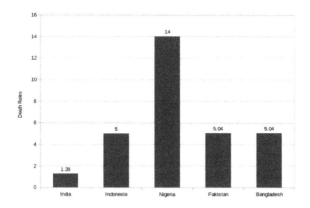

Fig. 1. Top 5 countries with the highest rate of snake bite deaths per 100,000 people

A analysis focused on 60 articles has reported that 363 victims with snake bites, both venomous (88%) and nonvenomous (12%) were diagnosed and treated if necrosis exists (15.2%) [30]. No infections were detected in patients although the antibiotics were not used. Thus, based on the analysis, it can be implied that antibiotics are present in the snake, considering the fact that very little raw data is given. Inability to identify snake from the visible characteristics is an important cause of mortality due to snake bite.

For centuries, snake venom, particularly in Chinese culture, have also been used as medicine tools. Any of the leading drugs for high blood pressure, cardiovascular disease, and heart attacks used snake venom as a blueprint. As a consequence, snake venom is often known as a mini-drug repository, with each medicine being clinically effective. For example, the FDA has licensed medicines relying on snake venom, such as Captopril® (Enalapril), Integrilin® (Eptifibatide), and Aggrastat® (Tirofiban) [24]. Aside from these approved medicines, various other snake venom materials for numerous therapeutic applications are presently in pre-clinical or clinical trials.

Snakebite envenoming is a well-known tropical disease exacerbated by a venomous snake accidentally injecting an extremely modified poison into humans. The snake's fangs, that are remodeled teeth attached to a poison glands via a inlet are used to extract the potion. Nearly 2 million residents in Asia are poisoned by snakes every year, although there are approximately 435,000 to 580,000 snake bites annually in Africa that require medication. Women, children and farmers in vulnerable remote regions in low and middle-income countries are affected by envenoming. The greatest risk exists in places where health care services are inadequate and medical facilities are insufficient.

The detection of snake types is a key aspect of the diagnosis process. Classification and detection of venomous and non-venomous snake has many dynamic applications such as: It can help the health professional in determining the best anti-venom to use. Snake venom is often known as a mini-drug repository, so by classifying the venomous snake from the non venomous snake the venom can be used to produce more drugs for mankind.

2   Related Work

The Deep Convolution Neural Network (CNN) has carried out in previous decades a number of groundbreaking findings on image recognition, object identification, semantic classification etc. [21]. Now it has become prominent in research for some day because it can handle an immense number of data [4]. CNN outperforms the machine learning approach in terms of efficiency. Classification and identification of images was an iconic machine learning issue, which was overcome through deep learning. In particular, technologies dealing with the visual information, including the biggest image classification data set (Image Net), computer vision and NLP analysis were quite impressive and the outcomes have been obtained is extraordinary. That is why we choose CNN for out study. The algorithms of deep learning are designed to imitate the role of the human brain [8]. In biological data [22,23] deep learning has been used. Also in object detection CNN has shown outstanding performance [11,27,37]. CNN has already shown remarkable effectiveness in diagnostic image recognition, such as the detection of lung cancer [14], skin cancer [28], oral cancer [18], brain tumors [10], and other diseases.

By Using object detection and a machine learning method focused on Mask Region-based Convolutional Neural Network (Mask R-CNN) has been implemented for snake species classification [7]. To discern reptile species from images, deep learning, specifically CNN, has been used [5]. Snake sting marks images were also used to identify poisonous and non-poisonous snakes using the CNN method [20].

James et al. [16] presented a semiautomatic method in order to differentiate six distinct organisms by eliminating taxonomical characteristics from the photos. There were 1,299 photographs in the dataset and 88 photos in the lowest frequent level. The outer edge taxonomical characteristics are least essential for organism recognition than the into front and side-view characteristics, according to various feature detection techniques.

In object detection and image processing, various model architectures have been evaluated. To discern 5 specific snake varieties Abdurrazaq et al. [2] used 3 distinct Convolutional Neural Network (CNN) frameworks. In this study they worked with a set of 415 pictures. There were 72 photos required for the less common snake type. The maximum outcomes were achieved by a medium-sized classification framework.

The Siamese network was used by Abeysinghe et al. [3] to categorize a comparatively limited data set that contains 200 photographs of 84 organisms from the WHO. The method discussed in their paper focuses on one-shoot learning, as 3 to 16 photos per habitat were provided in the collection of data. The outcomes collected by the automatic categorization process is lower than the exactness of human identification accuracy.

Snakebite poisoning is an overlooked environmental diseases which murders over 100,000 inhabitants and slaughters over 400,000 per year [36]. Snakebite is a frequent workplace hazard for citizens who make their living in cultivation, including those in South-East Communities in asia. An automated identification of a species of snake depending on its photograph has already been constructed, as previously mentioned. As a classifier, a several supervised machine learning technique has been implemented like Naive Bayes, Decision Tree J48, k-Nearest Neighbors, or Back-Propagation Neural Network. The requirements in the features extraction process, on the other hand, are not easy to train in conventional machine learning techniques and must be manually calibrated. As a result, throughout this study, important contributions has made in the following areas:

- A CNN based model has been proposed to classify venomous and non-venomous snake.
- Various architectures have been compared in terms of performance.
- K-fold cross validation has been applied on our proposed model with three different optimizer to improves generalization capacity.
- The system can detect both venomous and non-venomous snakes in real time, allowing non-experts to recognize snake species with greater accuracy than previously mentioned approaches.

3   Data Pre-processing

At first, we will discuss about the dataset. To initiate, the data set and model creation plan will be discussed in depth to aid in the planning of the proposed model. Following that, we'll go through the proposed model architecture simulation method in detail, as well as the training methodology for determining the best parameter modifications. Ultimately, we'll use modeling approaches to demonstrate critical flaws in visual indicators in addition to creating a reported snake more identifiable.

3.1   About Dataset

The set of data comes from kaggle.com and contains about 1766 snake images. Per photo was assigned to a category and was divided into groups by the respective class labels such as non-venomous and venomous. Since reformatting is among the most important phases of data preprocessing, all images are reformatted to 224×224 pixels. Figure 3 and Fig. 4 depicts several photographs from the benchmark dataset. Figures 3 and 4 demonstrate that there are numerous differences between venomous and non-venomous snakes in terms of physical appearances such as head structure, eye shape, skin colour, and so on. The mentioned features will aid our proposed model in learning the distinctions between poisonous and non-poisonous snakes. The set of data has been split into train, validation, and test segments in an appropriate proportion

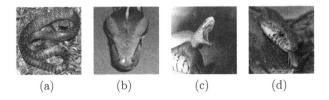

(a)   (b)   (c)   (d)

Fig. 2. Non-venomous snake image

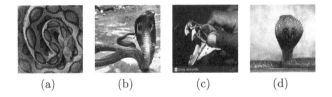

(a)   (b)   (c)   (d)

Fig. 3. Venomous snake image

3.2 Data Augmentation

It is well established that even a massive quantity of data in the datasets is needed to achieve a better result for a CNN model. The data augmentation techniques is necessary for correctly implementing a CNN architecture. This methodology prevents data manipulation and maintains the initial reliability. This technique is often used during the training process to increase the efficiency of the architecture by fixing overfitting problems. If the dataset is large enough, several features can be extracted from it and compared to unidentified data. However, if there is insufficient data, data augmentation may be implemented to boost the model's accuracy [9,15,26,33]. Through applying augmentation operations to training images, such as random rotation, shift, zoom, noise, flips, and so on, data augmentation will generate multiple pictures [33]. Every parameter has the ability to represent photos in a number of aspects and come up with particular features during the training phase, increasing the framework's effectiveness. Since our dataset is smaller in size, we implemented a variety of augmentation functions on it. For the augmentation, Image Data Generator was utilized. Figure 5 represents the primary picture as well as the augmented photos created from that. We implemented the model with 80% of the overall of the pictures and used the remaining 20% to validate the system throughout evaluation. The settings for image augmentation used in our experiment can be seen in Table 1.

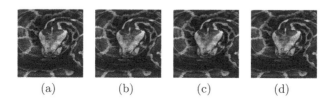

(a)   (b)   (c)   (d)

Fig. 4. Data augmentation

Table 1. Images augmentation settings

Augmentation setting	Range
Rotation	0.2
Zoom	0.1
Contrast	0.1
Horizontal flip	*True*

4   Methodology

Convolutional neural networks is inspired by neurological mechanisms. A convolutional neural system is made up of many layers, including convolution layers, pooling layers, and fully connected layers, and it uses a back-propagation algorithm to obtain features to train the model properly. Figure 6 depicts the overall research's system flow chart.

4.1   Model Construction

In this study, the framework was implemented using a Convolutional Neural Network (CNN) and data augmentation. First, the architecture uses the dataset to take the pictures. Then preprocessing begins. Then some augmentation parameters are used to enlarge the dataset. Ultimately, the enlarged set of data is

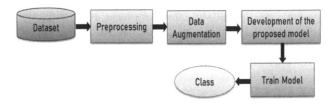

Fig. 5. System flowchart

used to forecast the class by the CNN architecture. The pictures were standardised to some extent to be properly categorized. CNN itself performed the characteristic retrieval of the pictures. We'll describe our recommended model architecture in detail in this section. The proposed method includes three basic components: feature extraction, identification, and classification. In the beginning, we include synchronized layers of convolution, activation, and max-pooling in our system design. The features are then passed into a flattened layer. The flattened attributes or features are then transferred into dense layers. In the dense layer dropout has been used to avoid overfitting. The classification process was then completed by the ultimate layer, which stated the softmax layer. The photos were provided to the model for the training process after the data augmentation. There is a CBr = iconv block in the system built, accompanied via a max pooling stratum that is three times in consonance in sequential format. Maxpooling is an efficient way of downsizing the tightly-scale photos, requiring maximal rates for each stratum, since most of the features generated are ignored by utilizing a 3×3 filter size. As discussed during the preceding analysis superimposed max pooling frames do not significantly increase over the nonoverlapping windows, so the max pooling layers used during our experiment was 2×2 with stride 2. It consists of 3 convolutionary layers, with 16 filters of 3×3 in the first convolutional layer,32 filters in the second convolutional layers and the third layer is 64 layers 3×3 in dimension. The scale of the kernel is 2. The produced features are reused by the attached activation function in the early stages to construct an unique feature map as output just after the convolution layer. In equation, convolution over an image q(x, y) is defined using a filter p(x, y).

$$p(x,y) * q(x,y) = \sum_{y=-j}^{j} \sum_{y=-k}^{k} w(m,n)f(x-m, y-n) \tag{1}$$

To generate the low-level features all layers of convolution was accompanied by the ReLU activation function. Following the previous convolution layers, the ReLU activation function was used in the hidden layer as well. ReLU has a number of advantages, the most notable of which is its ability to quickly distribute gradients. As a result, calculating the essential characteristics of CNN in the provisional mass ,reduces the chances of gradient extinction. The activating mechanism tends to perform component-by-component operations on this given input feature map, since the result tends to be the identical dimension as

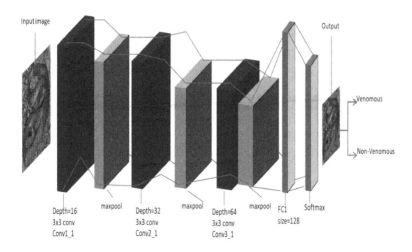

Fig. 6. Model architecture

the origin. As a result, among the most common activation functions, ReLU is being used in the all layers. ReLU [12] has been included to demonstrate that the architecture does not experience linearity, as shown in the corresponding formula:

$$R(x) = max(0, x) \tag{2}$$

The architecture is then exposed in the flattened layers to convert the feature map. From feature map generated by the previous convolution layers to complete the categorization task, a single dimensional feature vector has been constructed by flattened layer. A drop-out layer is linked following the Fully connected or hidden layer and the size of the fully connected layer is 128. This dropping layer will dump the weights of the Fully connected layer at random during training to mitigate unnecessary weight and overfitting. For our CNN model, we choose 0.2 as the dropout range for the drop out layer. The dropout layer's job is to discard 20% of the nodes in each FC layer in order to prevent overfitting [29]. The hyperparameters were fine-tuned by layering again until fault did not radically alter. In addition, the range of the dropout for the proposed model was determined by experimenting for several constants. The drop - outs range of 0.2 was considered as the best amount of the dropout layer because it tended to prevent overfitting rather than others value. In order to maximize the outcome the parameters are being adapted. Ultimately, since there are two categories the output layer contains two nodes. The softmax [32] activation function was used just after the FC layer, as shown in the following equation, to classify snake images into non-venomous and venomous categories. Figure 8 portrays the representations of the suggested model's layers.

$$Softmax(x) = \frac{e^i}{\sum_{i=0}^{i} e^i} \tag{3}$$

Model Contest	Details
1st Convolution Layer 2D	Filter Size=16,karnel size=3x3,activation=ReLU
1st MaxPooling Layer	Pooling Size= 2x2
2nd Convolution Layer 2D	Filter Size=32,karnel size=3x3,activation=ReLU
2nd MaxPooling Layer	Pooling Size= 2x2
3rd Convolution Layer 2D	Filter Size=64,karnel size=3x3,activation=ReLU
3rd MaxPooling Layer	Pooling Size= 2x2
Dropout Layer	Excludes 20% of the neurons at random
Flatten Layer	--
Fully connected Layer	Filter size=128 ,activation = ReLU
Dropout Layer	Excludes 20% of the neurons at random
Softmax Layer	2

Fig. 7. The proposed model's detailed layer representation

4.2   The Implementation Procedure

The coding for the framework was produced and implemented in Google Colab [6] using the python programming language. Keras [13], Tensorflow [1], NumPy [35], and Matplotlib [31] were the libraries utilized in the whole study. The backend of the framework was chosen as Tensorflow, and keras has been utilized to offer additional built-in functionality such as activation functions, optimizers, layers, and so on. Keras API was used to enhance the dataset. NumPy is a Python library for mathematical evaluation. Confusion matrix, split train and test files, modelcheckpoint, callback mechanism, as well as other schematic representation like confusion matrix, loss against epochs graphs, accuracy against epochs curves, and many more, are all generated using Sklearn. The matplotlib library is also needed to create visual representations of the previously mentioned diagrams, such as the confusion matrix.

5   Experimental Evaluation

The performance of the implemented model to classify photos of snakes specifically grouped into two groups, non-venomous and venomous, will be covered in this section. In addition, we will compare our proposed model to other traditional models such as Inception Net, Resnet50, VGG 16, VGG 19, Xception, MobileNet v2 and Inception Resnet V2. The outcomes of our model's k fold cross validation for different optimizers will also be articulated.

5.1   Tuning of the Hyper-parameters

Since fine-tuned hyper-parameters also have major impact on the CNN architecture's performance and they are are essential because they strongly impact the model's attitude. The Adam, Adamax, and SGD optimizers were utilized to trainIing 100 epochs for the proposed model, with a learning rate of 0.0001 with the batch size of 32. K fold cross validation has also been performed for the various optimizers. As the loss function categorical cross entropy was being used, the loss of class probability caused by the softmax function was also determined by this loss function. Finally, calculate each category's probability of occurrence. ModelCheckpoint has been added as a callback function as well.

5.2   K-Fold Cross Validation

To test our model, we attempt 5 fold cross-validation. Due to the general operational overhead, this phase is normally avoided in CNNs. The dataset is divided into three sections using K-folds cross-validation. Fold1 is composed of part 1 as a training set, part 2 as a validation set, and part 3 as testing set, while fold2 is consists of part 2, part 1 and part 3 as a training, validation and testing set respectively. Thus, the fold continues until it reaches 5 folds, with each fold containing unique training, validation, and testing datasets. The K-fold cross validation approach accounts for the utilization of various training and testing data, which reduces overfitting and improves generalization capacity. As a consequence, we may generalize our outcomes over the dataset.

5.3   Result

Figure 8 depicts the accuracy of the proposed model as compared to other standard Convolution neural networks like Inception Net, VGG 19, Resnet50, Xception Net, MobileNet v2, Inception Resnet V2 and VGG 16. Despite providing a dataset with a limited number of photographs, the designed model produces a high categorization accuracy cpmpared to other CNN models. As shown in the Fig. 9 Inception Net, VGG 19, Resnet50, Xception Net, MobileNet v2, Inception Resnet V2 and VGG 16 has 82.38%, 43.75%, 81.81%, 80.94%, 82.35%, 89.62% and 62.50% accuracy respectively. Our model outperformed then these models with 90.50% accuracy. The best result corresponds to the model we introduced, based on the current Inception Net, VGG 19, Resnet50, Xception Net, MobileNet v2, Inception Resnet V2, and VGG 16 models. As a result, it can be concluded that the developed framework outperforms the other ones. The performance of all evaluation models, as seen in Fig. 8, indicate that the method is superior to others. Figure 9 compares the proposed model's accuracy and loss curve to those of other traditional CNN models. From the shape of the curves in this mentioned figure, we can see that other convolutional models have a propensity to overfit or underfit, while our proposed model seems to have a good fit. Our proposed model's high accuracy and low loss have already been considered the best case scenario for any CNN model. Figure 10 shows the detection performance of the

Model Name	Accuracy
Inception Net	82.38
VGG19	43.75
Resnet50	81.81
Xception Net	80.94
MobileNet v2	82.35
Inception-Resnet-v2	89.62
VGG16	62.50
Proposed Model	90.50

Fig. 8. Accuracy of proposed model & other traditional models

proposed model and shows the detection result of the test dataset's in two classes: venomous and nonvenomous. In comparison to the previously listed other CNN models, 40 images were arbitrarily checked and 9 of those being seen in Fig. 6. The identification performance for the developed method is really exceedingly decent. The confusion matrices of the Inception Net, VGG 19, Resnet50, Xception Net, MobileNet v2, Inception Resnet V2, and VGG 16 models, as well as the suggested system, are shown in Fig. 11. For our adapted CNN model, the diagonal magnitude of the confusion matrices in both classes is greater than the other models. That is, the proposed model will precisely distinguish the same number of test samples from our test dataset as the current Neural network model. As a result, our model successfully outperformed the other conventional Neural network model in this area as well. Finally, Fig. 12 demonstrates the K-fold cross validation result of the proposed model utilizing three optimizers: Adamax, Adam, and SGD. By using adamax optimizer for K fold cross validation the validation accuracy and the testing accuracy for fold-1 is 83.58% & 86.87%, for fold-2 it is 81.83% & 82.52%, for fold-3 it is 77.44% & 80.07%, for fold-4 it is 84.24% & 84.96& and for fold-5 it is 86.87% & 83.20% respectively. For adam optimizer the validation accuracy and the testing accuracy for fold-1 is 86.56% & 89.22%, for fold-2 it is 87.57% & 88.04%, for fold-3 it is 83.35% & 84.42%, for fold-4 it is 87.78% & 90.48% and for fold-5 it is 84.36% & 88.43% respectively. For SGD optimizer the validation accuracy and the testing accuracy for fold-1 is 84.85% & 85.78%, for fold-2 it is 88.30% & 89.67%, for fold-3 it is 84.78% & 85.61%, for fold-4 it is 83.77% & 88.04% , and for fold-5 it is 87.73% & 91.30 respectively. The SGD optimizer in fold-5 produces better outcomes for the implemented model, as well as the other results are also quite satisfactory. Also it demonstrates that the accuracy of the classification model is unaffected by the training data.

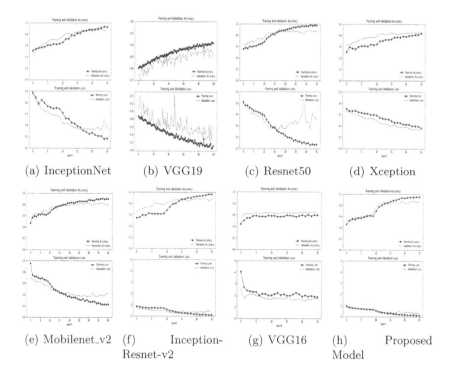

Fig. 9. Accuracy and loss curve

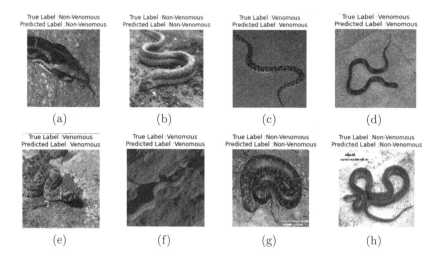

Fig. 10. Result of detection produced by the proposed model

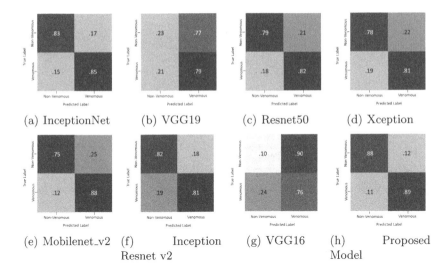

Fig. 11. Confusion matrix of the models

	Optimizer	Validation Accuracy	Testing Accuracy
Fold 1	Adamax	83.58	86.87
Fold 2	Adamax	81.83	82.52
Fold 3	Adamax	77.44	80.07
Fold 4	Adamax	84.24	84.96
Fold 5	Adamax	86.87	83.20

(a) adamax Optimizer

	Optimizer	Validation Accuracy	Testing Accuracy
Fold 1	Adam	86.56	89.22
Fold 2	Adam	87.57	88.04
Fold 3	Adam	83.35	84.42
Fold 4	Adam	87.78	90.48
Fold 5	Adam	84.36	88.43

(b) Adam Optimizer

	Optimizer	Validation Accuracy	Testing Accuracy
Fold 1	SGD	84.85	85.78
Fold 2	SGD	88.30	89.67
Fold 3	SGD	84.78	85.61
Fold 4	SGD	83.77	88.04
Fold 5	SGD	87.73	91.30

(c) SGD Optimizer

Fig. 12. K-Fold cross validation for proposed model using different optimizer

6   Epilogue and Future Work

A new convolutional neural network-based architecture for detecting and classifying venomous and non-venomous snakes was suggested during this whole study. The framework's ability to acquire snake features using neural network blocks is clearly demonstrated. In comparison to the various possibly the best Convolutional neural network frameworks Inception Net, VGG 19, Resnet50, Xception Net, MobileNet v2, Inception Resnet V2, and VGG 16, the architecture has remarkable categorization accuracy.

This study looks at how to develop and create a venomous and nonvenomous snake classification model that could help mankind. Snake venomous can be used as medicinal tools by distinguishing between venomous and non-venomous snakes. Snakebite disease may be minimized by identifying the species of snake and administering appropriate treatment.

The suggested solution greatly outshines state-of-the-art frameworks, with a dramatic increase in accuracy of 90.50%, according to the experimental research review. In addition, the model performs admirably in terms of K fold cross validation outcomes. It would have been more useful in upcoming analysis if we perform a grid hunt on the hyper-parameters and find the most suitable number of parameter values for K fold cross validation. Finally, we believe that the current findings would hopefully resolve unique stimulation in recognizing additional snake images and categorizing them in Artificial intelligence based environments, particularly in medical application. To create our suggested structure more reliable and authenticated, more analysis should be done to evaluate and gather a diverse data set with significant quantities of information about snake photographs. Furthermore, many additional Neural networks, such as DenseNet, EfficientNet, and others, can be used to enhance information horizons, and the model's output can be compared to that of other mainstream machine learning techniques. We will try to include more pictures of snake in future captured in different environment and lightening to analyze the model performance on those images. Also an integration of data-driven (CNN) and knowledge-driven (BRBES) approach can be proposed to analyze risk assessment of a snake bite in the human body [17,19,25,34].

References

1. Abadi, M., et al.: Tensorflow: a system for large-scale machine learning. In: 12th {USENIX} Symposium on Operating Systems Design and Implementation ({OSDI} 2016), pp. 265–283 (2016)
2. Abdurrazaq, I.S., Suyanto, S., Utama, D.Q.: Image-based classification of snake species using convolutional neural network. In: 2019 International Seminar on Research of Information Technology and Intelligent Systems (ISRITI), pp. 97–102. IEEE (2019)
3. Abeysinghe, C., Welivita, A., Perera, I.: Snake image classification using siamese networks. In: Proceedings of the 2019 3rd International Conference on Graphics and Signal Processing, pp. 8–12 (2019)
4. Albawi, S., Mohammed, T.A., Al-Zawi, S.: Understanding of a convolutional neural network. In: 2017 International Conference on Engineering and Technology (ICET), pp. 1–6. IEEE (2017)
5. Annesa, O.D., Kartiko, C., Prasetiadi, A., et al.: Identification of reptile species using convolutional neural networks (CNN). Jurnal RESTI (Rekayasa Sistem Dan Teknologi Informasi) 4(5), 899–906 (2020)
6. Bisong, E.: Google colaboratory. In: Building Machine Learning and Deep Learning Models on Google Cloud Platform, pp. 59–64. Springer (2019)
7. Bloch, L., et al.: Combination of image and location information for snake species identification using object detection and efficientnets. CLEF working notes (2020)
8. Chauhan, R., Ghanshala, K.K., Joshi, R.: Convolutional neural network (CNN) for image detection and recognition. In: 2018 First International Conference on Secure Cyber Computing and Communication (ICSCCC), pp. 278–282. IEEE (2018)

9. Chowdhury, R.R., Hossain, M.S., Ul Islam, R., Andersson, K., Hossain, S.: Bangla handwritten character recognition using convolutional neural network with data augmentation. In: 2019 Joint 8th International Conference on Informatics, Electronics & Vision (ICIEV) and 2019 3rd International Conference on Imaging, Vision & Pattern Recognition (icIVPR), pp. 318–323. IEEE (2019)

10. Díaz-Pernas, F.J., Martínez-Zarzuela, M., Antón-Rodríguez, M., González-Ortega, D.: A deep learning approach for brain tumor classification and segmentation using a multiscale convolutional neural network. In: Healthcare, vol. 9, p. 153. Multidisciplinary Digital Publishing Institute (2021)

11. Galvez, R.L., Bandala, A.A., Dadios, E.P., Vicerra, R.R.P., Maningo, J.M.Z.: Object detection using convolutional neural networks. In: TENCON 2018–2018 IEEE Region 10 Conference, pp. 2023–2027. IEEE (2018)

12. Glorot, X., Bordes, A., Bengio, Y.: Deep sparse rectifier neural networks. In: Proceedings of the fourteenth international conference on artificial intelligence and statistics, pp. 315–323. JMLR Workshop and Conference Proceedings (2011)

13. Gulli, A., Pal, S.: Deep Learning with Keras. Packt Publishing Ltd., Birmingham (2017)

14. Heuvelmans, M.A., et al.: Lung cancer prediction by deep learning to identify benign lung nodules. Lung Cancer **154**, 1–4 (2021)

15. Islam, M.Z., Hossain, M.S., Ul Islam, R., Andersson, K.: Static hand gesture recognition using convolutional neural network with data augmentation. In: 2019 Joint 8th International Conference on Informatics, Electronics & Vision (ICIEV) and 2019 3rd International Conference on Imaging, Vision & Pattern Recognition (icIVPR), pp. 324–329. IEEE (2019)

16. James, A.P., Mathews, B., Sugathan, S., Raveendran, D.K.: Discriminative histogram taxonomy features for snake species identification. HCIS **4**(1), 1–11 (2014)

17. Jamil, M.N., Hossain, M.S., Ul Islam, R., Andersson, K.: A belief rule based expert system for evaluating technological innovation capability of high-tech firms under uncertainty. In: 2019 Joint 8th International Conference on Informatics, Electronics & Vision (ICIEV) and 2019 3rd International Conference on Imaging, Vision & Pattern Recognition (icIVPR), pp. 330–335. IEEE (2019)

18. Jeyaraj, P.R., Nadar, E.R.S.: Computer-assisted medical image classification for early diagnosis of oral cancer employing deep learning algorithm. J. Cancer Res. Clin. Oncol. **145**(4), 829–837 (2019)

19. Kabir, S., Islam, R.U., Hossain, M.S., Andersson, K.: An integrated approach of belief rule base and deep learning to predict air pollution. Sensors **20**(7), 1956 (2020)

20. Kamalraj, R.: Deep learning model for identifying snakes by using snakes' bite marks. In: 2020 International Conference on Computer Communication and Informatics (ICCCI), pp. 1–4. IEEE (2020)

21. Li, Y., Hao, Z., Lei, H.: Survey of convolutional neural network. J. Comput. Appl. **36**(9), 2508–2515 (2016)

22. Mahmud, M., Kaiser, M.S., McGinnity, T.M., Hussain, A.: Deep learning in mining biological data. Cogn. Comput. **13**(1), 1–33 (2021)

23. Mahmud, M., Kaiser, M.S., Hussain, A., Vassanelli, S.: Applications of deep learning and reinforcement learning to biological data. IEEE Trans. Neural Netw. Learn. Syst. **29**(6), 2063–2079 (2018)

24. Mohamed Abd El-Aziz, T., Soares, A.G., Stockand, J.D.: Snake venoms in drug discovery: valuable therapeutic tools for life saving. Toxins **11**(10), 564 (2019)

25. Monrat, A.A., Islam, R.U., Hossain, M.S., Andersson, K.: A belief rule based flood risk assessment expert system using real time sensor data streaming. In: 2018 IEEE 43rd Conference on Local Computer Networks Workshops (LCN Workshops), pp. 38–45. IEEE (2018)
26. Progga, N.I., Hossain, M.S., Andersson, K.: A deep transfer learning approach to diagnose covid-19 using x-ray images. In: 2020 IEEE International Women in Engineering (WIE) Conference on Electrical and Computer Engineering (WIECON-ECE), pp. 177–182. IEEE (2020)
27. Ren, S., He, K., Girshick, R., Sun, J.: Faster r-cnn: Towards real-time object detection with region proposal networks. arXiv preprint arXiv:1506.01497 (2015)
28. Rezaoana, N., Hossain, M.S., Andersson, K.: Detection and classification of skin cancer by using a parallel CNN model. In: 2020 IEEE International Women in Engineering (WIE) Conference on Electrical and Computer Engineering (WIECON-ECE), pp. 1–7. IEEE (2020)
29. Srivastava, N., Hinton, G., Krizhevsky, A., Sutskever, I., Salakhutdinov, R.: Dropout: a simple way to prevent neural networks from overfitting. J. Mach. Learn. Res. **15**(1), 1929–1958 (2014)
30. Terry, P., Mackway-Jones, K.: Antibiotics in non-venomous snakebite. Emerg. Med. J. **19**(2), 142–142 (2002). https://emj.bmj.com/content/19/2/142.1
31. Tosi, S.: Matplotlib for Python Developers. Packt Publishing Ltd., Birmingham (2009)
32. Tüske, Z., Tahir, M.A., Schlüter, R., Ney, H.: Integrating gaussian mixtures into deep neural networks: softmax layer with hidden variables. In: 2015 IEEE International Conference on Acoustics, Speech and Signal Processing (ICASSP), pp. 4285–4289. IEEE (2015)
33. Uddin Ahmed, T., Hossain, M.S., Alam, M., Andersson, K., et al.: An integrated CNN-RNN framework to assess road crack. In: 2019 22nd International Conference on Computer and Information Technology (ICCIT) (2019)
34. Ul Islam, R., Andersson, K., Hossain, M.S.: A web based belief rule based expert system to predict flood. In: Proceedings of the 17th International conference on information integration and web-based applications & services, pp. 1–8 (2015)
35. Van Der Walt, S., Colbert, S.C., Varoquaux, G.: The numpy array: a structure for efficient numerical computation. Comput. Sci. Eng. **13**(2), 22–30 (2011)
36. Warrell, D.A., et al.: Guidelines for the management of snake-bites. Guidelines for the management of snake-bites (2010)
37. Yanagisawa, H., Yamashita, T., Watanabe, H.: A study on object detection method from manga images using CNN. In: 2018 International Workshop on Advanced Image Technology (IWAIT), pp. 1–4. IEEE (2018)

Recognition of Dysfluency in Speech: A Bidirectional Long-Short Term Memory Based Approach

N. A. Vinay[1]($\boxtimes$), S. H. Bharathi[1], and V. N. Manjunath Aradhya[2]

[1] School of ECE, REVA University, Bangalore, India
bharathish@reva.edu.in
[2] Department of Computer Applications, JSS Science and Technology University,
Mysuru, Karnataka, India
aradhya@sjce.ac.in

Abstract. Speech recognition plays a significant role in the human-machine interaction process, in which the first machine will search suitable keywords to act with help of Automatic Speech Recognition (ASR) system. But, if there is any discontinuity or dysfluency in speech then the Automatic Speech Recognition (ASR) system considers those words as out of vocabulary words, for such irregular structured speech machines cannot be able to perform the task as per the commands. In this paper, recognition of such speech discontinuity or dysfluency is done by using Bidirectional Long-Short Term Memory (Bi-LSTM) Recurrent Neural Network (RNN). The proposed work concentrates on recognition of dysfluency based on Mel-frequency Cepstral Coefficients- Shifted Delta Cepstral (MFCC-SDC) feature vectors. The datasets consist of 14 female speakers and 6 Male speakers taken from UCLASS database for testing and training the neural network. The proposed algorithm can recognize dysfluencies like prolongation, repetition, and blockage effectively with the highest accuracy of 96%.

Keywords: Bi-LSTM · MFCC-SDC · RNN · Prolongation · Repetition · Blockage

1 Introduction

Speech is one of the useful ways of communication which allows us to communicate effectively; this enhances the sharing of information or knowledge among individuals or group. It is defined as a group of words or phonemes, called Vocabulary. In general, as given by experts that an ordinary person can understand and use an average of 60K words oh his local language for communication. But in the recent development of technology this communication is extended up to the recognition of speech by Machines, which will work according to human commands. In machines the recognition of speech is handled by Automatic Speech Recognition (ASR) system, if the machine is not trained properly the work

© Springer Nature Switzerland AG 2021
M. Mahmud et al. (Eds.): AII 2021, CCIS 1435, pp. 232–244, 2021.
https://doi.org/10.1007/978-3-030-82269-9_18

assigned for a particular command to the machine will be affected. This happens when speech consists of out of vocabulary words, due to some noise or discontinuity is speech. The proposed work mainly concentrates on the identification of such dysfluent speech using Neural Networks. The neural networks consist of Artificial Neurons (Same as human Biological Brain Neurons), to process the speech and recognize properly, by using mathematical models. The neural network processes the features in three different layers in which the first layer is Input layer which can take the features of speech as an input, the intermediate layer is hidden layer which process the output of first layer and it maps m-dimensional vector to n-dimensional space to the output layer in proper order, thus it is referred as Self Organizing Map (SOM). The process of speech recognition flow is as shown in Fig. 1.

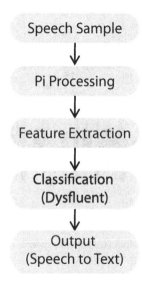

Fig. 1. Speech processing steps

The speech is recorded in an acoustic room with a frequency 41 kHz, but it is down sampled to 8 kHz because at higher and lower frequencies the sound is not audible for the human ear. Speech pre-processing normally includes noise filtering, smoothing, endpoint detection, framing, windowing, reverberation canceling an echo removing. From the preprocessed speech sample, the features re extracted using the most commonly used feature extraction technique Mel-frequency Cepstrum Coefficient which detects the endpoint of each phrase. Then, dysfluent speech is classified using Neural Network and converted to fluent or continuous speech for real-time applications.

2   Feature Extraction

2.1   Speech Representation

The best way to represent the speech is, in the time domain as a signal and as a spectrogram in the frequency domain. But, in time domain will get the duration of speech, in the frequency domain the relevant information like the pitch is obtained. The complete speech sample is split into different frames with a 50% overlap for feature extraction in frequency domain. The representation of speech in time domain and frequency domain is as shown in Fig. 2.

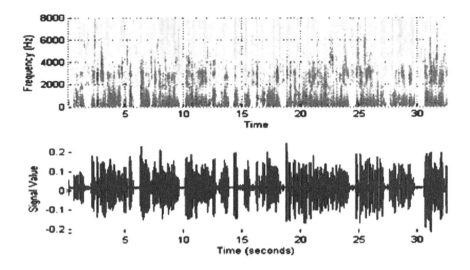

Fig. 2. Spectrogram of speech sample.

2.2   Mel-Frequency Cepstrum Coefficient

The frequency of recorded speech sample 44100 Hz, but the speech signal constantly varies concerning both time and amplitude, thus insertion of high-frequency speech sample in a short time scale is very difficult, hence it is down sampled to 8 KHz, for which human ears are sensitive. Thus, if the frequency of the speech sample is above or below 8 kHz spectral feature estimation is not conceivable. Thus, the complete speech sample is split into frames of total frame length 240 (120 frames are overlapped) each. After splitting up in to frames, the spectral density of a spectrum is computed for each frame, which is referred to as Power Spectral Density (PSD). The value of PSD changes as frequency changes, PSD gives more information required for Automatic Speech Recognition (ASR) system. Since the human ear cannot differentiate the phonemes of two closely spaced frequencies, the PSD of all the frames is summed up and total energy is calculated at different frequencies [23]. Let $X_i(n)$, $n = 1, 2, \ldots N$, the energy of the i-th frame audio sample of length N, is calculated according to the equation [11].

$$E(i) = \frac{1}{N} \sum_{n=1}^{N} |X_i(n)|^2 \tag{1}$$

C_i is the spectral centroid of the i-th frame defined at the center spectrum [21].

$$C_i = \sum_{n=1}^{N} \frac{(k+1)X_i(K)}{X_i(K)} \tag{2}$$

Where, $i = 1, 2, ... N$ the DFT coefficient of i-th small frame is represented by $X(k)$, length of the frame by N. Energy features of higher values indicates the presence of voice; therefore, the value of spectral centroid varies rapidly for speech regions or voiced regions in the sample of consideration.

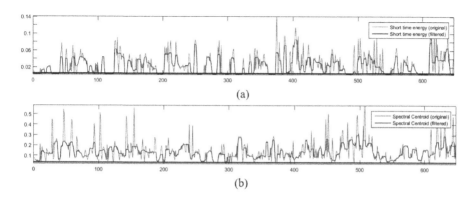

Fig. 3. Spectral centroid of original and filtered speech.

Based on these energy features silent/un-voiced regions and voiced regions are identified easily because the energy value of the voiced region is greater than the un-voiced segments. Figure 3 (a) shows the sequence of the signal's energy. In Fig. 3 (b), the spectral centroid sequence is presented also the endpoint of each phrase is recognized based on energy values. The Voice Activity Detection (VAD) [13,24], gives endpoint of each frame of speech; initially it differentiates the voiced and non-voiced regions, then determine the starting point and ending point of the speech. The detection of endpoint plays a major role in speech recognition because 50% of the errors are occurred in speech recognition due to inefficient recognition of endpoints. In the proposed work endpoint of each frame is determined based on its Energy and spectral centroid.

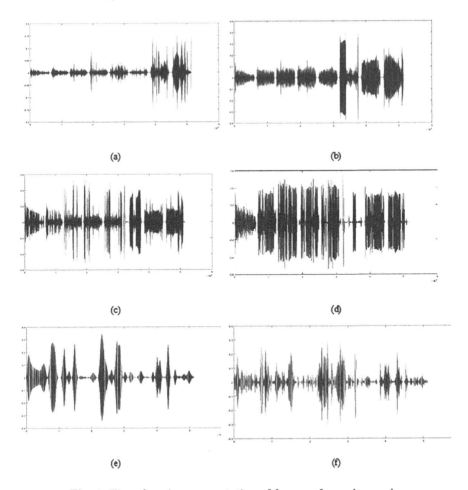

Fig. 4. Time domain representation of frames of speech sample.

The speech samples taken for identification of dysfluency includes repetition and prolongation of syllables. The process of recognition endpoint of each sample is done by fixing the thresholds: T1 T2, T3..., based on the energy sequence and the spectral centroid sequence respectively as shown in Fig. 4 from (a) to (f). In Mel-Filter Bank initially, filters are very narrow and gives the energy value 0 Hz and as the frequency increases the width of filters are also get wider, which affects the loudness of the speech (in linear scale) to avoid this logarithmic value of energy is considered which normalizes the variation of loudness of speech [22]. Normalization of loudnees is achived by keeping linear scale values in a Mel-Scale which relates received frequency and pitch of a processed speech to actual or original measured frequency. The compression from linear scale to Mel-scale incorporates the features to hear the sound properly. The conversion of a linear scale to Mel-scale is given by equation [1]:

$$f_{mel} = 2595 \log(f/100 + 1) \tag{3}$$

Since Mel filter banks are overlapped as in Fig. 4 the energy of the filter banks is quite interrelated with each other hence Discrete Cosine Transform (DCT) is applied to decor-relate the energies so that the performance of ASR is improved. The DCT is defined by [10]:

$$D_i(m) = \sum_{n=0}^{M} L(m) \cos\left[\pi m\left(\frac{n - 0.5}{M}\right)\right] \tag{4}$$

Where $L(m) = \ln \sum_{k=0}^{(N-1)} |PS|^2 B_m(k))$, indicates M-Number of filters and $0 < m \leq M$.

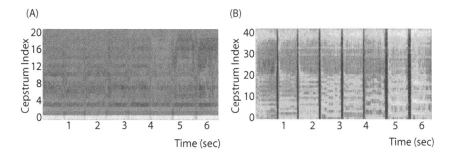

Fig. 5. Log Mel-filter bank energy and normalized MFCC's

The output of the Discrete Cosine Transform (DCT) gives a compressed form of the filter banks. In the proposed work 12 resultant cepstral coefficients are retained and the rest are discarded because the coefficients alter the filter bank coefficients rapidly and also do not contribute to Automatic Speech Recognition (ASR) process. The normalized MFCC's spectrum and lo Mel-Filter bank energy spectrum are shown in Fig. 5.

Finally, the MFCC's represents the auditory features which fed as input to the recognition system, but for dysfluent speech recognition shifted delta cepstral (SDC) coefficients are derived from the MFCC's calculated for dysfluent speech [1]. The native language recognition system, speech recognition system accuracy can be upgraded by using the SDCs as defined in Eq. (5) [6]. The shifted delta cepstral (SDC) coefficients for the N-dimensional cepstral feature vector are obtained by linking K blocks of delta coefficients as given in Eq. (5) [7].

$$\Delta a(t, i) = a(t + iV + d) - a(t + iV - d) \tag{5}$$

SDC features are typically written as N-d-P-k where: The number of cepstral coefficients in each speech frame is represented by N, advancement of time and delay for delta computation is represented by d, time difference between succeeding speech frames is represented by P and the number of frames that are linked to generate final vector is represented by K Finally, the structure of 12-1-9-12 SDC parameters are computed and linked with fixed coefficients, which gives 128-dimensional MFCC input vector. Then the resultant MFCC-SDC features are stored in vector as:

$$F_{CC} = F_{cc1}, F_{cc2}, F_{cc3}, F_{cc4}, \ldots, F_{cc56} \qquad (6)$$

Further, based on MFCC-SDC feature vectors continuous speech and dysfluent speech is classified by using Recurrent Neural Network.

3   Classification Using Recurrent Neural Networks

A Recurrent Neural Network (RNN) is a type of Artificial Neural Network (ANN) which is suitable to categorize progressive time data and use patterns to expect the following forthcoming consequence and application of neural network can be found in [14,15]. Hence, it is used widely in Speech Recognition and Natural Language Processing. Compare, to Deep Neural Network (DNN) and Multilayer Perceptron (MLP), in RNN weights and bias of the hidden layers are the same hence each of these layers performs conventionally and can combine each other [14,20].

For the prediction of the next word in sequence in a complete sentence, RNN utilizes the "memory cells", which stores the information about the word or a sequence that has been occurred. Also the application NN in detection infection in human body is explained in [15]. For example, to classify 5 words in a sentence, the network would be unfolded into a 5-layer where each layer is dedicated layer for each word. One demerit of standard RNN is, the newly generated gradients will replace the previous gradients, which damages the memory of the previous layers. Then it takes more time to compute one complete sentence and hence it becomes more expensive.

To avoid this, Long Short-Term Memory (LSTM) RRN is used, to categorize the data into short term and long-term memory cells. This allows RNN to identify which data is needed for further prediction and it decides which data has to be memorized and looped back into the network.

Hence LSTM is referred to as a special type of RNN, in LSTM each layer has inputs and outputs and the information in the network is controlled by input gates. The internal state (a^t) is the basic element of the cell which is controlled by the multiple units: input gates (g^t), output gates (h^t) and forward gate (e^t). The input of the LSTM block is represented by Eq. (5) and input, outputs, state unit and gates are given from Eqs. (7) to (12) respectively [9,16,16].

$$l^t = \tanh(w_z X^t + M_z d^{t-1} + n_z) \qquad (7)$$

$$g^t = \rho(w_1 X^t + M_1 d^{t-1} + V_1 \odot a^{t-1} + n_1) \qquad (8)$$

$$e^t = \rho(w_e X^t + M_f d^{t-1} + V_f \odot a^{t-1} + n_f) \qquad (9)$$

$$a^t = g^t \odot l^t + e^t \odot a^{t-1} \tag{10}$$

$$h^t = \rho(w_h X^t + M_h d^{t-1} + V_h \odot a^t + n_h) \tag{11}$$

$$d^t = h^t \odot \tanh(a^t) \tag{12}$$

Where ρ is a logistic sigmoid function, g^t is an input, h^t is an output, e^t is forget gate and a^t is an internal state vectors, n is a bias vector, weight vectors are represented as V and recurrent weight matrices are represented as M, at time t input vectors are represented by X^t, w are input weight vectors, tanh and $\odot$ is the element-wise product of the vectors. In the human and machine communication process, each frame i.e., previous, present and future of speech plays a significant role hence it is necessary to use Bidirectional LSTM (Bi-LSTM) in speech recognition. The Bi-LSTM is a multi-layer neural network, which process the frames in two distinct hidden layers (i.e., forward layer and backward layer). The first hidden layer will take input features as-it-is and the second layer will take the sequence in reverse order. Then the output layer will concatenate the values generated by these two separate hidden layers [9].

When the various layers of LSTM RNN are arranged on one above the other it results in the forming of Deep LSTM RNN structure. In the deep network, the output of one layer will be given input to the next layer; layer certifies that it receives the input from forward and backward layers of the previous layer.

In recent years recurrent neural network and LSTM has gained popularity in various applications [2–5,8,17–19] To process the classified data and more complex data in deep Bi-LSTM RNN, multiple hidden layers are adopted. Therefore, in this proposed work 256 hidden layers are fixed for forward and backward direction LSTM. The performance of a neural network depends on the number of hidden units used. A good machine learning model aims to simplify the trained to predict future data, but few hidden units affect the performance of a model in terms of Overfitting and Underfitting. Overfitting problem occurs when the random fluctuation in training data is provided to network and if the model is get trained for that noisy data only, this affects the performance of the network while testing the model [3–5]. Underfitting refers to a model that can neither model the training data nor simplify to new data, this will create errors while training and validating the data. Thus the number of hidden units should be optimized to reduce these kinds of errors, For this optimization, much research has been carried out but in most cases, the neural network is optimized with a different combination of hidden units and layers [12]. In the proposed work, this problem is fixed by adjusting the number of neurons during the testing process. In Fig. 6, the voice and non-voiced region of a speech are classified effectively using Bi-LSTM RNN as shown in Fig. 6(d). A type dysfluency that hampers the human-machine interaction is Blockage (silence or pause) is recognized effectively by using Bi-LSTM RNN as shown in Fig. 6(d) and another kind dysfluency specifically prolongation of a word is identified based on Zero Crossing Rate (ZCR). For this experiment, a female speech sample is taken from the UCLASS database.

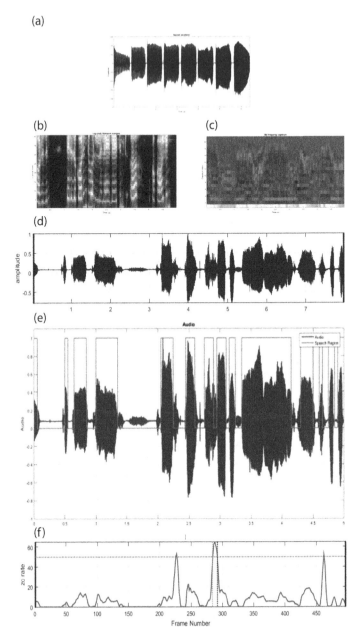

Fig. 6. (a) Original speech (b) log spectrum of energy in Mel scale (c) MFCC's spectrum (d) speech sample having blockage or silence as dysfluency (e) identification of dysfluency (blockage) of speech sample (a) (f) identification of prolongation based on ZCR.

Likewise, this approach is carried out for different speech samples for identification of dysfluency for speakers which is tabulated in Table 1.

Table 1. Training and testing of different dysfluencies

Utterance taken	Utterances trained	Utterances tested	Type of dysfluency detected
1280	430	384	Prolongation
589820	58982	17694	Prolongation and repetition
518889	51888	1556	Blockage and prolongation
8000	800	240	Blockage

For testing and training the network, totally 13 speech samples are collected from different speakers (14 to 28 is 1 s to 5 s. For the period of experimentation for the recognition of dysfluency, the accuracy of recognition depends on the number of hidden layers adopted. The accuracy and number of hidden layers used as shown in Fig. 7(a). From Fig. 7(a), it is observed that the accuracy is improved as the number of hidden layers increases and the highest accuracy is obtained with 3 hidden layers.

The minimum number neurons required in each layer are decided after identifying the number of hidden layers. During the testing process, neurons are distributed equally in each layer and for MFCC features 3 layers are used. Figure 7(b) shows the hidden layer comparison with the number of neurons; from this figure it is observed that 3 layers with 256 neurons perform better with MFCC features.

The recognition accuracy achieved by the enhanced MFCC SDC feature-based BiLSTM model on the training and validation data at different training epochs is shown in Fig. 7(c).

The accuracy of system with respect to duration of test dysfluent utterances is shown in the Fig. 7(d). The accuracy of each tested data is computed by segmenting the tested data into six groups based on its duration. It is apparent from Fig. 7(d) that accuracy of the speech recognition system improves with the duration of test utterances, so a consistent system can be developed when lengthier test utterances are available.

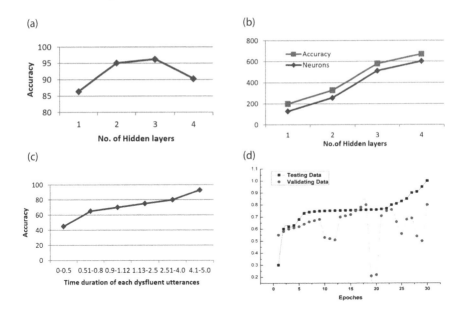

Fig. 7. (a) Effect of hidden layers on accuracy, (b) number of hidden layers and number of neurons, (c) recognition accuracy (d) accuracy of recognition of dysfluent utterances.

4   Conclusion

This proposed work recognized the three dysfluencies (prolongation, repetition, and blockage) effectively with 512 neurons at the third hidden layer for 14 female speakers and 6 Male speakers and gives efficiency of 96%. Further, it can be extended to recognize the same dysfluency in more real-time samples with a noisy environment and also concentrate on articulatory features can significantly improve the performance of automatic speech recognition systems.

References

1. Adeeba, F., Hussain, S.: Native language identification in very short utterances using bidirectional long short-term memory network. IEEE Access **7**, 17098–17110 (2019)
2. Al Banna, M.H., et al.: Attention-based bi-directional long-short term memory network for earthquake prediction. IEEE Access **9**, 56589–56603 (2021)
3. Al Banna, M.H., et al.: Application of artificial intelligence in predicting earthquakes: state-of-the-art and future challenges. IEEE Access **8**, 192880–192923 (2020)
4. Al Nahian, M.J., et al.: Towards artificial intelligence driven emotion aware fall monitoring framework suitable for elderly people with neurological disorder. In: Mahmud, M., Vassanelli, S., Kaiser, M.S., Zhong, N. (eds.) BI 2020. LNCS, vol. 12241, pp. 275–286. Springer, Cham (2020). https://doi.org/10.1007/978-3-030-59277-6_25

5. Al Nahian, M.J., et al.: Towards an accelerometer-based elderly fall detection system using cross-disciplinary time series features. IEEE Access **9**, 39413–39431 (2021)
6. Chen, X., et al.: Recurrent neural network language model adaptation for multi-genre broadcast speech recognition. In: Sixteenth Annual Conference of the International Speech Communication Association (2015)
7. Dinkel, H., Qian, Y., Yu, K.: Investigating raw wave deep neural networks for end-to-end speaker spoofing detection. IEEE/ACM Trans. Audio Speech Lang. Process. **26**(11), 2002–2014 (2018)
8. Fabietti, M., et al.: Artifact detection in chronically recorded local field potentials using long-short term memory neural network. In: 2020 IEEE 14th International Conference on Application of Information and Communication Technologies (AICT), pp. 1–6. IEEE (2020)
9. Gelly, G., Gauvain, J.L.: Optimization of RNN-based speech activity detection. IEEE/ACM Trans. Audio Speech Lang. Process. **26**(3), 646–656 (2017)
10. Gundogdu, B., Yusuf, B., Saraclar, M.: Generative RNNs for OOV keyword search. IEEE Sig. Process. Lett. **26**(1), 124–128 (2018)
11. Kim, M., Cao, B., Mau, T., Wang, J.: Speaker-independent silent speech recognition from flesh-point articulatory movements using an LSTM neural network. IEEE/ACM Trans. Audio Speech Lang. Process. **25**(12), 2323–2336 (2017)
12. Li, Y., Li, X., Zhang, Y., Liu, M., Wang, W.: Anomalous sound detection using deep audio representation and a BLSTM network for audio surveillance of roads. IEEE Access **6**, 58043–58055 (2018)
13. Ma, Z., Yu, H., Chen, W., Guo, J.: Short utterance based speech language identification in intelligent vehicles with time-scale modifications and deep bottleneck features. IEEE Trans. Veh. Technol. **68**(1), 121–128 (2018)
14. Mahmud, M., Kaiser, M.S., McGinnity, T.M., Hussain, A.: Deep learning in mining biological data. Cogn. Comput. **13**(1), 1–33 (2021)
15. Mahmud, M., Kaiser, M.S., Hussain, A., Vassanelli, S.: Applications of deep learning and reinforcement learning to biological data. IEEE Trans. Neural Netw. Learn. Syst. **29**(6), 2063–2079 (2018)
16. Namburete, A.I., Xie, W., Yaqub, M., Zisserman, A., Noble, J.A.: Fully-automated alignment of 3D fetal brain ultrasound to a canonical reference space using multi-task learning. Med. Image Anal. **46**, 1–14 (2018)
17. Orojo, O., Tepper, J., McGinnity, T., Mahmud, M.: A multi-recurrent network for crude oil price prediction. In: 2019 IEEE Symposium Series on Computational Intelligence (SSCI), pp. 2940–2945. IEEE (2019)
18. Orojo, O., Tepper, J., McGinnity, T., Mahmud, M.: Time sensitivity and self-organisation in multi-recurrent neural networks. In: 2020 International Joint Conference on Neural Networks (IJCNN), pp. 1–7. IEEE (2020)
19. Satu, M.S., Rahman, S., Khan, M.I., Abedin, M.Z., Kaiser, M.S., Mahmud, M.: Towards improved detection of cognitive performance using bidirectional multilayer long-short term memory neural network. In: Mahmud, M., Vassanelli, S., Kaiser, M.S., Zhong, N. (eds.) BI 2020. LNCS, vol. 12241, pp. 297–306. Springer, Cham (2020). https://doi.org/10.1007/978-3-030-59277-6_27
20. Sharma, M., Ray, K., Yupapin, P., Kaiser, M., Ong, C., Ali, J.: Comparative analysis of different classifiers on EEG signals for predicting epileptic seizure. In: Kaiser, M.S., Bandyopadhyay, A., Mahmud, M., Ray, K. (eds.) Proceedings of International Conference on Trends in Computational and Cognitive Engineering. AISC, vol. 1309, pp. 193–204. Springer, Singapore (2021). https://doi.org/10.1007/978-981-33-4673-4_17

21. Shi, L., Ahmad, I., He, Y., Chang, K.: Hidden Markov model based drone sound recognition using MFCC technique in practical noisy environments. J. Commun. Netw. **20**(5), 509–518 (2018)
22. Shin, I., Kim, J.J., Lin, Y.S., Shin, Y.: One-cycle correction of timing errors in pipelines with standard clocked elements. IEEE Trans. Very Large Scale Integr. (VLSI) Syst. **24**(2), 600–612 (2015)
23. Zhang, J., Du, J., Dai, L.: Track, attend, and parse (tap): an end-to-end framework for online handwritten mathematical expression recognition. IEEE Trans. Multimedia **21**(1), 221–233 (2018)
24. Zheng, K., Yan, W.Q., Nand, P.: Video dynamics detection using deep neural networks. IEEE Trans. Emerg. Top. Comput. Intell. **2**(3), 224–234 (2017)

Application of AI and Informatics in Network, Security, and Analytics

Distributed Denial of Service Attack Detection Using Machine Learning and Class Oversampling

Sakib Shahriar Shafin[1], Sakir Adnan Prottoy[1], Saif Abbas[1],
Safayat Bin Hakim[1], Abdullahi Chowdhury[2(✉)], and Md. Mamunur Rashid[3]

[1] Islamic University of Technology (IUT), Gazipur, Bangladesh
safayat.b.hakim@iut-dhaka.edu
[2] Federation University Australia, Ballarat, Australia
Abdullahi.Chowdhury@federation.edu.au
[3] Central Queensland University, Rockhampton, Australia
m.rashid@cqu.edu.au

Abstract. Distributed Denial of Services (DDoS) attack, one of the most dangerous types of cyber attack, has been reported to increase during the COVID-19 pandemic. Machine learning techniques have been proposed in the literature to build models to detect DDoS attacks. Existing works in literature tested their models with old datasets where DDoS attacks are not specific. These works mainly focus on detecting the presence of an attack rather than the type of DDoS attacks. However, detection of the attack type is vital for the review and analysis of enterprise-level security policy. Cyber-attacks are inherently an imbalanced data problem, but none of the models treated DDoS attack detection from this perspective. In this work, we present a machine learning model that takes the imbalance nature of the DDoS attack data into consideration for both presence/absence and the type of DDoS attack detection. Extensive experiment analysis with the recent and DDoS attack-specific dataset shows that the proposed technique can effectively identify DDoS attacks.

Keywords: Cyberattacks · DDoS attack · Machine learning

1 Introduction

As computer technologies are evolving, we are becoming increasingly dependent on the Internet, cloud systems, and sophisticated applications for corporate business, e-government functions, health services, industry operation, transportation services and everyday tasks at the personal level. The Covid-19 has demonstrated and increased our reliance on computers system even more. The smooth operation of all these services depends on the secured environment through which services can be delivered. The ubiquitous use of computing devices (including sensors in the Internet of Things) and services using those devices have made them an inevitable target of cyber-crime exploiting vulnerabilities in the system.

© Springer Nature Switzerland AG 2021
M. Mahmud et al. (Eds.): AII 2021, CCIS 1435, pp. 247–259, 2021.
https://doi.org/10.1007/978-3-030-82269-9_19

DDoS is one of the most dangerous threats on network security, specially many attacks have targeted cloud systems on which many medium and large organizations depend [1]. A report by Kaspersky [2] suggests that DDoS attacks in the second Quarter of 2020 have increased by three-fold compared to the same time in 2019, and a recent survey showed that nearly 70% of the organizations surveyed suffered 20 to 50 DDoS attacks per month and each attack incurred $50,000 in financial loss. The objective of the DoS or DDoS attack is to consume all resources of the target server and deprive the legitimate users of using the service. In this attack, attackers employ thousands of comprised hosts (slave servers) at their disposal which are distributed over the internet to simultaneously launch a coordinated attack making use of some legitimate services and exploiting the weakness in the network protocol. TCP SYN flood, UDP flood, Ping flood, Ping O' Death, smurf attack are some examples of DDoS attacks. The large number of requests send to the server within a very short time exhausts the victim's available bandwidth and memory resources, and the generated traffic prevents legitimate users to send a request.

To counter the DDoS attacks, it is important to identify an attack as early as possible and then adopt mitigation strategies as per the enterprise security policy. For this purpose, we need a detection technique that is can identify an attack with high accuracy at the early stage. In recent years, many works have been presented in literature which attempted to devise an automatic detection system for DDoS. In general, those works can be categorized into three approaches: signature-based, anomaly-based and their hybrid. In signature-based approaches, a signature is extracted from a known attack and then a database of signatures is created. Similarly, a signature is extracted from the current activities and pattern matching is done with the existing signatures in the database. In anomaly-based approaches, a significant deviation from normal behaviors (e.g., network traffic, port activities, IP addresses) signals an attack. Anomaly-based approaches can again be divided into statistical, machine learning and SDN (Software-defined network)- based approaches.

Recently, like many other domains, machine learning approaches have been applied to build models for DDoS attack detection. These works (detailed in next section) have used several machine learning algorithms, like ANN (artificial neural networks), SVM (support vector machine), decision tree (DT), Random Forest (RF), etc. A detailed discussion on related works published in recent years is presented in the next section. However, there is always scope to improve the detection accuracy of the proposed methods. One limitation of the proposed methods is the only a few works have been tested on the DDoS-specific datasets and most works were evaluated on old datasets. Furthermore, most works ignore detecting the type of the DDoS attack which is important to review and evaluate the current intrusion detection system of an organization. Lastly, DDoS attack dataset used to build models can be viewed as an imbalanced data problem, and to the best of our knowledge, no work has treated model building from this perspective. In addressing this problem, in this work, we present a robust machine learning based detection system considering imbalanced data samples among classes. In particular, the work makes the following contribution:

- Introduce a robust detection model taking class imbalance into account. The model demonstrates high detection accuracy and consideration of class imbalance shows further improvement.
- The model is evaluated on DDoS attack specific recent dataset while most reported works used old generic intrusion datasets.
- Our works also detects attack type instead of simply identifying the presence of an attack.

2   Related Works

In recent years, several notable works have been presented in literature which are described in this section. Since our work falls into the machine learning based anomaly detection approach, we limit our discussion on literature within this category and due to space limitations within recently reported works.

In [3], Kasim used a combination of autoencoder (AE) and support vector machine (SVM) to detect DDoS attacks. The approach attained an accuracy of 99.41% on CICIDS dataset and 99.5% on the NSL-KDD dataset. The method is shown to achieve better results than a standalone model built on SVM. The work claims to have reduced false positive rate (i.e., false alarms) significantly, however, it is the false negative rate (i.e., failing to detect an attack) that is more important to prevent cyberattack. One limitation of the method is that it needs extensive hyper-parameter tuning and the model's performance is highly dependent on the hyper-parameters and the number of hidden units used in the AE. Another issue is that, in many applications, the system administrators want to know the type of DDoS attack that was launched. The model was not extended to multi-class attack detection.

In [4], Gopal & Virender proposed an extreme machine learning (ELM)-based method called voting ELM (V-ELM) to DDoS attack detection in a cloud computing environment. This work is an extension of their previous work in [5] where a single ELM was used but here the authors used multiple ELMs and the detection decision of those ELMs were combined through a simple majority voting mechanism. Tested on NSL-KDD and ISCX datasets, their method reported 99.18% and 92.11% accuracy, respectively. Though overall accuracy is somewhat improved because of the use of multiple ELMs with voting, the detection sensitivity and specificity had very marginal improvement as the expense of 6 to 32-fold increase in the training time. The method's performance in detection the type of attack was also not investigated.

Sahi et al. [6] proposed a DDoS TCP flood attack detection and prevention by analyzing the income packets to a cloud providers. They used simple packet statistics including source and destination IP addresses to create feature vector and four classifiers, namely, Least Square-SVM (LS-SVM), KNN, naïve-Bayes, and multilayer perceptron to identify attack traffic. They simulated a TCP flood attack in a virtual cloud network and reported an overall accuracy of about 97% for a single source attack and 94% accuracy for multi-source attack on the capture data when LS-SVM was used.

Very recently Maranhao et al. [7] has worked with the latest DDoS called CicDDoS-2019 dataset containing 12 attack types and is the first work with this dataset. They proposed a combination of multiple denoising, tensor decomposition and classifiers to detection attack and reported an accuracy over 99% on binary classification for various types of denoising techniques. However, these work does not cover multi-class classification, i.e., detecting DDoS attack type which is an important task for security practitioners.

In [8], Aamir and Zaidi devised a method, using network flow traffic data as feature vectors, based on a combination of clustering and machine learning technique. It works in two stages and is applicable to unlabbelled data also. At the first stage, unlabbelled data goes through two clustering algorithms (one with Agglomerative clustering and another PCA+K-means custring) and labelling of data is done via the voting outcomes of these algorithms. Next, a model is built using the labelled data and a classifier of either KNN, SVM or RF. Their method attained an overall accuracy of 96.66% on their own dataset and 82% on CICIDS-2017 dataset. Accuracy on the later dataset is low. In [9] Kachavimath et al. applied co-relation based feature selection method on DSL-KDD dataset and extract 8 features out of 41 features. They reported 98.51% and 91.31% accuracy by KNN and Naive Bayes classifiers, respectively. The datasets contain multiple types of attacks and none of these two works tested their models' accuracy in identifying attack type.

3 Proposed Model

3.1 Datasets

To gain deeper understanding of the characteristics of pre-existing and newer cyberattacks, choice of datasets to study on holds immense value. Recent datasets created on DDoS attacks give a clearer picture of the variety of DDoS attacks and this motivates us to select two recent and extensive datasets, namely, CICIDS-2017 and CicDDoS-2019.

CICIDS-2017: This dataset was provided by the Canadian Institute of Cybersecurity (CIC). It includes the result of the network traffic analysis using CICFlowMeter (unb.ca). The dataset contains approximately 2.8 million samples with 78 features describing each sample. Although the dataset does not completely focus on DDoS type attacks, but these attacks are dominant in size. Besides DDoS, the set contains DoS, PortScan and very small amount of infiltration and other attack types.

CicDDoS-2019: Also created by the CIC, this dataset focuses completely on a wide variety of DDoS attacks. With over 50 million samples, 81 attack attributes and 13 attack types, the dataset can be used for thorough analysis of machine learning methods. Not relying on pre-existing attacks, it uses TCP/UDP based protocols at the application layer to provide new attack taxonomies. The dataset contains reflection based attacks like DNS, LDAP, NETBIOS, and SNMP and exploitation based attacks such as SYN, UDP and UDP-Lag.

3.2   Pre-processing

Dataset Preparation: Due to the large volume of datasets and limited computational resources, working with 2.8 and 50 million samples was not feasible. The datasets needed to be scaled down, while retaining their original characteristics. The dataset was scaled down by randomly choosing samples from each class proportionately in a way so that the reduced dataset still retains the same ratio of samples between classes as the original dataset. For CICIDS-2017, 10% and for CicDDoS-2019, 2% of the original dataset were retained. The final sizes were 0.28 million and 0.5 million samples for two sets, respectively. For the case of CICDDoS-19, an attack type named WebDDoS had extremely low number of samples compared to other classes and could not be evaluated properly. Hence, the class was excluded, bringing the total class to 13, with 12 attack and one benign type.

Feature Selection: The inclusion of less significant features in model training results in reduced detection capacity. To extract the most significant features, we used Random Forest Regression feature selection technique. It uses cross-validation technique which helps in reducing unnecessary features. When using a dataset with a sizeable number of samples, the features start correlating with each other after some iteration, creating bias, and leads to greater False Positive rate. Running the features through Random Forest Regression, it creates a number of trees, adjusts for the missing values in any feature and creates an iterative tree method, where it adjusts and compares samples and gradually creates a forest where the top tree shows the most effective features. Employing this techniques, 32 features were selected for CICIDS-2017 and 24 features for CICDDoS-2019.

Class Oversampling: Chawla et al. [10] proposed Synthetic Minority Oversampling Technique (SMOTE) that creates artificial minority class samples. It has been shown in literature undersampling the majority class losses valuable information. SMOTE proposes a method where a combination of undersampling and oversampling is used, the majority class being under-sampled and the minority class being over-sampled. In oversampling minority class, new synthetic samples are created rather than by over-sampling with replacement. For each minority class sample, this method takes a number of nearest KNN neighbours and interpolates feature values between that sample and one of its neighbours to create a new sample. Taking each minority samples ($\mathbf{x}$) and identifying k nearest neighbours using KNN (k = 5), randomly select one of them ($\mathbf{x}_{ch}$) and create a new synthetic sample using interpolation:

$$\mathbf{x}_{new} = \mathbf{x} + (\mathbf{x}_{ch} - \mathbf{x}) \times random(0, 1) \tag{1}$$

where $random(0,1)$ creates random number between 0 and 1. This process is repeated until desired number of synthetic samples are generated.

3.3   Machine Learning Models

We used six machine learning techniques to determine their efficacy in detecting DDoS attack and their types. These techniques are briefly described below.

Logistic regression (LR) is a linear binary classification algorithm that uses a supervised machine learning approach to categorize data into distinct number of classes. An input values (x) are directed to predict an output value (y), which is a binary value (0 or 1), using the following equation

$$y = \frac{e^{(b_0 + b_1 x)}}{1 + e^{(b_0 + b_1 x)}} \tag{2}$$

Here, y is the predicted output, b_0 is the bias or intercept term and b1 is the coefficient value of (x).

Support Vector Machines (SVM) is an effective tool in classifying data and regression tasks [11]. SVM tries to find an optimal separating hyperplane (OSH). It also transforms data into a higher dimensional space for the construction of OSH through the use of a kernel function. The rule of thumb here is limiting a higher bound on the normalization as opposed to limiting the rate of error is required to perform better. Considering the hyperplane $\mathbf{w}.\mathbf{x} + b = 0$, the output y_i in response x_i

$$y_i(w.x_i + b) \geq 1 - \varepsilon_i, \triangledown i \tag{3}$$

where $\varepsilon_i(>0)$ are often called slack variables. This equation shows how the optimum solution is achieved.

Decision Tree (DT) has nodes and leaves which are generated during learning, i.e., tree building [12]. Each node of the tree operates on an attribute and the branch out leaves from this attribute and analyze the class label depending on the value of the attribute. The sequence continues until the final class label traversing through all leaves is calculated. The tree construction is based on the information gain calculated by the entropy of sample S and attribute A_j as

$$Infogain(A_j) = Entropy(S) - Entropy(A_j) \tag{4}$$

Random Forest (RF) uses bagging to train the tree learners [13]. Bagging is a strategy to produce a training dataset by arbitrarily chosen substitution of N examples, where N is the size of the main training set. Where DT uses nodes of a tree, RF uses a forest of trees and bagging technique to reduce bias and correlation which can happen in case of large number of samples.

Artificial Neural Network (ANN) is an iterative method where the output learns about the input through prediction error and gradually maps the input-output relation by learning [14]. An ANN consists of neurons, arranged in layers. The input layer takes in values from the sample. The next layer is the hidden layer, whose every node is connected to every node at the input layer, and the hidden layer is connected to the output layer. The connection weights between layers are updated using backpropagation learning algorithm (Rumelheart, 1986). By iterating with X set of inputs ($\mathbf{X1,X2,\ldots,Xp}$) and Y set of outputs, the final output looks as below.

$$o_{kp} = f(net_{kp}) = f(\sum_{j} \omega_{kj} o_{jp} + \theta_k) \tag{5}$$

where o_{kp} is the output of neuron 'k', o_{jp} is the output of neuron 'j' at the preceeding layer, ω_{kj} is the weight between the neurons 'k', θ_k is the bias for 'k'.

k-Nearest Neighbors (KNN) is a non-parametric learning method which doesn't make any estimation about the data distribution rather designs algorithm based on the dataset. The classification of KNN works on a majority vote system based on the number of k. Performance of KNN depends on two factors, choice of the number k and selection or scaling of features to improve classification. Large value of k makes the decision boundaries vague, some preliminary knowledge about the dataset may be useful.

4   Performance Evaluation

We used the following widely used performance metrics to evaluate the detection capability of the proposed detection system.

Classification Accuracy (ACC): It simply states the rate of correctly predicting classification type, such as attack or benign.

$$ACC = \frac{TP + TN}{N} \times 100 \tag{6}$$

Precision: It shows the model's the accuracy of detecting attack signal. The higher the precision, the better.

$$Precision = \frac{TP}{TP + FP} \times 100 \tag{7}$$

Recall: It indicates the percentage of attack signals that were correctly classified. It is also known as sensitivity.

$$Recall = \frac{TP}{TP + FN} \times 100 \tag{8}$$

F1-Score: It is the measure of a model's accuracy on a dataset as a whole. The model is better and more accurate when it is higher.

$$F1 - Score = \frac{2 * Sensitivity * Precision}{Sensitivity + Precision} \tag{9}$$

ROC and AUC: ROC (Receiver Operating Curve) is a widely used tool for visualizing model performances. It gives another measure called AUC which is the area under curve of ROC plot.

Here, True Positive (TP) means the model predicts an attack as attack, False Positive (FP) mean a benign sample is incorrectly predicted as an attack, True negative (TN) means a benign sample is predicted as benign and False Negative (FN) means an attack sample is predicted as benign. The above is based on 2 × 2 confusion matrix for binary classification. For multiclass classification, we used an mxm confusion matrix, where m is the number of classes.

4.1   Detection Performance

In our first experiment, we evaluated the capability of the proposed method in distinguishing an attack from a benign application (i.e., binary classification) using the six machine learning techniques discussed above. To test the performance of the proposed model, each dataset was split into 80%/20% training/test sets. The performance metrics for experiments with CICIDS-17 and CICDDoS-2019 datasets are shown in Table 1 and 3, respectively. Table 2 and Table 4 shows the confusion matrix for CICIDS-17 and CICDDoS-2019 datasets, respectively. Note that for binary classification, data balancing technique was not employed as good performance was achieved by classifiers.

As shown in Table 1, for binary classification with CICIDS-17 dataset, RF attained the highest performance for accuracy, precision, recall and F1-score which are 99.86%, 1.00, 1.00, 1.00. RF is followed by DT, KNN and ANN. The lowest accuracy (89.06%) was observed for SVM. RF and KNN acquired the highest ROC (1.00), while LR and SVM attained the lowest (0.96).

Table 1. Attack/benign detection (binary class) performance on CICIDS-2017 dataset

Model	Accuracy (%)	Precision	Recall	F1-Score	AUC
Logistic Regression	90.64	0.90	0.91	0.90	0.96
Support Vector Machines	89.06	0.88	0.89	0.88	0.96
Decision Tree	99.81	1.00	1.00	1.00	0.99
Random Forest	99.86	1.00	1.00	1.00	1.00
Artificial Neural Network	97.12	0.97	0.97	0.97	0.99
K-Nearest Neighbours	98.80	0.99	0.99	0.99	1.00

Table 3 shows the binary class detection performance on the CICDDoS-2019 dataset. The overall accuracy, precision, recall and F1-score were highest for RF at 99.99%, 1.00, 1.00, 1.00, followed by ANN, DT and KNN. The RF also demonstrated the highest ROC (1.00). The lowest accuracy (99.34%), precision (0.98) and ROC (0.97) were observed for LR. From Table 1 and 3, it can be seen

Table 2. Confusion matrix for CICIDS-2017 dataset

Actual class	Prediction class	
	Negative	Positive
Negative	**10975**	**45**
Positive	**33**	**45562**

Table 3. Attack/benign detection (binary class) performance on CICDDoS-2019 dataset

Model	Accuracy (%)	Precision	Recall	F1-Score	AUC
Logistic Regression	99.34	0.98	0.99	0.99	0.97
Support Vector Machine	99.82	0.99	1.00	1.00	0.99
Decision Tree	99.95	1.00	0.99	0.99	0.99
Random Forest	99.99	1.00	1.00	1.00	1.00
Artificial Neural Network	99.96	1.00	1.00	1.00	0.99
K-Nearest Neighbours	99.93	1.00	0.99	0.99	0.98

Table 4. Confusion matrix for CICDDoS-2019 dataset

Actual class	Prediction class	
	Negative	Positive
Negative	**111315**	**3**
Positive	**4**	**204**

that RF and LR classifiers demonstrated the best and least performance respectively for both datasets. Our overall accuracy (99.96%) is better that the recently reported performance in [7] which is 99.68% with CICDDoS-2019 dataset.

The second experiment was done on CICDDoS-2019 dataset to identify the type of an attack as well as benign class (i.e., multiclass classification of 12 attack types and benign class). This dataset was chosen for multiclass classification as it contains various types of DDoS specific attacks. This experiment was done without SMOTE and with SMOTE for class balancing. Table 5 shows the performance metrics for multiclass classification when SMOTE is not employed. The accuracy, precision, recall and F1-score were highest for RF at 88.54%, 0.86, 0.88, 0.86, followed by KNN, ANN and DT. The lowest accuracy (75.36%) was observed for LR. Both RF and ANN attained the highest AUC (0.94). Similar to binary classification, LR attained the least precision (0.73) and F1-score (0.72) while SVM demonstrated the least recall (0.73).

Since RF demonstrated the best performance so far, further experiment for class balancing was done with this classifier. While addressing class imbalance, we tried two methods for class balancing with SMOTE. One with data balanced and another with selected class weights. Balanced weight is defined as: $B_{wc} =$

Table 5. Multiclass classification (attack types and benign) on CICDDoS-2019 dataset without class balancing

Model	Accuracy (%)	Precision	Recall	F1-Score	ROC
Logistic Regression	75.36	0.73	0.75	0.72	0.89
Support Vector Machine	78.63	0.77	0.73	0.75	0.85
Decision Tree	84.94	0.85	0.85	0.85	0.86
Random Forrest	88.54	0.86	0.88	0.86	0.94
Artificial Neural Network	84.97	0.85	0.85	0.82	0.94
K-Nearest Neighbours	87.98	0.84	0.86	0.86	0.90

Table 6. Multi-class classification using without and with SMOTE using Random Forest classifier

Type	Precision			Recall			F1-score		
	Original	SMOTE (Bal.)	SMOTE (Sel.)	Original	SMOTE (Bal.)	SMOTE (Sel.)	Original	SMOTE (Bal.)	SMOTE (Sel.)
Benign	0.93	0.94	0.96	0.99	0.99	0.99	0.96	0.96	0.97
DNS	0.81	0.81	0.82	0.49	0.76	0.86	0.61	0.67	0.76
NTP	0.99	0.99	0.99	1	1	1	0.99	0.99	0.99
SNMP	0.82	0.82	0.82	0.84	0.84	0.84	0.83	0.83	0.83
SSDP	0.44	0.44	0.45	0.42	0.43	0.46	0.43	0.47	0.52
UDP	0.55	0.55	0.56	0.57	0.63	0.74	0.56	0.61	0.64
LDAP	0.37	0.55	0.7	0.69	0.72	0.77	0.48	0.49	0.57
MSSQL	0.99	0.99	0.99	0.99	0.99	0.99	0.99	0.99	0.99
NetBIOS	0.9	0.9	0.9	0.91	0.94	0.99	0.9	0.91	0.94
Portmap	0.09	0.18	0.25	0.15	0.12	0.01	0.11	0.18	0.21
SYN	0.94	0.94	0.94	0.94	0.97	0.99	0.94	0.94	0.96
TFTP	1	1	1	0.99	0.99	0.99	1	1	1
UDPLAG	0.19	0.19	0.2	0.23	0.18	0.04	0.21	0.24	0.27
Overall	86	87	88	88	88	89	86	87	89

$s/(t \times s_c)$, where B_{wc} is the balanced weight of class c, s is the number of samples, s_c is the number of class c samples, and t is the total number of classes.

For selected weight classes, we tested with different values for different classes. We also over-sampled the minority class data using SMOTE. This improved the overall accuracy increases from 88.54% to 88.75% for without and with SMOTE respectively. We observed that the precision, recall, and F1-score are lower in some specific classes (e.g., SSDP, UDP, LDAP attack types) as shown in the columns marked with 'without SMOTE' in Table 6.

Table 7 and Table 8 show the confusion matrix for the CICDDoS-2019 dataset without and with applying SMOTE, respectively. When we applied SMOTE and used balanced weight (SMOTE (Bal.)) the performance increased. For example, the precision, recall, and F1-score for LDAP increased from 0.37, 0.69, and 0.48 to 0.55, 0.72, and 0.49 for 'without SMOTE' and balanced class weights with SMOTE (SMOTE (Bal.)) in learning, respectively. When we selective weights for the classes with lower performance and also used SMOTE, these classes' performance increased further. The above metrics for LDAP increased to 0.70, 0.77, and 0.49, respectively, when we applied SMOTE oversampling with selective class weight, demonstrating our method's efficacy in identifying attack types.

Table 7. Confusion matrix for CICDDoS-2019 dataset without SMOTE

Classes	Benign	DNS	NTP	SNMP	SSDP	UDP	LDAP	MSSQL	NetBIOS	Portmap	SYN	TFTP	UDPLAG
Benign	226	0	0	0	0	0	0	0	0	0	0	0	0
DNS	2	8859	13	1118	0	0	151	0	18	8	1	1	1
NTP	0	12	2451	0	0	0	0	0	0	0	0	0	0
SNMP	1	1037	0	8747	9	1	64	1	267	152	0	0	0
SSDP	0	2	1	67	753	4246	0	107	0	0	0	0	13
UDP	1	1	2	6	696	5355	0	68	0	1	1	1	19
LDAP	0	2766	0	594	0	482	1	0	0	0	0	0	0
MSSQL	0	2	0	4		35	0	11444	0	2	6	15	10
NetBIOS	0	14	0	55	0	0	0	0	4541	2776	1	0	0
Portmap	0	0	0	0	1	0	0	1	212	186	2	0	0
SYN	1	0	1	1	0	0	0	0	0	0	11540	41	1403
TFTP	4	1	1	3	0	0	0	1	0	0	154	39818	131
UDPLAG	1	1	0	1	8	88	0	3	0	0	285	13	377

Table 8. Confusion matrix for attack identification in CICDDoS-2019 dataset using SMOTE

Classes	Benign	DNS	NTP	SNMP	SSDP	UDP	LDAP	MSSQL	NetBIOS	Portmap	SYN	TFTP	UDPLAG
Benign	229	0	0	0	0	0	0	0	0	0	0	0	0
DNS	1	6726	17	1117	1	0	176	3	14	11	1	2	0
NTP	0	5	2432	1	0	0	0	0	0	0	0	4	0
SNMP	0	1043	0	8688	9	2	63	1	234	155	1	0	0
SSDP	0	10	2	68	1147	3854	2	76	0	1	0	1	14
UDP	1	2	0	8	1270	4915	0	67	0	1	0	3	26
LDAP	0	2728	0	604	0	578	2	0	0	0	0	0	0
MSSQL	0	4	0	2	23	26	0	11466	1	0	3	9	16
NetBIOS	0	7	0	37	0	0	0	0	3973	3301	0	0	0
PortMap	0	0	0	2	0	0	0	2	138	204	0	0	0
SYN	0	0	0	1	1	1	0	2	0	0	11517	47	1280
TFTP	3	1	5	1	0	0	0	0	0	0	171	40036	104
UDPLAG	0	1	1	1	14	63	0	4	0	0	331	9	302

Also method with SMOTE and class weight shows improved overall precision, recall and F1-score averaged over all classes.

Note that, due to the lack of works on identifying attack types in CICDDOS dataset, we could not compare our results with similar works in literature.

5 Conclusion

In this paper, we have proposed a machine learning model that can detect DDoS attacks and their type by considering the class imbalance nature of the dataset. Here, we have used SMOTE with selected weights for each class in addressing the class imbalance issue in the DDoS dataset. Experiment results with a recent DDoS attack-specific dataset show that the proposed model based on machine learning has a better capability of detecting DDoS attacks and their type in terms of widely used metrics. Our future work will explore ensemble (e.g., [15]) and/or deep learning and reinforcement learning techniques (e.g., [16], [17]) to enhance DDoS attack detection performance further. Adversarial sample generation and model retraining (e.g., [18]) is another approach to enhance performance that remains the focus of our future study.

References

1. Chowdhury, A.: Recent cyber security attacks and their mitigation approaches – an overview. In: Batten, L., Li, G. (eds.) ATIS 2016. CCIS, vol. 651, pp. 54–65. Springer, Singapore (2016). https://doi.org/10.1007/978-981-10-2741-3_5
2. Kaspersky DDoS attack report. https://securelist.com/ddos-attacks-in-q2-2020/98077/. Accessed 19 Mar 2021
3. Kasim, O.: An efficient and robust deep learning based network anomaly detection against distributed denial of service attacks. Comput. Netw. **180**, 107390 (2020)
4. Kushwah, G.S., Ranga, V.: Voting extreme learning machine based distributed denial of service attack detection in cloud computing. J. Inf. Secur. Appl. **53**, 102532 (2020)
5. Kushwah, G.S., Ali, S.T.: Distributed denial of service attacks detection in cloud computing using extreme learning machine. Int. J. Commun. Netw. Distrib. Syst. **23**(3), 328–351 (2019)
6. Sahi, A., Lai, D., Li, Y., Diykh, M.: An efficient DDoS TCP flood attack detection and prevention system in a cloud environment. IEEE Access **5**, 6036–6048 (2017)
7. Maranhao, J.P.A., et al.: Tensor based framework for distributed denial of service attack detection. J. Netw. Comput. Appl. **174**, 102894 (2021)
8. Aamir, M., Zaidi, S.M.A.: Clustering based semi-supervised machine learning for DDoS attack classification. J. King Saud Univ.-Comp. Info. Sci. (2019)
9. Kachavimath, A., Nazare, S.V., Akki, S.S.: Distributed denial of service attack detection using Naive Bayes and K-Nearest Neighbor for network forensics. In: Conference of ICIMIA, pp. 711–717. IEEE, Bangalore (2020)
10. Chawla, N.V., Bowyer, K.W., Hall, L.O., Kegelmeyer, W.P.: SMOTE: synthetic minority over-sampling technique. J. Artif. Intell. Res. **16**, 321–357 (2002)
11. Vapnik, V.N.: The Nature of Statistical Learning Theory. Springer, New York (1995). https://doi.org/10.1007/978-1-4757-2440-0

12. Quinlan, J.R.: C4.5: programs for machine learning. vol. 1, Morgan Kaufmann, San Francisco (1993)
13. Breiman, L.: Random forests. J. Mach. Learn. **45**(1), 5–32 (2001). https://doi.org/10.1023/A:1010933404324
14. Rumelhart, D.E., McClelland, J.L. and PDP Research Group: Parallel Distributed Processing, vol. 1, MIT Press (1986)
15. Rashid, M.M., Kamruzzaman, J., Hassan, M.M., Imam, T., Gordon, S.: Cyberattacks detection in IoT-based smart city applications using machine learning techniques. Int. J. Environ. Res. Public Health **17**(24), 9347 (2020)
16. Mahmud, M., Kaiser, M.S., McGinnity, T.M., Hussain, A.: Deep learning in mining biological data. Cogn. Comput. **13**(1), 1–33 (2021). https://doi.org/10.1007/s12559-020-09773-x
17. Mahmud, M., Kaiser, M.S., Hussain, A., Vassanelli, S.: Applications of deep learning and reinforcement learning to biological data. IEEE Trans. Neural Netw. Learn. Syst. **29**(6), 2063–2079 (2018)
18. Khoda, M.E., Imam, T., Kamruzzaman, J., Gondal, I., Rahman, A.: Robust malware defense in industrial IoT applications using machine learning with selective adversarial samples. IEEE Trans. Ind. Appl. **56**(4), 4415–4424 (2019)

Scientific Metrological Analysis of Government Services Based on Big Data Analysis and Visualization Software Driven by Information Technology

Wei-Keng Zhou, Yan-Tong Lin[✉], Zhi-Xiang Zhou, Xin Bai, Yi-Lin Yu, and Yu-Wen Pan

Sun Yat-Sen University Nanfang College, Guangzhou, China

Abstract. In recent years, Guangdong Province has made remarkable achievements in implementing the work of openness in government affairs, which has been rated as excellent in the evaluation. The digital government reform and construction of Guangdong Province also promotes the deep integration of government affairs openness and government services. However, for people from overseas, such as Hong Kong, Macao, Taiwan and foreign nationals or enterprises, there is no perfect service system and mechanism, which undoubtedly becomes one of the obstacles to the construction of the Guangdong-Hong Kong-Macao Greater Bay Area and is not conducive to the efficient development of the Greater Bay Area. At present, there is a gap in the bibliometric analysis of this topic. In this paper, 908 articles were retrieved from the Web of Science database, and the cited literatures on "e-government", "management", "social Science", "business economy", "Science and technology" were reviewed. With the use of big data analysis technology and visualization software, the author's key words, major research institutions, countries and sources of publications are analyzed in detail, revealing the current situation related to the work of government affairs openness, so as to provide a more complete picture. To a certain extent, it will promote the improvement of the government service level and ability of Guangdong Province as a first-tier city and region with close exchanges with overseas compatriots and foreign friends, and encourage it to absorb more talents.

Keywords: E-government · Management · Social sciences · Business economy · Science and technology

1 Introduction

Since the reform and opening up, China's economy has been deeply integrated into the global system, which has brought a tsunami-like impact on the global existing industrial economic pattern. On February 18, 2019, the CPC Central Committee and the State Council officially issued the Outline of the Development Plan for the Guangdong-Hong Kong-Macao Greater Bay Area. The issuance of this outline demonstrates China's confidence and determination to build a dynamic world-class city cluster, an international

© Springer Nature Switzerland AG 2021
M. Mahmud et al. (Eds.): AII 2021, CCIS 1435, pp. 260–267, 2021.
https://doi.org/10.1007/978-3-030-82269-9_20

center of science and technology innovation, a high-quality living area that is livable, suitable for business and travel, and a model of high-quality development in the world. Up to now, with industrial upgrading and value chain rising, the Greater Bay Area has gradually become a gathering place for high-tech enterprises. As a means of transforming public governance, e-government is increasingly recognized by people [1]. General Secretary Xi Jinping has stressed that talent is the primary resource for innovation. In the development process of the Greater Bay Area, the introduction of talents and follow-up services are particularly important. At the policy level, the gathering of high-level innovative talents in the Guangdong-Hong Kong-Macao Greater Bay Area has entered a white-hot stage [2]. At present, countries have made a lot of efforts to attract and serve overseas talents. The United States, Germany, Japan, South Korea, Singapore, Russia and other countries have established a series of relatively perfect laws to attract and serve overseas talents. Among them, Singapore has incorporated talent legislation into the framework of its immigration law, focusing not only on attracting practical talents, but also on future development [3]. In Germany, the government actively matches businesses with individuals. The German Labour Bureau has specially established an exchange platform between German IT enterprises and foreign IT talents on its website, produced an annual report, analyzed the employment development trend of various industries, and provided authoritative guidance information for senior talents' employment [4]. Within the Greater Bay Area of China, two-way flows of financial markets are also relatively frequent. The entire region has a rapid transport network, a port group of Guangzhou-Shenzhen-Hong Kong and a group of airports. The Hong Kong-Zhuhai-Macao Bridge has also been put into operation. The Greater Bay Area system coordination and breakthrough under the background of "one country, two systems" has been continuously explored and innovated in the process of comprehensively deepening reform and opening up on the mainland. The integrated economic development of the Guangdong-Hong Kong-Macao Greater Bay Area is a typical example of the introduction, development and upgrading of global industrial transfer in China from the middle and late 20th century, and eventually becomes an important level of the world economy. It is also a typical example of the connection and optimization of the economic development system and mechanism with Chinese characteristics and the world industrial economic system. The thoughts, theories and models of China's economic development contained in them are important contributions to the innovation of economic theories [5]. Marc et al. (2011) believe that in many service design projects, collaborative design is seen as the key to success, and collaborative design can bring a series of benefits. They have outlined the benefits of collaborative design in service design projects, which can help relevant personnel to clarify their goals more accurately and clearly [6]. Gang & Tony(2006) The application of mobile technology in the government sector not only provides an alternative channel for communication and public service delivery, but more importantly, it can solve the government's own mobility problem and transcend the traditional e-government service delivery model by bringing personalization. Localization and context awareness services are close to their citizens [7].

In a word, just as life scientists need complex data-intensive machine learning technology to mine a large amount of data for pattern recognition [8], the innovation of government services is necessary, and the innovation of government services and the improvement of government services facing overseas people are of great significance for the promotion of "One Core, One Belt, One Region" in Guangdong Province. At present, the government service has become a hot topic, but the research on the internal relationship of the government service field does not have the vision of seeing the tree and seeing the forest. In this study, the literature of e-government, management, social science, business economy, technology and other specific fields were reviewed by scientific metrology. Based on this, this paper screened 908 literatures from the Web Of Science (WOS) database, mapped the coword cluster, and analyzed their annual trend, topic scope, literature sources, etc. With the help of big data analysis technology and visualization software function, scientometrics is used to demonstrate the possibility and feasibility of the research contents in relevant fields, and to produce cutting-edge academic achievements with insight. In order to accelerate the reform of electronic government affairs in Guangdong Province to make forward-looking contributions.

2   Scientometric Approach and Data

As of January 5, 2021, we had retrieved and collected 908 papers from the WOS database of the WOS Core Collection(including SCI-Expanded, SSCI, A&HCI, ESCI), and used Python scripts to clean up and analyze the data. Delete duplicate keywords.Then, based on the multiple interactions of word clusters, the research contents are classified and summarized. Finally, VosViewer is used for visual analysis and drawing. Track spatial connections between keywords, disciplines, topics, and resources to create a dynamic network of interactive results.

We perform advanced search operations in the WOS core set: TS = ("Electronic government" OR "E-Governmant" OR "E-Government" OR "Digital government" OR "Mobile government" OR "Eletronic governance" OR "e-governance" OR "e-governor") AND SU = ("Management" OR "Social Sciences" OR "Business &" Economics" OR "Technology").

Arrange all the retrieved documents in order of high to low citations, export them as tabbed delimiter files, and then clean up the data using Python to produce 898 valid articles, based on which VosViewer is used for bibliographic coupling.

3   Research Findings

This paper introduces the research trends, major countries, institutions, publications and author keywords related to the topic and performs statistical and visual analysis.

3.1   Annual Trends

According to the statistical data in Fig. 1, the number of publications in this research field shows a fluctuating rise, especially when its popularity peaks in 2020. As can be seen from Fig. 2, the citation rate of related papers is also increasing year by year, and the two articles with the highest citation rate are:*Trust and Risk in E-Government Adoption* and *Trust* and *Electronic Government Success: An Empirical Study.*

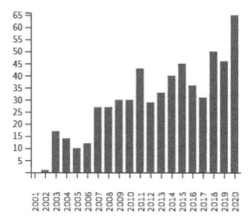

Fig. 1. The number of publications

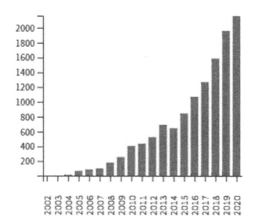

Fig. 2. The number of citations

3.2 Major States and Institutions

As shown in Fig. 3, the field described the relationship between the five groups involved, including 25 countries, green line represents the node of "American" in the middle of the picture, including "American" green country South Korea, Spain, wales, New Zealand, including Italy and Brazil, these data not only data have close relations with China, Also linked to the Dutch data system, the green group, shown in yellow, also plays a role in linking the two regions of society in red. The red countries, including China, include Denmark, Pakistan, Egypt, Indonesia, Malaysia, Switzerland, Australia and the United Arab Emirates, which are the middle points connecting the citizens of the two countries. The purple branches of Germany, including Sweden and India are closely related not only to the blue people, but also to the green people and the red people. The blue peoples on the right of the photo are Poland, Republic of South Africa, Ireland, etc. Although the proportion is relatively small, it cannot be ignored. Other data subjects in the picture include people of the yellow race, representing the Netherlands and Singapore.

Although the proportion of data is small, it also plays a role in connecting green and red nationalities.

Figure 4 shows the co-citation relationship of epidemic organizations. The whole chart is composed of six different groups. Among these numerous epidemic organizations, they are mainly concentrated in six groups: National University of Singapore, Bruna University, Nanyang Technological University, University of Manchester, Royal Melbourne Institute of Technology University and Seoul National University. The green group is the only country that can share the relationship with the four ethnic groups, and it is also the largest. Secondly, the blue and red residents are mainly concentrated in the nodes. Like the green group, the blue group acts as a bridge between the yellow and light blue groups. The yellow and purple groups are subgroups of the green groups, which deserve special attention.

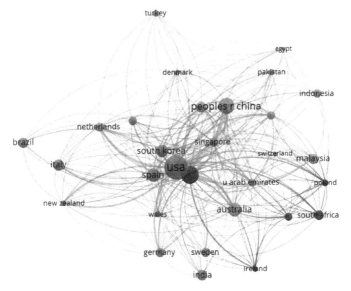

Fig. 3. Coupling visualization of major national literature (Color figure online)

3.3 Major Publications

Figure 5 shows the 15 publishing channels, with Social Science Computer Review, Public Administration Review, European Journal of Information, Research in Electronic Commerce, and Journal of Electronic Information taking the most important positions. However, the fact that the Social Science Computer Review is the largest shows its importance and its active engagement with the outside world. Compared with other ethnic groups, the red ethnic group accounts for the highest proportion and is the intermediate bridge between the yellow ethnic group and the green ethnic group. The second is the blue nationality, which spreads to other nationalities and plays a role of connecting the green nationality and the yellow nationality. Finally, although the proportion of yellow-green ethnic groups is small, it is a key link that cannot be ignored.

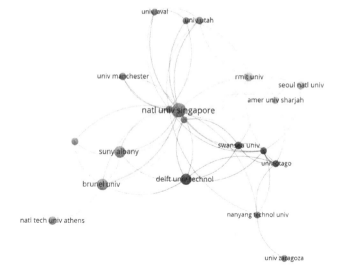

Fig. 4. Coupling visualization of literature of major institutions (Color figure online)

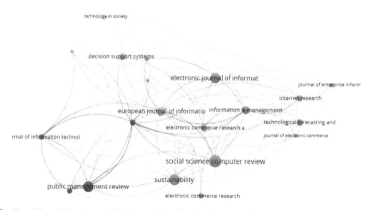

Fig. 5. Top 23 publications: Bibliographic Coupled Web Visualization (Color figure online)

3.4 Key Words Analysis of Authors

Figure 6 shows that this paper uses VosViewer software to build co-citation maps of author keywords and tests the links between these keywords and topics. It can show the development and development of specific fields on the knowledge map, help researchers to conduct intuitive analysis to determine the research direction of the field and the leading direction of the statistical field, visual analysis of the first 30 keywords, and divide them into four groups of colors.

Most of the key words in the picture are in the red group. It is often mentioned that keywords such as "e-government", "satisfaction", "e-government", "user acceptance", "information technology" and "system" are frequently cited, indicating that researchers attach great importance to this field when promoting information technology.

The green group in the upper right corner is the second largest keyword group in the image; "E-government" keyword nodes is the most important green group node, node is also the most closely contact with the outside world, it represents the minority of "social media", "information", "information and communications technology", "Internet", such as node, provides a way to contact with the outside world, and connect blue and red intersection of two nations.

The blue panel includes topics such as "innovation", "change", "implementation", "mechanism" and "management". It not only has close relation with green nation, but also has close relation with yellow nation and red nation. Although the number of keywords and the number of citations is small, it is also a detail that cannot be ignored. For the yellow group with the least keywords, although there is only one theme, "determinants", it is a bridge between the red nation and the blue nation, and it is also a detail that cannot be ignored.

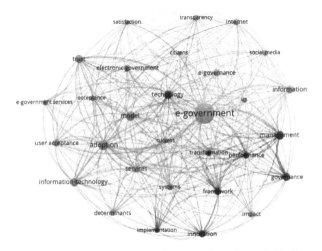

Fig. 6. Visualization of clustering results by the main authors (Color figure online)

4   Conclusion

Through the above literature review, data processing and visualization charts, it is more intuitive to show the cross and penetration of multiple structures in the field of e-government and service design. Based on different research methods, this paper draws the following conclusions:

(1) By applying the new thinking of government service design, service design combines the principles of customer experience and business process design to help public sector agencies improve three key tasks: task efficiency, productivity and customer satisfaction.

(2) The innovation of government services and the improvement of government services for overseas people are of great significance to the promotion of "One Core, One Belt, One Region" in Guangdong Province. At present, countries, including the United States, Singapore and China, are making continuous efforts to attract and serve overseas talents.

(3) In this paper, the research content based on the electronic government affairs, management, social sciences, business, economy and science and technology, the study found that with the content at the same time, cited most frequently keywords are "information technology", "system", "Internet", etc., it also shows that the development of information technology push scholars focus on government affairs service and research to new heights.

(4) The future work will be devoted to publishing the research report of "New Thinking Based on Government Design – Research on the Development Strategy of Guangdong Government Construction" in the Third World Ecological Design Conference.

(5) The difference between the current work and the key lies in the following points. Firstly, the knowledge of the end user is limited. Many government agencies lack detailed demographic and behavioral knowledge of the citizens and organizations they serve; Secondly, the service has been disconnected. Poor communication between different organizations and limited consolidation of processes and systems within the same organization can lead to disjointed service delivery.

In summary, as a current research hotspot, government services are attracting the attention of scholars. This article can familiarize readers with relevant research progress in existing research disciplines and provide ideas for follow-up researchers so that future research can find more meaningful and meaningful results. Our research conclusions will help future scholars to better study government services and related fields, and promote government service innovation.

References

1. Kuang, X.: The main problems and countermeasures of the integration of Guangdong-Hong Kong-Macao greater bay area. Mod. Mark. **4**, 12 (2020)
2. Lai, Y., Liang, X.: Exploration on the introduction of high-level innovative talents in the Guangdong-Hong Kong-Macao greater bay area. Innov. Entrep. **35**(9), 105–118 (2020)
3. Cao, D.: Attracting talents by foreign talents legislation. Chinese Talents (2013)
4. Jia, M.: Aspects of attracting talents abroad. High Technol. Ind. **3**, 311–331 (2004)
5. Wai, N., Zhou, P., Painting, W., Zhiyu, C.: Research on the economic integration development of Greater Bay area – based on the analysis of Guangdong-Hong Kong-Macao greater bay area. Shanghai Econ. Res. **7**(02), 275–283 (2020)
6. Steen, M., Manschot, M., De Koning, N.: Benefits of co-design in service design projects. Int. J. Design **5**(2), 53–60 (2011)
7. Song, G., Cornford, T.: Mobile government: towards a service paradigm. In: Proceedings of the 2nd International Conference on e-Government, University of Pittsburgh, USA, October, pp. 208–218 (2006)
8. Mahmud, M., Kaiser, M.S., McGinnity, T.M., Hussain, A.: Deep learning in mining biological data. Cogn. Comput. **13**(1), 1–33 (2020). https://doi.org/10.1007/s12559-020-09773-x

Violent Video Event Detection: A Local Optimal Oriented Pattern Based Approach

B. H Lohithashva(iD) and V. N Manjunath Aradhya$^{(\boxtimes)}$(iD)

Department of Computer Applications, JSS Science and Technology University,
Mysuru, Karnataka, India
{lohithashva.bh,aradhya}@sjce.ac.in

Abstract. Video/Camera-based monitoring is a prominent and difficult research problem in the field of machine learning and pattern recognition and posed much interest in our safety in the private and public sectors. Therefore, surveillance cameras have been deploying to control suspicious activity. Consequently, many researchers have worked on developing an automatic surveillance system to detect violent events and assists security guards to take the right decision at the right time. Still, violent event detection is difficult to detect because of illumination, complex background, scale variation, blurriness, occlusion, and low resolution in a surveillance camera. In this paper, the Local Optimal Oriented Pattern (LOOP) texture-based feature descriptor is proposed. Eventually, eminent features are used with a support vector machine (SVM) classier for violent event detection. Experiments are conducted on the Hockey Fight dataset and Violent-Flows dataset. The five-Fold Cross-Validation approach is used to analyze the performance of the proposed method. The data and results are promising and encouraging.

Keywords: Violent event · Texture features · Spatio-temporal · LOOP descriptor

1 Introduction

Video surveillance is often seen as the process of analyzing violent event scenes in the video. The actions conducted by humans can be analyzed with the help of a surveillance camera that can be manual or automated. An intelligent video surveillance system intends at detecting, tracking, and recognizing objects of interest and further analyzing and interpreting the video activities of the scenes, despite the substantial amount of videos collected by surveillance cameras. Nowadays, we see plenty of surveillance cameras being installed throughout the private and public sectors. The reason behind this is for the safety of human beings and also for the hardware equipment available in the markets at reasonable prices. As indicated by the way that visual information is generally accessible in surveillance systems, we focus on strategies used vision information [7]. The automatic

© Springer Nature Switzerland AG 2021
M. Mahmud et al. (Eds.): AII 2021, CCIS 1435, pp. 268–280, 2021.
https://doi.org/10.1007/978-3-030-82269-9_21

surveillance system reduces the risk of security persons monitoring prolonged videos. Violent event detection is a difficult action recognition task and it is a branch of computer vision. The pattern, facial expression, and actions to be detected unusual events in the video scenes. A terrorist attack, bomb detection, fraud detection, loitering, slip and fall event, and many more are action recognition problems [22]. Detection of the violent events is highly uncertain to resolve the difficult task. Once the system has experienced violent and non-violent events, we apparently gave the test label to detect the classification of events. This is a more challenging scenario when the normal event drastically alters and it is difficult to learn due to blurriness, variations in scale, complex background, occlusion, and illumination. In this work, we have used the LOOP descriptor to detect violent events in the video sequences.

The Contributions of the Paper are as Follows

- LOOP descriptor used to extracts salient features to detect violent events
- Spatial-temporal post-processing approach is used to improve the accuracy of violent event detection.
- To evaluate the efficiency of the proposed method, Five-Fold Cross-Validation approach is used and results are compared with the state of the art techniques.

The rest of the paper is structured as follows. Section 2 is connected with the previous research work. The proposed texture-based descriptors are discussed in Sect. 3. Experimentation results are described in Sect. 4. Finally conclude the research paper in Sect. 5.

2 Previous Works

In recent years, the research community has established a survey on a variety of algorithms based on the handcrafted features [2,5], deep learning features [27,28,30,39] and classifiers [3,18] are used to resolve the major issues of violent event detection [29,32]. Quasim et al. [33] introduced the Histogram of Swarms (HOS) descriptor. The method used the variance of Optical Flow (OF) to extract spatio-temporal information in the sequence of video frames. Ant Colony Optimization (ACO) is used to cluster moving object and it separate salient and non-salient features, finally OF technique is used to extract prominent features to detect normal and violent events. Febin et al. [12] presented a combination of Motion Boundary Scale Invariant Features Transform (MoB-SIFT) and movement filter algorithm. The movement filter algorithm extracts temporal information features of the non-violent event and avoids the normal event. Furthermore, the combination of motion boundary, optical flow, and SIFT feature extract eminent features to detect violent events. Esen et al. [36] used Motion Co-Occurrence Feature (MCF) to detect abnormal events in the video. The method used a block matching algorithm to extract the direction and magnitude of motion features and fed it to the KNN classifier to categorize normal and abnormal events. Recently, Lohithashva et al. [23] introduced the integration of texture features to detect violent activity. The method extracts prominent texture features to detect suspicious activity. Song et al. [37] introduced the fusion of multi-temporal analysis and multi-temporal perceptron layers to detect unusual events. Zhang et al. [41] presented an entropy model to measure the distribution of enthalpy for abnormal event detection. The authors have used an enthalpy model in the micro point of view to describe crowd energy information. Ryan et al. [35] proposed optical flow and Gray Level Co-occurrence Matrix (GLCM) feature descriptor to detect abnormal events in the video sequence. Lloyd et al. [21] proposed a GLCM texture feature descriptor detect non-violent and violent activity detection. Pujol et al. [10] described events based on features fusion extraction technique of local eccentricity which includes the combination of Fast Fourier Transform, radon transform, projection, and ellipse eccentricity. Deepak et al. [9] introduced the extraction of both spatio-temporal information from texture based feature descriptor. The method extracts local geometric characteristics such as gradients and curvatures which are basic space-time movement properties used to detect normal and abnormal events. Li et al. [20] introduced OF based feature descriptor to detect violent events in the video scene. Initially, they have used background subtraction to remove low variation and noise in the frame and extract the Histogram of Maximal Optical Flow Projection (HMOFP) features. Reconstruction cost (RC) is used to detect violent events in video scenes.

Imran et al. [16] introduced a deep learning method to detect a violent event in surveillance video. MobileNet is used to extract spatio-temporal information from the moving objects after that dominant features are given to a gated recurrent unit (GRU) to detect suspicious events in the video scene. Hason et al. [14] introduced spatiotemporal information using a Spatiotemporal Encoder, Bidirectional Convolution Long Short Term Memory (BCLSTM) deep-learning feature extraction technique to detect unusual events in the video sequence. Asad et al. [4] presented violent event detection based on the spatio-temporal features from a video's uniformly spaced sequential frames. Multi-level processes for two consecutive frames, obtained from the top and bottom layers of the convolutional layers neural network, are integrated using optimized feature fusion strategy, finally, features are fed to Long short term memory (LSTM) to distinguish between violent and non-violent event. Sabokrou et al. [11] introduced Fully Convolution Neural Networks (FCNs) to detect and localize violent events in a sequence of video. Accatolli et al. [1] introduced a 3D-CNN to detect suspicious activity in video. CNN architecture extracts salient features without any prior knowledge and fed them to the SVM classifier to segregate violent and non-violent events. Zhou et al. [36] applied hybrid auto-encoder architecture to extract spatio-temporal features from the crowd and discriminate normal and abnormal events in video frames. Song et al. [38] introduced a modified 3D-CNN to detect an aggressive incidence throughout the video. The method is used a uniform sampling method to reduce the redundancy and conquest the motion coherence and they have illustrated the efficacy of the sampling method.

3   Proposed Methodology

We demonstrate an overview of the proposed approach in this section. The LOOP descriptor extracts prominent texture features from the input video and fed them to the SVM classifier to detect violent events. Figure 1 shows the workflow of violent event detection using the proposed LOOP descriptor. The approach suggested in the sections that follow illustrates the detection of violent events.

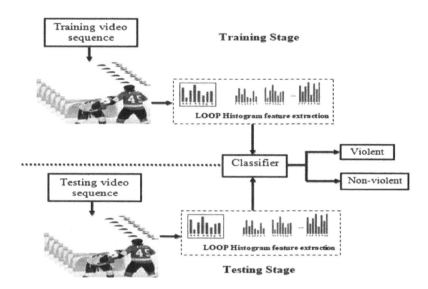

Fig. 1. The description of the proposed method

3.1   LOOP Feature Descriptor

LOOP [6] is a scale and rotational invariance texture-based feature descriptor. To overcome the drawback of previous binary descriptors the LOOP descriptor has used and it is an upgrade of the Local Binary Pattern (LBP) and Local Directional Pattern (LDP) descriptors. Consider p_c be the intensity of the frame F at pixel (a_c, b_c) and $p_n (n = 0, 1, ..., n - 1)$ and pixel intensity of 3×3 neighborhood of (a_c, b_c) except for the middle pixel p_c. The eight Kirsch masks used previously for the LDP [17] are located in the direction of these eight adjacent pixels $p_n (n = 0, 1, ..., n - 1)$. Therefore, it provides a measure of the severity of the degree of variability in the direction, separately. The Kirsch eight directions mask as shown in Fig. 2.

The eight respondents of the Kirsch masks are k_n response to the pixels of the intensity $p_n (n = 0, 1, ..., n - 1)$. Each pixel is assigned an exponential e_n by the size of k_n output of eight Kirsch masks.

$$\begin{bmatrix} -3 & -3 & 5 \\ -3 & 0 & 5 \\ -3 & -3 & 5 \end{bmatrix} \quad \begin{bmatrix} -3 & 5 & 5 \\ -3 & 0 & 5 \\ -3 & -3 & -3 \end{bmatrix} \quad \begin{bmatrix} 5 & 5 & 5 \\ -3 & 0 & -3 \\ -3 & -3 & -3 \end{bmatrix} \quad \begin{bmatrix} 5 & 5 & -3 \\ 5 & 0 & -3 \\ -3 & -3 & -3 \end{bmatrix}$$

East   North East   North   North West

$$\begin{bmatrix} 5 & -3 & -3 \\ 5 & 0 & -3 \\ 5 & -3 & -3 \end{bmatrix} \quad \begin{bmatrix} -3 & -3 & -3 \\ 5 & 0 & -3 \\ 5 & 5 & -3 \end{bmatrix} \quad \begin{bmatrix} -3 & -3 & -3 \\ -3 & 0 & -3 \\ 5 & 5 & 5 \end{bmatrix} \quad \begin{bmatrix} -3 & -3 & -3 \\ -3 & 0 & 5 \\ -3 & 5 & 5 \end{bmatrix}$$

West   South West   South   South East

Fig. 2. Kirsch eight directions mask

$$LOOP(a_c, b_c) = \sum_{n=0}^{n-1} s(p_n - p_c) * 2^{k_n} \tag{1}$$

$$s(a) = \begin{cases} 1 & if \ a \geq 0 \\ 0 & otherwise \end{cases} \tag{2}$$

The LOOP outcome about the pixel (a_c, b_c) is stated as in (1 & 2) and s(a) represents neighborhood pixels intensity values. Therefore, the LOOP descriptor computes the rotational invariance in the major method. Eventually, pixel intensities are evaluated over the cell at each number that has prominently featured. This descriptor is measured as a $2^8 = 256$ dimensional features for each frame.

3.2   Classification Based on Support Vector Machine (SVM)

SVM [8] is a binary classification approach which is widely used in regression and classification applications. Initially, SVM is introduced for classification and regression and subsequent kernel methodologies are used to implement non-linear classification by processing input information via a high-dimensional feature space. SVM attempts to optimize the distance of the distinguishing borderline among violent and non-violent events by trying to maximize the distance of the separating plane from each of the features. In the binary classification problem, data from a two-class are considered. In our research work, the Gaussian kernel function in SVM is used to violent video scene.

3.3   Post-processing

The post-processing technique [34] significantly increases the accuracy and reduces the false-positive rate. In this work, for the post-processing technique, we have taken 30 frames for the detection of frames which significantly improves the performance.

4   Experiment Results and Discussion

In this section, we summarize the detailed experimentation study to evaluate the use of violent event detection approaches in two standard benchmark datasets. Thereafter, the experimentation parameter setting is explained. Finally, the results obtained are compared with the existing feature descriptors.

4.1   Violent Datasets

The Hockey Fight (HF) dataset and Violent-Flows (VF) dataset experimentation are conducted to demonstrate the effectiveness of the proposed method and both datasets have complex backgrounds, illumination, blurriness, scale changes, and occlusion. This dataset comprises 1000 action videos of the National Hockey League (NHL) (500 fights and 500 no-fights), initially used to distinguish violent event detection processes [31]. For each clip, there have been battles to fight between two or hardly any hockey players. Each video clip is approximately equal to 1.75 s.

Fig. 3. Violent datasets sample frames. First row: Normal scenes, Second row: Fight scenes.

The Violent-Flows dataset contains 246 action videos (123 fights and 123 no-fights). Maximum possible people to seeing aggressive events that occurred inside the football ground during the match. This dataset is used to assess the detection of violent events [15]. All violent videos in the angered circumstances, each video is roughly equivalent to 3.5 s. Figure 3 illustrates the following frame sequences comprising Hockey Fight and Violent-Flows dataset sample frames of fights and no fight scenes.

4.2 Experimental Setting

In this section, we have used a Five-fold cross-validation test. We have compared our experimental results with existing methods using Hockey Fight and Violent-Flows dataset. Therefore, five different divisions were partitioned into each dataset: four for training and one for evaluation testing. The average accuracy result is estimated each time and the Precision (P), Recall (R), F-measure (F), Accuracy (Acc), and Area Under Curve (AUC) have used as an evaluation method. we employed an SVM classifier with a Gaussian kernel function to differentiate violent and non-violent events in the video sequences.

4.3 Result

In the experiment, we have used the LOOP descriptor to demonstrate for detection of unusual events in the video sequence. Our proposed method shows impressive results compared to existing methods. HF dataset ROC curves with SVM classifier using LOOP descriptor is compared with the existing methods as shown in Fig. 4. The Precision of 94.48%, Recall of 94.09%, F-measure of 94.28%, the accuracy of 92.25%, and AUC of 95.11% as illustrated in Table 1. VF dataset ROC curves SVM classifier using LOOP descriptor compared with the previous methods as shown in Fig. 5. The obtained Precision, Recall, F-measure, Accuracy, and AUC result are successively, 95.64%, 93.38%, 95.17%, 91.54%, and 93.81% on the Violent-Flows dataset as shown in Table 1. Comparative analysis of the proposed method for HF and VF Datasets as shown in Fig. 6. It is noticed that our proposed feature descriptor is capable to detect violent events even if there is a cluttered background, varied illumination, little motion, and scale changes.

Table 1. Performance evaluation metrics is illustrated in percentage

Dataset	P	R	F	Acc	AUC
Hockey Fight	94.48	94.09	94.28	92.25±1.77	95.11
Violent-Flows	95.64	93.83	95.17	91.54±3.42	93.84

4.4 Discussion

Our proposed LOOP descriptor gives good result than Histograms of Oriented Gradients (HOG), Histogram of Optical Flow (HOF), Local Ternary Pattern (LTP), Violent Flow (ViF), Oriented Violent Flow (OViF), ViF+OViF, Distribution of Magnitude Orientation Local Interest Frame (DiMOLIF), GHOG+GIST, LBP+GLCM and Histogram of Optical flow Magnitude and Orientation (HOMO) for both HF and VF datasets. HOG, HOF, LTP, and ViF descriptors can not work if orientation changes. Therefore, these feature extraction methods are failed to detect violent event detection. The OViF feature extraction method extracts orientation features and obtains good performance for the HF dataset but does not perform well for the VF dataset. To resolve this problem the ViF+OViF feature extraction technique is used to extracts both magnitude and orientation features to detect suspicious behavior and is superior to ViF and OViF descriptors. DiMOLIF descriptor extracts magnitude and orientation from the optical flow feature descriptor to detect violent events. This descriptor gives substantial results as compared to ViF and OViF. The GHOG+GIST descriptor uses the fusion of global gradient and texture features. GHOG descriptor is poorly performed if there is a cluttered background and the GIST descriptor does not work for violent crowd activity in the video sequence. LBP+GLCM descriptor uses the fusion of texture features to detect aggressive behavior. The main drawback of LBP is the arbitrarily defined set of binary weights that depend on direction. GLCM feature extraction limitations are the high dimensional of the matrix and the high correlation of the features. HOMO is based on multiple scaling factors being applied to the magnitude and orientation variations of the optical flow. LOOP descriptor is effective for illumination changes, scale, and rotational invariance.

Table 2. Performance comparision result on Hockey Fight and Violent-Flow dataset

Method	HF dataset		VF dataset	
	Acc (±SD)	AUC	Acc (±SD)	AUC
HOG [19]	87.8	-	57.43±0.37	61.82
HOF [19]	83.5	-	58.53±0.32	57.60
LTP [40]	71.90±0.49	-	71.53±0.17	79.86
ViF [15]	81.60±0.22	88.01	81.20±1.79	88.04
OViF [13]	84.20±3.33	90.32	76.80±3.90	80.47
ViF+OViF [13]	86.30±1.57	91.93	86.00±1.41	91.82
DiMOLIF [25]	88.6±1.2	93.23	85.83±4.2	89.25
GHOG+GIST [24]	91.18 ± 2.95	93.45	88.86 ±5.12	92.00
LBP+GLCM [23]	91.51±1.51	93.60	89.06±3.32	93.00
HOMO [26]	89.3±0.91	95.18	76.83±1.76	82.84
LOOP	**92.25±3.13**	**95.19**	**91.54±1.32**	**93.84**

We have demonstrated the efficiency of our proposed model and this is an immensely important task. We compare our experimental results with existing methods using HF and VF datasets. In the experiment, we have used the LOOP descriptor to demonstrate for violent event detection. Our proposed method shows impressive results compared to existing methods as illustrate in Table 2.

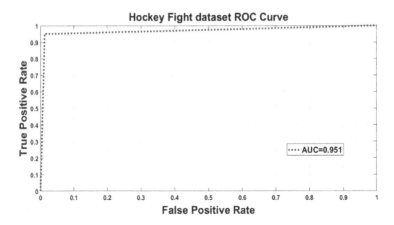

Fig. 4. Hockey Fight dataset ROC Curves of proposed feature descriptor with SVM classifier

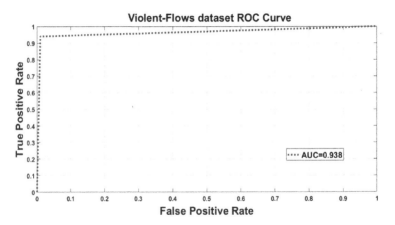

Fig. 5. Violent-Flows dataset ROC Curves of proposed feature descriptor with SVM classifier

It is noticed that our proposed feature descriptor is capable to detect violent event even if there is a cluttered background, varied illumination, little motion, and scale changes. Actually, there are six attributes that need to be intimate for suspicious event detection. Some of the intimates are, magnitude, orientation, the spatial arrangement of the moving objects, number of the objects moving in a video scene, mass, and acceleration. Certainly, our proposed method based on the scale and orientation of the object apparent motion using the extraction of LOOP features to improve the performance of the proposed method. Eventually, we deduce that our proposed method significantly performs well for both Hockey Fight and Violent-Flows dataset.

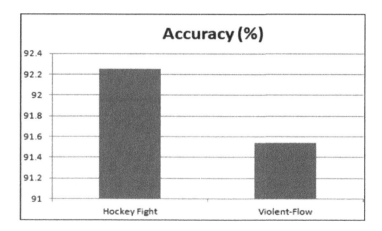

Fig. 6. Comparative analysis of the proposed method for Hockey Fight and Violent Flows Dataset

5 Conclusion

Video monitoring is used as a mechanism of scrutinizing videos to recognize suspicious behavior. Human behavior can be examined with the help of a surveillance video that could be manual or automatic. The research community has failed to develop an effective algorithm because of complex background, illumination, scale changes, etc. Experiments are conducted on the HF dataset and VF dataset and the experimental result shows that our proposed method performs an effective and preferable result to the previous feature descriptors. In the future, we intent to conduct experimentation on complex videos, endeavor to optimize the proposed method to improve the accuracy and reduce the time computation.

Acknowledgment. The first author would like to thank UGC under RGNF for supporting financially, Letter no.F1-17.1/2014-15/RGNF-2014-15-SC-KAR-73791 /(SA-III/Website), JSS Science and Technology University, Mysuru, Karnataka, India.

References

1. Accattoli, S., Sernani, P., Falcionelli, N., Mekuria, D.N., Dragoni, A.F.: Violence detection in videos by combining 3d convolutional neural networks and support vector machines. Appl. Artif. Intell. **34**(4), 329–344 (2020)
2. Aradhya, V.M., Basavaraju, H., Guru, D.S.: Decade research on text detection in images/videos: a review. Evolut. Intell. 14, 1–27 (2019)
3. Aradhya, V.M., Mahmud, M., Guru, D., Agarwal, B., Kaiser, M.S.: One-shot cluster-based approach for the detection of covid-19 from chest x-ray images. Cognit. Comput. **22**, 1–9 (2021)
4. Asad, M., Yang, J., He, J., Shamsolmoali, P., He, X.: Multi-frame feature-fusion-based model for violence detection. Vis. Comput. **37**(6), 1415–1431 (2020)

5. Basavaraju, H., Aradhya, V.M., Pavithra, M., Guru, D., Bhateja, V.: Arbitrary oriented multilingual text detection and segmentation using level set and gaussian mixture model. Evolut. Intell. **14**(2), 881–894 (2020)
6. Chakraborti, T., McCane, B., Mills, S., Pal, U.: Loop descriptor: local optimal-oriented pattern. IEEE Signal Process. Lett. **25**(5), 635–639 (2018)
7. Cong, Y., Yuan, J., Liu, J.: Sparse reconstruction cost for abnormal event detection. In: CVPR 2011, pp. 3449–3456. IEEE (2011)
8. Vapnik, V., Cortes, C.: Support vector machine. Mach. Learn. **20**(3), 273–297 (1995)
9. Deepak, K., Vignesh, L., Chandrakala, S.: Autocorrelation of gradients based violence detection in surveillance videos. ICT Express **6**(3), 155–159 (2020)
10. Denoeux, T.: A k-nearest neighbor classification rule based on dempster-shafer theory, vol. 25, pp. 804–813. IEEE (1995)
11. Esen, E., Arabaci, M.A., Soysal, M.: Fight detection in surveillance videos. In: 2013 11th International Workshop on Content-Based Multimedia Indexing (CBMI), pp. 131–135. IEEE (2013)
12. Febin, I., Jayasree, K., Joy, P.T.: Violence detection in videos for an intelligent surveillance system using MoBSIFT and movement filtering algorithm. Pattern Anal. Appl. **23**, 611–623 (2020)
13. Gao, Y., Liu, H., Sun, X., Wang, C., Liu, Y.: Violence detection using oriented violent flows. Image Vis. Comput. **48**, 37–41 (2016)
14. Hanson, A., Pnvr, K., Krishnagopal, S., Davis, L.: Bidirectional convolutional lstm for the detection of violence in videos. In: Proceedings of the European Conference on Computer Vision (ECCV) (2018)
15. Hassner, T., Itcher, Y., Kliper-Gross, O.: Violent flows: real-time detection of violent crowd behavior. In: 2012 IEEE Computer Society Conference on Computer Vision and Pattern Recognition Workshops, pp. 1–6. IEEE (2012)
16. Imran, J., Raman, B., Rajput, A.S.: Robust, efficient and privacy-preserving violent activity recognition in videos. In: Proceedings of the 35th Annual ACM Symposium on Applied Computing, pp. 2081–2088 (2020)
17. Jabid, T., Kabir, M.H., Chae, O.: Local directional pattern (LDP)-a robust image descriptor for object recognition. In: 2010 7th IEEE International Conference on Advanced Video and Signal Based Surveillance, pp. 482–487. IEEE (2010)
18. Kaiser, M.S., et al.: iworksafe: towards healthy workplaces during Covid-19 with an intelligent phealth app for industrial settings. IEEE Access **9**, 13814–13828 (2021)
19. Laptev, I., Marszalek, M., Schmid, C., Rozenfeld, B.: Learning realistic human actions from movies. In: 2008 IEEE Conference on Computer Vision and Pattern Recognition, pp. 1–8. IEEE (2008)
20. Li, A., Miao, Z., Cen, Y., Zhang, X.P., Zhang, L., Chen, S.: Abnormal event detection in surveillance videos based on low-rank and compact coefficient dictionary learning. Pattern Recognit.**108**, 107355 (2020)
21. Lloyd, K., Rosin, P.L., Marshall, D., Moore, S.C.: Detecting violent and abnormal crowd activity using temporal analysis of grey level co-occurrence matrix (GLCM)-based texture measures. Mach. Vis. Appl. **28**(3-4), 361–371 (2017)
22. Lohithashva, B.H., Manjunath Aradhya, V.N., Basavaraju, H.T., Harish, B.S.: Unusual crowd event detection: an approach using probabilistic neural network. In: Satapathy, S.C., Bhateja, V., Somanah, R., Yang, X.-S., Senkerik, R. (eds.) Information Systems Design and Intelligent Applications. AISC, vol. 862, pp. 533–542. Springer, Singapore (2019). https://doi.org/10.1007/978-981-13-3329-3_50

23. Lohithashva, B., Aradhya, V.M., Guru, D.: Violent video event detection based on integrated LBP and GLCM texture features. Rev. d'Intell. Artif. **34**(2), 179–187 (2020)
24. Lohithashva, B.H., Manjunath Aradhya, V.N., Guru, D.S.: Violent event detection: an approach using fusion GHOG-GIST descriptor. In: Komanapalli, V.L.N., Sivakumaran, N., Hampannavar, S. (eds.) Advances in Automation, Signal Processing, Instrumentation, and Control. LNEE, vol. 700, pp. 881–890. Springer, Singapore (2021). https://doi.org/10.1007/978-981-15-8221-9_82
25. Mabrouk, A.B., Zagrouba, E.: Spatio-temporal feature using optical flow based distribution for violence detection. Pattern Recognit. Lett. **92**, 62–67 (2017)
26. Mahmoodi, J., Salajeghe, A.: A classification method based on optical flow for violence detection. Expert Syst. Appl. **127**, 121–127 (2019)
27. Mahmud, M., Kaiser, M.S., McGinnity, T.M., Hussain, A.: Deep learning in mining biological data. Cognit. Comput. **13**, 1–33 (2021)
28. Mahmud, M., Kaiser, M.S., Hussain, A., Vassanelli, S.: Applications of deep learning and reinforcement learning to biological data. IEEE Trans. Neural Netw. Learn. Syst. **29**, 2063–2079 (2018)
29. Majumder, S., Kehtarnavaz, N.: A review of real-time human action recognition involving vision sensing. In: Real-Time Image Processing and Deep Learning 2021. vol. 11736, p. 117360A. International Society for Optics and Photonics (2021)
30. Naveena, C., Poornachandra, S., Manjunath Aradhya, V.N.: Segmentation of brain tumor tissues in multi-channel MRI using convolutional neural networks. In: Mahmud, M., Vassanelli, S., Kaiser, M.S., Zhong, N. (eds.) BI 2020. LNCS (LNAI), vol. 12241, pp. 128–137. Springer, Cham (2020). https://doi.org/10.1007/978-3-030-59277-6_12
31. Bermejo Nievas, E., Deniz Suarez, O., Bueno García, G., Sukthankar, R.: Violence detection in video using computer vision techniques. In: Real, P., Diaz-Pernil, D., Molina-Abril, H., Berciano, A., Kropatsch, W. (eds.) CAIP 2011. LNCS, vol. 6855, pp. 332–339. Springer, Heidelberg (2011). https://doi.org/10.1007/978-3-642-23678-5_39
32. Pareek, P., Thakkar, A.: A survey on video-based human action recognition: recent updates, datasets, challenges, and applications. Artif. Intell. Rev. **54**, 2259–2322 (2021)
33. Qasim, T., Bhatti, N.: A hybrid swarm intelligence based approach for abnormal event detection in crowded environments. Pattern Recognit. Lett. **128**, 220–225 (2019)
34. Reddy, V., Sanderson, C., Lovell, B.C.: Improved anomaly detection in crowded scenes via cell-based analysis of foreground speed, size and texture, pp. 55–61. IEEE (2011)
35. Ryan, D., Denman, S., Fookes, C., Sridharan, S.: Textures of optical flow for real-time anomaly detection in crowds. In: 2011 8th IEEE international conference on advanced video and signal based surveillance (AVSS), pp. 230–235. IEEE (2011)
36. Sabokrou, M., Fayyaz, M., Fathy, M., Moayed, Z., Klette, R.: Deep-anomaly: fully convolutional neural network for fast anomaly detection in crowded scenes. Comput. Vis. Image Underst. **172**, 88–97 (2018)
37. Song, D., Kim, C., Park, S.K.: A multi-temporal framework for high-level activity analysis: violent event detection in visual surveillance. Inf. Sci. **447**, 83–103 (2018)
38. Song, W., Zhang, D., Zhao, X., Yu, J., Zheng, R., Wang, A.: A novel violent video detection scheme based on modified 3d convolutional neural networks. IEEE Access **7**, 39172–39179 (2019)

39. Ye, L., Liu, T., Han, T., Ferdinando, H., Seppänen, T., Alasaarela, E.: Campus violence detection based on artificial intelligent interpretation of surveillance video sequences. Remote Sens. **13**(4), 628 (2021)
40. Yeffet, L., Wolf, L.: Local trinary patterns for human action recognition. In: 2009 IEEE 12th International Conference on Computer Vision, pp. 492–497. IEEE (2009)
41. Zhang, X., Shu, X., He, Z.: Crowd panic state detection using entropy of the distribution of enthalpy. Phys. A Stat. Mech. Appl. **525**, 935–945 (2019)

Human Age Estimation Using Deep Learning from Gait Data

Refat Khan Pathan[1] , Mohammad Amaz Uddin[1] , Nazmun Nahar[1] ,
Ferdous Ara[1] , Mohammad Shahadat Hossain[2(✉)] , and Karl Andersson[3]

[1] BGC Trust University Bangladesh Bidyanagar, Chandanaish, Bangladesh
nazmun@bgctub.ac.bd
[2] University of Chittagong, Chittagong, Bangladesh
hossain_ms@cu.ac.bd
[3] Lulea University of Technology, 931 87 Skellefteå, Sweden
Karl.andersson@ltu.se

Abstract. Identifying people's ages and events by the use of gait information is a popular issue in our daily applications. The most popular application is health, security, entertainment and charging. A variety of algorithms for data mining and deep learning have been proposed. Many different technologies may be used to keep track of people's ages and behaviors. Existing approaches and technologies are limited by their performance, as well as their privacy and deployment costs. For example CCTV or Kinect sensor technology constitutes a privacy offense and most people do not want to make pictures or videos when they are working every day. The inertial sensor-based gait data collection is a recent addition to the gait analysis field. We have identified the age of people in this paper from an inertial sensor-data. We obtained the gait data from the University of Osaka. Convolution Neural Network (CNN) and LSTM-Based Convolution Neural Network (LSTM-CNN) are two deep learning algorithms that have been used to predict people's ages. The accuracy of age prediction via CNN is around 71.45%, while it is around 65.53% via CNN-LSTM, according to the experimental results.

Keywords: Gait · Inertial sensor · Age estimation · Deep learning

1 Introduction

Age-prediction is an important analytical factor in deep learning system. Currently, the age of a person may be predicted by measure and analysis of using teeth and bones with its acceptable error [1,2]. Human beings are systems of complex social cells and organisms that live in organized way to shape a living being that is a nebulous structure of atoms, of cells, of tissues, of organisms. The entirety of this instruction originates from the association of two cells. To tell the age of a living being a person could consider the cell divisions emphases of the framework and develop a standard morphology model for living frameworks all in all dependent on hereditary qualities and the cycle by emphasis development

© Springer Nature Switzerland AG 2021
M. Mahmud et al. (Eds.): AII 2021, CCIS 1435, pp. 281–294, 2021.
https://doi.org/10.1007/978-3-030-82269-9_22

of a life form. The images in this system have a few varieties in appearance, clamor, posture, and lighting which may influence the capacity of those physically planned computer vision techniques to precisely order the age of the images. Deep learning-based methods have demonstrated empowering execution in this field particularly on the age order of unfiltered face images [3,4].

Age assessment is a procedure of consequently marking the human face with a precise age or then again age gathering. This age can be either genuine age, appearance age, seen age, or assessed age [5]. Appearance and seen age are assessed dependent on visual age data depicted on the face while assessed age is a subject's age assessed by a machine from the facial visual appearance. Appearance age is thought to be steady with real age despite the fact that there are varieties due to the stochastic nature of maturing among people. Real age is the quantity of years one has assessed since birth to date, meant as a genuine number. Another method of age estimation is to look at a person's overall appearance and guess their age. Age estimation from facial images, on the other hand, is gaining popularity. As a result, facial characteristics are more accurate aging biomarkers than blood samples, and they can represent health conditions more than actual age.

Another method of age assessment is the classification machines which are performed with the age highlights. This can be arranged into three methodologies: single-level age assessment [6], hierarchical age assessment [7], and age group characterization [8]. The principal approach is the strategy that roughly predicts an age gathering, rather than assessing precise age. The first and second methodologies center around assessing the exact age.

These days, movable or wearable keen hardware devices are utilized as often as possible for various purposes and they are made with the different sort of sensors. Despite the fact that their request is a lot of high, these devices are grown quickly; furthermore, the assembling organizations are improving these tools as indicated by the interest of the proprietor and furthermore rely upon the wellbeing state of the customary individuals [9].

Even though the previous approaches can achieve effective estimation outcomes, they do have several drawbacks. Some of these problems include the impact on age prediction of gender differences, face, or the accuracy of captured photos.

In spite of the fact that these previous techniques can create great assessment results, they despite everything have numerous difficulties. Whatever difficulties incorporate the impact of sex contrasts, facial appearances, or the quality of caught pictures on age assessment. The appearance of the human face changes (both male and female) in both texture and shape.

There are many method and many types of data available [11–14] to classify age. In this paper, we have attempted to confront these difficulties and have showed the way toward predicting age from the inertial sensor-based gait dataset. The walk Inertial sensor which is remembering gyroscope or accelerometer or both for it is dynamically being appended in profitable movable electronic gadgets. Walk inertial sensor information was made by Osaka University-Institute of

Scientific and Industrial Research (OU-ISIR) [10]. We use a convolutional neural network in this case because it is an extremely noise-resistant model that can extract very detailed, deep features which are time-independent.

The main objective of this paper to classify human age is given below:

- • A CNN and CNN-LSTM based age classification is proposed where we used inertial based gait dataset.
- • We have compared our proposed CNN and CNN-LSTM model with other traditional machine learning method.
- • We have also compared our CNN method with other current work.

The remaining portions of the paper are divided into several parts. The Sect. 2 describes the related work. Section 3 discusses the methodology. Section 4 describes the experiment's results. The conclusion and future work are discussed in the final section.

2   Related Work

Kanij Mehtanin Khabir et al. [15] used an inertial sensor-based Dataset consist of 744 people for age identification. In this research, they analyzed twelve types of time-domain features such as mean, median, maximum, minimum, mean absolute deviation, kurtosis, skewness, standard deviation, variance, root mean square, standard error of the mean, vector sum. This research has some overfitting problems because the accuracy of the training data is higher than the test data.

The statistical features collected from accelerations and angular velocities [16] of 26 people to measure the age. The total 50 features estimated in this research, in each step. The diversity of biometric features was too small in this experiment.

The uniqueness of video-based gait features for four different classes, as for instance children, adult males, adult females, and the elderly were analyzed with static and dynamic components for age classification in [17].

Tim Van Hamme et al. [18] analyzed the age information from gait traces gained from IMU sensors and compared different machine learning algorithms, including both traditional and deep learning methods.

Thanh Trung Ngo et al. [19] organized a challenging competition on age prediction using wearable sensors. They used the largest inertial gait dataset to predict a person age which gained by using the IMUZ sensor. The proposed method and extracted features are not enough enriched.

Age classification based on gait analysis data was presented in [20]. They find out 50 hand-crafted spatio-spectral features by a sensor which was fixed at the chest. In the research, they used three different estimators to predict the age where random forest regressor performed well other than support vector regressor and Multi-layer perceptron. The number of data was not enough for deep learning so needed a larger dataset.

Multi-stage CNN based method proposed in [21] for age estimation. In this paper, they introduced CNN based model which manufactured with three stages of CNN and analyzed the large-scale gait OULP-age dataset.

In another work, a baseline algorithm using Gaussian process regression [22] has been used to estimate age. This proposed method achieved successes in the age classification. When the actual age and the gait age difference this proposed method failed to give good result.

3   Methodology

As seen in Fig. 1, this section describes the proposed methodology framework for classifying human age, which includes data collection, data preprocessing and applying deep learning method.This study has considered the dataset obtained using the 3-axis accelerometer and gyroscope sensor in the University of Osaka. The dataset was preprocessed to remove noise, which were then split into two datasets: training and testing. Deep learning methods were used to train the training dataset.The components of the proposed technique as seen in Fig. 1, are described below.

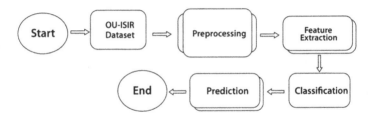

Fig. 1. Graphical illustration of proposed methodology.

3.1   Dataset Description

The University of Osaka generated OU-ISIR gait dataset. It is the biggest inertial gait dataset on a sensor [23], and is comparatively well built. Three IMU (inertial measurement unit) sensors known as IMUZ were used to collect gait signals in this dataset. A 3-axis accelerometer and a 3-axis gyroscope module were used in the IMUZ. Three sensors are located on the belt: one on the right, one on the left, and one on the center-back. These three sensors were attached to the belt in a variety of positions (90° for centre-left, center-right and 180° for right-left group). 745 visitors' gait data was gathered over the course of five days. Every visitor entered and exited the specified data collection tool only once. Triaxial accelerometer and triaxial gyroscope signals are recorded in each IMUZ sensor. And hence, 6D data from every signal is stored. Five actions data classified as: slope-up, slope-down, level walking, step-up and step-down walking have been gathered. Data were obtained for only level walking, Slope-up and slope-down for each subject. The data contains four categories, including identity, age, gender and activity. The signals of accelerometer data and gyroscope data are shown in Figs. 2 and 3.

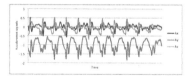 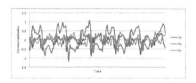

Fig. 2. Example of signals for accelerometer data.

Fig. 3. Example of signals for gyroscope data

3.2   Model Design

In this paper, we have used two deep learning model one is Convolutional neural network (CNN) and the other is LSTM-based Convolutional Neural Network (CNN-LSTM).

CNN Model Design. Table 1 illustrates the network structure of our proposed model. The CNN architecture is made up of four 1D convolution layers and a fully-connected layer. The first two 1D convolution layers are composed of 64 filters, each with a kernel size of 3. All of these filters create maps for extracting various data features. A MaxPooling layer with a pool size of 2 is included in order to find the maximum number of features. There are 128 filter with kernels of size 3 in the second and third convolution layers, each following the two previous layers. This time, a MaxPooling layer with the dimension of pool 2 has been added. Finally, the pooling layer is flattened into a single vector. The fully-connected layer, which is also known as the hidden layer, consists of 128 nodes. There is a drop-out layer after the hidden layer that modifies 50% of the active nodes so that the model does not show bias against the training result, thus preventing the model from overfitting. In all convolutions as well as the hidden layer, the activation function ReLU has been used. The final CNN layer is an output layer consisting of three nodes for three classes, and this layer is used as a SoftMax activation function.

LSTM-CNN Model Design. Table 2 shows the CNN-LSTM-based model. The CNN-LSTM has four convoluted layers, followed by two maximum pooling layers and two layers of the LSTM. First input data is fed into the LSTM layer. First LSTM layer consists of 64 nodes this layer is followed by another LSTM

Table 1. Description of the CNN system architecture.

Model contents	Details
First and second convolution layers	32 filters of size 3, ReLU, 85 × 1
Max pooling layer	Pooling size 2
Third and fourth convolution layers	64 filters of size 3, ReLU activation function
Max pooling layer	Pooling size 2
Hidden layer	64 nodes, ReLU activation function
Dropout layer	Deactivates 50% of node randomly
Output layer	3 nodes for 3 classes, SoftMax activation function
Optimization function	Adam
Learning rate	0.001
Loss function	Categorical cross entropy

layer which consists 128 nodes. Then these LSTM layer are fed into Convolutional layer. Convolution layers are used to create maps that are transferred into the nest layers. There are 64 filters for the first two 1D convolution layers, each with a kernel size of 3. There is a layer of MaxPooling with a pool of 2 size. In the second and third convolution layers, the filters have kernels of size3, following the previous two layersA MaxPooling layer with the dimension pool 2 has been applied this time. The pooling layer would finally be flattened into one vector. There are 32 nodes in the fully connected layer, which is also called the hidden layer. A drop-out layer following the hidden layer modifies 25% of the active nodes to prevent the model from overfitting. The last CNN layer is a three-class output layer composed of three nodes, and this layer is used SoftMax activation function.

4   Result and Discussion

In this section, we'll talk about the performances of the applied model identifies human age. Human age primarily classified into three groups which are child, adult and old. It discusses a brief description of the data collection used in the study and analysis process. In this paper, we have used OU-ISIR Gait Database, Large Population Dataset with Age (OULP-Age). The dataset has been split into 80–20% train-test section. We have used 80% (1244 samples) of the data to train our model with CNN and CNN-LSTM, remaining 20% (312 samples) data has been used for validation of the trained model.

Table 2. Description of the LSTM-CNN system architecture.

Model contents	Details
First and second LSTM layers	64 nodes, 85 × 1
First and second convolution layers	64 filters of size 3, ReLU activation function
Max pooling layer	Pooling size 2
Third and fourth convolution layers	32 filters of size 3, ReLU activation function
Max pooling layer	Pooling size 2
Hidden layer	32 nodes, ReLU activation function
Dropout layer	Deactivates 25% of node randomly
Output layer	3 nodes for 3 classes, SoftMax activation function
Optimization function	Adam
Learning rate	0.001
Loss function	Categorical cross entropy

4.1 System Configuration

We used the tensor-flow enabled GPU [24] for implementation of convolution neural network. A suitable GPU for the deep learning model training is required because there are many matrix multiplication operations in the neural network. Because of the processing power limitations in a CPU, the proposed CNN Architecture is designated for training on the Google Colaboratory cloud server. GPU and Jupyter Notebook environment shared by the Google Colab is specially designed to help the machine learner overcome the problem of the processing unit. Google Colab has been used to train and test our presented deep learning approach.

4.2 Tuning Hyperparameters

Hyperparameters are essential if they effect the behaviors of the system directly, as fine-tuned hyperparameters affect the performance of the model significantly. We used the Adam [25] optimizer to train 200 epochs, with a learning rate of 0.0001 for a batch size of 64. In addition, the categorical cross entropy loss function determines the class probability loss estimated by the softmax function. Lastly, calculate each age groups probability.

4.3 Performance Evaluation Matrix

In this paper, we evaluated the age estimation output with Accuracy, Loss and MAE (mean absolute error) [26]. We have compared the efficiency of the classification model to three metrics: accuracy, recall and F1-score. Accuracy can be defined as system capability to estimate the age against the ages of ground truth. Accuracy can be determined from.

$$Accuracy = \frac{TP + TN}{TP + TN + FP + FN} \times 100 \tag{1}$$

The average of absolute errors between the predicted ages and the age of ground truth can be known as MAE. MAE can be determined from

$$MAE = \frac{1}{n} \sum_{j=1}^{n} \mid y - y' \mid \tag{2}$$

4.4   Result

Table 3 shows the training accuracy and validation accuracy of CNN and CNN-LSTM. From the table we can see that the CNN algorithm's training accuracy is 91.56% and Validation accuracy is 71.86% and CNN-LSTM algorithm's training accuracy is 80.86% and validation accuracy is 65.53%. From the observation, we can see that validation accuracy is 20% less than the training accuracy in CNN algorithm and in CNN-LSTM validation accuracy is 15% less than the training accuracy.

Table 3. Training and validation accuracy.

Classifier name	Training accuracy	Testing accuracy	MAE
CNN	91.56%	71.45%	3.75%
CNN-LSTM	80.86%	65.53%	5.50%
Gradient boosting	92.15%	69.48%	5.0%
Bagging	96.48%	67.47%	5.94%
Extra tree classifier	98.92%	63.28%	6.21%

Figure 4 shows the training and validation accuracy at each stage for CNN algorithm. Here, green line shows the training accuracy and the red line shows the validation accuracy. From the figure we can see that at initial stage the training accuracy is 58% and validation accuracy is 51%. Gradually the training accuracy and validation accuracy is increasing with the number of epoch. At final epoch the training accuracy is approximately 90% and validation accuracy is approximately 70%. After the 200 epoch between training accuracy and validation accuracy is difference more than 20%.

Figure 5 shows the training and validation accuracy at each stage for CN-LSTM algorithm. Here, green line shows the training accuracy and the red line shows the validation accuracy. From the figure we can see that at initial stage the training accuracy is 55% and validation accuracy is 50%. Gradually the training accuracy and validation accuracy is increasing with the number of epoch. At

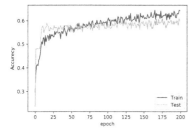

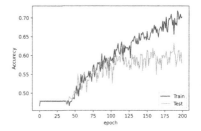

Fig. 4. Training and validation accuracy of CNN algorithm (Color figure online)

Fig. 5. Training and validation accuracy of CNN-LSTM algorithm (Color figure online)

final epoch the training accuracy is approximately 80% and validation accuracy is approximately 65%. Difference between the training and validation accuracy is approximately 15% after the 200 epoch.

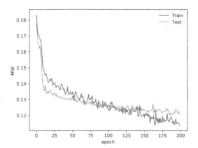

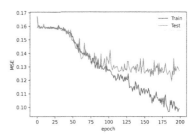

Fig. 6. Training and validation MSE of CNN algorithm (Color figure online)

Fig. 7. Training and validation MSE of CNN-LSTM algorithm (Color figure online)

Figures 6 and 7 shows the MSE of training and validation of the CNN and CNN-LSTM algorithm. In these figure the blue line shows the training MSE and orange line show the validation MSE. From Fig. 6 we can see that at initial epoch the training MSE is greater than 0.18 and while the epoch is increasing the loss is decreasing. At the epoch number 200 the MSE is less than 0.10. When the epoch number is increasing the difference between the training and testing MSE is become minimized. From Fig. 7 we can see that at initial stage the validation MSE is 0.16 and training MSE is greater than 0.17. The difference between the training and validation MSE is gradually increases while the epoch number is increasing.

Figures 8 and 9 illustrates the confusion matrix of CNN and CNN-LSTM based algorithm. The confusion matrix is applied to three classes: child, adult,

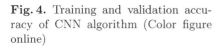

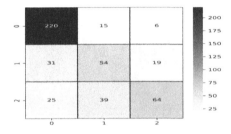

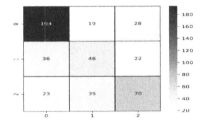

Fig. 8. Confusion matrix of CNN algorithm

Fig. 9. Confusion matrix of CNN-LSTM algorithm

and Old. The row of the table represents the true class, and the column represents the class that classifiers know. The value in the table shows the possibility of recognizing the real class.

Table 4. Age estimation performance matrices

Classifier name	Class level	Precision	Recall	F-score
CNN	Child	0.80	0.91	0.85
	Adult	0.50	0.52	0.51
	Old	0.72	0.50	0.59
CNN-LSTM	Child	0.77	0.70	0.89
	Adult	0.46	0.44	0.45
	Old	0.58	0.55	0.56
Gradient boosting	Child	0.72	0.82	0.79
	Adult	0.48	0.43	0.45
	Old	0.48	0.46	0.47
Bagging	Child	0.63	0.89	0.71
	Adult	0.48	0.38	0.42
	Old	0.66	0.54	0.59
Extra tree classifier	Child	0.72	0.92	0.84
	Adult	0.68	0.26	0.38
	Old	0.65	0.64	0.65

The Above Table 4 shows the precision, recall and f-measure of the CNN and CNN-LSTM based algorithm. From the table we can see that child class shows the better precision, recall and f-Score in two algorithms and adult class shows the worst precision, recall and f-score in two algorithms.

We have also compared our proposed CNN-LSTM with other existing work. Table 5 shows the comparison with other existing work. From the table we can see that the proposed method has the highest accuracy among the other work.

Table 5. Comparison of our proposed methodology with existing work.

Author	Method/Algorithm	Performance matrix (%)
[8]	Ensemble	MAE (5.94%)
[16]	TCN	MAE (12.29%)
[17]	Multu-layer perceptron	RMSE (9.72%)
[19]	Multi-stage CNN	MAE (5.84%)
Our proposed method	CNN	MAE (3.75%)

5 Conclusion and Future Work

In this study, the best deep learning algorithm has been attempted to estimate age in the inertial sensor gait dataset. This experiment analyzes the largest inertial sensor OU-ISIR gait dataset. The use of time and frequency domain characteristics is a key aspect of our paper and we also choose the most appropriate features for estimating age. These derived functions are used to train our chosen deep learning models successfully. Nevertheless, in this analysis, only 1100 training set data were used. We will collect more data for the training process in the future and we also try to build more deep learning model [27–32] and use some traditional machine learning model [33–39]. As our proposed deep learning does not give the better accuracy so in future we will apply some data preprocessing technique to improve our accuracy also to handle ambient conditions.

References

1. Hillewig, E., et al.: Magnetic resonance imaging of the sternal extremity of the clavicle in forensic age estimation: towards more sound age estimates. Int. J. Legal Med. **127**(3), 677–689 (2013)
2. Thevissen, P.W., Kaur, J., Willems, G.: Human age estimation combining third molar and skeletal development. Int. J. Legal Med. **126**(2), 285–292 (2012)
3. Ranjan, R., et al.: Unconstrained age estimation with deep convolutional neural networks. In: Proceedings of the IEEE International Conference on Computer Vision Workshops. pp. 109–117 (2015)
4. Szegedy, C., et al.: Going deeper with convolutions. In: Proceedings of the IEEE Conference on Computer Vision and Pattern Recognition, pp. 1–9 (2015)
5. Fu, Y., Guo, G., Huang, T.S.: Age synthesis and estimation via faces: a survey. IEEE Trans. Pattern Anal. Mach. Intell. **32**(11), 1955–1976 (2010)

6. Lanitis, A., Draganova, C., Christodoulou, C.: Comparing different classifiers for automatic age estimation. IEEE Trans. Syst. Man Cybern. Part B (Cybern.) **34**(1), 621–628 (2004)
7. Luu, K., Ricanek, K., Bui, T.D., Suen, C.Y.: Age estimation using active appearance models and support vector machine regression. In: 2009 IEEE 3rd International Conference on Biometrics: Theory, Applications, and Systems, pp. 1–5. IEEE (2004)
8. Gao, F., Ai, H.: Face age classification on consumer images with Gabor feature and fuzzy LDA method. In: Tistarelli, M., Nixon, M.S. (eds.) ICB 2009. LNCS, vol. 5558, pp. 132–141. Springer, Heidelberg (2009). https://doi.org/10.1007/978-3-642-01793-3_14
9. Muro-De-La-Herran, A., Garcia-Zapirain, B., Mendez-Zorrilla, A.: Gait analysis methods: an overview of wearable and non-wearable systems, highlighting clinical applications. Sensors **14**(2), 3362–3394 (2014)
10. Ngo, T.T., Makihara, Y., Nagahara, H., Mukaigawa, Y., Yagi, Y.: The largest inertial sensor-based gait database and performance evaluation of gait-based personal authentication. Pattern Recogn. **47**(1), 228–237 (2014)
11. Mahmud, M., Kaiser, M.S., McGinnity, T.M., Hussain, A.: Deep learning in mining biological data. Cogn. Comput. **13**(1), 1–33 (2021)
12. Mahmud, M., Kaiser, M.S., Hussain, A., Vassanelli, S.: Applications of deep learning and reinforcement learning to biological data. IEEE Trans. Neural Netw. Learn. Syst. **29**(6), 2063–2079 (2018)
13. Kaiser, M.S., et al.: iWorkSafe: towards healthy workplaces during COVID-19 with an intelligent pHealth app for industrial settings. IEEE Access **9**, 13814–13828 (2021)
14. Pathan, R.K., Uddin, M.A., Nahar, N., Ara, F., Hossain, M.S., Andersson, K.: Gender classification from inertial sensor-based gait dataset. In: Vasant, P., Zelinka, I., Weber, G.W. (eds.) ICO 2020. AISC, vol. 1324, pp. 583–596. Springer, Cham (2020). https://doi.org/10.1007/978-3-030-68154-8_51
15. Khabir, K.M., Siraj, M.S., Ahmed, M., Ahmed, M.U.: Prediction of gender and age from inertial sensor-based gait dataset. In: 2019 Joint 8th International Conference on Informatics, Electronics and Vision (ICIEV) and 2019 3rd International Conference on Imaging, Vision and Pattern Recognition (icIVPR), pp. 371–376. IEEE, May 2019
16. Riaz, Q., Vögele, A., Krüger, B., Weber, A.: One small step for a man: estimation of gender, age and height from recordings of one step by a single inertial sensor. Sensors **15**(12), 31999–32019 (2015)
17. Makihara, Y., Mannami, H., Yagi, Y.: Gait analysis of gender and age using a large-scale multi-view gait database. In: Kimmel, R., Klette, R., Sugimoto, A. (eds.) ACCV 2010. LNCS, vol. 6493, pp. 440–451. Springer, Heidelberg (2010). https://doi.org/10.1007/978-3-642-19309-5_34
18. Garofalo, G., Argones Rúa, E., Preuveneers, D., Joosen, W.: A systematic comparison of age and gender prediction on IMU sensor-based gait traces. Sensors **19**(13), 2945 (2019)
19. Ngo, T.T., et al.: OU-ISIR wearable sensor-based gait challenge: age and gender. In: 2019 International Conference on Biometrics (ICB), pp. 1–6. IEEE, June 2019
20. Riaz, Q., Hashmi, M.Z.U.H., Hashmi, M.A., Shahzad, M., Errami, H., Weber, A.: Move your body: age estimation based on chest movement during normal walk. IEEE Access **7**, 28510–28524 (2019)

21. Sakata, A., Takemura, N., Yagi, Y.: Gait-based age estimation using multi-stage convolutional neural network. IPSJ Trans. Comput. Vis. Appl. **11**(1), 1–10 (2019). https://doi.org/10.1186/s41074-019-0054-2
22. Makihara, Y., Okumura, M., Iwama, H., Yagi, Y.: Gait-based age estimation using a whole-generation gait database. In: 2011 International Joint Conference on Biometrics (IJCB), pp. 1–6. IEEE, October 2011
23. Lu, J., Tan, Y.P.: Gait-based human age estimation. IEEE Trans. Inf. Forensics Secur. **5**(4), 761–770 (2010)
24. Abadi, M., et al.: TensorFlow: a system for large-scale machine learning. In: 12th USENIX Symposium on Operating Systems Design and Implementation (OSDI 2016), pp. 265–283 (2016)
25. Kingma, D.P., Ba, J.: Adam: a method for stochastic optimization. arXiv preprint arXiv:1412.6980 (2014)
26. Sokolova, M., Lapalme, G.: A systematic analysis of performance measures for classification tasks. Inf. Process. Manag. **45**(4), 427–437 (2009)
27. Islam, M.Z., Hossain, M.S., ul Islam, R., Andersson, K.: Static hand gesture recognition using convolutional neural network with data augmentation. In: 2019 Joint 8th International Conference on Informatics, Electronics and Vision (ICIEV) and 2019 3rd International Conference on Imaging, Vision and Pattern Recognition (icIVPR), pp. 324–329. IEEE, May 2019
28. Ahmed, T.U., Hossain, S., Hossain, M.S., ul Islam, R., Andersson, K.: Facial expression recognition using convolutional neural network with data augmentation. In: 2019 Joint 8th International Conference on Informatics, Electronics and Vision (ICIEV) and 2019 3rd International Conference on Imaging, Vision and Pattern Recognition (icIVPR), pp. 336–341. IEEE, May 2019
29. Abedin, M.Z., Nath, A.C., Dhar, P., Deb, K., Hossain, M.S. : License plate recognition system based on contour properties and deep learning model. In: 2017 IEEE Region 10 Humanitarian Technology Conference (R10-HTC), pp. 590–593. IEEE, December 2017
30. Kabir, S., Islam, R.U., Hossain, M.S., Andersson, K.: An integrated approach of belief rule base and deep learning to predict air pollution. Sensors **20**(7), 1956 (2020)
31. Ahmed, T.U., Hossain, M.S., Alam, M.J., Andersson, K.: An integrated CNN-RNN framework to assess road crack. In: 2019 22nd International Conference on Computer and Information Technology (ICCIT), pp. 1–6. IEEE, December 2019
32. Chowdhury, R.R., Hossain, M.S., Hossain, S., Andersson, K.: Analyzing sentiment of movie reviews in bangla by applying machine learning techniques. In: 2019 International Conference on Bangla Speech and Language Processing (ICBSLP), pp. 1–6. IEEE, September 2019
33. Zisad, S.N., Hossain, M.S., Andersson, K.: Speech emotion recognition in neurological disorders using convolutional neural network. In: Mahmud, M., Vassanelli, S., Kaiser, M.S., Zhong, N. (eds.) BI 2020. LNCS, vol. 12241, pp. 287–296. Springer, Cham (2020). https://doi.org/10.1007/978-3-030-59277-6_26
34. Uddin Ahmed, T., Jamil, M.N., Hossain, M.S., Andersson, K., Hossain, M.S.: An integrated real-time deep learning and belief rule base intelligent system to assess facial expression under uncertainty. In: 9th International Conference on Informatics, Electronics and Vision (ICIEV). IEEE Computer Society (2020)
35. Islam, R.U., Hossain, M.S., Andersson, K.: A deep learning inspired belief rule-based expert system. IEEE Access **8**, 190637–190651 (2020)

36. Nahar, N., Hossain, M.S., Andersson, K.: A machine learning based fall detection for elderly people with neurodegenerative disorders. In: Mahmud, M., Vassanelli, S., Kaiser, M.S., Zhong, N. (eds.) BI 2020. LNCS, vol. 12241, pp. 194–203. Springer, Cham (2020). https://doi.org/10.1007/978-3-030-59277-6_18

37. Basnin, N., Nahar, L., Hossain, M.S.: An integrated CNN-LSTM model for micro hand gesture recognition. In: Vasant, P., Zelinka, I., Weber, G.W. (eds.) ICO 2020. AISC, vol. 1324, pp. 379–392. Springer, Cham (2020). https://doi.org/10.1007/978-3-030-68154-8_35

38. Hossain, E., Shariff, M.A.U., Hossain, M.S., Andersson, K.: A novel deep learning approach to predict air quality index. In: Kaiser, M.S., Bandyopadhyay, A., Mahmud, M., Ray, K. (eds.) Proceedings of International Conference on Trends in Computational and Cognitive Engineering. AISC, vol. 1309, pp. 367–381. Springer, Singapore (2021). https://doi.org/10.1007/978-981-33-4673-4_29

39. Nahar, N., Ara, F., Neloy, M.A.I., Barua, V., Hossain, M.S., Andersson, K.: A comparative analysis of the ensemble method for liver disease prediction. In: 2019 2nd International Conference on Innovation in Engineering and Technology (ICIET), pp. 1–6. IEEE, December 2019

An Error Resilient Video Transmission in Ad Hoc Network Using Error Diffusion Block Truncation Coding

S. Sasi Kumar[1], K. Siva Kumar[2], M. A. Jalil[3], J. Kavikumar[4(✉)], K. Ray[5], and D. Nagarajan[6]

[1] Department of Electronics and Communication Engineering, Hindustan Institute of Technology and Science, Chennai, India
ssasik@hindustanuniv.ac.in

[2] Department of Computer Science and Engineering, Roever Engineering College, Perambalur, India
sivakumarme2004@gmail.com

[3] Department of Physics, Faculty of Science, Universiti Teknologi Malaysia, 81310 Skudai, Johor, Malaysia
arifjalil@utm.my

[4] Fuzzy Mathematics and Applications, Faculty of Applied Sciences and Technology, Universiti Tun Hussein Onn Malaysia, Pagoh Campus, Pagoh, Malaysia
kavi@uthm.edu.my

[5] Amity School of Applied Sciences, Amity University, Jaipur 303001, Rajasthan, India
kanadray00@gmail.com

[6] Department of Mathematics, Hindustan Institute of Technology and Science, Chennai, India
dnrmsu2002@yahoo.com

Abstract. In this paper, a mesh Ad Hoc network of error-resilient video transmission allows evaluating two disjoint nodes from source to destination. The main drawback of this paper is that it is impossible to safeguard video transmission over reliable channels. An error-resilient video transmission method is utilized over a wide variety of network application needs by using a new method called error diffusion block truncation coding (EDBTC). It is used to remove index color video features creates two-color quantizers and bitmap video. The performance metrics provide both transmissions of videos and non-corresponding disjoint paths to enhance the quality of error concealment video decoder by using proposed EDBTC delivers better video encoder and decoder process than the existing system.

Keywords: Layered coding · Flexible macro block ordering · EDBTC · Error resilient · Video coding

This research was supported by the Ministry of Higher Education Malaysia, under FRGS Grant No: K179.

1   Introduction

In recent trends, video transmission through Ad Hoc networks is required to be concentrated plays a vital role in processing bandwidth and power for mobile Ad Hoc devices. An Ad Hoc network is defined as a group of devices that allows users to provide static infrastructure for exchanging consecutive data. Each node in the network will act as a router. As a result of a quick process Ad Hoc network, a video transmission becomes an additional feature than other video transmission systems. Video transmission is defined as a process of streaming and compressing transmitted videos through the internet. The drawback is that it requires sufficient distance to transmit those videos. One of the most stimulating tasks is making video communication through the Ad Hoc network more consistent. Both line breaks, as well as packet loss from video channel, will often get occurred because of mobility and the disappearing of nodes from particular channel video. In addition to this, the errors for compressed video bitstreams become delicate due to the dependency of temporal data and the variable length of coded ciphers. Each frame error has been transmitted into a various set of frames through which the quality of video gets degraded for some point. A forward error correction (FEC) method possesses a better choice to detect the channel error that is required. But redundancy of transmitted data gets affected because packet loss of transmitted video will not work properly. An automatic repeat request is an existing method is utilized to identify missing packets of the video channel [1]. It provides less overhead than forwarding error correction. It is utilized as one of the most effective applications for backchannel that provide sufficient availability of video decoder channels respectively. At a certain point, a retransmitted packet of video channel will not be suitable. When retransmitted video packet gets lost, then that particular part of the video frame gets hidden by other information video frames. On the other hand, a bursty error environment becomes a common part of Ad Hoc networks through hidden data is required to be efficient, In this case, Multiple Description Coding (MDC) makes a path to be effective. These distributed errors get occurred within a frame in a separate manner that makes hidden packet loss be executed more efficiently. A flexible macroblock ordering method in H.264 AVC video standard has been established. It denotes the process of arranging Macro-Blocks (MB) into several groups where each group description of the video was described based on a specific pattern [2]. A layered coding method [3] is utilized [4] to enhance error resiliency video and supports several network properties. It converts the base layer into many enhancement layers. It also delivers basic video quality to improve the quality of the base layer. This method encodes standard codecs of the enhancement layer autonomously based on the accessibility of the base layer. A base layer is much more essential than an enhancement layer as it is required to protect an error-prone network of video transmission [5]. A quality-of-service routing problem in a MANET, self-organizing mobile route network linked through a wireless network without access point that provides a real-time factor for multimedia applications. Aliyu et al. [6] proposed a multipath video transmission protocol that considers the path's route coupling effect to minimize interference between paths which is utilized to develop an interference-aware video streaming method considering angular driving statistics of vehicles. Asif-Ur-Rahman et al. [7] proposed a five-layered heterogeneous mist, fog, and cloud-based IoHT [8] framework capable of efficiently handling and routing (near-)real-time as well as offline/batch mode data. They have concluded that the designed network via its various components can achieve high QoS, with reduced end-to-end latency and packet drop rate, which is essential for developing next generation-healthcare systems.

The basic idea of this video transmission is to distribute the number of tickets from the source that could be separated into sub tickets to search satisfactory multi-path. Through simulations, the value of our multi-path protocol flexibility was maintained when the network bandwidth is very limited, it delivers a higher success rate to find satisfactory QoS route than those protocols that allow users to find uni-path, and also when network bandwidth is sufficient performs almost similar to those protocols from both routing overhead and success rate. An EDBTC bitmap video has been constructed to reward the brightness of nearby pixels. It separates the particular block of video into several non-overlapped videos. Each video has been processed individually to provide the EDBTC video encoder and decoder process. The main contribution of the paper are to encompass EDBTC video encoder method for encoding video and propose an EDBTC video decoder method for decoding video. The remaining section of the paper is ordered as follows: Sect. 2 presents a brief review of the existing research works related to both Ad Hoc network and unequal error packet technique and also its advantage and disadvantage were discussed briefly Sect. 3 shows the detailed explanation of the proposed EDBTC comparative analysis of proposed work. Section 4 involves the short discussion of the conclusion and future work of the proposed work.

2   Proposed Work

This section presented a proposed work of EDBTC extension from the video encoder and decoder process. An EDBTC video provides a better method for integrating the error diffusion kernel into the bitmap video that is produced. It contains two quantizers such as minimum and a maximum quantizer. It delivers low computational complexity for both bit map video and quantizers. In the EDBTC method, two quantizers and a video bit map have been created by computing several moment values to reduce high computational. Consider color video of size $M \times N$ that are separated into non-overlapping video block size $m \times n$. Assume $f(a,b) = \{f_R(a,b), f_G(a,b), f_B(a,b)\}$ as block of video, where $a = 1, 2, \cdots, m$ and $b = 1, 2, \cdots, n$. Every video, this proposed EDBTC creates single bit map video $bm(a,b)$ and also quantizerq_{min} and q_{max}. The size of the bit map video is similar to the size of the original video for both the encoder and decoder process. It is used to produce an error kernel representation of bit map video. To overcome the contour problem, an EDBTC property for error diffusion has been proposed. A blocking process of EDBTC in error kernel has been quantized from one part into another part of video encoded and decoded boundary. It has been determined by performing average threshold values along with the error kernel. In a block-based encoder and decoder process, the path moves from left to right and top to bottom for every pixel of a video given. Both $f(a,b)$ and $\bar{f}(a,b)$ represents original and average inter-band value respectively. It can be determined as

$$\bar{f}(a,b) = \frac{1}{3}\left(f_R(a,b) + f_G(a,b), +(a,b)\right) \tag{1}$$

The Eq. 1 states that $f_R(a,b), f_G(a,b), f_B(a,b)$ represents represents video pixels like red, green, and blue color channels. A gray scale video has been viewed by average inter-band video of encoder and decoder process. A minimum, maximum, and mean value for inter-band average can be computed as $a_{\min} = \min_{\forall a,b} \bar{f}(a,b)$, $a_{\max} = \max_{\forall a,b} \bar{f}(a,b)$ and $\bar{x} = \sum_{a=1}^{m}\sum_{b=1}^{n} \bar{f}(a,b)$. An video bit map $k(a,b)$ has been computed and determined as

$$k(a,b) = \begin{cases} 1 & \text{if } \bar{f}(a,b) \geq \bar{x} \\ 0 & \text{if } \bar{f}(a,b) \leq \bar{x} \end{cases}.$$

An intermediate value $l(a,b)$ for similar bitmap video time generation has been produced. This value $l(a,b)$ are determined as

$$l(a,b) = \begin{cases} a_{\max} & iif\ k(a,b) = 1 \\ a_{\min} & \text{if } k(a,b) = 0 \end{cases}.$$

An EDBTC residual quantization error of video can be calculated by given equation $g(a,b) = \bar{f}(a,b) - l(a,b)$. This EDBTC thresholding method from one pixel into another pixel of residual quantization error that has been diffused and accumulated to nearby unprocessed. An unprocessed pixel $\bar{f}(a,b)$ is updated and computed by using equation

$$\bar{f}_{new}(a,b) = \bar{f}(a,b) + g(a,b) * \mu \tag{2}$$

In Eq. 2, where μ where represents the error kernel that is used to diffuse the quantization residual method into neighboring pixels encoded into EDBTC thresholding. A symbol $*$ represents convolution operation. There are different error kernel diffusion operations is performed for Jarvis error kernel, Burkers, Floyd-Steinberg, Sierra, Stucki, and Stevenson. The purpose of selecting extreme values to represent video blocks is to produce a dithered result and also to reduce the annoying blocking effect or false contour of EDBTC video. An error at the boundary of the video block must be dispersed to their particular adjacent blocks. This could be estimated considerably reduced from reconstructed EDBTC video. It consists of information about RGB color video that can be obtained by finding minimum and maximum value for every color video block.

A two consecutive EDBTC color quantizers have been also calculated by observing every block or frame of a video

$$q_{\min}(i,j) = \{\min_{\forall a,b} f_R(a,b),, \min_{\forall a,b} f_G(a,b), \min_{\forall a,b} f_B(a,b)\} \tag{3}$$

$$q_{\max}(i,j) = \{\max_{\forall a,b} f_R(a,b), \max_{\forall a,b} f_G(a,b), \max_{\forall a,b} f_B(a,b)\} \tag{4}$$

In Eqs. 3 and 4, where $q_{\min}(i,j)$ and $q_{\max}(i,j)$ represents maximum and minimum quantizer of video encoding and decoding process $\min_{\forall a,b} f_R(a,b)$, $\min_{\forall a,b} f_G(a,b)$, $\min_{\forall a,b} f_B(a,b)$ and $\max_{\forall a,b} f_R(a,b)$, $\max_{\forall a,b} f_G(a,b)$, $\max_{\forall a,b} f_B(a,b)$ represents maximum and minimum video color coding.

Figure 1 represents the overall diagram for the proposed EDBTC video encoder and decoder system. It is unable to encode or decode video. Then, the index of a video is capable of obtaining values from the CBIR system. At the EDBTC encoding process, both color quantizers and bitmap video of the decoder have been sent through a transmission channel. It replaces the video bit map as 1 and 0. Here the value 1 represents the maximum quantizer and the value o represents the minimum quantizer. In the encoding process, the EDBTC process sends video bit map value into the encoder through a transmission channel. It converts the original video into a reconstructed video of a transmitted video channel. In the decoder process, there is no such computation required that makes the user understandable in real-time applications. An EDBTC encoder and decoder process both blocking effect and false contour through which the produced EDBTC video has been reconstructed.

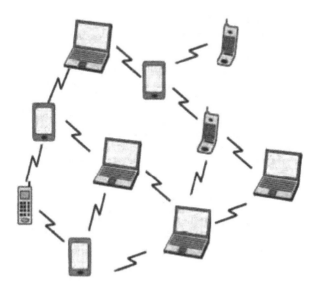

Fig. 1. Mobile adhoc network

3   Performance Analysis

In this section, the performance results of both existing and proposed techniques LC_JCM, LC_JSVM, and EDBTC are analyzed and evaluated based on PSNR values for various Paris sequences. To prove the advantage of the proposed system, LC_JM is compared with some of the existing techniques like LC_JCM, LC_MDC1, and LC_MDC2. In those consequences, Paris sequences for two consecutive 90-frame video test sequences were coded at 30 frames/s.

3.1   Peak Signal to Noise Ratio

The quality of the video has been calculated and measured by using the PSNR formula of the reconstructed video decoder. Here, where N number of pixel frames in PSNR can be calculated as follows

$$PSNR = 10 \log 10 \left[\frac{255^2}{\frac{1}{N} \sum_i \sum_j (Y_{ref(i,j)} - Y_{proc(i,j)})^2} \right] \tag{5}$$

where $Y_{ref(i,j)}$ and $Y_{proc(i,j)}$ represents pixel values for both reference and processed frames correspondingly. In this paper, the proposed EDBTC method has better performance than other existing systems such as LC_JM, LC_MDC1 and LC_MDC2. A single path for Paris sequence packet values of PSNR will be sent. The performance analysis for data loss PSNR and time coding Paris sequences in existing and proposed system graph values has been determined (Fig. 2).

PSNR Data Loss for Paris Sequence. The Fig. 3 represents PSNR data loss for Paris sequences. The x-axis denotes video data loss and y-axis denotes PSNR. The LC_MDC1 method provides good performance than LC_MDC2. If the error gets burst, then video information from different path becomes essential. A data loss value for video packet in x-axis ranges from 0 to 30 and PSNR value in y-axis ranges from 0 to 40. The LC_JM values from 0 to 30 are 37.5, 37, 36, 32.5, 32.7, 26, 22, 18 and 14.5. The LC_MDC1 and LC_MDC2 values from 0 to 30 are 37.2, 37, 36, 33.5, 32, 28, 24.5, 21, 17, 37.5, 37.1, 36.2, 34.2, 33, 29, 25.2, 21.8 and 18. Finally, the LC_JSVM values from 0 to 30 are 38, 37.8, 37, 34.3, 32.5, 28, 24, 20 and 16.5.

Comparative Study: Time Coding for Paris Sequence. The Fig. 4 represents time coding for Paris sequence. The x-axis represents rate and y-axis represents time. A rate value in x-axis ranges from 200 to 1900 and Time value in y-axis ranges from 0 to 300. A coding time frame for video encoder and decoder contains two process like buffering and arranging MBs. The proposed LC_MDC method achieves high scalability performance than existing system like LC_JM and LC_JSVM. A rate and time frame from 200 to 1900 in LC_JM are 60, 70, 90, 100, 115, 140, 175, 210, 240 and 255. Similarly, rate and time from 200 to 1900 for both LC_MDC1 and LC_MDC2 are 55, 65, 85, 92, 107,

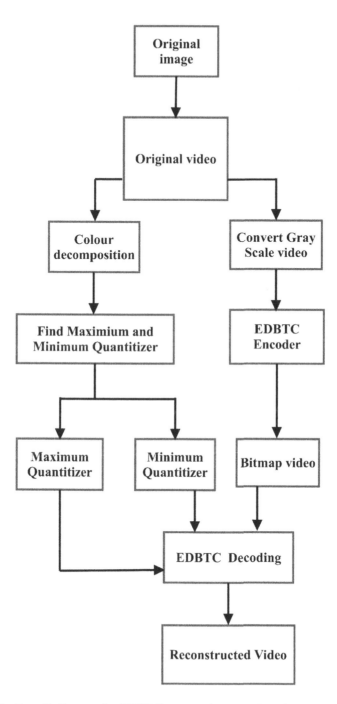

Fig. 2. Overall diagram for EDBTC proposed system in video transmission

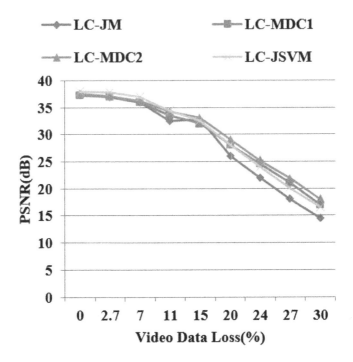

Fig. 3. PSNR data loss for Paris sequence

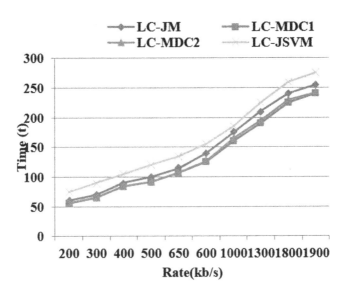

Fig. 4. Time coding for Paris sequence

125, 127, 160, 165, 190, 195, 225, 230, 240 and 242. Finally, the rate and time frame from 200 to 1900 in LC_JSVM are 75, 90, 105, 120, 135, 155, 185, 225, 260 and 275. Figure 5 depicts the deforming coding rate of the HERP versions and the proposed with variable Bit Error Ratio. It is observed that for less value of BFR (i.e. >0.000005), the proposed and the two HERP versions deliver the same decodable frame rate that states the non-utilizable redundancy at this level of an error on HERP performance protection. Consequently for higher Bit Error Ratio values i.e., >0.00001 the DFR values of the HERP version decrease to avoid transmission delay. As per the above results, the THL value is fixed as 0.00005. Figure 6 illustrates the average delay in transmission attained by the solution. When BER is less than 0.002, HERP attains a low average delay when compared with UDP-SPFEC. Due to network overload that disturbs the delay in transmission the performance of UDP-SPFEC is reduced. In contrast, HERP possesses a low transmission delay since the maximum redundancy rate is not used to circumvent the overload of the network and the transmission rate is not reduced at a similar time error. Consequently, as the BER is more than 0.002, UDP-SPFEC achieves less average delay than HERP, since the HERP mechanism lowers the rate of transmission to evade the blocking issue and also because of a large number of I-frame retransmission of video packets. Figure 5 demonstrates that UDP attains minimum average delay than UDP-SPFEC, proposed and HERP with BER since the jamming problem faced by UDP-SPFEC and the reduction in the rate of transmission by HERP was not faced by UDP. Figure 7 depicts the average PSNR of every video structure for the pretended protocols. It is observed that when the Bit Error Ratio is less than 0.002, the HERP possesses high PSNR than UDP, proposed and HERP due to HERP's PDR is high than the other compared protocols that deliver high DFR.

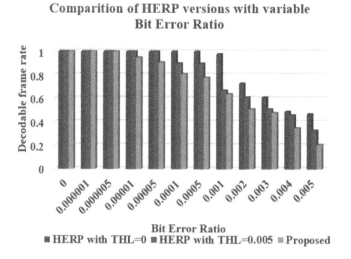

Fig. 5. Comparison of HERP versions with variable Bit Error Ratio.

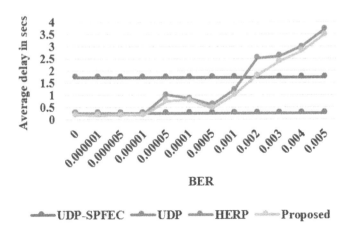

Fig. 6. Comparison of BER with average delay in seconds.

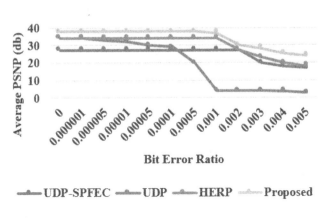

Fig. 7. Comparison of BER with average PSNP.

4   Conclusion

In this paper, a layered coded video transmission by disjoint paths in the Ad Hoc network is proposed to increase the video layer of the error-prone network. It is a method that separates a given video into several non-overlapped video blocks. Every video block is processed separately to acquire two extreme quantizers. A layered coding is also known as a scalable video coding method that is utilized to extract the encoded and decoded quality of the video. To generate a sketch for a single layer of video, a flexible macroblock ordering method is utilized to protect the base layer. To overcome existing methods, a new EDBTC method is proposed to achieve indexing color video transmission of both encoding and decoding processes. It is used to represent encoded data for both quantizers and bit map video. The performance analysis for both PSNR data loss and time coding for the Paris sequence has been determined and executed.

References

1. Mao, S., Lin, S., S. Panwar, S., Wang, Y.: Reliable transmission of video over Ad Hoc networks using automatic repeat request and multipath transport. In: IEEE 54th Vehicular Technology Conference. VTC Fall 2001. Proceedings (Cat. No. 01CH37211), pp. 615–619 (2016)
2. Ghahremani, S., Ghanbari, M.: Error resilient video transmission in Ad Hoc networks using layered and multiple description coding. Multimedia Tools Appl. **76**, 9033–9049 (2017)
3. Hellge, C., Gómez-Barquero, D., Schierl, T., Wiegand, T.: Layer-aware forward error correction for mobile broadcast of layered media. IEEE Trans. Multimedia **13**, 551–562 (2011)
4. Sullivan, G.J., Ohm, J.-R., Han, W.-J., Wiegand, T.: Overview of the high efficiency video coding (HEVC) standard. IEEE Trans. Circuits Syst. Video Technol. **22**, 1649–1668 (2012)
5. Liao, W.-H., Wang, S.-L., Sheu, J.-P., Tseng, Y.-C.: A multi-path QoS routing protocol in a wireless mobile Ad Hoc network. Telecommun. Syst. **19**, 329–347 (2002)
6. Aliyu, A., et al.: Interference-aware multipath video streaming in vehicular environments. IEEE Access **6**, 47610–47626 (2018)
7. Asif-Ur-Rahman, M., et al.: Toward a heterogeneous mist. fog, and cloud-based framework for the internet of healthcare things. IEEE Internet Things J. **63**, 4049–4062 (2019)
8. Kaiser, M.S., et al.: 6G Access network for intelligent internet of healthcare things: opportunity, challenges, and research directions. In: Kaiser M.S., Bandyopadhyay A., Mahmud M., Ray K. (eds.) Proceedings of International Conference on Trends in Computational and Cognitive Engineering. Advances in Intelligent Systems and Computing, vol. 1309. Springer, Singapore (2021). https://doi.org/10.1007/978-981-33-4673-4_25

ALO: AI for Least Observed People

Shamim Al Mamun$^{1(\boxtimes)}$ ⓘ, Mohammad Eusuf Daud^2, Mufti Mahmud^3,
M. Shamim Kaiser^1, and Andre Luis Debiaso Rossi^4

^{1} Institute of Information Technology, Jahangirngar University,
Savar, Dhaka 1342, Bangladesh
`shamim@juniv.edu`
^{2} Consultant, Ministry of finance, Naples, Italy
^{3} University of Nottingham, Nottingham, England
^{4} Universidade Estadual Paulista, Itapeva, Brazil

Abstract. In recent years, visual assistants of humans are taking place in the consumer market–the eye-line of humans equipped with a see-through optical display. Computer Vision Technology may play a vital role in visually challenged people to carry out their daily activities without much dependency on others. In this paper, we introduce ALO (AI for Least Observed) as an assistive glass for blind people. It can listen as a companion, read from the internet on the fly, detect surrounding objects and obstacles for freedom of movement, and recognize the faces he is communicating with. This glass can be a virtual companion of the users for social safety from unknown people, reduce the dependency of others. This system uses the camera for identifying human faces using MTCNN deep learning technique, bone conduction microphone, and google API (Application Programming Interface) for translating voice to text and text to bone conduction sound. A Market Valuable Product (MVP) has already been developed depending on our survey of over 300 visually impaired persons in Europe and Asia.

Keywords: Smart glass · Blind vision · Face recognition · Object detection

1 Introduction

Globally, at least 2.2 billion people have a vision impairment or blindness. The majority of these populations face moderate or severe distance vision impairment or blindness due to refractive error, cataracts, glaucoma, corneal opacities, diabetic retinopathy, and trachoma. In terms of regional differences, blindness in low and middle-income countries projects to be four times higher than in developed countries. In the Asian region, the blindness problem is 10% lower than the developed region [1].

The healthcare industry is in the midst of a transformative period, thanks to the emergence of sensor technology and the rapid implementation of the Internet of Things (IoT) [2–4]. These sensors and IoT devices provide researchers with

© Springer Nature Switzerland AG 2021
M. Mahmud et al. (Eds.): AII 2021, CCIS 1435, pp. 306–317, 2021.
https://doi.org/10.1007/978-3-030-82269-9_24

several opportunities to develop assistive products for people with special needs in a variety of ways [5–8].

In recent years, researchers have attempted to develop innovative gadgets that will be of assistance to visually impaired people in their daily lives. Nevertheless, since the end-users are real blind people, finding a solution must be based on empathy for the situation. The standard survey method will never be effective in identifying their life's most difficult challenges. The process of prototyping hardware and software involves a great deal of thinking and iteration to be successful. There are unique problems in each and every fundamental domain of Artificial Intelligence – Machine Learning, Cognitive Vision, and Natural Language Processing, for example – from data preparation to attaining high accuracy levels using performance measurements [18,19]. Though the challenges, researchers and startup industries are trying to develop vision assistance to blind people. We are proposing an intelligent eyeglass for blind people that can assist them in indoor environments. In indoor, the blind or low visioned person needs daily activity like pouring water into the glass for drinking. In this scenario, users need to find the glass and water bottle first and know its location in indoor premises [16]. Therefore, they need a companion or ask help from family members to serve them. In addition, in the developed country, blind people have many community services in a working hour, but in the Asian region, that kind of service is rare. So, they need to help themselves to find someone by oral communication. If glass demonstrate someone around them like in [20,21], it would be great. In this context, researchers and startup companies come up with some solutions with the help of AI. One of the widespread products provided by google's X lab. This intelligent glass uses primary navigation and localizes information based on the mobility of the mobile user on the road. It uses an optical head-mounted display connected via wi-fi or pairing with an android mobile phone to assist the user in getting information surrounding them. It also uses its Speech to Text/Text to Speech (GTTS) for communication with users. According to our study, researchers try to assist real blind people by innovating technology for oral communication (OC). Moreover, gives observability of the surrounding through the camera, object detection (OD), face detection/identification (FDI), optical character recognition, and bone conduction (BC) for ear free hearing. The summary of our findings from different research groups describes in tabular form in Table 1.

Table 1. System review for blind people assistive product.

Product	Developer	OC	NAV	OD	FDI	BC
Google glasses [9]	Google Inc	Yes	Yes	Yes	Yes	No
Aira [10]	Suman Kanuganti	Yes	Yes	Yes	No	No
eSights [11]	CNETs	No	No	Yes	Yes	No
[12]	CCES, PMU	Yes	Yes	No	No	No
ALO	Yes	Yes	Yes	Yes	Yes	Yes

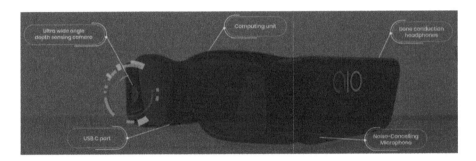

Fig. 1. Overall system specification

In this paper, we are proposing an intelligent goggle named ALO (AI for Least Observed) that can communicate with blind people or user with the help of the internet. It can able to read text from any newspapers. We use "google text to speech (gTTS)" service API for reading the text and send it to our bone conduction microphone because we want to free the user's ear from hearing bud. It can recognize the object around the user so that s/he can find their necessary things without the help of companions or family members. Our glass also trained to recognize the user's family members or acquaintances with whom they communicate in their daily lives. These features make them self-dependent when they go outside. When blind people are in their comfort zone, users want to do their work like finding water glass and bottle, TV remote, finding the dress to wear, etc. Our system acts as a complete companion in their life to give them freedom of movement in an indoor scenario. Figure 1 illustrated the overall system features and real market valuable product (MVP) unit. In the subsequent Sects. 2, 3 will describe ALO briefly with our survey over 300 blind participants from Asia and European regions.

2   AI for Least Observed (ALO)

We are proposing ALO in collaboration with the Ministry of Economic Development, Italy, and the ICT division of the Bangladesh government by conducting a survey of 300 participants from both countries. Among them, 158 are male participants, and 142 are female in 6 different age groups illustrated in Table 2. Our survey illustrated that 60% male and 40% female are suffering from low vision due to accident or disease. We have also interviewed them personally by social interaction method in the park, road, or home. 88.2% of the sample population feels lack of autonomy in aspect to

- Dependency on assistance,
- Not understanding the Surrounding,
- Inability to recognize the facial expression of others,
- Inability to find Objects, and,
- Inability to understand Distance and Direction.

Table 2. Survey sample size of 300 participants

Age	Sample size	Male	Female
<20	18	12	6
21–30	25	14	11
31–40	64	34	30
41–50	67	35	32
51–60	76	38	38
61–70	50	25	25

Moreover, 81.2% feels worried in the aspect of 1: Lack of visual information, 2: Unable to determine risks, 2: person/kids/pets in the vicinity, Obstacles/risks around the path, 3: Unable to see the facial expression of others and 4: Inability to understand texts/reading materials. Moreover, we found that lack of self-esteem, Inability to develop a desired life or career, Forced to follow a routine without any exception, Psychological health condition of the subject, Gradual disconnect from society (example: Friends or colleagues), and Self-isolation by the subject [22]. Therefore, Fig. 1 ALO gives them a chance to lead their own life without dependency, communicate with other persons, remember acquainted persons in the next meet, measure the object's distance to avoid or pick up, and read contents from the internet.

3 System Overview

Our goal is to make a Market Valuable Product (MVP) for the slightest vision or blind user. So that, they can read text from internet resources like Wikipedia or any daily newspaper, detect and recognize the faces of family members or acquainted person at home or roadside walking, detection of an object for using or avoiding hazardous. ALO uses Raspberry pi zero W model with 8 Mega Pixel camera module (Sony IMX219 image sensor) supported by 850 mAh battery for 2 h of continuous energy supply. It also uses a 2.4 GHz wi-fi module for home use. Noise cancellation MIC and used Remax earphones wireless audio driver circuit running a bone conduction module. The dimension of ALO is 154 mm × 43 mm and 147 mm from the side view angle and 154 mm × 40 mm from the front view. Total weight is average 80 gm only, which will give comfort for the users (Fig. 2).

3.1 Real Time Messaging

Our system also proposes a high level of service integration ecosystem to support blind users through this glass illustrated in Fig. 4. ALO uses a contextual chatbot for a live conversation with users. Users give voice commands through noiseless MIC using a real-time messaging protocol like person detection or object detection using Google speech API services. Moreover, Contextual chatbot API then

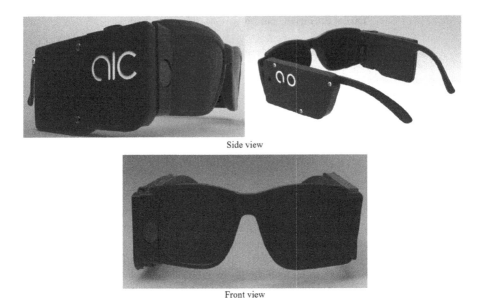

Side view

Front view

Fig. 2. Side and front view of ALO

hooks the scheduler model update service to get the API for other services. Model builder and model service layer are separated because of continuous update of the model when ALO gets new objects or persons. ALO assists the different users simultaneously from the web. Hence it will open API services for real-time messaging among targeted users and storage of ALO. For real-time messaging, ALO uses Mesibo [13] frameworks for building on system FnF APP which can open instantaneous replies from the chatbot. The working procedure of Mesibo illustrates in Fig. 3. Moreover, the chatbot model continuously updates its model depends on the conversations. Users to ALO real-time communication makes extremely simple by Mesibo. mesibo know about each of ALO end user. Mesibo will create an access token for each user and give it to the unit using the internet (using mesibo Server-side Admin API) to give respective access tokens to the users. Therefore, users use this access token in Mesibo SDK to create a real-time connection with the mesibo server to send and receive real-time messages. Using this system, users can communicate with the glass by voice command. To implement this task, we use Google Speech-to-Text (gSTT), which interfaced with a python library to get the message into our Mesibo architecture for real-time execution of the command. gSTT has a multi-language support API for convert the ultimate length of voice to text. This API recognizes over 120 languages and variants to support the user base. gSTT uses deep natural language machine learning techniques to identify the languages for instant translation to text. In our system, we use only English and Bangla for MVP purposes. We have used a simple questionnaire in fig that the user may ask to find an object or person.

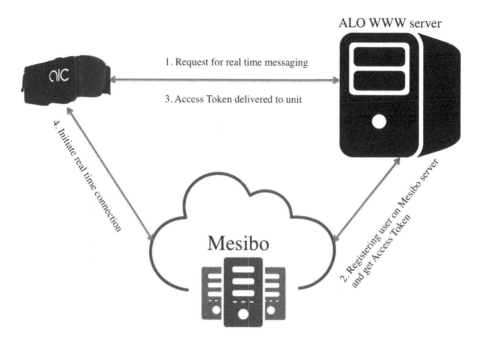

Fig. 3. Mesibo works flow

```
ques1 = "Where are we"
ques2 = "Why you think so"
ques3 = "No thanks"
ques4 = "Let us get introduced with these person"
ques5 = "What is in front of me"
b_ques5 = 'সামনে কি আছে' # 'এটা'
ques6 = "What are the items on the table"
b_ques6 = "টেবিল কি আছে"
```

Fig. 4. Question ask by the user to the system

3.2 Bone Conduction Unit

The regular headphone uses wired or wireless passes through the ear canal to the eardrum for making a spectrum of voice. The bone conduction unit of our system works by vibrating against the bones in our cheeks or upper jaw, passing the ear canal to direct hit on the eardrum. Therefore, users are independently listening to system output as well as surrounding events. We included HBQ-Q25C TWS Wireless Bluetooth Headphones Ergonomic Waterproof Earbuds Ear Hook Bone Conduction (BC) Earphones module. This particular module has 10 m of transmission distance with a sensitivity range 50–180 KHz. In Fig. 5 exhibit our BC unit attached to ALO, modified to be compatible with our system for connecting it. We opened the bought bone conduction product and tried to reset up it. We have changed the battery and circuit of the bone conduction unit and attached it with our glass handle. So, this BC module is no more wireless Bluetooth, and it now acts as a System on a chip (SOC) (Fig. 6).

Fig. 5. ALO Bone Conduction Module

3.3   Object Detection

Our system can successfully detect objects in an indoor situation to find out the objects like water bottles, cups etc., for daily uses. We used Look Only Once (YOLO) [16] for object detection based on VGG-16 deep learning architecture. Though most Image Recognition Systems (IRS) use GPUs, we use the tiny version of YOLO's cpuNet that runs on a CPU at 15 FPS, which is quite good for detecting only 80 classes of objects using COCO dataset [14]. COCO dataset contains 82,783 training, 40,504 validation, and 40,775 testing images split into train, validation, and test data. There are nearly 270k segmented people and 886k segmented object instances in the 2014 train and validation data alone. The cumulative 2015 release will contain 165,482 train, 81,208 val, and 81,434 test images. Moreover, we use VGG-16 net to train the model developed in Keras and the google TensorFlow framework. The system is identifying an object with 98% of accuracy. In addition, when a user gives a voice command like "What is in front of me?" using mesibo framework, it takes a camera feed. It feeds into our IRS model to identify object and labeling as categories and name it. The user gets feedback sound through a bone conduction microphone which is attached to our unit. Figure 7 shows the accuracy of detecting objects using our system.

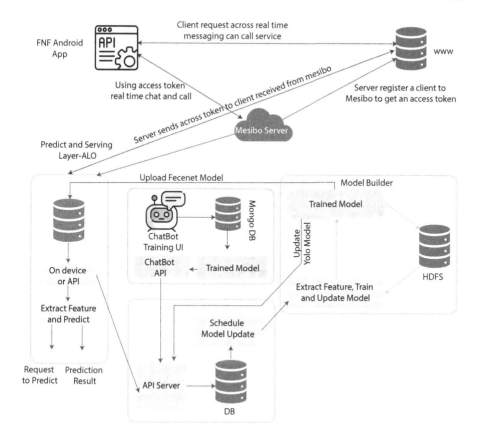

Fig. 6. System Architecture of ALO

3.4 Face Detection and Identification

Humans are using feature-based techniques to solve vision problems. The machine also uses the same process, such as the cascade classifier. Nowadays, deep learning methods have achieved state-of-the-art results on standard benchmark face detection datasets like Multi-task Cascade Convolutional Neural Network (MTCNN). In the traditional feature engineering method, we need thousands of features or kernels to detect the facial point to identify the face. But, in MTCNN, face detection and face alignment are done jointly, in a multi-task training fashion. Face alignment allows the model to detect better faces that are initially not aligned. MTCNN model structure uses three networks; at the first stage of this system, the image is resized to a range of different sizes called an image pyramid. And, then the first model (Proposal Network or P-Net) proposes candidate facial regions, the second model (Refine Network or R-Net) filters the

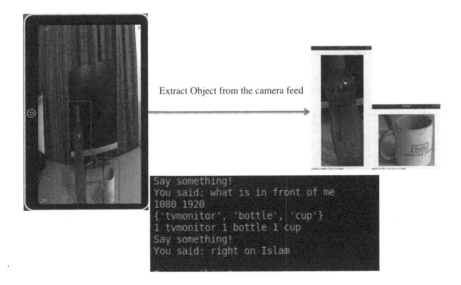

Extract Object from the camera feed

Say something!
You said: what is in front of me
1080 1920
{'tvmonitor', 'bottle', 'cup'}
1 tvmonitor 1 bottle 1 cup
Say something!
You said: right on Islam

Fig. 7. System performance of ALO for object detection.

bounding boxes, and the third model (Output Network or O-Net) offers facial landmarks. There are three types of prediction uses in MTCNN; face classification, bounding box regression, and facial landmark localization. Three models are not directly connected and act as a lap of a sprint race. When one round finishes, the next one starts, and so on until the 3rd lap finished. The additional processing is performed between stages; for example, non-maximum suppression (NMS) is used to filter the candidate bounding boxes proposed by the first-stage P-Net, the input feeder R-Net model. Figure 8 shows the camera feed of faces and extract faces from the feed, and Fig. 9 illustrated that our system could recognize those two faces using MTCNN framework. In our system, we use OpenCV library with python to implement the model. As we are considering multiple models in our architecture to work simultaneously and recognize the acquainted person's faces, we have developed multi-layer trained deep CNN for cascading the facial images in training and validation. Our system also teaches individual models with a single image instead train the whole model for classification. Moreover, multiple users can update their model on-the-fly mode to store and prepare their model without dormant the previous weight file rather than update it concurrently.

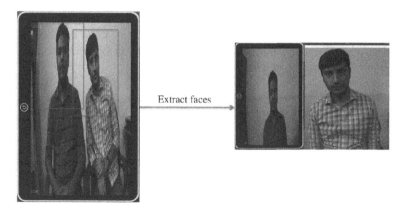

Fig. 8. Face detection using MTCNN

```
Say something!
You said: what is in front of me

1080 1920
{'person'}
Start Recognition!
Face Detected: 1
[534 378]
yes
[[0.03438325 0.04981384 0.88569597 0.03010695]]
best class probabilities [0.88569597]
['Akshay Kumar', 'Salman Khan', 'Tushar', 'kazi']
Tushar
Start Recognition!
Face Detected: 1
[492 359]
yes
[[0.04501446 0.04126357 0.0085204  0.90520156]]
best class probabilities [0.90520156]
['Akshay Kumar', 'Salman Khan', 'Tushar', 'kazi']
Tushar kazi
Tushar kazi 2 person
Say something!
```

Fig. 9. System output for MTCNN face detection

4   Conclusion

In this paper, we propose communicative assistive tools for blind people found
by the survey of 300 participants of real blind users. Our system gives level
up the user's confidence level in their daily life. ALO also gives them a comfort zone to communicate with another person whether they are unknown to
them. Hence, also improve their security when they are communicating with
an unknown person at home or road. We will do more experiments in natural

environment scenarios shortly and find their comfort level for using ALO. Additionally, implement improved circuitry for resizing the glass at the minimum size and weight. We will train our system with different objects, languages and enhance the voice-to-text accuracy also.

Acknowledgment. This work was financial supported by the Information and Communication Technology Department of the Bangladesh Government through startup Bangladesh Program and ALO Limited.

References

1. Blindness and Vision Impairment. https://www.who.int/news-room/fact-sheets/detail/blindness-and-visual-impairment. Accessed on 24 Feb 2020
2. Noor, M.B.T., Zenia, N.Z., Kaiser, M.S.: Challenges ahead in healthcare applications for vision and sensors. In: Ahad, M.A.R., Inoue, A. (eds.) Vision, Sensing and Analytics: Integrative Approaches. ISRL, vol. 207, pp. 397–413. Springer, Cham (2021). https://doi.org/10.1007/978-3-030-75490-7_15
3. Esha, N.H., Tasmim, M.R., Huq, S., Mahmud, M., Kaiser, M.S.: Trust IoHT: a trust management model for internet of healthcare things. In: Proceedings of International Conference on Data Science and Applications, pp. 47–57. Springer, Singapore (2021).https://doi.org/10.1007/978-981-15-7561-7_3
4. Farhin, F., Kaiser, M.S., Mahmud, M.: Secured smart healthcare system: blockchain and bayesian inference based approach. In: Kaiser, M.S., Bandyopadhyay, A., Mahmud, M., Ray, K. (eds.) Proceedings of International Conference on Trends in Computational and Cognitive Engineering. Advances in Intelligent Systems and Computing, vol. 1309. Springer, Singapore (2021). https://doi.org/10.1007/978-981-33-4673-4_36
5. Kaiser, M.S., et al.: 6G access network for intelligent internet of healthcare things: opportunity, challenges, and research directions. In: Kaiser, M.S., Bandyopadhyay, A., Mahmud, M., Ray, K. (eds.) Proceedings of International Conference on Trends in Computational and Cognitive Engineering. Advances in Intelligent Systems and Computing, vol. 1309. Springer, Singapore (2021). https://doi.org/10.1007/978-981-33-4673-4_25
6. Kaiser, M.S., Al Mamun, S., Mahmud, M., Tania, M.H.: Healthcare robots to combat COVID-19. In: Santosh, K., Joshi, A. (eds.) COVID-19: Prediction, Decision-Making, and its Impacts. Lecture Notes on Data Engineering and Communications Technologies, vol. 60. Springer, Singapore (2021). https://doi.org/10.1007/978-981-15-9682-7_10
7. Farhin, F., Kaiser, M.S., Mahmud, M.: Towards secured service provisioning for the internet of healthcare things. In: 2020 IEEE 14th International Conference on Application of Information and Communication Technologies (AICT), pp. 1–6. IEEE (2020)
8. Jesmin, S., Kaiser, M.S., Mahmud, M.: Artificial and internet of healthcare things based Alzheimer care during COVID 19. In: Mahmud, M., Vassanelli, S., Kaiser, M.S., Zhong, N. (eds.) Brain Informatics. BI 2020. Lecture Notes in Computer Science, vol. 12241. Springer, Cham (2020). https://doi.org/10.1007/978-3-030-59277-6_24

9. Google Inc.: Google glasses. Retrieved from https://en.wikipedia.org/wiki/Google_glasses. Accessed on 28 Feb 2020
10. Aira: By Your Side Throughout Life's Journey. Accessed on 28 Feb 2020
11. Electronic Glasses for the Blind. https://esighteyewear.com/. Accessed on 28 Feb 2020
12. AlSaid, H., et al.: Deep Learning Assisted Smart Glasses as Educational Aid for Visually Challenged Students. In: 2019 2nd International Conference on new Trends in Computing Sciences (ICTCS). IEEE (2019)
13. https://www.mesibo.com/what. Accessed on 27 Feb 2020
14. Al Mamun, S., Lam, A., Kobayashi, Y., Kuno, Y.: single laser bidirectional sensing for robotic wheelchair step detection and measurement. In: Huang, D.S., Hussain, A., Han, K., Gromiha, M. (eds.) Intelligent Computing Methodologies. ICIC 2017. Lecture Notes in Computer Science, vol. 10363. Springer, Cham (2017). https://doi.org/10.1007/978-3-319-63315-2_4
15. Lin, T.-Y., et al.: Microsoft coco: Common objects in context. In: Fleet, D., Pajdla, T., Schiele, B., Tuytelaars, T. (eds.) Computer Vision – ECCV 2014. ECCV 2014. Lecture Notes in Computer Science, vol. 8693. Springer, Cham (2014). https://doi.org/10.1007/978-3-319-10602-1_48
16. Al Mamun, S., et al.: Autonomous bus boarding robotic wheelchair using bidirectional sensing systems. In: Bebis, G., et al. (eds.) Advances in Visual Computing. ISVC 2018. Lecture Notes in Computer Science, vol. 11241. Springer, Cham (2018). https://doi.org/10.1007/978-3-030-03801-4_64
17. Zhang, K., et al.: Joint face detection and alignment using multitask cascaded convolutional networks. IEEE Signal Process. Let. **23.10**, 1499–1503 (2016)
18. Kaiser, M.S., et al.: iWorkSafe: towards healthy workplaces during COVID-19 with an intelligent pHealth App for industrial settings. IEEE Access **9**, 13814–13828 (2021)
19. Kaiser, M.S., Al Mamun, S., Mahmud, M., Tania, M.H.: Healthcare robots to combat COVID-19. In: Santosh, K., Joshi, A. (eds.) COVID-19: Prediction, Decision-Making, and its Impacts. Lecture Notes on Data Engineering and Communications Technologies, vol. 60. Springer, Singapore (2021). https://doi.org/10.1007/978-981-15-9682-7_10
20. Rahman, M.M., Mamun, S.A., Kaiser, M.S., Islam, M.S., Rahman, M.A.: cascade classification of face liveliness detection using heart beat measurement. In: Kaiser, M.S., Bandyopadhyay, A., Mahmud, M., Ray, K. (eds.) Proceedings of International Conference on Trends in Computational and Cognitive Engineering. Advances in Intelligent Systems and Computing, vol. 1309. Springer, Singapore (2021). https://doi.org/10.1007/978-981-33-4673-4_47
21. Tabassum, T., Tasnim, N., Nizam, N., Al Mamun, S.: anonymous person tracking across multiple camera using color histogram and body pose estimation. In: Kaiser, M.S., Bandyopadhyay, A., Mahmud, M., Ray, K. (eds.) Proceedings of International Conference on Trends in Computational and Cognitive Engineering. Advances in Intelligent Systems and Computing, vol. 1309. Springer, Singapore (2021). https://doi.org/10.1007/978-981-33-4673-4_52
22. Asif-Ur-Rahman, M., Afsana, F., Mahmud, M., Kaiser, M.S., Ahmed, M.R., Kaiwartya, O., James-Taylor, A.: Toward a heterogeneous mist, fog, and cloud-based framework for the internet of healthcare things. IEEE Internet Things J. **6**(3), 4049–4062 (2018)

Emerging Applications of AI and Informatics

COVID-Hero: Machine Learning Based COVID-19 Awareness Enhancement Mobile Game for Children

Md. Shahriare Satu[1]([✉])(iD), K. Shayekh Ebne Mizan[2](iD), Syeda Anika Jerin[2](iD),
Md Whaiduzzaman[2,3](iD), Alistair Barros[3](iD), Kawsar Ahmed[4](iD),
and Mohammad Ali Moni[5](iD)

[1] Department of Management Information Systems, Noakhali Science
and Technology University, Sonapur, Noakhali 3814, Bangladesh
shahriarsetu.mis@nstu.edu.bd
[2] Institute of Information Technology, Jahangirnagar University,
Savar, Dhaka 1342, Bangladesh
[3] School of Information Systems, Queensland University of Technology,
Brisbane, Australia
[4] Department of Information and Communication Technology, Mawlana Bhashani
Science and Technology University, Santosh, Tangail 1902, Bangladesh
[5] WHO Collaborating Centre on eHealth, UNSW Digital Health,
Faculty of Medicine, University of New South Wales,
Sydney, NSW 2052, Australia
m.moni@unsw.edu.au

Abstract. In this pandemic, children are affected heavily by lockdown
and quarantine worldwide. Hence, children's awareness of COVID-19 and
passing a joyful time at home are necessary for their mental health. In
this work, we developed a mobile gaming app named COVID-Hero, which
intends to learn and create awareness among children about COVID-19.
Using this app, they obtain scores/points by grabbing the right objects
from their superhero-shaped player, which are fun, attractive, and psy-
chologically helpful during this pandemic. However, we designed a questionnaire and conducted a user survey of different aged people who gave
their opinions about this game. Finally, numerous significant features
were extracted and prioritized using machine learning regression models
that enhance children's COVID-19 awareness and tolerable behavior in
this pandemic.

Keywords: COVID-19 · Machine learning · COVID-Hero · Regression
models · Features

1 Introduction

On December 31, 2019, Wuhan Municipal Health Commission (WMHC)
reported that a cluster of pneumonia cases had been identified in Wuhan, Hubei

M. Mahmud et al. (Eds.): AII 2021, CCIS 1435, pp. 321–335, 2021.
https://doi.org/10.1007/978-3-030-82269-9_25

province, China. Then, the coronavirus disease (COVID-19) was first identified there [4,20] and eventually spread it throughout the world [26]. To transmit coronavirus human to human, different types of medium are considered, such as close contact, sneezing, coughing, and respiratory droplets for both symptomatic and asymptomatic individuals [9]. However, the symptoms of COVID-19 can be expressed from 2 to 14 d [7]. Later, the World Health Organization (WHO) proclaimed this outbreak as a Public Health Emergency of International Concern (PHEIC) on February 28, 2020 [22,25]. In this situation, various precautions are followed, such as staying in the home, using masks, frequently washing hands, restrictions at travels, avoiding social gatherings, and sanitizing places to get rid of this pandemic [28]. Again, many countries are imposing lockdowns to prevent COVID-19 by restricting the movement of their citizens.

While the adults are followed the precautions of deadly COVID-19, it is not easy for children to keep up them at home because they are less susceptible about this infection. However, a recent study showed that children aged from newborn to 21 years old were admitted to pediatric intensive care units (PICUs) in the United States and Canada due to COVID-19 [27]. So, children should not go outside and no longer accompany with their friends in this pandemic situation. Besides, they need to get worried and conscious about COVID-19. Hence, a lot of enjoyable activities like various kinds of sports, songs, dances, and humors can be used to concise children about this disease. Many digital applications (i.e., computer/smartphone apps) are not only assisted to create real-time solutions [12,32] but also used to build awareness against COVID-19 [24,25]. Likewise, game playing is a fun and accessible way to demonstrate this threat more precisely. On the other hand, machine learning is an emerging field to estimate unknown aspects about various issues more precisely [14,15]. Recently, this tool is widely employed to explore significant facts about COVID-19 [5,25]. A study showed that video games are inspiring, innovative, and fruitful things to impart implicit knowledge and carry out persuasive messages [3]. The rationale of work is to aware kids about COVID-19 through game playing and extract noteworthy factors about its impact using machine learning.

In this work, we proposed a machine learning framework where a 2D survival smartphone based gaming app named COVID-Hero has been developed. In this app, a protagonist character is used as a player and numerous components are passed from left to right in the screen. In this situation, the player can be grabbing them by jumping from bottom to top. However, he should avoid virus to save their lives. To justify impact of this game, a survey was conducted to get public (i.e. specially the guardians of children) reactions. Afterwards, various regression models were implemented on these instances to extract significant features of this game's effects. Therefore it can be seemed as a reliable platform for children to learn about familiar positive and negative objects of this disease in the subconscious mind. Hence, some following research questions (RQ) are arisen about this work which are:

- **RQ1:** How can we design and develop interesting games for children?
- **RQ2:** How this interactive game enhance children awareness about COVID-19?
- **RQ3:** How machine learning techniques impact children performance and awareness about this pandemic through this game?

This paper is organized as follows: Sect. 2 describes several works about COVID-19 game development. Section 3 narrates some step by step procedure, how we can develop this app, conduct the survey, and extract significant features using machine learning methods. Section 4 explains the experimental results and Sect. 5 evaluates the performance of this work. Finally, Sect. 6 summarizes the outcomes and provides some future instructions that enhance this task.

2 Related Works

However, there were happened some works related to manufacturing associated gaming applications to learn and make interaction about this pandemic situation. The first coronavirus game for children was recently developed by Richard Weizmann named "Can You Save the World" [8]. It showed how children could avoid pedestrians, cyclists, coughing people on busy roads, and maintain social distance. Also, they rescued more people and got a higher score for defending themselves. Meanwhile, only 9 years old Italian child named Lapo Daturi had stunned the world by making a funny game for children called "Cerba-20" [1]. In this app, a spacecraft was fighting against its COVID-19 opponent and required to kill all the coronaviruses for winning the battle. Then, a mobile game entitled "COVID Run" had been launched by the developers of department of Health, Kerala, where a young boy is considered the central character to clear multiple obstacles including the coronavirus, infected people, gorges and reach his destination [2]. Suppan et al. [29] developed a serious game named "Escape COVID-19" to boost safe infection prevention and control (IPC) practices among health workers within the Geneva University Hospitals. They [30] also build a gamified e-learning module to increase knowledge about the usage of personal protective equipment (PPE) among prehospital health care workers. Gasper et al. [10] developed a serious game named "COVID-19-Did You Know?" which provided science based, personal care information and also assessed players' knowledge about COVID-19–related topics. Laato [13] used location based games to investigate the responses of game developers and players and observe human movement during COVID-19 applying netnography method. Venigalla et al. [31] proposed a 2D survival game named "Survive Covid-19" to educate individuals about taking stable precausions in the outside their homes (i.e., how can we use masks, sanitizers and maintaining social distance) against COVID-19.

3   Methods and Materials

This proposed methodology consists of several parts to explain how children can learn about COVID-19 through game playing app and investigate its impact using machine learning. The details of this framework is shown briefly in Fig. 1.

3.1   Requirement Analysis

Requirement Analysis is a crucial part of system development that specifies to design this app as the expectations of users. First of all, we need to fix how we can build this gaming app and what tools should be required to use. Consequently, android which is the most common platform has been used for planning and developing this app (see details Sect. 3.2). To realize the performance of this game, we prepared a questionnaire about COVID-19 oriented gaming app and taken a survey. Then, various machine learning models have been employed into survey data to estimate which aspects are more significant to make children aware about COVID-19.

3.2   COVID-Hero

Numerous media such as television, smartphones, tablets, and others are affecting children minds in positive or negative ways. COVID-Hero makes an opportunity for kids to interact with real-life tools and learn about precautions of this pandemic with fun. The working procedure of this app how can it operate and make scores are provided as follows.

1. When COVID-Hero is run, it shows a splash screen message and a symbol of fighting against COVID-19. Then, the enter button is needed to access the game. This app has been made for the children more flexible way where they do not requisite extra instructions to play it.
2. The background of this game is entirely astral. Moreover, several protagonist characters are used (e.g., superheroes like Superman, Thor), which draw more attention to the kids. Also, different items are symbolized as positive (i.e., wearing a mask, washing hands, and maintaining distance) and negative objects (i.e., crowd, virus, etc.) that assist to learn such things with fun.
3. Recently, children are more enthusiastic, compassionate and fight against coronavirus. Hence, there are considered three levels namely, level 1 (easy), 2 (medium) and 3 (hard) to make COVID-Hero more thrilling. In these levels, a virtual avatar appears like a superhero that symbolizes the player. In this game, the player can jump up and down vertically as well as catch individual symbolic positive objects to gather points. But, grabbing the negative objects are warned kids that they are harmful for losing scores (i.e., reduce 0.25 score in each touch) or their life. However, the player have three lives to stay in the game. If he touch the symbol of coronavirus, one life is overlooked at a time. Moreover, he can stay in this game until losing all of his lives. Finally, when the player drops all of his life to stay game, this app shows final scores and finishes the game. Again, he can start a new session to play this game.

4. If the player obtains 500 scores without losing life, he reaches to the level 2 and asks to play in this session. Meanwhile, a superhero character and another positive objects such as a doctor, oranges, food containing vitamin C, stay home are used to catch them in the same way. Like level 1, the player must avoid negative objects to keep scores and lives. If he touches the virus objects at most three times, the game is terminated to display final scores. In addition, the player can also run this game to play new session.

5. When the player gain almost 1000 scores, he comes into level 3 and can play it in this session. Almost all positive or negative objects of both levels are passed from left to right more rapidly and the player can touch them to get scores. Like other levels, player have to avoid the negative objects specially virus. Likewise, if the game is terminated in level 3, the final score is shown and given the option to play again.

6. However, he can pause the running session at any stage and save the final scores of this game. However, the lifelines are fully retrieved while shifting to the individual levels of the game.

Developing Platform and UI/UX Design. In the Human Computer Interaction (HCI) model, a well-designed user interface (UI) is used to maximize the usability of application. On the other hand, User Experience (UX) depicts an application by supporting the desire and behavior of users. In this work, the whole apps has been developed at android studio v4.0.1 (i.e.,Android version 10, API level 29).

- **User Interface (UI):** COVID-Hero is developed using Java programming language in android platform. Different classes and interfaces were used to organize UI in this apps. Therefore, Canvas class is employed for hosting the draw calls and Paint class is applied for style and color information about drawing geometries, text and bitmaps. Alongside Bitmap class depicts bitmap images as well as BitmapFactory deploys these images as resource, inputStream or file.

- **User Experience (UX):** In COVID-Hero, the background, protagonist characters (i.e., the players) and other objects are important to grow flexible user experience about this app. The main characters are considered as the Marvel and detective comics (DC) characters alike Superman and Thor in different levels. Alongside the signs of different objects (e.g., mask man, doctor, hand-washing, virus, distancing, vitamin C, staying home etc.) are quite enchanting to enthrall the children. Moreover, every loss of life makes a heart from red to fade where the lifelines are fully recoverable at the different levels in the game. However, the moving sign and flying of the players create this gaming environment more dynamic. In the change of levels, notification message makes children more amicable to play this game.

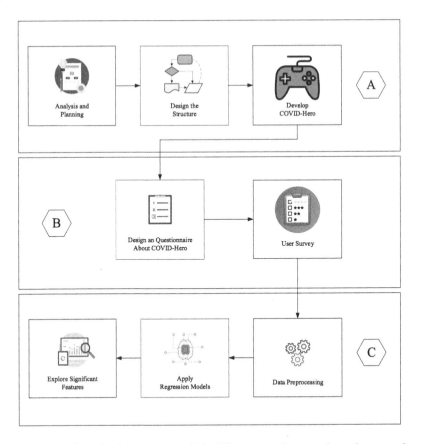

Fig. 1. Proposed methodology where (A) different requirement have been analyzed, designed the structure and developed smartphone-based gaming app named COVID-Hero, (B) prepared a questionnaire to assess the performance of COVID-Hero and take a survey from various users (C) preprocessing survey instances, implemented regression models and explored the priority list of individual features

3.3 Survey Works

After releasing the prototype of this app, we gathered several participants to get user feedback about COVID-Hero. First, a survey questionnaire had been prepared and validated by a psychological expert [23]. These comments were taken using two steps namely pre-survey (before playing/observing) and post survey after playing. Pre-survey was needed to extract general knowledge and usefulness about this kinds of game. In this session, there are considered five questions (F1–F5) to get opinions about the usefulness of this type of game. Consequently, post-survey was used to take comments about how COVID-Hero is useful to create awareness and learn about this disease among children. In this light, it contains eight questions (F6–F13), where we took user reactions after playing/observing this game. Due to the COVID-19 situation, the data collection procedures are too much difficult from the users. Hence, a working video clip was useful to take responses about this game before and after observing it. Therefore, it was not efficient way to take responses from under-aged kids. So, we took responses from children's legal guardians (e.g., parents, siblings, teachers or others) on behalf of them where the audience (i.e., adolescents, adults, and mobile game experts) age limits were found within 17–42 years old. Further, some enthusiastic and interested people are also observed and give their feedback about this app. Each response contains several options: strongly agree, agree, neutral, disagree, and strongly disagree. Again, some of them are considered different options like strongly satisfactory, satisfactory, neutral, not satisfactory, and strongly not satisfactory. We shared the questionnaire and guided videos with children via the participant's email or social media respectively.

Table 1. Demographic description of survey data

Features	Mean	SE	Median	Mode	SD	Skewness	Kurtosis
Age	22.245	0.210	22.15	23.000	3.035	1.901	9.132
Awareness (F1)	4.024	0.055	4.120	4.000	0.795	−1.207	2.312
Psychological Affect (F2)	4.096	0.043	4.130	4.000	0.622	−0.675	2.750
Habit (F3)	3.875	0.050	3.900	4.000	0.725	−0.574	0.548
Educational (F4)	3.986	0.050	4.050	4.000	0.726	−0.898	1.422
Attractivity (F5)	3.784	0.056	3.800	4.000	0.802	−0.551	0.635
Enjoyably (F6)	3.760	0.057	3.820	4.000	0.822	−0.949	1.249
Content (F7)	3.673	0.059	3.730	4.000	0.845	−0.726	0.385
Graphical Curiosity (F8)	3.423	0.064	3.500	4.000	0.924	−0.532	−0.376
Behavioral Changes (F9)	3.409	0.055	3.440	4.000	0.787	−0.264	−0.248
Mental Health (F10)	2.514	0.065	2.440	2.000	0.943	0.622	0.134
Experience (F11)	3.529	0.059	3.570	4.000	0.851	−0.685	0.860
Adaptability (F12)	3.288	0.068	3.390	4.000	0.980	−0.544	−0.343
Rate (F13)	3.678	0.059	3.750	4.000	0.855	−0.824	0.639

Legend: SE: Standard Error of Mean; SD: Standard Deviation

3.4   Machine Learning Based Analysis

In this section, we applied various machine learning methods to the user responses and prioritized individual features about children's behavioral changes for COVID-Hero/this types of of games. The workflow of this procedure is described briefly as follows:

Data Preprocessing. After gathering numerous user's comments, duplicate and missing instances were removed from this dataset. The primary questionnaire is contained 18 features with 13 qualitative and 4 general features like name, age, gender, and mail address. A few attributes (e.g., name and mail address) had not shown any behavioral effects, hence they were lessen from this work. Then, we calculated the average of each instance o determine the ultimate responses respectively. Table 1 shows the demographics details of numerical values of this survey data. Then, we encoded categorical instances (i.e., gender) into numeric values for further analysis.

Applying Regression Models. Several machine learning based regression models [6,16] such as linear regression (LR), decision tree (DT), random forest (RF), XGBoost (XGB), and k-nearest neighbour (KNN) were used to investigate this survey dataset. Many works were previously happened where these models were widely implemented. For instance, Satu et al. [21] used LR to select significant attributes about adolescent career decision difficulties. Then, Howlader et al. [11] employed different DT models to extract factors about diabetes mellitus. Further, Prakash et al. [18] were identified some essential features and ranked them to monitor hydraulic cooling circuit applying XGB. However, Sanchez et al. [19] proposed a methodological framework to diagnose multifaults in rotating machinery by ranking its features using RF and KNN.

Evaluation Metrics. In this work, several performance metrics such as max error (ME), mean absolute error (MAE), mean squared error (MSE) and R2 score were used to verify these regression models which are described as follows:

– **Max Error (ME)** denotes as the maximum residual error that computes the worst distance between predicted and desired samples. The associated formula is defined as follows:

$$\mathrm{Max\,Error}(y, \hat{y}) = \max\left(|y_i - \hat{y}_i|\right) \tag{1}$$

Where y_i and $\hat{y}_i$ indicates real and predicted instances respectively.
– **Mean Absolute Error (MAE)** computes the average inaccuracy and does not measure trending issue. Therefore, all singular variances are considered as similar weighted. The matrix values of MAE are begun from 0 to infinity, and low scores are represented the good performance of machine learning models.

$$MAE = \frac{1}{n}\sum_{j=1}^{n}|y_j - \hat{y}_j| \tag{2}$$

Where n is the number of records including y_i and $\hat{y}_i$ indicates real and predicted instances respectively.

– **Mean Square Error (MSE)** manipulates the average magnitude of the residuals that indicates how the predicted result is fitted properly with real instances by ignoring unexpected large errors.

$$MSE = \frac{1}{n}\sum_{j=1}^{n}(y - \hat{y})^2 \tag{3}$$

Where n is the number of tuples along with y_i and $\hat{y}_i$ indicates real and predicted instances respectively.

- **R-Squared** measures the relational strength among dependent variables and models. Again, the degree around the prediction line is defined that perfectly fits with it. A high R^2 value has represented the goodness of model.

$$R^2 = 1 - \frac{SS_{RES}}{SS_{TOT}} = 1 - \frac{\sum_i (y_i - \hat{y}_i)^2}{\sum_i (y_i - \bar{y})^2} \tag{4}$$

Where SS_{RES} and SS_{TOT} generates the sum of regression and total sum of regression error. Besides, y_i, $\hat{y}_i$ and $\bar{y}$ denotes as real, predicted and mean values instances, respectively.

4 Experimental Result

In this work, we developed a gaming smartphone app named COVID-Hero which helps kids to learn precaution steps about COVID-19 with fun. Various comments were gathered from users to realize the effects of this app on children's behavior. Therefore, some machine learning regression models were implemented into this survey dataset for identifying relevant significant features (i.e. which enhances the quality of the game). To conduct this work, scikit learn machine learning library [17] had been used to investigate these instances using python. Hence, the performance of individual regression models were evaluated using various metrics, such as ME, MAE, MSE, and R2 Score respectively.

Table 2. Experimental result of different regression models

Classifier	ME	MAE	MSE	R2 score
LR	6.080	2.330	7.730	0.990
DT	1.154	0.166	0.054	0.727
RF	0.630	0.110	0.020	0.890
XGB	0.410	0.070	0.009	0.950
KNN	1.030	0.130	0.030	0.840

The outcomes of individual regression models are given at Table 2. In such a situation, XGB showed the lowest ME (0.410), MAE (0.070), and MSE (0.009) and RF showed the second lowest ME (0.630), MAE (0.110), and MSE (0.020), respectively. Later, KNN provided the third lowest residuals for ME (1.030), MAE (0.130), and MSE (0.030). In comparing residuals between the rest of the models, DT showed the lowest residuals than LR. Besides, we required to compare the results of R2 score with another metrics for identifying the best

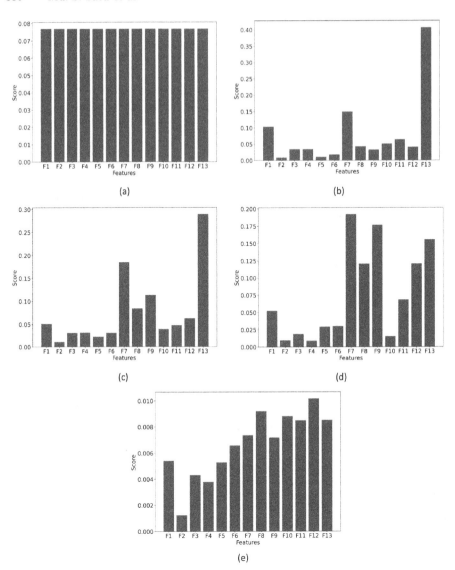

Fig. 2. The feature ranking plots are generated using (a) LR (b) DT (c) RF (d) XGB (e) KNN regression models and estimate individuals to extract significant features about COVID-19

model that prioritized individual features as well. LR showed the highest R2 value (0.990), but its residual values (Max Error, MAE, and MSE) were higher than other models. So, it was not seemed as the best model. Instead, XGB showed the maximum R2 value (0.950) and the lowest residuals respectively. Therefore, XGB is estimated as the best regression model in this experiment. Then, RF provided the second-best model because it gave higher R2 score (0.890) and lower residuals except for XGB. Further, KNN generated higher R2 value than DT. When we compared DT and LR, LR represented larger residuals than DT except for the R2 value.

We inspected the findings of different regression models to determine the importance of individual features and indicated how they effected the behavior of children about COVID-19. From the perspective of their performance, XGB is the best model to analyze the user survey dataset. The feature ranking of individual regression models is shown in Fig. 2. As the best model, XGB ranked individual features such as F13, F7, F9, F12, F8, F11, F1, F6, F5, F3, F10, F4, and F2 respectively (see Fig. 2(d)). Also, other models have been predicted user scores and prioritized individual features as well (see Fig. 2(a–c, e)). Then, we averaged the ranks of different features of individual regression models and sorted them according to the smallest to largest values. The features were organized as F13, F7, F12, F8, F9, F1, F11, F10, F6, F3, F4, F5, and F2 respectively. Afterward, two feature ranking lists were gathered where the weights (i.e., 1, 2, 3, 4,......) has been serially assigned to the features of these lists, summed up the ranks both of similar features and originated a sequential list. Hence, the final feature list is provided by the following sequence, F13, F7, F12, F9, F8, F11, F1, F6, F10, F3, F5, F4 and F2.

When we describe the effect of ranked variables from right to left, the prerequisite criteria can be detected. First, the psychological effect (F2) is an essential variable where most of the users were given the highest marks to it. So, they are confident to change the psychological condition of children for COVID-19/this types of game. Later, F4 is identified as the second prior feature that indicates COVID-Hero is a more educational game to learn about this pandemic. Then, F5 and F3 are prioritized where F5 symbolizes attractiveness, and F3 denotes the changes of children's habits. Nevertheless, F10 and F6 are ranked wherever F10 represents the worrisome issues about the game's negative impact and F6 exemplifies the joyfulness of it. Thus, F1 and F11 provide equal priority because their summation was equal. These features were associated with the effectiveness and shared criteria of children. Then, F8 displays user's graphical interface and F9 shows the behavioral changes of children after playing/observing this game. Therefore, the adaptability of children on COVID-Hero have been pondered as F12 as well. Besides, F7 and F13 are less important, where F7 indicates the contents, and F13 shows this app's rate, respectively.

5   Discussion

Most of the children are not conscious about the harmful effects of COVID-19. It is a challenging task to realize about this pandemic because they are not perceived related information as adult people. Numerous ways are used to identify and make awareness to the kids. Game playing is useful way to make aware and learn about COVID-19 for children. Recently, several games [1,2,8] had been developed which had not efficiently functioned. Therefore, we built a smartphone-based gaming app named COVID-Hero that is more flexible to learn precaution steps about this pandemic. Both pre and post-survey of this app were mingled to investigate its performance. Thus, machine learning models were used to scrutinize which features are more critical to change children's behaviors. Two schemes are used to optimize features such as XGB and average feature rankings. Then, the final feature priority list are generated to understand the effects of COVID-Hero about changing behavioral activities. Although some research questions (RQ) has been raised that defines the feasibility of gamification for the awareness of COVID-19. According to above explanation, it is one of the best approaches to change relevant habitual facts with fun, and perhaps they do not understand the general instructions about COVID-19 properly. By playing game, children are able to learn precautions and follow them as usual (i.e., mostly it happens due to changing their behavioral activities). Thus, these issues cover RQ1. Due to the lockdown situation, children cannot go outside and enjoy the usual games and other activities. As a result, they may addict to watch inappropriate contents which make them disgusting and hamper their mental and health conditions severely. Also, most of online materials are not provided sufficient things to aware kids about COVID-19 pandemic. This app provides children with such services where they can learn about handling COVID-19 with funny games. Therefore, RQ2 is accomplished from this response. In addition, machine learning is needed to investigate significant features about how this game can affect children about COVID-19. Besides, we explore the prioritized list of features and determine how various features are significant for children correspondingly. Thus, RQ3 is covered for this reason.

6   Conclusion and Future Work

The WHO imposed and recommended several essential prohibitions of COVID-19 during this pandemic period and called for compliance. The aim of this work is to create awareness and enhance their knowledge about COVID-19 among children by educating them through mobile games. Hence, we designed and developed an attractive mobile app-based game named COVID-Hero in this purpose. By playing this game, kids are encouraged to develop various healthy habit such as "cleaning their hands and face", "not touching eyes", "nose and mouth", "wearing masks", and "maintaining social distance" etc. to cope with this outbreak. Additionally, machine learning based regression analysis is used to extract relevant factors which indicate why COVID-Hero/Related games are useful to change behavioral activities of children against COVID-19. Besides, COVID-Hero is one of well-organized gaming app where no related apps were not originated and evaluated to estimate children's activities in this situation. Like other mobile apps, we should be aware of excessive game playing tendencies (i.e., COVID-Hero/related games) among children. In future, we will include comparatively more intelligent features and functionality to this game for in-depth understanding among children about COVID-19.

Acknowledgements. The authors acknowledge that this research is partially supported through the Australian Research Council Discovery Project: DP190100-314, "Re-Engineering Enterprise Systems for Microservices in the Cloud".

References

1. 9-year-old italian boy creates "cerba-20", video game on covid-19 (2020). https://cutt.ly/3bMvdvl
2. Covid 19 with corona run (2020). https://cutt.ly/8bMcAG4
3. Video games benefit quarantined kids in covid-19 pandemic (2020). https://cutt.ly/RbMvj2h
4. Adhikari, S.P., et al.: Epidemiology, causes, clinical manifestation and diagnosis, prevention and control of coronavirus disease (COVID-19) during the early outbreak period: a scoping review. Infect. Dis. Poverty **9**(1), 29 (2020). https://doi.org/10.1186/s40249-020-00646-x
5. Ahamad, M.M., et al.: A machine learning model to identify early stage symptoms of SARS-Cov-2 infected patients. Expert Syst. Appl. **160**, 113661 (2020). https://doi.org/10.1016/j.eswa.2020.113661
6. Ahammed, K., Satu, M.S., Khan, M.I., Whaiduzzaman, M.: Predicting infectious state of hepatitis C virus affected patient's applying machine learning methods. In: 2020 IEEE Region 10 Symposium (TENSYMP), pp. 1371–1374 (2020). https://doi.org/10.1109/TENSYMP50017.2020.9230464, iSSN: 2642-6102
7. Anastassopoulou, C., Russo, L., Tsakris, A., Siettos, C.: Data-based analysis, modelling and forecasting of the COVID-19 outbreak. PLOS ONE **15**(3), e0230405 (2020). https://doi.org/10.1371/journal.pone.0230405. (publisher: Public Library of Science)
8. Batha, E.: Coronavirus computer game teaches children social distancing (2020). https://cutt.ly/gbMcUfe
9. Dhand, R., Li, J.: Coughs and sneezes: their role in transmission of respiratory viral infections, including SARS-CoV-2. Am. J. Resp. Crit. Care Med. **202**(5), 651–659 (2020). https://doi.org/10.1164/rccm.202004-1263PP. (publisher: American Thoracic Society - AJRCCM)
10. Gaspar, J.D.S., et al.: A mobile serious game about the pandemic (COVID-19 - did you know?): design and evaluation study. JMIR Ser. Games **8**(4), e25226 (2020)
11. Howlader, K.C., Satu, M.S., Barua, A., Moni, M.A.: Mining significant features of diabetes mellitus applying decision trees: a case study In Bangladesh. bioRxiv p. 481994 (2018). https://doi.org/10.1101/481994. (publisher: Cold Spring Harbor Laboratory Section: Contradictory Results)
12. Kaiser, M.S., et al.: iWorksafe: towards healthy workplaces during COVID-19 with an intelligent phealth app for industrial settings. IEEE Access **9**, 13814–13828 (2021). https://doi.org/10.1109/ACCESS.2021.3050193
13. Laato, S., Laine, T.H., Islam, A.N.: Location-based games and the COVID-19 pandemic: an analysis of responses from game developers and players. Multimodal Technol. Interact. **4**(2) (2020). https://doi.org/10.3390/mti4020029, https://www.mdpi.com/2414-4088/4/2/29
14. Mahmud, M., Kaiser, M.S., McGinnity, T.M., Hussain, A.: Deep learning in mining biological data. Cogn. Comput. **13**(1), 1–33 (2020). https://doi.org/10.1007/s12559-020-09773-x

15. Mahmud, M., Kaiser, M.S., Hussain, A., Vassanelli, S.: Applications of deep learning and reinforcement learning to biological data. IEEE Trans. Neural Networks Learn. Syst. **29**(6), 2063–2079 (2018). https://doi.org/10.1109/TNNLS.2018.2790388. (conference Name: IEEE Transactions on Neural Networks and Learning Systems)

16. Nurjahan, Rony, M.A.T., Satu, M.S., Whaiduzzaman, M.: Mining significant features of diabetes through employing various classification methods. In: 2021 International Conference on Information and Communication Technology for Sustainable Development (ICICT4SD), pp. 240–244 (2021). https://doi.org/10.1109/ICICT4SD50815.2021.9397006

17. Pedregosa, F., et al.: Scikit-learn: machine learning in python. J. Mach. Learn. Res. **12**, 2825–2830 (2011)

18. Prakash, J., Kankar, P.K.: Health prediction of hydraulic cooling circuit using deep neural network with ensemble feature ranking technique. Measurement **151**, 107225 (2020). https://doi.org/10.1016/j.measurement.2019.107225

19. Sánchez, R.V., Lucero, P., Vásquez, R.E., Cerrada, M., Macancela, J.C., Cabrera, D.: Feature ranking for multi-fault diagnosis of rotating machinery by using random forest and KNN. J. Intell. Fuzzy Syst. **34**(6), 3463–3473 (2018). https://doi.org/10.3233/JIFS-169526. (publisher: IOS Press)

20. Sarkodie, S.A., Owusu, P.A.: Investigating the cases of novel coronavirus disease (COVID-19) in China using dynamic statistical techniques. Heliyon **6**(4), e03747 (2020). https://doi.org/10.1016/j.heliyon.2020.e03747

21. Satu, M.S., Ahamed, S., Chowdhury, A., Whaiduzzaman, M.: Exploring significant family income ranges of career decision difficulties of adolescents in Bangladesh applying regression techniques. In: 2019 International Conference on Electrical, Computer and Communication Engineering (ECCE), pp. 1–6 (2019). https://doi.org/10.1109/ECACE.2019.8679415

22. Satu, M.S., et al.: Convolutional neural network model to detect COVID-19 patients utilizing chest X-ray images. medRxiv p. 2020.06.07.20124594 (2021). https://doi.org/10.1101/2020.06.07.20124594. (publisher: Cold Spring Harbor Laboratory Press)

23. Satu, M.S., et al.: Prottoy: a smart phone based mobile application to detect autism of children in Bangladesh. In: 2019 4th International Conference on Electrical Information and Communication Technology (EICT), pp. 1–6 (2019). https://doi.org/10.1109/EICT48899.2019.9068815

24. Satu, M.S., et al.: Short-term prediction of COVID-19 cases using machine learning models. Appl. Sci. **11**(9), 4266 (2021). https://doi.org/10.3390/app11094266. (number: 9 Publisher: Multidisciplinary Digital Publishing Institute)

25. Satu, M.S., et al.: TClustVID: a novel machine learning classification model to investigate topics and sentiment in COVID-19 tweets. Knowl.-Based Syst. 107126 (2021). https://doi.org/10.1016/j.knosys.2021.107126

26. Satu, M.S., et al.: Diseasome and comorbidities complexities of SARS-CoV-2 infection with common malignant diseases. Brief. Bioinform. **22**(2), 1415–1429 (2021). https://doi.org/10.1093/bib/bbab003

27. Shekerdemian, L.S., et al.: International COVID-19 PICU collaborative: characteristics and outcomes of children with coronavirus disease 2019 (COVID-19) infection admitted to US and Canadian pediatric intensive care units. JAMA Pediat. **174**(9), 868–873 (2020). https://doi.org/10.1001/jamapediatrics.2020.1948

28. Sujath, R., Chatterjee, J.M., Hassanien, A.E.: A machine learning forecasting model for COVID-19 pandemic in India. Stoch. Env. Res. Risk Assess **34**(7), 959–972 (2020). https://doi.org/10.1007/s00477-020-01827-8

29. Suppan, M., et al.: A serious game designed to promote safe behaviors among health care workers during the COVID-19 pandemic: Development of "Escape COVID-19." JMIR Ser. Games **8**(4), e24986 (2020)
30. Suppan, M., et al.: Teaching adequate prehospital use of personal protective equipment during the COVID-19 pandemic: development of a gamified e-learning module. JMIR Ser. Games **8**(2), e20173 (2020)
31. Venigalla, A.S.M., Vagavolu, D., Chimalakonda, S.: SurviveCovid-19 - an educational game to facilitate habituation of social distancing and other health measures for covid-19 pandemic. arXiv:2004.09759 (2020)
32. Whaiduzzaman, M., et al.: A privacy-preserving mobile and fog computing framework to trace and prevent COVID-19 community transmission. IEEE J. Biomed. Health Inf. 1–1 (2020). https://doi.org/10.1109/JBHI.2020.3026060

Literature Classification Model of Deep Learning Based on BERT-BiLSTM——Taking COVID-19 as an Example

Zhi Li[✉]

School of Management, Harbin Institute of Technology, Harbin 150001, China

Abstract. [Objective] In the beginning of 2020, the outbreak of covid-19 epidemic occurred, and the number of literatures related to it increased rapidly. In order to meet the increasing needs of literature classification, this paper will explore an automated literature classification model. [method] firstly, more than 20000 articles related to covid-19 in CNKI were collected as the marked data set, and the title, keyword and abstract information of the articles were extracted. Then, different combinations of the title, keyword and abstract were used as the input of different features of the model, and the support vector machine (SVM) based literature classification model and BERT-LSTM based literature classification model were trained respectively and the effect of the model was compared. [Results] The accuracy of the feature combination of "title + keyword + abstract" in the BERT-BiLSTM model was 85.79%, which was higher than the accuracy of the feature combination of "title + keyword" and "keyword + abstract". The accuracy of the benchmark model (SVM) with the combination of "title + keyword + abstract" is 78.79%, so the model based on BERT-BiLSTM can significantly improve the classification effect. [limitation] this paper only classifies four categories, which are classified under R category, so the classification is very few.

Keywords: Deep learning · BERT · Literature classification · Covid-19

1 Introduction

In early 2020, the outbreak of New Coronavirus (COVID19) in Wuhan region of China. Then it rapidly evolved into a global pandemic. On the night of January 30, 2020, the WHO (WHO) announced that it would list COVID-19 as a public health emergencies of international concern. In response to the outbreak of New Coronavirus, a great deal of research has been carried out around the world. It is estimated that only about 2000 articles were collected in CNKI in January 1, 2020 alone. Literature is the basis of further research, and the classification of literature is the basis of making full use of existing literature. Based on this situation, this paper will explore an automatic document classification model to cope with the growing work of document classification.

There are five basic classification methods in China, which are: Chinese Library Classification, China Library Classification, Library Classification of Chinese Academy of Sciences, library of Renmin University of China and International Book Integration

M. Mahmud et al. (Eds.): AII 2021, CCIS 1435, pp. 336–348, 2021.
https://doi.org/10.1007/978-3-030-82269-9_26

classification. Among them, the classification method of Chinese library [1] is the most widely used. The classification method of Chinese library is initiated by Beijing Library, which is divided into five basic categories, and 22 categories. The mark adopts the mixed number of Chinese pinyin and Arabic numerals. Such classification often involves manual participation and complicated classification rules, which costs more resources and is difficult to cope with the urgent need of document classification during COVID-19.

Since the 21st century, deep learning algorithm is more and more used in document classification. Compared with traditional machine learning algorithm, deep learning method has the significant advantage of high classification efficiency and can quickly deal with the classification needs of a large number of data. Therefore, this paper will take the COVID-19 related literature which has been classified in CNKI as the data, extract some features of these literature, and compare the classification effect of machine learning and deep learning algorithm, design a document automatic classification model based on deep learning.

2 Review of Related Research

2.1 Research on Text Classification Algorithm

Text classification technology has experienced the transition from expert system to machine learning and then to deep learning [2]. Text classification is a classic problem in natural language processing (NLP). In the 1950s, text classification was mainly carried out through expert system. In the 1980s, knowledge engineering was used to establish expert system. For example, Li Ming and Liu Lu [3] proposed a multi knowledge domain expert recommendation method based on fuzzy text classification. However, the common disadvantages of these methods are high cost and poor portability. Since the 1990s, machine learning has been developed and widely used in the field of text classification. Since the 21st century, the application of deep learning algorithm in the neighborhood of text classification has greatly improved the effect of text classification.

(1) Traditional machine learning algorithm.
    Text classification using traditional machine learning algorithms requires two steps of artificial feature engineering and shallow classification models. In terms of feature selection, feature selection methods for text classification were proposed by Dasgupta A [4] et al. In terms of shallow classification models, the commonly used algorithms are Naive Bayes (NB), random forest (RF), support vector machine (SVM), maximum entropy and nearest neighbor (KNN), etc. The process of utilizing SVM for text classification is illustrated by Joachims T [5]. Nigam K [6] et al. use maximum entropy to build a classification model. McCallum A [7] et al. compared the effect of multivariate Bernoulli model and polynomial model based on Naive Bayes model. Soucy P [8] et al. searched for features through a feature interaction approach based on word dependency and conducted text classification with the KNN method.
    At the same time, many scholars have improved these basic methods to deal with the problems in reality. For example, scholars such as Qiu Ningjia [9] proposed a weighted naive Bayes algorithm for the problem that the independence assumption

of naive Bayes would reduce the classification effect. Zou Dingjie [10] proposed a Bayesian classifier based on knowledge mapping to solve the problem that paper books have low performance of automated classifiers due to scarcity of metadata.

(2) Deep learning algorithms

The main drawbacks of traditional learning algorithms are high dimensionality and highly sparse text representation as well as weak feature expressivity. Whereas the properties of deep learning algorithms adapted to handle continuous and dense data compensate for this shortcoming. This makes it suitable for addressing the problem of text classification on a large scale. The application of deep learning is embodied in two aspects, the directed quantitative representation of text and the text classification model.

In terms of the directed quantitative representation of text, two typical deep learning algorithms are Word2Vec and BERT. The Word2Vec model was proposed in 2013 by Mikolov T [11] et al. The model was extended with skip-gram model and continuous bag-of word model (CBOW). Subsequently Mikolov T [12] proposed the training method for Word2Vec, i.e., Negative Sampling and Hierarchical softmax. The skip-gram model uses a single word as input to predict the context around it. The continuous bag-of word model takes as input the context of a word to predict that word itself. The primary use of Word2Vec is the acquisition of word vectors. Its main advantages are two points. First it takes context into account, and second it has a smaller dimension of its generative vector. It is therefore more versatile and suitable for more natural language processing tasks. It has the disadvantage that words and vectors are one-to-one relationships. The 2018 Google team [13] proposed the BERT model. The model used transformer as the main framework of the algorithm and used the multitask training goal of mask model (MLM) and next sentence prediction (NSP) The advantage of BERT is that it employs a combination of pre-training with fine-tuning. This allows it greater flexibility to accommodate more downstream tasks. The disadvantage of BERT is that the number of parameters is huge, and pre-training requires substantial computational resources. In text classification models, the commonly used algorithms for text classification are convolutional neural network (CNN), recurrent neural network (RNN), and long and short memory network (LSTM). For example Xie Kinbao [14] et al. applied convolutional neural networks in the classification of multi-fields texts. Wu Hanyu [15] et al. combined attention mechanism, convolutional neural network and long and short memory network to construct classifiers. And Mahmud used this technology in medical domain [27] and biological data analysis [28].

2.2 Related Research on the Application of Text Classification

Besides the improvement of algorithms for text classification, many scholars are also exploring the application of text classification. The classification of texts has been widely used in the column division of press publications, classification of web pages, personalized recommendation, filtering of harmful information and retrieval of information classification. Chen Deyi, Zhang Hongyi [16] and so on used keywords information to construct a CNN network to identify harmful information. Ma Zhanghua [17] analyzed the characteristics of different network retrieval systems constructed based on literature taxonomy in terms of resource selection, class table survey, and retrieval method. Jia Haijun and Liao Chenyang [18] introduced the text classification technology into the government convenient service system to make the personalized recommendation of government documents Gao Fei [19] used text classification technique to detect malicious codes. Liu Gaojun and Wang Xiaobin [20] et al. used CNN and LSTM to classify marketing news. But most of the studies have problems as follows: Most of the studies used machine learning algorithms, but the classification effect is poor; Part of the literature used deep learning algorithms, but the used deep learning algorithms are not advanced enough; Less literatures involved in multiple classification problems. Meanwhile, in the field of literature classification, there are many problems such as low accuracy and consistency of literature classification [21] and incompatibility of literature classification system [22] Therefore, this paper proposed a literature classification model based on BERT-BiLSTM, which can solve the above problems to some extent.

3 The Text Classification Model Based on BERT-BiLSTM

3.1 The Description of Text Classification Problem

The purpose of this paper is to construct a multi classifier and use the classifier to classify literature about COVID-19. In this paper, title, key words and abstract were used as characteristics. With the Chinese library classification number as the output target value. Thus let the literature Pi = {Ti, Ki, Ai, Ci}, where Ti denote title, Ki denote keywords, Ai denote summary, Ci denote classification number. The above formula illustrates that a literature sample consists of four values: title, keywords, abstract, and classification number. In this paper, we will build a classification g. By using mapping $\hat{C}_i = g(Ti, Ki, Ai)$, to predict the true value of C_i.

3.2 Pre Training Language Model—BERT

In this section, we will introduce BERT and its detailed implementation. There are two steps in the framework of BERT: pre training and fine-tuning. The model is pre trained with unlabeled data. Use the lable data in the downstream task to fine tune all parameters. Therefore, although each downstream task has the same pre training model, the model of each downstream task is different. The composition of the BERT model is described below.

(1) Input of the model
   One advantage of the BERT model is that the BERT model takes "word" as the unit, so it can improve the problem of polysemy. The input to BERT can be a single sentence or a pair of sentences. BERT transforms the sentence into a sequence label, which is used as the input of the self-attention layer. The sequence label is completed by following steps: (1) A special label ([CLS]) is added at the beginning of the sentence, another special label ([SEP]) is added between two sentences, and each word is converted into a word embedding (2) For two sentences, fragment embedding should be used to further distinguish them, such as EM_A stands for the

first sentence,EM_B means the second sentence. (3) Position embedding is introduced to represent the position information of words. The input of self-attention layer can be obtained by adding the word embedding, fragment embedding and position embedding. The whole process is shown in Fig. 1.

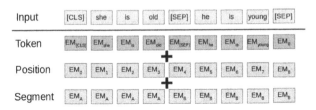

Fig. 1. Generating principle of BERT input sequence

(2) The layer of self-attention
The self-attention layer is based on the encoder of transformer model [23], which is composed of 12 layers based on the same structure. The layer with the same structure is composed of three parts: multi attention layer, full link layer and normalization layer. In the multi attention layer, we first define the dot product attention as follows:

$$\text{Attention}(Q, K, V) = \text{softmax}\left(\frac{QK^T}{\sqrt{d_k}}\right)V \tag{1}$$

Where q is the query matrix, K is the key matrix, V is the value matrix, and d_k is the dimension of Q and K matrices. After that, we can define multi attention as follows:

$$\text{MultiHead}(Q, K, V) = \text{contact}(head_1, \ldots, head_h)W^o \tag{2}$$

Among them $head_i = Attention\left(QW_i^Q, KW_i^K, VW_i^V\right)$. This is the final output.
In addition, there are normalization layer and full link layer in self attention mechanism. The main structure is shown in Fig. 2.
Compared to Word2Vec, BERT has the following advantages: (1) The word vector generated by BERT is dynamic, which can better solve the problem of polysemy (2) BERT embodies the complex characteristics of words, such as semantic and grammatical characteristics. (3) BERT uses the way of pre-training and fine-tuning, which makes it more widely used.

3.3 BiLSTM

In recent years, deep learning algorithm is widely used in text classification. The deep learning models for text classification include convolutional neural network (CNN), recurrent neural network (RNN), long short memory network (LSTM) and bidirectional

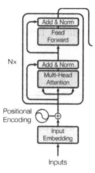

Fig. 2. Structure chart of BERT

long short memory network (BiLSTM). The following will introduce the deep learning methods used in this paper: LSTM and BiLSTM.

LSTM was first proposed by Hochreiter and Schmidhub [24] in 1997 to solve the long-term dependence problem in RNN. The reason of long-term dependence is that after multi-stage calculation, the characteristics of the long time slice have been covered. The solution to the long-term dependence of long and short memory network is the introduction of gating unit. The basic structure of long short memory network is shown in Fig. 3.

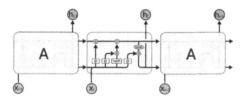

Fig. 3. LSTM schematic diagram

The long-term and short-term memory network is composed of special neural network units, which plays a role in maintaining long-term and short-term memory. The long short memory network can be expanded into a series of cells as shown in Fig. 3. Each cell has three types of gating components: input gate, forgetting gate and output gate. The function of forgetting gate is to judge how much information needs to be forgotten according to the given input. The input gate consists of two parts for updating information. The output gate, also known as update gate, affects the output of the gating unit at time t and the input at time t + 1.

A key part of LSTM is the state of the cell. The input of the cell at time t is the splicing of the vector representation of the data and the vector output at the previous time. The gating components in every cell have an effect on the state of the cell. The state of the cell is like a production line, which processes and outputs the information of T-1 time.

However, one disadvantage of LSTM is that it can't encode the information from back to front. BiLSTM is a combination of forward LSTM and backward LSTM, that is, the input of forward LSTM and backward LSTM are spliced as model input. So this method can capture bidirectional semantics better.

3.4 Support Vector Machine (SVM)

Support vector machine is a statistical learning theory, which was first proposed in the 1960s. Support vector machine (SVM) is a binary classification model, which tries to find a hyperplane and divide samples into two classes. The principle of finding hyperplane is to maximize the classification interval. Support vector machine (SVM) was first applied to linear separable problems, and then with the introduction of kernel method, it can also deal with non linear separable problems.

For the linear separable problem, let the classifier be $y_i = w^T x_i + b$, support vector machine is essentially to solve the optimization problems which is shown in formula (3):

$$\max \frac{1}{2} \|w\|_2^2 \tag{3}$$

$$\text{s.t. } y_i \left(w^T x_i + b\right) \geq 1$$

The parameters of the solution are w and b, the objective function is a quadratic function of w, and the constraint condition is linear. Therefore, the optimization problem is a quadratic programming problem, and the global optimal solution can be obtained.

Support vector machine (SVM) can't solve the linear non separable problem directly. For this kind of problem, we can use kernel function to map the original vector to a higher dimensional space and make it separable in a higher dimensional space. In this case, the classifier is $y_i = w^T \phi(x_i) + b$ In this case, the optimization problem is shown in formula (4).

$$\max \frac{1}{2} \|w\|_2^2 \tag{4}$$

$$\text{s.t. } y_i(w^T \phi(x_i) + b) \geq 1$$

It is difficult to solve the problem directly, so kernel function is introduced to solve the problem conveniently. The commonly used kernel functions are linear kernel, Gaussian kernel, Laplace kernel and so on. But in reality, it is difficult to determine which kernel function can make the original problem linearly separable, so a soft interval support vector machine will be used in practice. Soft interval support vector machine is mainly realized by relaxing variables. At this time, the optimization problem is shown in formula (5).

$$\max \frac{1}{2} \|w\|_2^2 + P \sum\nolimits_{i=1}^{n} \zeta_i \tag{5}$$

$$\text{s.t. } y_i(w^T x_i + b) \geq 1 - \zeta_i$$

Where p > 0 is the penalty parameter, the greater the P is, the greater the penalty for misclassification, and the smaller the P is, the smaller the penalty for misclassification.

Support vector machine is usually used to solve binary classification problem. But this paper is faced with multi classification problem. The method to deal with multi classification is to transform the original optimization problem into a multi-objective optimization problem, and solve multiple hyperplanes to divide the feature space at the same time. However, this method needs a lot of calculation and is difficult to achieve in reality. Therefore, the following three methods can be used to realize multi classification of SVM in reality.

(1) One to many training method.
In this method, one class is taken as one class, and the other class is taken as another class to train SVM. If there is a k-classification problem, the method needs to train K SVM. The main drawback of this method is that there will be problems of repeated classification and unclassifiability. The so-called repeated classification means that multiple classes claim that the sample belongs to it. Unclassifiable means that all classes claim that the sample does not belong to it.
(2) One to one training method.
In this method, all classes are combined in pairs to train multiple support vector machines, and then the final class of samples is determined by statistical frequency. If there is a k-classification problem, this method needs to train $\frac{k*(k-1)}{2}$ support vector machines. This method can avoid the phenomenon of unclassifiability, but it still has the problem of repeated classification.
(3) Hierarchical support vector machine.
The structure of this method is similar to the decision tree. Firstly, all categories are divided into two categories, and then each sub category is subdivided until each individual category can be determined.

3.5 Model Framework

Therefore, this paper proposes a literature classification model based on BERT-BiLSTM, as shown in Fig. 4.

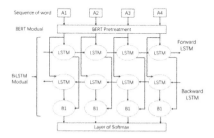

Fig. 4. Schematic diagram of BERT-BiLSTM model

Based on the BERT-BiLSTM model, the input can be any combination of summary, title and keyword. The input is first processed by BERT and converted to the data type that BiLSTM can process, and then processed by BiLSTM layer and input into softmax layer. After softmax layer output, we get the category of literature.

4 Experimental Setup

This experiment includes three steps: experimental data collection and processing, experimental model design and experimental results comparison. Compare the model based on BERT-BiLSTM with the benchmark SVM model to illustrate the effect of the model based on BERT-BiLSTM.

4.1 Collection and Processing of Experimental Data

The purpose of this experiment is to realize the automatic classification of documents. Therefore, the corpus of this paper is R-type Chinese literature related to cowid-19 on CNKI. Because there are many subcategories under R category, it needs a lot of computing resources to include each subcategory into the model, so this experiment only selects the class with more literature for the experiment. The specific experimental steps are as follows:

(1) Data collection: Search "covid-19" in the advanced retrieval function of "CNKI", select Chinese literature, extract the title, key words and abstract information of literature, and export them. A total of 18598 literatures were exported. All literatures were published from January 15, 2020 to February 10, 2021.
(2) Data preprocessing: remove the category labels of non-R categories in the classification number of Chinese Library Classification. Non-Chinese literatures were deleted. Delete the literature that abstract or keyword is empty. The literatures with the same integral part of the classification number are merged into one category. According to the category, the category with more samples is selected. Finally, we get the following four categories: R563, R197, R259, R181. Their meanings are: R563 represents the category of lung disease. R197 stands for medical and health systems and institutions. R259 represents the diseases of modern medicine. R181 represents the basic theory and method of epidemiology. The number of samples in each category is shown in Fig. 5.

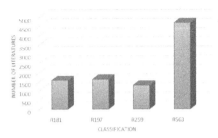

Fig. 5. Literature distribution map

4.2 Experimental Model Design

Due to the excellent performance of BERT on many data sets [25], the experiment uses the BERT-BiLSTM model. Three combinations of "abstract + key words", "topic + key words" and "topic + key words + abstract" were used as features to compare the effects of these three combinations. Then the best model is compared with the traditional machine learning model. Traditional machine learning methods include SVM, logistic regression and so on. In this paper, SVM is selected as the contrast.

(1) Design of classification model based on BERT-BiLSTM.

Due to the limitation of computing resources, this paper uses the downloaded Chinese pre training model (Chinese_ L-12_ H-768_ A-12 model, which has 12 layers, 768 hidden layer neurons and 12 Attention heads).

Deep learning models for text classification include convolutional neural network (CNN), recurrent neural network (RNN) and long short memory network (LSTM). RNN is suitable for processing data with continuous features, but its main disadvantage is that it is difficult to train for long sequences. Moreover, the influence of the preceding words on the following words is decreased by degrees. Long short memory network is a special kind of recurrent neural network, which improves the shortcomings of recurrent neural network. Long short memory network is controlled by gate structure, including input gate, output gate and forgetting gate. The long-term and short-term memory can be effectively maintained through the gate cycle unit. However, LSTM does not make full use of the information from the back to the front. Therefore, this paper uses bi-directional long and short memory network (BiLSTM) to model.

The specific experimental steps are as follows: first of all, the BERT pre training model is optimized. In this paper, we use bert4keras to implement the BERT model. Dropout layer is added to the BERT model to prevent over fitting. After that, the bidirectional long short memory network layer is added, and the output dimension of this layer is 300. Finally, the output layer is added, softmax function is used as the activation function, and the output dimension is 4. Finally, the test set data is used to evaluate the model, and the accuracy is used as the evaluation index. Perform the above steps for the three combinations of "abstract + keyword", "topic + keyword" and "topic + keyword + abstract".

(2) Design of classification model based on SVM.

First, we extract the words from the sentences in the test set. Because Jieba is not effective in Chinese English mixed sentences, this paper uses Chinese Academy of Sciences' pynlpir to extract words from sentences. After extracting words from sentences, feature extraction is carried out by using the hot bag feature and TF-IDF feature respectively. Then, the SVM model is constructed by using the model in sklearn package.

4.3 Comparison of Experimental Results

Next, the experimental results are compared, and the accuracy rate is used as the evaluation index of the model.

In the classification model based on BERT-BiLSTM, the accuracy of three combinations of "abstract + keyword", "keyword + topic" and "abstract + topic + keyword" is shown in Fig. 6. It can be seen from Fig. 6 that the best combination is "abstract + keyword + title", with an accuracy of 85.79%. The second is the combination of "title + keyword", the accuracy rate is 84.74%. The accuracy of "abstract + keywords" combination was the lowest, which was 82.56%. Because the combination of "abstract + keyword + title" contains more information, the model trained with it as feature also has strong generalization ability. Therefore, the combination of "abstract + keyword + title" is selected as the feature to further compare the effect of the model based on BERT-BiLSTM and the traditional machine learning model SVM.

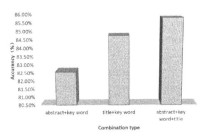

Fig. 6. Comparison of accuracy of different combination models

Using the combination of "abstract + keyword + title" as the feature, we compare the effects of the classification model based on BERT-BiLSTM, the SVM model based on hot word bag and the SVM model based on TF-IDF. The accuracy of the three models is shown in Fig. 7. It can be seen from the figure that the BERT-BiLSTM model has the highest accuracy which is 85.79%. The accuracy rate of SVM model using hot word bag as feature extraction method is 78.79%. The accuracy of SVM model based on TF-IDF is 78.41%. From the results of this experiment, it can be seen that the effect of the model based on BERT-BiLSTM is better than that of SVM model. Because SVM mainly deals with two classification problems, it needs to build multiple SVM when dealing with multi classification problems, so the deviation is large. The text classification model based on BERT-BiLSTM is pre trained on the basis of deep network and attention mechanism. At the same time, BiLSTM model can better capture two-way semantics, so the experimental effect is better.

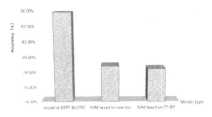

Fig. 7. Comparison of accuracy of different models

5 Epilogue

From the experiments, it can be seen that using the combination of "abstract + key words + title" has a better effect than using only "title + key words" or only "abstract + key words" for classification. Therefore if more information is included in the input, such as including references, author related information, etc. [26], the classification may be improved.

Besides that the complexity of deep learning model is higher, which easily leads to overfitting. Therefore the sample size needs to be increased to reduce the risk of overfitting. This paper has a sample size of just over 9000 due to the limitation of computing resources. Since part of the data was again extracted from it to be used as a test set and a validation set, the number of training samples was low. Increasing the number of training samples might improve model fit.

This paper model is used to solve is four classification problem and only four classes R563, R197, R259, R181 are considered, while there are 16 classes under R class. This limits the use of the model as more classes are not considered and the fine classification of these four classes is not considered. In further studies, the scope of the study should be extended to enhance the usefulness of the model.

The model also does not take into account domain crossover issues of the literature. A literature related to COVID-19 may not be limited to category R. It may also produce crossovers with other major categories. More broad categories should also be included in the model in future studies.

More models can be tried in subsequent studies. Using different models for different data may achieve different classification effects. In the pre training process of BERT, the data within a field can also be used for pre training if the computational resources allow it. This action can also affect the model classification effect.

References

1. Chinese Library Classification. Sci. Technol. Inf. **18**(36), 171 (2020)
2. He, L., Zheng, Z., Xiang, F., et al.: Research progress of text classification technology based on deep learning. Comput. Eng. **47**(2), 1–11.021 (2021)
3. Ming, L., Liu, L., Jun, W.: Approach to expert recommendation with multiple knowledge areas based on fuzzy text categorization. J. Beijing Univ. Aeronaut. Astronaut. **35**(10), 1254–1257 (2009)
4. Dasgupta, A., Drineas, P., Harb, B., et al.: Feature selection methods for text classification. In: Proceedings of the 13th ACM SIGKDD International Conference on Knowledge Discovery and Data Mining, 230–239 (2007)
5. Joachims, T.: Transductive inference for text classification using support vector machines. Icml. 99, 200–209 (1999)
6. Nigam, K., Lafferty, J., McCallum, A.: Using maximum entropy for text classification. IJCAI-99 Workshop Mach. Learn. Inform. Filtering. 1(1), 61–67 (1999)
7. McCallum, A., Nigam, K.: A comparison of eventmodels for naive bayes text classification. AAAI-98 Workshop Learn. Text Categorization, **752**(1), 41–48 (1998)
8. Soucy, P., Mineau, G.W.: A simple KNN algorithm for text categorization. In: Proceedings 2001 IEEE International Conference on Data Mining. IEEE, 647–648 (2001)

9. Qiu, N., He, J., Xue, L., Wang, P., Zhao, J.: Weighted Naive Bayes classification algorithm fusing semantic features. Comput. Eng. Des. **41**(09), 2523–2529 (2020)
10. Dingjie, Z.: Book classification based on knowledge map and Bayesian classifier. Comput. Eng. Des. **41**(06), 1796–1801 (2020)
11. Mikolov, T., Chen, K., Corrado, G., et al.: Efficient estimation of word representations in vector space. arXiv preprint arXiv:1301.3781 (2013)
12. Mikolov, T., Sutskever, I., Chen, K., et al.: Distributed representations of words and phrases and their compositionality. arXiv preprint arXiv:1310.4546 (2013)
13. Devlin, J., Chang, M.W., Lee, K., et al.: BERT: pre-training of deep bidirectional transformers for language understanding. arXiv preprint arXiv:1810.04805 (2018)
14. Xie, J., Li, J., Kang, S., Wang, Q., Wang, Y.: A multi-domain text classification method based on recurrent convolution multi-task learning. J. Electr. Inf. Technol. 1–9[2021–03–03]. http://kns.cnki.net/kcms/detail/11.4494.TN.20210302.1140.008.html
15. Wu, H., Jiang, Y., Huang, S., Li, R., Jiang, M.: CNN-BiLSTM-attention hybird model for text classification. Comput. Sci. 47(S2), 23–27+34 (2020)
16. Chen, D., Zhang, H., Liu, C., Zhang, G.: Classification of Chinese text harmful information based on keywords strategy and convolutional neural network. J. Jimei Univ. (Natural Sci.) **25**(05), 392–400 (2020)
17. Zhanghua, M.: Library classification used in network resources organization. Libr. Inf. Serv. **12**, 24–29 (1999)
18. Haijun, J., Liao Chengyang, D., Jingsong, S.Y.: Applied research on TextCNN technology in government OA system. Off. Inform. **25**(14), 45–48 (2020)
19. Gao, F.: Application of malware detection tool based on text classification technology. Technol. Econ. Guide, **28**(27), 23+22 (2020)
20. Gaojun, L., Xiaobin, W.: Marketing news text classification incorporating CNN+LSTMAttention. Comput. Technol. Dev. **30**(11), 59–63 (2020)
21. Jianhua, D.: Probe into the accuracy and consistency of literature classifying and indexing of the literatures belong to the category of writing——the comparison of the classifying and indexing of the collection data of the main domestic libraries. Sci-Tech Inf. Dev. Econ. **24**(02), 32–33 (2014)
22. Yang, M.: Analysis and countermeasures of common problems in book classification. Manage. Observ. (16), 184–185 (2015)
23. Vaswani, A., Shazeer, N., Parmar, N., et al.: Attention is all you need. arXiv preprint arXiv: 1706.03762 (2017)
24. Hochreiter, S., Schmidhuber, J.: Long short-term memory. Neural Comput. **9**(8), 1735–1780 (1997)
25. Adhikari, A., Ram, A., Tang, R., et al.: Docbert: BERT for document classification. arXiv preprint arXiv:1904.08398 (2019)
26. Pengcheng, L., Yibo, W., Jimin, W.: Automatic displine classification for scientific papers based on a deep pre-training language model. J. China Soc. Sci. Tech. Inf. **39**(10), 1046–1059 (2020)
27. Mahmud, M., Kaiser, M.S., McGinnity, T.M., Hussain, A.: Deep learning in mining biological data. Cogn. Comput. **13**(1), 1–33 (2020). https://doi.org/10.1007/s12559-020-09773-x
28. Mahmud, M., Kaiser, M.S., Hussain, A., Vassanelli, S.: Applications of deep learning and reinforcement learning to biological data. IEEE Trans. Neural Networks Learn. Syst. **29**(6), 2063–2079 (2018). https://doi.org/10.1109/TNNLS.2018.2790388

Identifying Relevant Stakeholders in Digital Healthcare

Nasrin Sultana Nipa[1], Mehnaz Alam[2], and Md Sanaul Haque[3,4,5](✉)

[1] Department of Computer Science, University of Memphis, Memphis, USA
nnipa@memphis.edu
[2] Department of Development Studies, Bangladesh University of Professionals,
Dhaka, Bangladesh
[3] Research Unit of Medical Imaging, Physics and Technology, University of Oulu, Oulu, Finland
md.haque@oulu.fi
[4] Department of Software Engineering, LUT University, Lappeenranta, Finland
[5] gameCORE Research Centre, Institute of Technology Carlow, Carlow, Ireland

Abstract. In recent times, considerable attention has been given to digital services, mainly digital healthcare, i.e., health and well-being applications and services by health organizations, practitioners, and researchers. One of the significant challenges for today's digital health and well-being applications and services is that they are not sustainable and focusing less on relevant stakeholders. However, to the best of our knowledge, little is known about relevant stakeholders in the digital health and well-being applications and services, precisely identifying them using an appropriate method. This paper seeks to define and identify the relevant stakeholders in the digital health and well-being applications and services. A literature review is conducted based on relevant articles on stakeholders within the health domain. Hence, the narrative synthesis literature review approach has been used with a combination of the Bryant model of stakeholder-issue interrelationship. We identified relevant stakeholders who may build a better future to enhance the efficacy of the digital health and well-being applications and services in the long run and suggested a future study on value propositions.

Keywords: Relevant stakeholders · Digital healthcare · Narrative synthesis literature review · Bryant model · Sustainability

1 Introduction

The United Nations Sustainable Development Goals: goal three is intended to "ensure healthy lives and promote well-being for all ages" [1]. In the modern operating environment of work, various actors need to collaborate to build a successful occupational digital healthcare. These multiple actors with apparent interests ('stakes') in the work and operations within a workplace are known as stakeholders [2].

Nowadays, services for all stakeholders cover the broad area of the new IT and its utilization which we call the "digital service", mixing knowledge with technology. Deploying digital services in supporting health and well-being is expanding rapidly.

M. Mahmud et al. (Eds.): AII 2021, CCIS 1435, pp. 349–357, 2021.
https://doi.org/10.1007/978-3-030-82269-9_27

Thousands of digital health and well-being applications and services for the users are accessible. An example, Teveyshelppi: A digital telephone mediated free healthcare service for LähiTapiola personal insurance customers in Finland. It is expected that various advanced digital services, i.e., digital health and well-being applications and services, will be readily available in the future. But not all these services are fulfilling stakeholders' value expectations or preferences.

Out of 196 countries, 78 countries expense more than 7% of total GDP (Gross domestic product) in healthcare costs, which covers the delivery of health and well-being applications and services [3]. The digital health and well-being applications and services are struggling to focus on stakeholders' needs and preferences, particularly relevant stakeholders. It means digital health and well-being services are not relevant stakeholders' oriented even though it costs a high budget. Involving users and communities is essential to improve digital healthcare [4].

Moreover, researchers [5] examined that healthcare service providers face difficulties in improving the performance of digital health and well-being applications and services. Collaborating with relevant stakeholders to work to create value is still a challenge [6]. Considering the obstacles mentioned earlier, involving the relevant stakeholders, and focusing on their needs may bring positive aspects for the sustainable development of digital health and well-being applications and services. This leads to the research question:

- *To what degree relevant stakeholders can be identified, and who are the relevant stakeholders in digital healthcare?*

To answer the question, we proposed a technique and identified relevant stakeholders, which is based on a narrative synthesis review of literature on relevant stakeholders' topic of interest and adopting Bryant model of stakeholder-issue interrelationship. The results of this study could support adding an advantage to digital health and well-being applications and services involving the relevant stakeholders.

2   Relevant Stakeholders

The term "Stakeholder" was formed based on the word Stockholder in 1960 [7]. It was suggested that in the process of decision making of publicly held, contemporary corporations and other parties are present to have the "stake". Stanford Research Institute introduced the term "stakeholders" in 1963, but Freeman [8] developed the stakeholder concept by defining stakeholders as the team or group of members or an individual in an organization, and this organization's performance is affected by stakeholders, for example, consumers, suppliers, creditors, competitors, employees, communities, incubators, financial institutions, government, universities, and research institutes etc. Moreover, Philips and his colleagues, in their work [9] identified a few internal stakeholders or primary stakeholders (customers, suppliers, employers, shareholders or financiers, and communities or dropping competitors) and added external stakeholders or secondary stakeholders (NGOs, governments, environmentalists, critics, media, and others). Our study named the users and other stakeholders as the "relevant stakeholders" due to their relativity in the digital health and well-being applications and services. Stakeholders help organizations to save time, effort and integrate resources [10], and it is, therefore, important to find other stakeholders who are related to achieve the objectives.

Previous research highlighted the importance of identifying stakeholders [11, 12]. A stakeholder identification methodology was implemented over two phases in trans-disciplinary research [11]. First phase was a design phase where the researchers worked with other researchers involved in the same project to develop a tool to identify stake-holders in the second phase of implementation. They then worked with the case study leaders to confirm their interests and skills were accounted for. The resultant tool such as a questionnaire was then implemented by case study leaders with the help from the central researcher of the project [11].

Others identified stakeholders generally in healthcare IT projects but not deliberated a method to define and identify relevant stakeholders of digital health and well-being applications and services. In their work [12], Nilsen and his colleagues have employed longitudinal qualitative and interpretive methodological approach in their research to design the case study to find stakeholders. For the stakeholder analysis, an analytical framework has been applied to define different aspects (decisions-making fields, roles, and levels) of stakeholder's participation in healthcare decision-making [13]. However, to the best of our knowledge, little is known about relevant stakeholders in the digital health and well-being applications and services, precisely identifying them using appropriate method and techniques.

3   Method

Our approach in identifying relevant stakeholders in digital healthcare might be one effective method for sustainable digital health and well-being applications and services. The approaches applied are a combination of the narrative synthesis literature review and integrating Bryant model [14] of stakeholders-issue interrelationship. We categorized of relevant stakeholders' identification process as a set expressed by,

- Relevant stakeholders in digital healthcare = {Narrative synthesis literature review + incorporation of Bryant model}

3.1   Narrative Synthesis Literature Review

The literature search presented in this study was performed using conference and jour-nal papers in the context of relevant stakeholders and health-based information systems. A narrative literature review search was conducted using the online repository systems: ACM digital library, science direct, web of science, Scopus, and EBSCO Database. Addi-tionally, we scanned the reference lists of selected articles (snowballing). We searched for literature using the combination of search terms "stakeholders", "relevant stakehold-ers", and "stakeholders and digital healthcare". The second literature search specifically targeted the conference and journal papers in the context of health-based information systems. The second search had been conducted using web addresses dealt with health and well-being conference proceedings and journal papers. Relevant titles and abstracts on English literature were reviewed, published between January 2007 and January 2021. This review search was started at the beginning of August 2020 and finished at the end of January 2021.

Eligibility Criteria
Eligibility CriteriaArticles were included in this systematic review if the abstract or title showed the results of original research studies related to stakeholders and healthcare services and related approaches. Electronic citations, including accessible abstracts of all articles recovered from the search, were selected by one author to choose articles for full-text review. From the initial search, duplicates were eliminated. However, publication and language bias has been analysed during the search process of the article election. Nevertheless, full texts of possibly relevant studies were examined to ascertain eligibility for inclusion. In the following Table 1, inclusion and exclusion criteria for the studies are listed.

Table 1. Criteria for inclusion and exclusion of studies

Criteria	Inclusion	Exclusion
Time period	Jan 2007 – Jan 2021	Before 2007
Language	English	Other languages
Type of studies	Primary studies	Reports, commentaries, letters
Aim: to identify relevant stakeholders	Literature points out possible stakeholders	Literature does not cover

Subsequently, we summarized the main outcomes and key results. The variances were set by consensus. Finally, a narrative synthesis literature review of studies that meet the inclusion criteria was conducted. We used reference management software MENDELEY (Windows 10 Version 1803) to categorize and store the literature.

Data Extraction and Synthesis
The data extraction in the form of a framework was applied to summarize the study results. The literature was deliberated and synthesized into themes after the data extraction. To synthesize the findings of the studies, a narrative synthesis was performed. We decided that a narrative synthesis literature review establishes as the fit instrument to synthesize the findings of the studies. This was done due to the choice of different studies that were incorporated in this narrative review. The findings from the search resulted in eight unique literature studies (Fig. 2). These eight literature studies revealed that researchers had identified some relevant stakeholders in the health and well-being applications and services.

3.2 Adopting Bryant Model

To analyze the results of relevant stakeholders, we integrated the Bryant model to the identified eight pieces of literature studies (Fig. 2). Stakeholders differ according to their issues of interest [15]. As relevant stakeholders have related issues and these stakeholders are interlinked to each other. Bryant depicted a stakeholder-issue interrelationship diagram [14] where different issues connect a group of stakeholders, and then these stakeholders are defined as relevant stakeholders. Therefore, we examined whether these relevant stakeholders from the eight literature studies define the Bryant model, such as whether they are connected based on similar topics of interest in digital health and well-being applications and services. We found out that these relevant stakeholders are directly or indirectly interlinked to each other.

Relevant stakeholders can be primary stakeholders or secondary stakeholders, or both if they are relevant and related to achieve their objectives. Stakeholders differ according to their issues of interest [15]. They can have related issues, and they can be interlinked to each other. Bryant depicted stakeholder-issue interrelationship diagram [14]. On the diagram, stakeholders' interests have been indicated by arrow signs and stakeholders interlinked by issues or important topics to discourse, e.g., value and value related actions in the digital health and well-being applications and services.

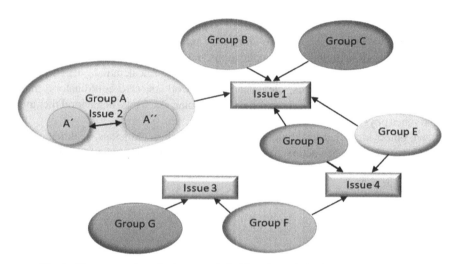

Fig. 1. The connection of relevant stakeholders through the lens of Bryant model

Figure 1 represents the stakeholder-issue interrelationship, and seven stakeholder groups (Group A, Group B, Group C, Group D, Group E, Group F, Group G) are interlinked by four issues (Issue1, Issue 2, Issue 3, Issue 4). Group A has two members (A' and A"), and they are connected by issue 2, i.e., they have similar topics to discuss. Issue 1 is surrounded by Group B, C, D and E due to similar topic approaches of the group stakeholders. On the other hand, Group F is connected with Group D and E by issue 4. Group F and G are connected by issue 3. The above diagram describes the relationship among a group of stakeholders associated with the key issues or topic and the member of groups. When different issues connect a group of stakeholders, these stakeholders are defined as relevant stakeholders. Relevant stakeholders might be involved in any subjective matter. They can be identified if and only if their issues of interest are focused on values and value-related actions, such as whether these stakeholders co-create value in the digital health and well-being applications and services.

4 Results

The findings from searching resulted in eight unique literature studies of relevant stakeholders, which are presented below.

- Researchers mentioned the relevant stakeholders as patients or users, families of patients, health professionals (clinicians and nurses, employees), health institutions and organizations, payer and authorities [10].
- Researchers listed stakeholders as acceptors, providers, supporters, and controllers [16].
- Others identified patients, clinicians, nurses, residents, interns, specialists, physicians, and administrators as the key stakeholders [17]. Value has been described in digital health and well-being applications and services by considering the relevant stakeholders: patients, employers, providers, payers, and manufacturers [18].
- Relevant stakeholders are listed as clinicians, nurses, employees, patients, and other parties engaged in digital health applications and services [19].
- Scholars coined out relevant stakeholders as patients, surgical, radiation, gynecologic, medical oncologists, nurses, dieticians, social workers, care coordinators, mental health professionals, nurses, practitioners, physician assistants, behavioral therapists, and other physicians' extenders [20, 21].
- Later, others identified stakeholders as patients, families, clinicians, healthcare facilities, researchers, policy actors, payors and purchasers, employees, vendors, suppliers, distributors, small-to-medium enterprise applications and services developers and consultants [22].

5 Discussion

Based on narrative synthesis literature review and integrating Bryant model of stakeholders-issue interrelationship [14], the study's main findings are presented in Fig. 2.

Figure 2 represents our technique of identifying relevant stakeholders. The identified relevant stakeholders are patients or users, families of patients, health professionals (clinicians, nurses, administrators, and employees), health institutions and organizations, researchers, payers' organizations and authorities, health care policymakers, health care facilities, small-to-medium service developers and consultants, and consumer advocates. However, this is not to say that this is the end of relevant stakeholders in digital healthcare. In upcoming years, more research should be conducted to add more of them to the list.

To co-create value, value propositions convey users and other stakeholders' solutions, i.e., by involving relevant stakeholders in one body network [23]. Thus, value propositions are a potential approach [24] for sustainable digital health and well-being applications and services. These relevant stakeholders can add value to identify the key

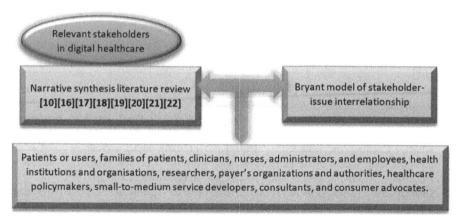

Fig. 2. The proposed technique of identifying relevant stakeholders in digital healthcare.

value propositions [24] for digital healthcare research, particularly in the context of developing countries.

To avoid human error and to reduce time and effort, the literature search could have been conducted using an AI-based online literature review and data extraction search machine such as irish.ai. Though this was a limitation due to not having a licensed or registered AI-based searching tool; and using an AI-based tool is a new approach which the authors and researchers of the present study might have found challenging to implement. Our identified relevant stakeholders in digital healthcare are limited to literature, and expert validation (such as in-depth interviews) is not involved.

This is a work-in-progress paper. Further study needs more attention on the extract version of these key relevant stakeholders to underline their value for different digital healthcare applications and services. In future, expert validation of pertinent stakeholders of digital healthcare should be performed. Focusing on future expert validation, an impact framework can be proposed. This framework can be focused on the sustainable development of digital health and well-being applications and services. As examples, involving relevant stakeholders and design thinking for sustainable solutions [25, 26].

6 Conclusion

This paper was aimed to identify relevant stakeholders in digital healthcare, i.e., digital health and well-being applications and services. This was conducted by proposing a method followed by the Bryant model and narrative synthesis review of literature based on their topic of interest and recommendation from the literature study. We also believe that digital healthcare applications and services providers and other relevant stakeholders will work together to provide quality and efficient service to users to boost digital health and well-being applications and services.

References

1. UN. Goal 3: Ensure healthy lives and promote well-being for all at all ages. United Nation Report. (2019) UN. https://www.un.org/sustainabledevelopment/health/. Accessed 22 April 2021
2. Auvinen, A.: Understanding the stakeholders as a success factor for effective occupational health care. (2017). https://doi.org/10.5772/66479
3. World bank report.: Health expenditure total GDP (2013) world bank. http://data.worldbank.org/indicator/SH.XPD.TOTL.ZS. Accessed on 22 Feb 2021
4. KPMG.: Creating new value with patients. KPMG (2014). https://www.kpmg.com/Global/en/IssuesAndInsights/ArticlesPublications/what-works/creating-new-value-with-patients/Documents/creating-new-value-with-patients.pdf. Accessed on 22 Feb 2021
5. Chakraborty, S., Dobrzykowski, D.: Examining value co-creation in healthcare purchasing: a supply chain view. Bus. Theor. Pract. **15**(2), 179–190 (2014)
6. Boyer, K.K., Pronovost, P.: What medicine can teach operations: what operations can teach medicine. J. Oper. Manag. **28**(5), 367–371 (2010)
7. Goodpaster, K.E.: Business ethics and stakeholder analysis. Bus. Ethics Q. **1**(1), 53–73 (1991). https://doi.org/10.2307/3857592
8. Freeman, R.E.: Strategic Management: A Stakeholder Approach. Pitman, Marshfield (1984)
9. Philips, R.A., Freeman, R.E., Wicks, A.: What stakeholder theory is not. Bus. Ethics Q. **13**(4) (2003). https://doi.org/10.2307/3857968
10. Gronroos, C., Vioma, P.: Critical service logic: making sense of value creation and co-creation. Acad. Mark. Sci. **41**(2), 133–150 (2013)
11. Leventon, J., Fleskens, L., Claringbould, H., Schwilch, G., Hessel, R.: An applied methodology for stakeholder identification in transdisciplinary research. Sustain. Sci. **11**(5), 763–775 (2016). https://doi.org/10.1007/s11625-016-0385-1
12. Nilsen, E.R., Stendal, K., Gullslett, M.K.: Implementation of eHealth technology in community health care: the complexity of stakeholder involvement. BMC Health Serv. Res. 395 (2020)
13. Chambers, M., Storm, M.: Resilience in healthcare: a modified stakeholder analysis. In: Wiig, S., Fahlbruch, B. (eds.) Exploring Resilience. SAST, pp. 113–119. Springer, Cham (2019). https://doi.org/10.1007/978-3-030-03189-3_14
14. Bryant, J.: The Six Dilemmas of Collaboration: Inter-Organizational Relationships as Drama, Chichester. John Wiley and Sons, England (2003)
15. Bryson, A.: What to do when stakeholders matter: stakeholder identification and analysis techniques. Public Manag. Rev. **6**(1), 21–53 (2007)
16. Mantzana, V.M., Themistocleous, M., Irani, V.M.: Identifying healthcare actors involved in the adoption of information systems. Eur. J. Inf. Syst. **16**(1), 91–102 (2007)
17. Macloed, D., larke, N.: Engaging for Success: Enhancing Performance Through Employee Engagement. Office of Public Sector Information, London (2009)
18. Yong, P.L., Olsen, L., McGinnis, J.M.: Value in Healthcare: Accounting for Cost, Quality, Safety, Outcomes, and Innovation. National Academy of Sciences, Washington D.C (2010)
19. Epstein, R.M., Street, R.L.: The values and value of patient-centered care. Ann. Fam. Med. **9**(2) (2011)
20. Joiner, K.A., Robert, F.L.: Evolving to a new service-dominant logic for health care. Innov. Entrepreneurship in Health (2016)
21. HTA Core Model report. HTA (2014). www.hiqa.ie/HTAGuidelinesStakeholderManagement. Accessed 21 Apr 2021
22. Petersen, C., Adams, S.A., DeMuro, P.R.: mHealth: don't forget all the stakeholders in the business case. Medicine 2.0 **4**(2), e4 (2015). https://doi.org/10.2196/med20.4349

23. Gummesson, E.: Customer centricity: reality or a wild goose chase? Eur. Bus. Rev. **20**(4), 315–330 (2008)
24. Haque, M.S., Arman, A., Kangas, M., Jämsä, T., Isomursu, M.: Towards value propositions for persuasive health and wellbeing applications. In: Maglaveras, N., Chouvarda, I., de Carvalho, P. (eds.) Precision Medicine Powered by pHealth and Connected Health. IP, vol. 66, pp. 217–221. Springer, Singapore (2018). https://doi.org/10.1007/978-981-10-7419-6_36
25. Haque, M.S.: Persuasive mHealth behavioural change interventions to promote healthy lifestyle. University of Oulu Graduate School. University of Oulu, Faculty of Medicine. University of Oulu, Faculty of Information Technology and Electrical Engineering. Medical Research Center Oulu. Oulu University Hospital (2020)
26. Haque, M.S., Kangas, M., Jämsä, T.: A persuasive mHealth behavioral change intervention for promoting physical activity in the workplace: feasibility randomized controlled trial. JMIR Formative Res. **4**(5), e15083 (2020). https://doi.org/10.2196/15083

COVID-19 Detection Using Chest X-Ray Images with a RegNet Structured Deep Learning Model

Md. Kawsher Mahbub[1], Milon Biswas[1], Abdul Mozid Miah[1],
Ahmed Shahabaz[2], and M. Shamim Kaiser[3(✉)]

[1] Department of Computer Science and Engineering,
Bangladesh University of Business and Technology, Dhaka, Bangladesh
[2] University of South Florida, Tampa, USA
shahabaz@usf.edu
[3] Institute of Information Technology, Jahangimagar University, Dhaka, Bangladesh
mskaiser@juniv.edu

Abstract. AI-based medical image processing has made significant progress, and it has a significant impact on biomedical research. Among the imaging variants, Chest x-rays imaging is cheap, simple, and can be used to detect influenza, tuberculosis, and various other illnesses. Researchers discovered that coronavirus spreads through the lungs, causing severe injuries during the COVID19 pandemic. As a result, chest x-rays can be used to detect COVID-19, making it a more robust detection method. In this paper, a RegNet hierarchical deep learning-based model has been proposed to detect COVID-19 positive and negative cases using CXI. The RegNet structure is designed to develop a model with a small number of epochs and parameters. The performance measurement found that the model takes five periods to reach a total accuracy of 98.08%. To test the model, we used two sets of data. The first dataset consists of 1200 COVID-19 positive CXRs and 1,341 COVID-19 negative CXRs, and the second dataset consists of 195 COVID-19 positive CXRs and 2,000 COVID-19 negative CXRs; all of these are publicly available. We obtained precision of 99.02% and 97.13% for these datasets, respectively. As a result of this finding, the proposed approach could be used for mass screening, and, as far as we are aware, the results achieved indicate that this model could be used as a screen guide.

Keywords: COVID-19 · Chest X-Rays · Deep learning · RegNet · CNN · Image processing

1 Introduction

Coronavirus was first discovered in late 2019 in Wuhan, Hubei Province, China, and is now the most feared name in the world. According to the World Health Organization (WHO), in mid-April 2021, 138 million people were infected, and

M. Mahmud et al. (Eds.): AII 2021, CCIS 1435, pp. 358–370, 2021.
https://doi.org/10.1007/978-3-030-82269-9_28

2.97 million people have died. COVID-19 is distributed from person to person through respiratory transmission. In most cases, it is spread through direct contact with people who have COVID-19, such as through air or hand contact. The most common symptoms include fever, dry cough, exhaustion, sore throat, headache, nausea, muscle pain, and shortness of breath [1]. COVID-19 causes pneumonia in humans, which affects the lungs and results in severe injury. Real-time reverse transcription-polymerase chain reaction (RT-PCR) is the most widely used detection method for COVID-19 diagnosis. Since people infected with COVID-19 develop pneumonia, chest radiological screening, such as X-rays and computed tomography (CT) scans, can be used to diagnose the infection [3,4]. After all, when the virus spreads to the lungs, it causes serious injuries. As a result, radiographic imaging of the chest may be used to diagnose disease [5].

In recent months, several researchers have successfully contributed to the early detection methodology of COVID-19 infection. This was possible as recent developments in artificial intelligence (AI) [1] and Machine Learning (ML) [6] and computational techniques. Through the study of computed tomography (CT) lung imaging, chest x-ray images, workplace employee safety, symptom identification using fluid systems, and hospital support for robots, several AI and ML-driven approaches to help COVID-19 were created [8–12]. It's difficult to create a classifier with a small number of details. Overcome this problem by considering unique class-specific features that need to be learned if the experience of common features can be imported or borrowed. RegNet Structured Deep Learning Model can be used to do this. Our contribution in this work is listed below:

- A ML model for classifying COVID-19-infected patients based on their chest x-ray images has been suggested.
- The model is trained and tested on an open dataset of COVID-19 infected chest x-ray images.
- A RegNet Structured deep learning model is proposed to learn features from the chest x-ray images.
- The proposed approach is higher than state-of-the-art learning algorithms available in the literature.

The remainder of the study is summarized as follows: The related works explaining COVID-19 detection using a Machine Learning Model are presented in Sect. 2. COVID-19 Chest X-Ray is included in Sect. 3. The proposed COVID-19 detection model is introduced in Sect. 4 of the imaging datasets. Model evaluation is covered in Sect. 5. The findings and discussion are described in Sect. 6. Finally, Sect. 7 brings the work to an end

2   Related Works

Severe Acute Respiratory Syndrome Coronavirus 2 (SARS-CoV-2) causes Coronavirus Disease 2019 (COVID-19). Using a chest X-ray image, A.K. Jaiswal et al. [2] used deep learning to recognize pneumonia in the lungs. The researcher [7] used three different deep learning models to classify the pneumonia patient using X-ray images: fine-tuned model, model without fine-tuning, and scratch-trained model. Another research obtained an average of 82.2% accuracy using the ResNet model and Multi-Layer Perception (MLP) as a classification tool. S.S. Yadav et al. [13] used X-Ray images of natural, bacterial, and viral pneumonia to classify pneumonia using classification algorithms such as SVM, InceptionV3, and VGG-16 models as a deep learning approach. To detect COVID-19 positive patients, we have used a chest X-Ray image data processing method. The study aims to develop a technique that uses image recognition and deep learning to detect the COVID-19 coronavirus. The suggested procedure is validated on a data collection of chest X-Ray photographs and Covid positive and negative chest images and provides tailored findings. In CXRs, K.C. Santosh et al. [14] used Faster R-CNN to locate foreign objects such as surgical tubing, instruments, and jewelry. The proposed DNN had a precision of 97%, a recall of 90%, and an F1 score of 93%. In another work, K.C. Santosh [15] addressed that AI-driven tools will facilitate to spot COVID-19 outbreaks and predict their nature of spread across the world. Dipayan Das et al. [16] suggested an AI-driven screening method that uses a Truncated Inception Net Convolutional Neural Network (CNN) model to distinguish COVID-19 positive cases from chest x-ray images and found 99.96% accuracy. Himadri Mukherjee et al. [17] proposed a lightweight (9 layered) CNN-tailored deep neural network model to identify COVID-19 for both CT Scans and Chest X-rays images, and they achieved 96.28% accuracy. The authors [18] developed a shallow CNN-tailored architecture model with fewer parameters that can automatically identify COVID-19-positive cases with no false negatives using chest X-rays and achieved the highest precision of 99.69%. To diagnose COVID-19 cases using chest x-rays, Mesut Togaçar et al. [19] used the Fuzzy color approach, Stacking technique, Social mimic, and Deep learning approaches where the average accuracy rate was 99.27%. In their article, Ali Narin1 et al. [20] used five pre-trained convolutional neural network-based models (ResNet50, ResNet101, ResNet152, InceptionV3 and Inception-ResNetV2) to diagnose coronavirus positive cases using chest X-ray images and achieved 96.1%, 99.5% and 99.7% accuracy for three separate datasets. Huang C et al. [21] published a paper on COVID-19's therapeutic and paraclinical dimensions in January 2020. They claimed that Ground-Glass Opacity (GGO) anomalies could be detected using chest CT scans (based on 41 positive cases). CT scans are commonly used to recognise irregular trends in COVID-19 confirmed cases [22–24]. Li and Xia [25] tested 51 CT scans (images) and found that COVID-19 could be identified in 96.1% of the cases. Zhou S et al. [26] tested 62 COVID-19 and Pneumonia mice, and their findings revealed a variety of trends that resemble lung parenchyma and interstitial diseases. Author of [27] and [28] addressed a convolutional neural network with transfer learning to detect for COVID-19 positive cases. Tulin Ozturk et al. [29] proposed a deep learning model called DarkCovidNet, which can detect COVID-19 cases with 98.08% accuracy using CXRs. Jing Xu et al. [30] proposed a self-regulated network for image classification. They used RNN and followed RegNet architecture. Emtiaz Hussain et al. [31] introduced a deep learning model called CoroDet to detect COVID-19 by using plain chest X-rays and CT scan images with up to 99.1% accuracy. In a few recent works, authors' [32] proposed model is a multi-class classification model since it divides photos into four categories: bacterial pneumonia, viral pneumonia, natural, and COVID-19. In another work, authors [33] proposed a COVID-19 infection detection pipeline based on CXR images and achieved a classification accuracy of 99.65%. Deep learning methods are used to extract meaningful results from medical records. A Designing Network Design Spaces had introduced by Ilija Radosavovic et al. [35] they proposed a network called RegNet. The purpose of the network is to design a network with a low-compute, low-epoch regime using a single network block type on ImageNet. The authors [37] of this paper provided a concise overview of the use of DL, RL, and deep RL strategies in biological data mining. Finally, they explored future architecture viewpoints and open questions in this challenging research field. In another article, authors [38] proposed a hybrid deep learning model for diagnosing the virus from chest X-rays that combines a convolutional neural network (CNN) and a gated recurrent unit (GRU) (CXRs). The model was developed using 424 CXRs images divided into three groups(COIVD-19, Pneumonia, and Normal) and obtained promising results of 0.96, 0.96, and 0.95.

3   Dataset

In Artificial intelligence-based work, data is essential, and to achieve substantial efficiency, we need to analyze a large quantity of data. Data has been collected from several resources. We collected more than two thousand five hundred images from multiple sources for the COVID-19 dataset. COVID-19 was diagnosed in this study primarily using X-ray images collected from two separate sources. Tawsifur Rahman [32,33] has developed a COVID-19 X-ray image dataset that is open access to everyone, and this dataset is available in Kaggle. This database is constantly updated with images shared by researchers from different regions. At present, there are 1200 COVID-19 positive X-ray images, 1341 normal X-Ray images. Sample CXRs given in Fig. 1 (Table 1).

Table 1. Data collection publicly available

Collection	Positive cases	Negative cases
C1: COVID-19 Radiography Database	1200	1341
C2: COVID-XRay-5K DATASET	195	2000

Another source of COVID-19 X-ray image collection was COVID-XRay-5K DATASET [34] is an open-source dataset, which is made and maintained by Shervin Minaee and his team. At the time of the present study, it comprises 184 COVID-19 positive Chest X-ray and some other CXRs of diseases like viral

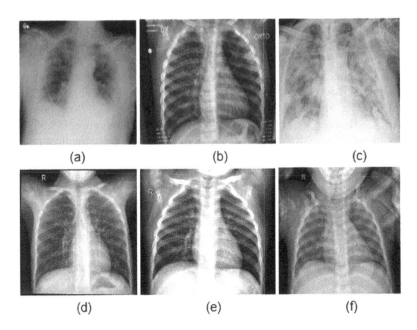

Fig. 1. Sample images of data set. (a–c) COVID-19 positive cases CXRs and (d–f) COVID-19 negative cases CXRs

Pneumonia, Normal, Fracture, Edema, etc. Our purpose is to use COVID-19 positive and negative CXRs images from this dataset.

These images had been collected from different published papers available online or from pdfs. Other qualities and sizes of images were noisy, skewed, and had different orientations. Moreover, the various grades and sizes of image handling was an extremely challenging task. We prepossessed each image before train our deep learning models. In this prepossessing, the data set was reconstructed using greyscale conversion. Then, we trained the two data sets using our deep learning models.

4 Proposed Model Architecture

Deep learning methods have been used for image processing in many fields, including medical image processing. Many researchers have used deep learning models for image recognition, segmentation, identification, and diagnosis of diabetes, brain tumors, and skin cancer using MRI, CT, and X-ray. We have followed the RegNet network to develop our deep learning model. We designed the model with CNN, consisting of three layers: a convolutional layer, pooling layer, and fully connected layer to perform these operations effectively. The feature extraction process takes place in both convolutional and pooling layers.

Our proposed model has nine convolution layers with three simple blocks of conv2d layer followed by ReLu. The block we used in our model, visually

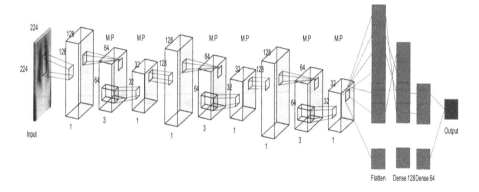

Fig. 2. The architecture of the RegNet structured proposed model.

presented in Fig. 3 is based on the standard residual bottleneck block with group convolution. Each block consists of a 1×1 conv2d, a 3×3 group conv2d, and a last 1×1 conv2d and ReLU follow each conv2d layer. The second layer after the convolutional layer is the pooling layer. The pooling layer is usually applied to the created feature maps for reducing the number of feature maps and network parameters by applying corresponding mathematical computation. In this study, we used max-pooling with stride $(s = 1)$. The number of neurons was 128,64,32, respectively. To attain further knowledge about our model, see Fig. 2, Fig. 3 and Table 2. A fully connected layer is the last and most important layer of any deep learning model. This fully connected layer functions like a multi-layer perceptron, and Rectified Linear Unit (ReLU) activation function is most commonly used on a fully connected layer. In contrast, the Sigmoid activation function predicts output images in the last layer of a fully connected layer. We used 50% dropout on a fully connected layer.

We trained our model with five epochs, which is very few epochs compared to other trained deep learning models. Our model consists of input size 224×224, which ideal input size for RegNet structured network. In Table 2 we used 9 conv2d layer with filter size 128,64,32 and 1 flatten layer two dense layer for our model. The total number of learning parameters is 194,903,073 for 224×224 images.

5   Model Evaluation

The reason for using CNN to build our model is feature engineering is not required. CNN can extract features automatically from the image. CNN performs well, and it gives better accuracy compared to handcrafted features. It is covering local and global features. It also learns different features from images. CNN effectively uses adjacent pixel information to down-sample the image first by convolution and then uses a prediction layer at the end, and CNN is easy to implement. Our main target was to achieve higher accuracy with a few epochs and learning parameters, and we just used five epochs to get 99.02% accuracy.

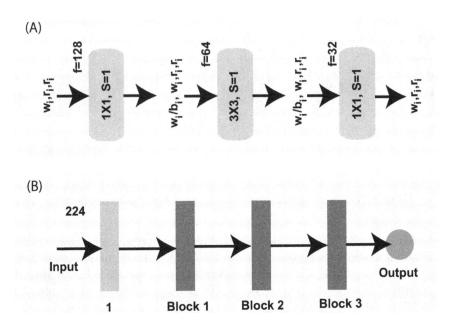

Fig. 3. Block diagram of the RegNet structured proposed model.

Table 2. Number of learning parameter of our proposed model for 224×224 image

Number of layer	Layer name	Output shape	Params
1	Conv2d	[224, 224, 128]	256
2	Conv2d	[222, 222, 64]	73792
3	Conv2d	[222, 222, 32]	2080
4	Conv2d	[222, 222, 128]	4224
5	Conv2d	[220, 220, 64]	73792
6	Conv2d	[220, 220, 32]	2080
7	Conv2d	[220, 220, 128]	4224
8	Conv2d	[218, 218, 64]	73792
9	Conv2d	[218, 218, 32]	2080
10	Flatten	[1520768]	0
11	Dense	[128]	194658432
12	Dense	[64]	8256
13	Linear	[1]	65
Total parameters			194,903,073

To validate our model, we used two distinct data set and k-10 fold validation. The primary purpose was to design a model with low-compute, low-epoch, and gain higher accuracy using a single network block. We just used five epochs to train our model. We obtain 99.02% validation accuracy for the first dataset, and for the second dataset, we receive 97.13% validation accuracy. The average accuracy is 98.075% which is promising compare to other deep learning models. The training and validation accuracy for both data sets are given below.

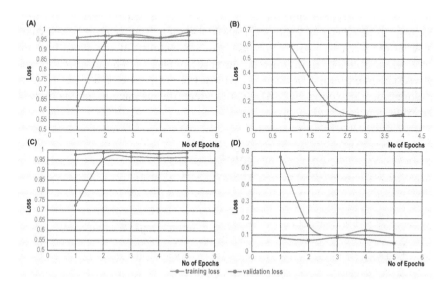

Fig. 4. Training/Validation Accuracy/loss. (A) the training and validation accuracy (B) training and validation loss as a function of epoch using for dataset named COVID-19 Radiography Database [32,33] (C) the training and validation accuracy (D) training and validation loss as a function of epoch using for dataset named CoronaHack -Chest X-Ray-Dataset [34]

There were 1200 COVID-19 positive cases in the first data set and 1341 COVID-19 negative chest x-ray images. We split the data set into 70 and 30 ratios for training and validation. The training set consists of 960 COVID-19 positive CXRs and 1072 COVID-19 negative CXRs. The validation set contains 240 COVID-19 positive CXRs and 402 COVID-19 negative CXRs. We obtained 99.02% accuracy for this dataset, and we can see from Fig. 4 the training and validation accuracy and loss for every epoch of our model.

There were 195 COVID-19 positive cases and 2000 COVID-19 negative chest x-ray images in the second data set. We split the data set into 70 and 30 ratios for training and validation. The training set contains 156 COVID-19 positive CXRs and 1400 COVID-19 negative CXRs. The validation set includes 58 COVID-19 positive CXRs and 600 COVID-19 negative CXRs. We obtained 97.13% accuracy for this dataset, and we can see from Fig. 4 the training and validation accuracy and loss for every epoch of our model.

6   Result Analysis

In this section, we will present an analysis of our model and a comparison with other deep learning models presented in our literature review.

Intending to present more information on the performance of our classifiers on test images, we provide a receiver operating characteristic curve (ROC) curve Fig. 5 below. A receiver operating characteristic curve (ROC) curve is a graphical plot that illustrates the model performance evaluation. We have presented a ROC curve of 2 distinct dataset. AUC - ROC curve display estimation for the classification problems at various threshold settings. ROC is a probability curve, and AUC depicts the degree or measure of separability. It describes how much the model is proficient in differentiating between classes. The proposed classifier achieved the maximum AUC score (1.00) for the both dataset. The AUC score of our model for identifying COVID-19 is 1, which means our model has high-class separation capability whatsoever.

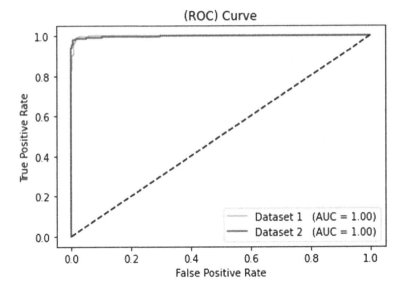

Fig. 5. ROC curve of proposed model.

From Table 3, we can see our model achieved 99.02% accuracy, and the authors of [15, 18, 19] presented models have more accuracy than our model's accuracy. On the other hand author of [17, 20, 25, 29] presented models have less accuracy than our model. So we can conclude that our model gave a promising result for the detection of COVID-19 positive cases.

Table 3. Comparison table

Ref	Author name	Model name	Accuracy rate
[16]	Das et al.	Truncated Inception Net	99.96
[17]	Himadri Mukherjee et al.	CNN-tailored network	96.28
[18]	Himadri Mukherjee et al.	Shallow CNN-tailored network	99.69
[19]	Mesut Togaçar et al.	Deep learning	99.27
[20]	Ali Narin1 et al.	ResNet	96.01
[25]	Li and Xia	Deep learning	96.10
[27]	Bassi & Attux	ImageNe	100.0
[28]	Majeed, T et al.	CNN transfer learning	97.86
[29]	Tulin Ozturk et al.	DarkCovidNet	98.08
[31]	Hussain et al.	CoroDet	99.10
[32]	Chowdhury, M. E. et al.	ImageNet	99.70
[33]	Rahman, T. et al.	Deep learning	99.65
[38]	P. M. Shah et al.	Deep GRU-CNN model	96.00
	Our proposed model	RegNet Structured	**99.02**

7 Conclusion and Future Work

In this paper, we propose a lightweight (12-layer) RegNet structured deep learning model for detecting COVID-19 positive patients using chest X-ray images. In this project, we used two types of images; one type was COVID-19 positive, and the other type was COVID-19 negative images. For validation, experimental tests were done on two different experimental datasets by combining COVID-19 positive and COVID-19 negative CXRs. We have trained and tested the proposed model, and we have achieved an overall accuracy of 98.08%. Besides, considering the number of parameters and the number of epochs used in our proposed model, it is computationally efficient compared to many other established models and other works presented in the literature review. It is important to note that our study has no clinical implications and has not been reviewed by any medical experts. We aimed to check whether our proposed RegNet structured model could detect COVID-19 positive cases using CXRs with high accuracy. Our developed model is only able to perform binary classification with an overall accuracy of 98.08%. In future, this work could be extended by fusing the decisions of multiple transfer learning models.

References

1. Kaiser, M.S., et al.: iWorkSafe: towards healthy workplaces during COVID-19 with an intelligent pHealth app for industrial settings. IEEE Access **9**, 13814–13828 (2021)
2. Jaiswal, A.K., et al.: Identifying pneumonia in chest X-rays: a deep learning approach. Measurement **145**, 511–518 (2019)
3. Aradhya, V.M., Mahmud, M., Guru, D.S., Agarwal, B., Kaiser, M.S.: One-shot cluster-based approach for the detection of COVID-19 from chest X-ray images. Cogn. Comput. **1–9** (2021). https://doi.org/10.1007/s12559-020-09774-w
4. Mahmud, M., Kaiser, M.S.: Machine learning in fighting pandemics: a COVID-19 case study. In: Santosh, K., Joshi, A. (eds.) COVID-19: Prediction, Decision-Making, and Its Impacts, vol. 60, pp. 77–81. Springer, Singapore (2021). https://doi.org/10.1007/978-981-15-9682-7_9
5. Singh, A.K., Kumar, A., Mahmud, M., Kaiser, M.S., Kishore, A.: COVID-19 Infection detection from chest X-ray images using hybrid social group optimization and support vector classifier. Cogn. Comput. 1–13 (2021). https://doi.org/10.1007/s12559-021-09848-3
6. Mahmud, M., Kaiser, M.S., McGinnity, T.M., Hussain, A.: Deep learning in mining biological data. Cogn. Comput. **13**(1), 1–33 (2021). https://doi.org/10.1007/s12559-020-09773-x
7. Baltruschat, et al.: Comparison of deep learning approaches for multi-label chest X-ray classification. Sci. Rep. **9**(1), 1–10 (2019)
8. Noor, M.B.T., Zenia, N.Z., Kaiser, M.S., Al Mamun, S., Mahmud, M.: Application of deep learning in detecting neurological disorders from magnetic resonance images: a survey on the detection of Alzheimer's disease, Parkinson's disease and Schizophrenia. Brain Inform. **7**(1), 1–21 (2020). https://doi.org/10.1186/s40708-020-00112-2
9. Ruiz, J., Mahmud, M., Modasshir, M., Kaiser, M.S.: 3D DenseNet ensemble in 4-way classification of Alzheimer's disease. In: : Mahmud, M., Vassanelli, S., Kaiser, M.S., Zhong, N. (eds.) International Conference on Brain Informatics, pp. 85–96. Springer, Cham (2020). https://doi.org/10.1007/978-3-030-59277-6_8
10. Mahmud, M., et al.: A brain-inspired trust management model to assure security in a cloud based IoT framework for neuroscience applications. Cogn. Comput. **10**(5), 864–873 (2018). https://doi.org/10.1007/s12559-018-9543-3
11. Rabby, G., Azad, S., Mahmud, M., Zamli, K.Z., Rahman, M.M.: TeKET: a tree-based unsupervised keyphrase extraction technique. Cogn. Comput. **12**(4), 811–833 (2020). https://doi.org/10.1007/s12559-019-09706-3
12. Kaiser, M.S., et al.: Advances in crowd analysis for urban applications through urban event detection. IEEE Trans. Intell. Transp. Syst. **19**(10), 3092–3112 (2017)
13. Yadav, S.S., Jadhav, S.M.: Deep convolutional neural network based medical image classification for disease diagnosis. J. Big Data **6**(1), 1–18 (2019). https://doi.org/10.1186/s40537-019-0276-2
14. Santosh, K.C., Dhar, M.K., Rajbhandari, R., Neupane, A.: Deep neural network for foreign object detection in chest X-rays. In: 2020 IEEE 33rd International Symposium on Computer-Based Medical Systems (CBMS), pp. 538–541. IEEE (2020)
15. Santosh, K.C.: AI-Driven tools for coronavirus outbreak: need of active learning and cross-population train/test models on multitudinal/multimodal data. J. Med. Syst. **44**(5), 1–5 (2020). https://doi.org/10.1007/s10916-020-01562-1

16. Das, D., Santosh, K.C., Pal, U.: Truncated inception net: COVID-19 outbreak screening using chest X-rays. Phys. Eng. Sci. Med. **43**(3), 915–925 (2020). https://doi.org/10.1007/s13246-020-00888-x

17. Mukherjee, H., Ghosh, S., Dhar, A., Obaidullah, S.M., Santosh, K.C., Roy, K.: Deep neural network to detect COVID-19: one architecture for both CT Scans and Chest X-rays. Appl. Intell. **51**(5), 2777–2789 (2020). https://doi.org/10.1007/s10489-020-01943-6

18. Mukherjee, H., Ghosh, S., Dhar, A., Obaidullah, S.M., Santosh, K.C., Roy, K.: Shallow convolutional neural network for COVID-19 outbreak screening using chest X-rays. Cogn. Comput. (2021). https://doi.org/10.1007/s12559-020-09775-9

19. Togacar, M., et al.: COVID-19 detection using deep learning models to exploit Social Mimic Optimization and structured chest X-ray images using fuzzy color and stacking approaches. Comput. Biol. Med. **121**, 103805 (2020)

20. Narin, A., et al.: Automatic detection of coronavirus disease (COVID-19) using X-ray images and deep convolutional neural networks. arXiv preprint arXiv: 2003.10849 (2020)

21. Huang, C., et al.: Clinical features of patients infected with 2019 novel coronavirus in Wuhan, China. The lancet **395**(10223), 497–506 (2020)

22. Fang, Y., et al.: Sensitivity of chest CT for COVID-19: comparison to RT-PCR. Radiology **296**(2), E115–E117 (2020)

23. Ng, M.Y., et al.: Imaging profile of the COVID-19 infection: radiologic findings and literature review. Radiol.: Cardiothorac. Imaging **2**(1), e200034 (2020)

24. Li, Y., Xia, L.: Coronavirus disease 2019 (COVID-19): role of chest CT in diagnosis and management. Am. J. Roentgenol. **214**(6), 1280–1286 (2020)

25. Ye, Z., Zhang, Y., Wang, Y., Huang, Z., Song, B.: Chest CT manifestations of new coronavirus disease 2019 (COVID-19): a pictorial review. Eur. Radiol. **30**(8), 4381–4389 (2020). https://doi.org/10.1007/s00330-020-06801-0

26. Zhou, S., Wang, Y., Zhu, T., Xia, L.: CT features of coronavirus disease 2019 (COVID-19) pneumonia in 62 patients in Wuhan, China. Am. J. Roentgenol. **214**(6), 1287–1294 (2020)

27. Bassi, P.R., Attux, R.: A deep convolutional neural network for COVID-19 detection using chest X-rays. arXiv preprint arXiv:2005.01578 (2020)

28. Majeed, T., Rashid, R., Ali, D., Asaad, A.: COVID-19 detection using CNN transfer learning from X-ray images. medRxiv (2020)

29. Ozturk, T., Talo, M., Yildirim, E.A., Baloglu, U.B., Yildirim, O., Acharya, U.R.: Automated detection of COVID-19 cases using deep neural networks with X-ray images. Comput. Biol. Med. **121**, 103792 (2020)

30. Xu, J., et al.: RegNet: Self-regulated network for image classification. arXiv preprint arXiv:2101.00590 (2021)

31. Hussain, E., et al.: CoroDet: A deep learning based classification for COVID-19 detection using chest X-ray images. Chaos, Solitons Fractals **142**, 110495 (2021)

32. Chowdhury, M.E., et al.: Can AI help in screening viral and COVID-19 pneumonia? IEEE Access **8**, 132665–132676 (2020)

33. Rahman, T., et al.: Exploring the effect of image enhancement techniques on COVID-19 detection using chest X-ray images (2020)

34. Minaee, S., et al.: Deep-COVID: predicting COVID-19 from chest X-ray images using deep transfer learning. Med. Image Anal. **101794** (2020). https://doi.org/10.1016/j.media.2020.101794

35. Radosavovic, I., et al.: Designing network design spaces. In: Proceedings of the IEEE/CVF Conference on Computer Vision and Pattern Recognition, pp. 10428–10436 (2020)

36. Aradhya, V.N.M., et al.: One-shot cluster-based approach for the detection of COVID–19 from chest X-ray images. Cogn. Comput. 1–9 (2021). https://doi.org/10.1007/s12559-020-09774-w

37. Mahmud, M., Kaiser, M.S., Hussain, A., Vassanelli, S.: Applications of deep learning and reinforcement learning to biological data. IEEE Trans. Neural Netw. Learn. Syst. **29**(6), 2063–2079 (2018)

38. Shah, P.M., et al.: Deep GRU-CNN model for COVID-19 detection from chest X-rays data. IEEE Access (2021). https://doi.org/10.1109/ACCESS.2021.3077592

Mixed Bangla-English Spoken Digit Classification Using Convolutional Neural Network

Shuvro Das[1]([✉]), Mst. Rubayat Yasmin[1], Musfikul Arefin[1], Kazi Abu Taher[1], Md Nasir Uddin[2], and Muhammad Arifur Rahman[3]

[1] Department of ICT, Bangladesh University of Professionals, Dhaka, Bangladesh
surojit.shuvro@gmail.com, tithirubayat@gmail.com, pollob96@gmail.com, kataher@bup.edu.bd
[2] Department of Neurology, University of Rochester, Rochester, NY 14642, USA
nasir_uddin@urmc.rochester.edu
[3] Department of Physics, Jahangirnagar University, Dhaka, Bangladesh
arif@juniv.edu

Abstract. In this era of the scientific revolution, speech recognition is an important field. People of the world are connecting by using technology. People are shifting from one country to another, sharing their culture and language. Speech recognition has made it easy by translating most of the languages into a readable format. Our world is moving forward through the era of the digital revolution. Still, there are rudimentary examples of research works on Bangla speech recognition with the advancement of automatic speech recognition (ASR). From a Bangladeshi perspective, we often feel the need of using mixed Bangla-English language in different use-cases, mostly in educational institutions and hospital environments. However, most research works focus on speech recognition in the English language, so we were motivated to develop a mixed Bangla-English language classifier to transcribe isolated mixed Bangla-English spoken digits. We have used an open-source dataset for English, and for Bangla, we created a dataset in a noisy environment by speakers of different ages, gender, and dialects. Finally, for the mixed dataset, we have used Mel Frequency Cepstral Coefficient (MFCC) for feature extraction and Convolutional Neural Network (CNN) classifier to train, test, and analyze data for two different experiments we found promising results.

Keywords: Bangla-English digit classification · MFCC · CNN · ASR

1 Introduction

Speech is one of the most important means of human communication. From ancient times, people did use established gestures to express their emotions and feelings, then over time, and through the evolution process, the language came

---

The original version of this chapter was revised: The wrong value and typographical errors in the caption of figure 9 have been corrected. The correction to this chapter is available at https://doi.org/10.1007/978-3-030-82269-9_31

M. Mahmud et al. (Eds.): AII 2021, CCIS 1435, pp. 371–383, 2021.
https://doi.org/10.1007/978-3-030-82269-9_29

into being. There are 7.6 billion people in the world. Of these, 379 and 228 million people use English and Bengali language respectively, as their first language [36]. With the change of era, computers, different programming languages, algorithms, and many more have been discovered. Speech recognition is one of them, which is a cross-sectional subfield of computer science and computational linguistics that includes techniques and methods to identify the spoken language. Speech is then converted to text via computer. There has been substantial improvement in speech recognition over the last few decades. Today's speech recognition first started from 'Audrey' (1952) which, was a single-speaker digit recognition system [31]. Plenty of research work has been carried out on English speech recognition than that of Bangla.

Fig. 1. Applications of speech recognition: it has been widely adopted from the purpose of entertainment to autonomous transportation, medical record-keeping to personal digital assistance and beyond.

Figure 1 shows the applications where speech recognition is being used. For entertainment, speech commands can be used to play a song or to play a movie. In hospitals, speech recognition can be beneficial to generate a prescription, find the medical record, and hospital staffs can be reminded of a given task or instruction, etc. At work, speech recognition can be used to start a conference, schedule a meeting, book an appointment, etc. [11]. In the automobile, voice commands are already being used. Since our world is connected through technology, people are taking immigration to their dearest country. For this immigration system, people are mixing up language and culture. Also, many Bangladeshi people are living in different foreign countries. People often are using mixed Bangla-English almost in every aspect of their daily communication. People commonly use 'please', 'sir', 'excuse me' in their normal conversation with Bangla. This paper aims to develop a Bangla-English mixed spoken digits (0–9) classifier that can be denoted as the first approach to building a system that can recognize Bangla-English mixed language in the future. Figure 2 shows the visual representation of our research work, where we put both genders as the speaker, then the spoken digits are preprocessed in a .JSON file (.wav format). MFCC technique is applied for

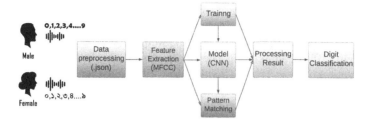

Fig. 2. Basic block diagram for digit classification

feature extraction, which is the most popular feature extraction method used in most speech recognition research works. It also works well with machine learning algorithms. The extracted information is then fed to a CNN architecture mode for training and testing purpose. It can be seen that CNN based models are popular and used for a variety of tasks from Music Genre Classification [6,9,38], Environment Sound Classification [3,8,14], Audio Generation [21,26]. Besides, in [29] CNN is used for Bangla digits classification and achieved an impressive result of 98% which was way better than the results that were found using the CNN model in paper [2,12,15,19] which motivates us to work with CNN architecture for this task. We have used a mixture dataset of Bangla-English where an open-source English isolated dataset [5] are mixed with recorded Bangla dataset from various area of Bangladesh. MFCC features are easily extracted from the 'librosa' module in python. Finally, we achieved classified digits as the system output extracted by CNN model architecture.

2   Literature Review

We live within the age of information, where everything around us is associated with one another based on the information, and this information is the processed facts of raw data. In this digital world, every single digital operation is based on data, for example, mobile data, business data, social media data, security data, health data, etc. There is no alter of Artificial Intelligence (AI) techniques that are performed through different machine learning algorithms to process this data. Articles [17,18] focused on the use of deep learning to analyze patterns in data from diverse biological domains; the work investigates different learning architectures applications to these data. Another article [27] presented a comprehensive comparison based on Machine Learning algorithms like Polynomial Regression (PR) and Multilayer Perception (MLP) and Long Short-Term Memory (LSTM) algorithm to predict the Infected and Recovered (SIR), projected comparative outcomes during the outbreak of COVID-19 in Bangladesh. Thus, machine learning algorithms have much diversity in solving real-World applications and setting up research directions [4,24]. Classification through machine learning algorithms is not new. Many articles work with the machine learning approach to develop various classification systems. In [1], Naive Bayes Classifier, a Bayesian approach of Machine Learning algorithm, has been applied to identify fake news. Satellite Image Classification with K-nearest neighbour (KNN) algorithm has been outperformed in [7]. Support vector machine (SVM) has been used in [10] for classifying the images using the feature vector in Facial Spoof Detection. Music Artist Classification with Convolutional Recurrent Neural Network in [20] is performed. But in our paper, we are focused on audio data based on the mixed voice. We have also reviewed some remarkable works that are associated with the English and Bangla voice-based dataset.

In the research work [32] presents a brief study of remarkable works done to develop the Automatic Speech Recognition (ASR) system for the Bangla language. It highlights information of available speech corpora for this language and reports major contributions made in this research paradigm in the last decade. Some important design issues, challenges, levels of recognition, vocabulary size, speaker dependency, and approaches for classifications have been reviewed in this paper in the order of complexity of speech recognition.

Taufik and Hanafiah [33] developed an automated visual acuity test (Auto-VAT) that can run on a computer using a microphone as an input device and monitor as an output device. The authors have used Snellen Chart with digit optotype to measure the visual acuity. They have collected a downloadable dataset that contains twenty isolated English words, including isolated spoken digits (0–9). After collecting the dataset, they have used a python package called librosa for the MFCC feature extraction. They got 20×8 matrix for each file as output after applying the MFCC. Finally, CNN is used for classification.

Paul et al. [22] proposed a system that can automatically recognise spoken numerals in regional language. The authors developed a Gaussian Mixture Model (GMM) for isolated Bengali spoken numerals and MFCC for feature extraction. They have achieved 91.7% accuracy in prediction for the Bangla numeral dataset.

Watt and Kostylev [35] used a newly proposed approach, spin-wave delay-line active-ring reservoir computer for spoken digit recognition. The authors have achieved 93% accuracy on spoken digit recognition. They also let the Reservoir Computer (RC) perform Short-Term Memory (STM) and Parity Check (PC) tasks to satisfy the two main properties of RC implementation.

Reddy and Kumar [25] made a comparison between CNN and NN in spoken digit recognition. The authors have noticed that accuracy increased in spoken digit recognition using CNN. They got 100% accuracy in spoken digit using CNN and 95%–99% using NN.

Sharmin et al. [29] proposed a Bengali digit classification approach using CNN. The authors used 1230 audio files (.wav format) from ten different people from different age groups, dialects, and gender. For feature extraction, MFCC was used, then they used the train, test, split method to train and test the dataset and claimed 98% accuracy comparatively on a smaller dataset.

Mahalingam and Rajakumar [16] used a different approach for spoken digit classification. Instead of the commonly used feature extraction approach MFCC, the authors used wavelet scattering for the initial extraction of useful information from the audio signal. Then, the extracted information was sent to the LSTM network for classification.

Zerari et al. [37] proposed a general framework using LSTM and NN for Arabic speech recognition. The authors have used both spoken Arabic digits (0–9) and spoken Arabic TV commands as a dataset. They have used both feature extraction techniques MFCC-dynamic and static features, and the Filter Banks (FB) coefficient. Their proposed system first extracts relevant features from the signal of natural speech using MFCC (dynamic and static features) and FB, and then the extracted information is padded to deal with the non-uniformity of the sequence. After that, LSTM or Gated Recurrent Unit (GRU) is used as an architecture to encode the sequences and then introduced to an MLP network to perform classification.

Gupta and Sarkar [13] represented a method that can recognize Bengali spoken digits in both noise-free and noisy environments. MFCC and PCA are used for feature extraction. The authors have used SVM, MLP, and Random Forest (RF) for the classification and made a comparison of their performance. They found that RF has a lower accuracy rate than MLP and SVM.

3   Methodology

3.1   Data Preproecessing

Speech preprocessing includes conversion of digital audio data from the analog audio data recorded by speakers, labeling speech files, and extraction of features. In our experiment, Data acquisition is done with the following recording parameters:

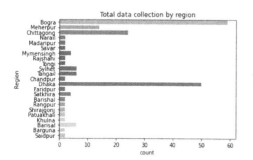 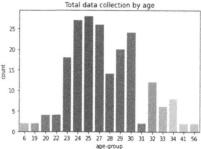

Fig. 3. Variations of the dataset in dialects and age respectively with 23 different regions of Bangladesh and an age range (6–56) years of people

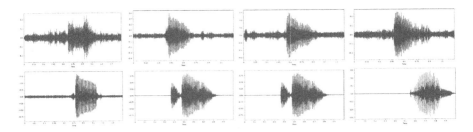

Fig. 4. Raw input audio signal: (top left to right) waveform of 'Shunno', 'Ek', 'Dui', 'Tin' and (bottom left to right) 'Chaar', 'Zero', 'One', 'Two' respectively.

- Encoding Format: Highest quality (PCM/WAV)
- Sampling Rate: 22050 (default with 'librosa' package)
- Environment: Less noisy for English and Noisy for Bangla

We have taken a mixture of 3500 data, where the English dataset containing 1500 audio files (.wav format) collected from Google AI blog [5] and for Bangla dataset, we have collected voice recordings of 200 people containing 2000 audio files(.wav format) for the experiment. For the Bangla dataset, the participation ratio of age-group and different dialects has been represented using the seaborn barplot.

Thus, Fig. 3(left), we have taken the count numbers in X-axis and in Y-axis and plotted the dialects of 23 different regions whereas Fig. 3(right) shows the representation of the age group ranging from six to fifty-six (6–56) years for the data we have collected. It is clearly noticeable that most of the dataset that we have collected is from Dhaka and Bogura regions, and between 24 to 27 age-group. Thus, Fig. 3 proves the data diversity of our collected data (Fig. 5).

English digits	Bangla digits	Pronunciation
0 (Zero)	০ (শূন্য)	SHUNNO
1 (One)	১ (এক)	EK
2 (Two)	২ (দুই)	DUI
3 (Three)	৩ (তিন)	TIN
4 (Four)	৪ (চার)	CHAAR
5 (Five)	৫ (পাঁচ)	PAACH
6 (Six)	৬ (ছয়)	CHOY
7 (Seven)	৭ (সাত)	SAAT
8 (Eight)	৮ (আট)	AAT
9 (Nine)	৯ (নয়)	NOY

Fig. 5. English-Bangla symbolic digits and pronunciation

We have taken a sample rate of 22050, which works better with 'librosa' packages. Then, the pre-processed data was saved as .json file, which has fed into our built model later. Figure 4 illustrates the waveform of some digits such as, 'shunno', 'ek', 'dui', 'tin', 'chaar', 'zero', 'one', and 'two' respectively. These waveforms were generated using 'librosa' python package with the help of 'matplotlib.pyplot'.

We have mixed the both data set of English-Bangla and kept them in a single folder path and labeled properly. For English, each data were labeled as- 'one', 'two', 'three', 'four', 'five' , 'six', 'seven', 'eight', and 'nine'. For Bangla, each data were labeled as- 'shunno', 'ek', 'dui', 'tin', 'chaar', 'paach', 'choy', 'saat', 'aat', and 'noy'.

3.2 Feature Extraction

MFCC is the most commonly used method of audio feature extraction. The reason behind using MFCC because it tells us a lot about the timbre of an audio signal. MFCC takes into account human perception for sensitivity at appropriate frequencies by converting the conventional frequency to Mel Scale, and are thus suitable for speech recognition tasks quite well. Figure 6 shows the process of feature extraction of a audio data. MFCC features were easily extracted from the audio files using the 'librosa' package of python [23] and appended into a python 'numpy'- array [28]. Figure 6 illustrates the spectrum of the audio signal before and after feature extraction.

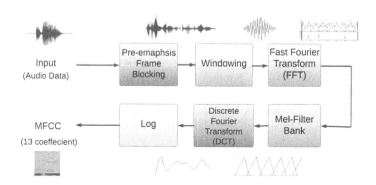

Fig. 6. Feature extraction technique of isolated digit taking 13 coefficient as output

3.3 Train and Test Data

After the feature extraction and labelling was completed, the dataset created was divided into 'train' and 'test' set. It was done using the *test_train_split*

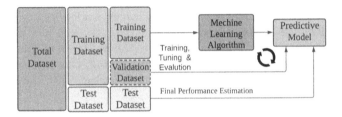

Fig. 7. Train, validation and test division of a dataset before processing in developed model and prediction analyses

method from the 'sklearn' module in python [30]. The dataset was divided by maintaining an 80:20 ratio, where 80% data was used for the training dataset and 20% data was used for the test dataset, 20% of the training dataset is taken as a validation set for the processing. Figure 7 shows the processing overview of the training, test and validation dataset in the model which will be used in prediction analysis of the test dataset with the trained model.

3.4   Feature Learning and Classification Using CNN

In this analysis, we have built a 3-layer sequential Convolutional Neural Network for feature learning and classification purposes. We have built 2 different models with different parameters in each convolution layers. It was made utilizing the 'Tensorflow and Keras' module in python [34]. Train data was passed through the first 2D-convolutional layer (conv2D) which comprises a filter size of 128 (model-1) and 64 (model-2) with (3, 3) kernel size, a RELU activation function and an 'L2' kernel regulizer for both models. The output of the first Conv2D layer was passed through the first batch normalization layer. After that, the output is sent into a 2D-max pooling layer. This process is done twice for each model using the second conv2D and third conv2D. For the first model, a size of 48 filters size batch normalization-pool size of (3, 3) is used and for the second model: the size of 32 filters are used keeping the other two parameters the same as before.

After the feature learning process, the classification procedure starts with transforming the resultant vector into a one-dimensional vector by using the flatten layer as 1-D vector is easier to use for classification purposes, and therefore, it has been used to flatten the data. The 1D vector that came out of the flatten layer is then passed through a series of layers consisting of a fully connected dense layer with 128 and 64 units of neurons along with the 'RELU' activation function for the first and second model respectively. The output from that layer is passed down to the dropout layer with a 0.3 dropout rate used to minimize the over-fitting issue. Then, the resultant vector is passed through a final fully connected dense layer with twenty units, which is the number of keywords for the Bangla-English mix dataset, and the softmax activation function. After that, we got the final output. We have used 'Sparse Categorical Cross-

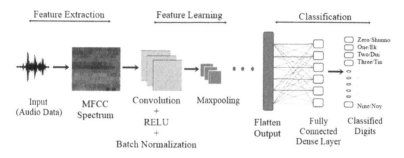

Fig. 8. CNN architecture used for digit classification using 'RELU' as activation funtion and (3 × 3) maxpooling for minimizing overfitting issues with a fully connected dense layer

entropy' as the loss function and 'Adam' as optimizer in this model. Figure 8 shows the basic architecture of our proposed model.

4   Result Analysis

We have performed two experiments with two different case scenario for the mixed Bangla-English model. In the first experiment, we implemented model-1 with a 90:10 and 80:20 training-test ratio which gives us a test accuracy of 87.24% and 81.04% respectively. Similarly, in the second experiment, we implemented model-2 with the same training-test ratios as before which gives us a test accuracy of 84.23% and 72.81% respectively. So, it has been marked that model-1 outperforms better than the other model in both experiments. Table 1 illustrates the comparison of test accuracy for the cases of experiment-1 and experiment-2.

Figure 9 shows performance evaluation with train vs validation accuracy and train vs validation loss for the best-suited model, i.e. experiment-1. We have acquired 87.25% & 81.04% test accuracy and test loss of 57.19% & 79.19% for (0:10 and 80:20 respectively while experimenting. Figure 10 compares our result with the previous research works for classification purposes. It can be seen that in 91.04% accuracy acquired which was developed by CNN model working with English digits and letters [33] and 93% accuracy acquired working with using TI46 corpus which was developed by STM [35]. Another work claimed extraordinary results on only Bangla digit classification and achieved an accuracy of 98% which was also developed by CNN as well [29]. However, they used only 1200 data samples. Compared to these works, though our model has not performed well, we have achieved a decent performance accuracy as a first tried method for mixed English-Bangla speech corpus, i.e. mixed digit classifications.

Figure 10 is the performance evaluation of our model with previous research work to classify audio digits in English and Bangla language. Model 1 to Model 4 is the outcome of our proposed work for mixed Bangla-English language. Though some of the existing model shown in the figure have higher accuracy than our

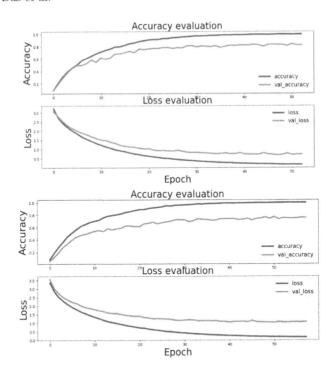

Fig. 9. The plots describe accuracy measure shows train and validation accuracy vs train and validation loss which has given the best outcome i.e Fig. 9 (top and 2nd top) for model-1 and Fig. 9 (3rd top and bottom) for model-2. Model-1 achieved 87.24% which involves 128, 48, 48 filters each conv2D layer and 128 active neurons taking 90% data for training the model, 10% for testing purpose and 10% for validation from the remaining train set whereas in model-2 we kept every other parameter the same as before but now we run 80% data for training the model, 20% for testing purpose and 20% for validation from the remaining 80% of train set which also can be seen by the Table 1 summery.

Table 1. A performance measurement comparison for individual run-time with different model and train-test ratio

Experiment no.	Dataset ratio		Train-test dataset ratio	Filters used in each layer	Active neurons	Test accuracy
	English digits	Bangla digits				
Exp. 1	1500	2000	90:10	128,48,48	128	87.24%
			80:20			81.04%
Exp .2	1500	2000	90:10	64,32,32	64	84.22%
			80:20			72.81%

obtained results, they are for individual languages, either English or Bangla. However, we worked on a mixed Bangla-English model, and till the present date, no mixed model was available to compare our results.

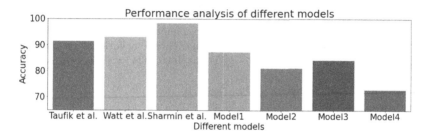

Fig. 10. Performance analysis of different models

5   Conclusion

As the days go by, speech recognition is becoming a necessary part of people's daily lives. Since speech recognition itself is a substantial and instrumental part of artificial intelligence and machine learning, spoken digit recognition is paramount. If we look at it from the Bangladeshi perspective, most people use mixed Bangla-English for daily communication. To take Bangla speech recognition a step forward, we have performed a mixed Bangla-English spoken digits classification. The main contribution of our work is to develop a Bangla isolated dataset of 2000 voices. A mixture model of the Bangla-English dataset is trained and test with CNN architecture with an accuracy of 87.24%, which is not up to the satisfactory level. However, the result is quite conceivable as the first approach on this topic has been carried out to the present date. We believe still better accuracy can be found in the future by tuning model parameters more appropriately and developing a more enriched Bangla dataset which can also be mentioned as one of the challenging issues. Besides, taking variation in the rest of the dialects for the other regions and age groups of the Bengali speaking people and a larger dataset for training the model could be helpful to attain a higher accuracy level.

References

1. Adiba, F.I., Islam, T., Kaiser, M.S., Mahmud, M., Rahman, M.A.: Effect of corpora on classification of fake news using naive bayes classifier. Int. J. Autom. AI Mach. Learn. Canada **1**, 80–92 (2020)
2. Sumon, S.A., Chowdhury, J., Debnath, S., Mohammed, N., Momen, S.: Bangla short speech commands recognition using convolutional neural networks. In: 2018 International Conference on Bangla Speech and Language Processing (ICBSLP), pp. 1–6 (2018). https://doi.org/10.1109/ICBSLP.2018.8554395
3. Aytar, Y., Vondrick, C., Torralba, A.: SoundNet: learning sound representations from unlabeled video. CoRR abs/1610.09001 (2016). http://arxiv.org/abs/1610.09001
4. Bishop, C.M.: Pattern Recognition and Machine Learning. Springer, Heidelberg (2006)

5. Blog, G.A.: Launching the speech commands dataset, August 2017. https://ai. googleblog.com/2017/08/launching-speech-commands-dataset.html//

6. Choi, K., Fazekas, G., Sandler, M.B., Cho, K.: Convolutional recurrent neural networks for music classification. CoRR abs/1609.04243 (2016). http://arxiv.org/abs/1609.04243

7. Das, T.R., Hasan, S., Sarwar, S.M., Das, J.K., Rahman, M.A.: Facial spoof detection using support vector machine. In: Kaiser, M.S., Bandyopadhyay, A., Mahmud, M., Ray, K. (eds.) Proceedings of International Conference on Trends in Computational and Cognitive Engineering. AISC, vol. 1309, pp. 615–625. Springer, Singapore (2021). https://doi.org/10.1007/978-981-33-4673-4_50

8. Demir, F., Abdullah, D., Sengur, A.: A new deep CNN model for environmental sound classification. IEEE Access **8**, 66529–66537 (2020)

9. Dong, M.: Convolutional neural network achieves human-level accuracy in music genre classification. CoRR abs/1802.09697 (2018). http://arxiv.org/abs/1802.09697

10. Ferdous, H., Siraj, T., Setu, S.J., Anwar, M.M., Rahman, M.A.: Machine learning approach towards satellite image classification. In: Kaiser, M.S., Bandyopadhyay, A., Mahmud, M., Ray, K. (eds.) Proceedings of International Conference on Trends in Computational and Cognitive Engineering. AISC, vol. 1309, pp. 627–637. Springer, Singapore (2021). https://doi.org/10.1007/978-981-33-4673-4_51

11. getsmarter: Applications of speech recognition, March 2019. https://getsmarter.com/blog/market-trends/applications-of-speech-recognition//

12. Ghanty, S., Shaikh, S., Chaki, N.: On recognition of spoken Bengali numerals. In: International Conference on Computer Information Systems and Industrial Management Applications (CISIM), pp. 54–59 (10 2010). https://doi.org/10.1109/CISIM.2010.5643692

13. Gupta, A., Sarkar, K.: Recognition of spoken Bengali numerals using MLP, SVM, RF based models with PCA based feature summarization. Int. Arab J. Inf. Technol. **15**(2), 263–269 (2018)

14. Hees, A.G.F.R.J., Dengel, A.: EsresNet: environmental sound classification based on visual domain models. arXiv (2020)

15. Huque, S., Rasel, A., Islam, B.: Analysis of a small vocabulary Bangla speech database for recognition. Int. J. Comput. Appl. **133**, 22–28 (2016). https://doi.org/10.5120/ijca2016907827

16. Mahalingam, H., Rajakumar, M.: Speech recognition using multiscale scattering of audio signals and long short-term memory 0f neural networks. Int. J. Adv. Comput. Sci. Cloud Comput. **7**, 12–16 (2019)

17. Mahmud, M., Kaiser, M.S., Hussain, A.: Deep learning in mining biological data. arXiv (2021)

18. Mahmud, M., Kaiser, M.S., Hussain, A., Vassanelli, S.: Applications of deep learning and reinforcement learning to biological data. CoRR abs/1711.03985 (2017). http://arxiv.org/abs/1711.03985

19. Muhammad, G., Alotaibi, Y., Huda, M.: Automatic speech recognition for Bangla digits. In: 12th International Conference on Computers and Information Technology, pp. 379–383, January 2010. https://doi.org/10.1109/ICCIT.2009.5407267

20. Nasrullah, Z., Zhao, Y.: Music artist classification with convolutional recurrent neural networks. In: International Joint Conference on Neural Networks (IJCNN), pp. 1381–1388 (2019)

21. van den Oord, A., et al..: WaveNet: a generative model for raw audio. CoRR abs/1609.03499 (2016). http://arxiv.org/abs/1609.03499

22. Paul, B., Bera, S., Paul, R., Phadikar, S.: Bengali spoken numerals recognition by MFCC and GMM technique. In: Mallick, P.K., Bhoi, A.K., Chae, G.-S., Kalita, K. (eds.) Advances in Electronics, Communication and Computing. LNEE, vol. 709, pp. 85–96. Springer, Singapore (2021). https://doi.org/10.1007/978-981-15-8752-8_9

23. PyPI: librosa.feature.mfcc librosa 0.8.0 documentation (www document) (2020). https://pypi.org/project/librosa/

24. Rahman, M.A.: Gaussian process in computational biology: covariance functions for transcriptomics. Ph.D. thesis, University of Sheffield (2018)

25. Reddy, P.V.N., Kumar, D.D.A.: Test accuracy improvement in spoken digit recognition using convolutional neural networks. Int. J. Adv. Sci. Technol. **29**(02), 1468–1477 (2020)

26. Roberts, A., Engel, J.H., Raffel, C., Hawthorne, C., Eck, D.: A hierarchical latent vector model for learning long-term structure in music. CoRR abs/1803.05428 (2018). http://arxiv.org/abs/1803.05428

27. Sadik, R., Reza, M.L., Noman, A.A., Mamun, S.A., Kaiser, M.S., Rahman, M.A.: Covid-19 pandemic: a comparative prediction using machine learning. Int. J. Autom. AI Mach. Learn. Canada **1**, 1–16 (2020)

28. Scipy: numpy.append numpy v1.20 manual (2020). https://docs.scipy.org/doc/numpy/reference/genrated/numpy.append.html

29. Sharmin, R., Rahut, S.K., Huq, M.R.: Bengali spoken digit classification: a deep learning approach using convolutional neural network. Proc. Comput. Sci. **171**, 1381–1388 (2020)

30. sklearn: sklearn.model_selection.train_test]_split scikit-learn 0.24.1 documentation-documentation (www document) (2020). https://scikit-learn.org/stable/modules/generated/sklearn.model_selection.train_test_split.html

31. Speaks, A.: Audrey: the first speech recognition system, October 2014. https://astaspeaks.wordpress.com/2014/10/13/audrey-the-first-speech-recognition-system//

32. Sultana, S., Rahman, M.S., Iqbal, M.Z.: Recent advancement in speech recognition for bangla: a survey. Int. J. Adv. Comput. Sci. Appl. **12**(3) (2021). https://doi.org/10.14569/IJACSA.2021.0120365 http://dx.doi.org/10.14569/IJACSA.2021.0120365

33. Taufika, D., Hanafiaha, N.: Autovat: An automated visual acuity test using spoken digit recognition with MEL frequency cepstral coefficients and convolutional neural network. In: 5th International Conference on Computer Science and Computational Intelligence 2020. vol. 179, pp. 458–467 (2021)

34. tensorflow: tensorflow.org/guide/keras/sequential_tensorflow core v2.4.1] (www document) (2020). https://www.tensorflow.org/guide/keras/sequential_model

35. Watt, S., Kostylev, M.: Spoken digit classification using spin-wave delay-line active-ring reservoir computing. arXiv (2020)

36. Wikiland: List of languages by total number of speakers (2019). https://wikiwand.com/en/List_of_languages_by_number_of_native_speakers//

37. Zerari, N., Samir, A., Hassen, B., Raymond, C.: Bidirectional deep architecture for Arabic speech recognition speech recognition using multiscale scattering of audio signals and long short-term memory of neural networks. Open Comput. Sci. **9**(1), 92–102 (2019)

38. Zhang, W., Lei, W., Xu, X., Xing, X.: Improved music genre classification with convolutional neural networks. In: INTERSPEECH (2016)

Sluggish State-Based Neural Networks Provide State-of-the-art Forecasts of Covid-19 Cases

Oluwatamilore Orojo[1(✉)], Jonathan Tepper[1,2], T.M. McGinnity[1,3], and Mufti Mahmud[1]

[1] School of Science and Technology, Nottingham Trent University, Nottingham NG11 8NS, UK
{oluwatamilore.orojo,mufti.mahmud}@ntu.ac.uk
[2] Perceptronix Ltd., Avon Way, Derby DE65 5AE, UK
jtepper@perceptronix.net
[3] Intelligent Systems Research Centre, University of Ulster, Magee Campus, Derry BT48 7JL, UK
tm.mcginnity@ulster.ac.uk

Abstract. At the time of writing, the Covid-19 pandemic is continuing to spread across the globe with more than 135 million confirmed cases and 2.9 million deaths across nearly 200 countries. The impact on global economies has been significant. For example, the Office for National Statistics reported that the UK's unemployment level increased to 5% and the headline GDP declined by 9.9%, which is more than twice the fall in 2009 due to the financial crisis. It is therefore paramount for governments and policymakers to understand the spread of the disease, patient mortality rates and the impact of their interventions on these two factors. A number of researchers have subsequently applied various state-of-the-art forecasting models, such as long short-term memory models (LSTMs), to the problem of forecasting future numbers of Covid-19 cases *(confirmed, deaths)* with varying levels of success. In this paper, we present a model from the simple recurrent network class, *The Multi-recurrent network (MRN)*, for predicting the future trend of Covid-19 confirmed and deaths cases in the United States. The MRN is a simple yet powerful alternative to LSTMs, which utilises a unique sluggish state-based memory mechanism. To test this mechanism, we first applied the MRN to predicting monthly Covid-19 cases between Feb 2020 to July 2020, which includes the first peak of the pandemic. The MRN is then applied to predicting cases on a weekly basis from late Feb 2020 to late Dec 2020 which includes two peaks. Our results show that the MRN is able to provide superior predictions to the LSTM with significantly fewer adjustable parameters. We attribute this performance to its robust sluggish state memory, lower model complexity and open up the case for simpler alternative models to the LSTM.

Keywords: ANN · RNN · Covid-19 · Multi-recurrent Neural Network · Time-series

Supported by organization Nottingham Trent University.

M. Mahmud et al. (Eds.): AII 2021, CCIS 1435, pp. 384–400, 2021.
https://doi.org/10.1007/978-3-030-82269-9_30

1   Introduction

The World Health Organisation (WHO) declared the Covid-19 outbreak a pandemic on the 11th of March 2020 [1]. From the 11th of March to date, the outbreak has spread rapidly to many countries and has had a drastic impact on our day-to-day lives. Accurate forecasting of Covid-19 cases is crucial for resource allocation to treat infected patients and to aid governments and scientist as they discuss tactics to mitigate the virus spread. A number of researchers, in an attempt to understand the virus, particularly the rate at which it spreads, have applied various forecasting models *(such as Susceptible-Exposed-Infectious-Recovered model, Long-Short Term Memory (LSTM)* to forecast the future cases *(death or confirmed).*

Artificial intelligence (AI) and machine learning (ML) techniques are notable for their predictive abilities in a number of fields such as anomaly detection [2,3], biological data mining [4], disease detection [5], financial prediction [6], text analytics [7] and urban planning [8]. This also includes methods to support Covid-19 [9] through analysing lung images acquired by means of computed tomography [10], chest x-ray [11], safeguarding workers in workplaces [12], identifying symptoms using fuzzy systems [13], and supporting hospitals using robots [14]. In particular, LSTMs have been widely applied for the Covid-19 prediction task given the currently held belief that they are state of the art for forecasting [15–18]. Others such as Shastri *et al.* [19] build on the premise that LSTMs are the most suitable tools for time-series processing and have endowed the LSTM to enhance performance.

In this paper, we compare the Multi-recurrent Network to current state-of-the-art, the LSTM to forecast future cases of Covid-19 in the USA. To the best of our knowledge, MRNs have not been presented or applied for the Covid-19 forecasting task. Both models are evaluated on publicly available data from the Centers for Disease Control and Prevention and assessed using the Mean Absolute Percentage Error. The structure of the paper is as follows. A brief summary of the modelling techniques applied for Covid-19 forecasting is given in Sect. 2. The methodology is given in Sect. 3. The results are given in Sect. 4 and Sect. 6 concludes.

2   Covid-19 Forecasting

Mathematical models have been historically applied for the modelling and prediction of infectious disease [20–22]. In particular, in an attempt to model Covid-19, the most basic Susceptible-Infectious-Recovered (SIR) model and variants *(such as Susceptible-Exposed-Infectious-Recovered (SEIR) model)* have been widely applied [23,24]. He *et al.* [25] propose the SEIR model to analyse the epidemic evolution in Hubei province demonstrating its usefulness to forecast Covid-19 epidemic. Tiwari *et al.* [26] employ an improvised five compartment mathematical model, SEIR-Death (SEIRD) model, to predict the peak of the epidemic considering the lockdown in India. Other mathematical models have been developed and adopted to model Covid-19. For example, Singhal *et al.* [27] apply Gaussian Mixture model and Fourier decomposition method (FDM) to predict Covid-19 cases. They show that the proposed models can be used to aid the continuous predictive monitoring of Covid-19. Bekiros and Kouloumpou [28] introduce a Stereographic Brownian Diffusion Epidemiology Model (SBDiEM) for modelling, forecasting and nowcasting for Covid-19.

Statistical models have been popularly used for time-series analysis, particularly due to their flexibility and ability to model stationary processes. For example, Ankarali *et al.* [29] apply different curves *(exponential, quadratic, power, cubic, logistic, and growth)* to model Covid-19. They found that the cubic model obtained the best results. Zuo *et al.* [30] propose a statistical model, they particularly study a sub-model, *flexible extended Weibull distribution*, they find these sub-models could describe the total death data of Covid-19 in Asian countries. Despite the success obtained with mathematical and statistical models, they are notably prone to inaccuracies. Mathematical models specifically i) assume the future is similar to the past (which is not always the case) and ii) model estimates are based *a priori*, so the models may miss changes over time thus limiting the usefulness of the model [31]. Similarly, statistical methods mostly assume linearity and are unable to predict the structural shifts found in non-linear data. This is unsuitable for the Covid-19 prediction task as current observations indicate non-linearity.

Machine learning has provided opportunities to better model non-linearities and co-dependencies in the signal that aids learning and enhances performance thus mitigating the limitations of mathematical and statistical model [32–34]. To harness the superiority of ML techniques, researchers have applied them for Covid-19 prediction and classification task. For example, Parbat and Chakraborty [35] propose a model based on a support vector regression model with Radial Basis Function to predict Covid-19 cases[1] in India. Their proposed methodology provides higher accuracy than a linear, polynomial, or logistic regression. Jibril *et al.* [36] develop models based on supervised learning algorithms[2] to predict Covid-19 infection in Mexico using labelled data. They find that models based on the Decision tree performed best based on accuracy while the SVM provides the best sensitivity[3] and finally the Naives Bayes obtains the best specificity[4].

Several researchers present a comparative analysis between different models. Kirbaş *et al.* [37] carry out a comparative analysis using the ARIMA, Nonlinear Autoregression Neural Network (NARNN) and LSTM approaches to predict the Covid-19 confirmed cases in 8 European countries[5]. The results show that the

---

[1] The total number of COVID19 infected cases, total number of daily new cases, total number of deaths and total number of daily new deaths.

[2] Logistic regression, Decision tree, Support vector machine, Naive Bayes, and Artificial neutral network.

[3] The percentage of Covid-19 positive patients correctly identified by the models.

[4] The percentage of Covid-19 negative patients correctly identified by the models.

[5] Denmark, Belgium, Germany, France, United Kingdom, Finland, Switzerland and Turkey.

LSTM has superior predictive abilities. Wang *et al.* [38] used a model built on LSTM along with a rolling update mechanism to forecast positive cases in Russia, Peru and Iran. The model provided very consistent results with actual values, demonstrating the suitability of the LSTM for modelling of Covid-19 cases. Yan *et al.* [39] propose a method based on the LSTM and compared to digital prediction models *(such as Logistic and Hill equations)*. Their proposed method produced smaller prediction deviation and provided a better fit.

Shahid *et al.* [40] assesses the performance of ARIMA, Support Vector Regression (SVR), LSTM, bidirectional LSTM (Bi-LSTM) for time-series prediction of confirmed, death and recovered cases in the top ten countries largely affected by the virus. Their experimental results demonstrate that the Bi-LSTM outperformed the other models as it enhances learning and memorizing of long sequences thus, they present the Bi-LSTM as an appropriate predictor. ArunKumar *et al.* [41] similarly presents deep learning Recurrent Neural Networks (RNN) models including the LSTM to predict the confirmed, recovered and death cases.

Arora *et al.* [42] apply LSTM variants *(Deep LSTM, Convolutional LSTM and Bi- LSTM)* to predict the number of positive cases in India. They also found that Bi-LSTM provided the best result. Vadyala *et al.* [43] predict confirmed cases using k-means-LSTM for short-term Covid-19 cases forecasting in Louisana, USA. They benchmark their model against traditional SEIR model and demonstrate that their model provides better results. Others enhanced predictive performance and modelling abilities using pre-processing techniques. Silva *et al.* [44] employ five machine learning models[6] for Covid-19 forecasting of the cumulative confirmed in five Brazilian and American states. They also employ the variational mode decomposition (VMD) for pre-processing. They demonstrate that using the hybridization of VMD enhances performance. Gautam [45] proposes transfer learning for Covid-19 cases and deaths forecast using LSTM networks. The LSTM has also been applied for other Covid-19 related task due to its popularity, for example, Demir [46] employ a deep LSTM for automated detection of Covid-19 cases from chest X-ray images which significantly improves performance compared to current radiology based approaches.

Specifically, LSTMs are believed to currently provide the best performance given the acclaimed track record with forecasting and mitigate limitations associated with RNNS. However, Nabi *et al.* [47] find that from the deep learning models employed, LSTMs were a poor candidate particularly as they aim to identify seasonality and periodic intervals which were absent in our studied countries. This demonstrates the lack of robustness with these models. However, Chen *et al.* [48] argue that LSTMs are not adaptable to new changes that occur as seen when they used it to predict oil prices. In addition, Le *et al.* [49] point out that although LSTMs provide accurate forecasts at specific points, they should however be combined with other models to obtain improved performance for

---

[6] Bayesian regression neural network (BRNN), Cubist Regression (CUBIST), k-nearest neighbours (KNN), Quantile Random Forest (QRF), and support vector regression (SVR).

long-term prediction. Danihelka *et al.* [50] point out the LSTM's limited ability with representation makes it a poor candidate for learning due to its lack of memory mechanism. Yu *et al.* [51] presented a systematic review on different LSTM cells and pointed to the need of 'external' memory to strengthen memory capacity. Ulbricht [52]'s proposed model, the Multi-recurrent network (MRN) has been shown to enhance prediction *(compared to Simple Recurrent Network, Echo-State Network)*. In this paper, the MRN is compared to the LSTM to identify if it offers better results and as such is a more reliable tool to inform decision-making and resource allocation.

3   Methodology

In this section, the data and the proposed modelling technique, the Multi-recurrent Network along with other notable techniques are presented for Covid-19 predictions. In addition, the error measurement, Mean Absolute Percentage Error (MAPE) is specified.

3.1   Covid-19 Dataset

In this paper, the data collection is like that in [19]. U.S. confirmed and death cases of Covid-19 are used for the monthly prediction task obtained from Centers for Disease Control and Prevention, U.S. Department of Health and Human Services[7]. The selection date is from the 7th of Feb 2020 to the 7th of July 2020 for the confirmed cases and from the 26th of Feb to the 7th of July 2020 for the death cases. The data was divided into training and testing sets, training data accounted for 80% of the data and the remaining 20% was out-of-sample testing. Both series were transformed using *MinMaxScaler*, such that the data is scaled to a given range on the training set [19].

Additional data from the 22nd of January to 22nd of December used for weekly of prediction of Covid-19 confirmed and death cases. Similarly, the data was divided into training and testing sets, training data accounted for 80% of the data and the remaining 20% was out-of-sample testing and transformed using *MinMaxScaler*.

3.2   Multi-recurrent Networks

Ulbricht [52] explored this notion that complexity and memory are key components for effective time-series processing and as a result introduced Multi-recurrent Networks. The MRN integrates features of both the Jordan and SRN model, along with input memory banks and variable layer-link and self-link recurrency. These properties enhance the model complexity sufficiently to encourage better processing without the added over-complexity associated with LSTM or

---

[7] https://www.cdc.gov/.

Gated Recurrent Units and as such are worthy of further exploration for appropriateness for time-series. In addition, the MRN enables and allows for different and flexible representation of past information unlike Jordan, SRN, ESN and LSTM which have a 'rigid' representation. Tepper *et al.* [53] more recently showed that this slightly more sophisticated class of SRNs, MRNs, is better able to capture the latent signal in time-series data and found that the MRN dynamics improved learning and achieved better accuracy (compared to the SRN, NARX and ESN networks).

The MRNs memory mechanism enables the network to 'forget' and 'retain' knowledge which is the catalyst for enhanced performance [52]. In addition, the MRNs memory state enables the formation of a comprehensive averaged history providing better insights and understanding of spatio-temporality in the data. More specifically, Ulbricht [52] and more recently [53] and Orojo *et al.* [6] demonstrated the MRNs superiority when compared with other techniques *(such as the Elman Network, Echo-State Network, LSTM)*. A detail description of this method is provided in [6].

An adapted MRN architecture from [53] is illustrated in Fig. 1 showing the flow of information through the network layers, employing the following feedback:

1. Layer-link recurrency: the units within each layer of the network copied to its respective memory bank at time, t, fed to the hidden layer at time, $t + 1$. The layer-level recurrency comprises the:
    - *Input layer recurrency*: the input layer's output at time, t is fed back to the relevant memory bank on the input layer at time, $t + 1$.
    - *Hidden layer recurrency*: the hidden layer's output at time, t is fed back to the relevant memory bank on the input layer at time, $t + 1$.
    - *Output layer recurrency*: the output layer's output at time, t is fed back to the relevant memory bank on the input layer at time, $t + 1$.
2. Self-link recurrency: the units within each memory bank on the input layer (referred to as either state units or context units) at time, t is fed back to itself at time, $t + 1$

The memory bank compositions for each layer are derived using the calculated layer-link and self-link ratios *(which determine the degree of rigidity and flexibility of the memory banks)*. More specifically, the number of memory banks for a layer is directly related to the granularity at which previous and current information is integrated and stored [53]. For each layer, the layer-link ratios are calculated from the allocated number of memory banks for the layer, n_M as: $\frac{i}{n_M}$ for $i = n_M, ..., 2, 1$. The self-link ratios are then calculated as: $1 - \frac{i}{n_M}$ for $i = n_M, ..., 2, 1$. For example, a network with for 4 output memory banks gives the following layer-link ratios: $\frac{4}{4}(1), \frac{3}{4}(0.75), \frac{2}{4}(0.5), \frac{1}{4}(0.25)$ and the following self-link ratios: $1 - \frac{4}{4}(0), 1 - \frac{3}{4}(0.25), 1 - \frac{2}{4}(0.5), 1 - \frac{1}{4}(0.75)$.

These combinations *(of varying layer- and self-link weights and thus memory banks)* form sluggish state-spaces within the memory mechanism of the MRN. These sluggish state spaces distinguishes the MRN from other networks in the simple recurrent network family [53]. More specifically, these sluggish

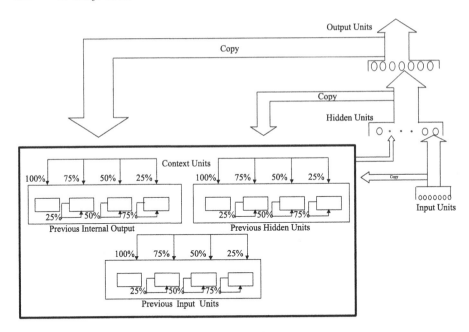

Fig. 1. The architecture of an MRN without noise injection (adapted from [53]).

state spaces aid the exploiting of information from both recent and distant past endowing the network with a 'longer averaged history' encouraging learning in long-term dependency tasks [53].

3.3   Forecasting Methodology

The MRN is coupled with a sliding window approach for prediction as applied by [6] *et al.* as this encourages better information processing in the MRN. The input sequences *(temporal input windows)* which are fed as inputs at any given time-step to predict the output are generated by a sliding window technique with a shift factor of 1 [6]. *Input window lengths are empirically established.* For each input sequence, the output is determined by the forecast horizon (that is the number of time-steps ahead the prediction is made) [6].

4   Results and Discussion

In this section, the MRN is applied for Covid-19 forecasting and its performance is compared to current state-of-the-art, the LSTM. Model forecasts are obtained using an averaging ensemble approach (that is a given number *(empirically established)* of models are trained and the average of the predictions are used as the final predictions and to assess performance. The models are assessed using the Mean Absolute Percentage Error (MAPE) score.

The MRN and LSTM are first trained and validated on data from early Feb to early June *for the confirmed cases* and late Feb to mid-June *for the death cases* to predict the monthly confirmed and death cases from early-June to early July *for the confirmed cases* and mid-June to early July *for the death cases*. The MRN and LSTM are then trained and validated on data from late January to mid-October to predict weekly confirmed and death cases from mid-October to late December.

4.1 Advance Monthly Predictions of Covid-19 Cases

The MRN and LSTM are trained to forecast the number of Covid-19 cases from mid-June to early July. Both models are trained with a number of parameter combinations to identify the best parameters. Note: both models have the same training and test set, however the MRN processes the data as input sequences and as such predictions start later than that of the LSTM as shown in Figs. 2 and 3.

MRN: The *MRN* is trained with 20 units and employs a sigmoid activation function for its hidden layer, a learning rate of *0.001* and momentum of *1.25*. Experiments with three window size [15, 25, 35] and a memory order of 4 *(that is, the maximum number of memory bank for any memory bank type is 4; [4, 4, 4])* are undertaken to identify the best model.

LSTM: The *LSTM* is trained with 20 units and employs a sigmoid activation function. Experiments with three optimisers; Stochastic Gradient Descent (SGD), Adam and RMSprop optimiser, three dropouts [0.1, 0.4, 0.7] and three batch sizes [20, 50, 100] are undertaken to identify the best model.

Table 1 presents the MAPE score *(for the test set)* for the best MRN and LSTM. The MRN is trained for 500 epochs whereas the LSTM is first trained for 500 epochs and then trained further for an additional 500 epochs *(1000 epochs in total)* as results show training for longer epochs enhances its performance and provides predictions closer to the observations). The MRN models performed best for both confirmed and death cases.

Table 1. MAPE Score on test set for USA Covid-19 cases *(with the number of trainable parameters shown in parentheses)*

Models	Epochs	Confirmed cases	Death cases
MRN	500	**4.11** *(1,261)*	**0.3** *(1,821)*
LSTM	500	7.03 *(5,061)*	22.67 *(5,061)*
	1000	6.99 *(5,061)*	7.62 *(5,061)*

Figure 2(a) and 2(b) visualises the number of observed confirmed cases against the predicted number of confirmed cases for the MRN and the LSTM *(respectively)* for the confirmed cases. The MRN appears to follow the trend of the confirmed cases closely; it does have an uptrend similar to that of the observed however it misses the sharp increase in the number of confirmed cases from late June. The LSTM on the other hand appears to follow the upward trend of the observed cases however, it overestimates the number of confirmed cases up to late June thus explaining the higher MAPE score it obtained in Table 1. *Note: Both models have the same training and test set, however the number of windows available to the MRN is dependent on the window size which determines the number of observations available, the MRN starts predicting from early April unlike the LSTM which processes the observations sequentially rather than in windows.*

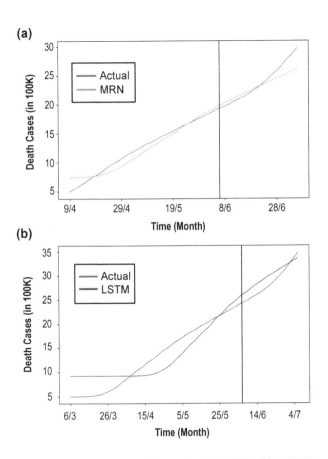

Fig. 2. Monthly confirmed cases for (a) MRN (b) LSTM.

The MRN and LSTM models are then used to forecast the number of Covid-19 death cases. Figure 3(a) and 3(b) visualises the number of observed death cases against the predicted number of death cases of the MRN and the LSTM *respectively.* The MRN appears to have learnt the underlying signal and predicts values for the death cases similar to those observed. The LSTM on the other hand appears to follow the trend however it overestimates the number of death cases compared to the observed number of death cases. *(Note: Both models have the same training and test set, however the number of windows available to the MRN is dependent on the window size which determines the number of observations available, the MRN starts predicting from late April.)*

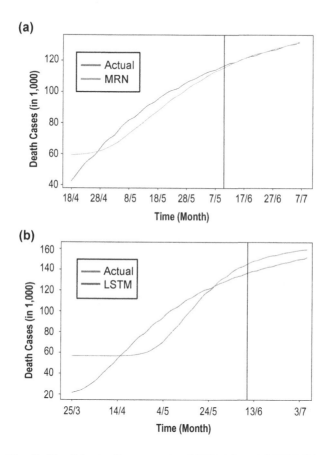

Fig. 3. Monthly death cases using MRN (a) and LSTM (b).

The MRN albeit a smaller framework has a lower MAPE score for both forecasting task and outperforms the LSTM *(see* Table 1*)*. The results demonstrate the predictive abilities of the MRN for time-series forecasting, specifically Covid-19 forecasting. To validate the superiority of the MRN, we then train it to forecast weekly Covid-19 cases over a longer period of time, roughly a year *(which reflects different underlying signals given the cyclical pattern observed with Covid-19 in 2020)*, we then benchmark its performance against the LSTM.

4.2 Advance Weekly Predictions of Covid-19 Cases

The MRN and LSTM are then trained to forecast the number of Covid-19 cases from mid-October to late December using weekly data from late-January to early-October. Like the monthly predictions, both models are trained with 20 hidden units and with several combinations to identify the best parameters. The models are trained for 500 epochs.

MRN: The *MRN* is trained with 20 units and employs a sigmoid activation function for its hidden layer, a learning rate of *0.001* and momentum of *1.25*. Experiments with three window size [15, 25, 35] and a memory order of 4 *(that is, the maximum number of memory bank for any memory bank type is 4; [4, 4, 4])* are undertaken to identify the best model and the results of which are presented in Table 2.

Table 2. MRN results for the test set *(number of trainable parameters shown in parentheses)*

Window size	Confirmed cases		Death cases	
	MAPE Score	Memory bank	MAPE Score	Memory bank
15	14.5 *(861)*	[0, 2, 0]	5.13 *(1,261)*	[0, 3, 0]
25	**12.78 (861)**	[0, 2, 0]	**4.86 (861)**	[0, 2, 0]
35	14 *(1,721)*	[0, 4, 3]	5.92 *(861)*	[0, 2, 0]

LSTM: The *LSTM* is trained with 20 units and employs a sigmoid activation function. Experiments with three optimisers; Stochastic Gradient Descent (SGD), Adam and RMSprop optimiser, three dropouts [0.1, 0.4, 0.7] and five batch sizes [20, 50, 100, 120, 150] are undertaken to identify the best model and the results of which are presented in Table 3.

Table 3. LSTM results for the test set *(number of trainable parameters shown in parentheses)*

Batch size	Confirmed cases	Death cases
20	35.22 *(5,061)*	24.02 *(5,061)*
50	23.44 *(5,061)*	16.34 *(5,061)*
100	20.75 *(5,061)*	12.51 *(5,061)*
120	**17.64 (5,061)**	12.57 *(5,061)*
150	18.15 *(5,061)*	**9.88 (5,061)**

As seen from Table 2 and Table 3, the best MRN model employed a window size of 25 for the confirmed and death cases. The best LSTM model employed a batch size of 120 for the confirmed cases and a batch size of 150 for the death cases. All the LSTM models performed best with a dropout of 0.1 and the LSTM models using a batch size of 100, 120 & 150 performed best with the *RMSprop* optimiser while those using a batch size of 20 & 50 performed best with the *adam* optimiser.

The MRN models performed best on both the confirmed and death cases, more specifically all the best MRN models for each window size performed better than the overall best LSTM models *(in bold in* Table 3*)*. Interestingly, the MRN models employ a significantly lower number of parameters *(in some cases over one-fifth less)* than the LSTM models.

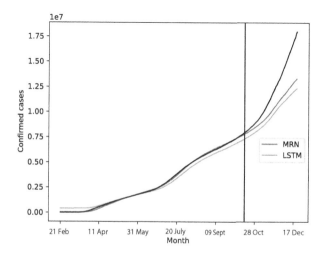

Fig. 4. Weekly confirmed cases

Figure 4 presents the MRN and LSTM predictions of weekly confirmed cases against the observed number of confirmed cases. Both models appear to follow the trend however miss the spike in confirmed cases from mid-late October. The MRN appears to accurately map and predict all the confirmed cases for the training set *(to the left of the black vertical line)* however for the test set, it follows the trend but underestimates the number of observed cases. The LSTM appears to map and accurately predict the training set till mid-June after which it underestimates the number of confirmed cases. For the test set, the LSTM underestimates the number of confirmed cases.

The weekly death cases are presented in Fig. 5 visualising the number of observed death cases against the MRN and LSTM predictions of weekly death cases. Like the confirmed cases, both models appear to follow the trend however missing the spike in death cases from mid-late October. The MRN appears to accurately map and predict most of the confirmed cases for the training set *(to*

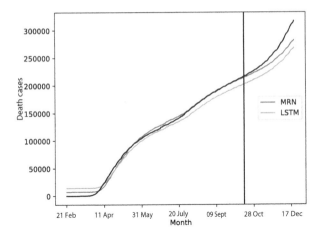

Fig. 5. Weekly death cases

the left of the black vertical line). However, for the test set, underestimates the number of observed cases. The LSTM appears to map and accurately predict some training data and for the test underestimates the number of confirmed cases.

5   Discussion

There has been a shift from simple recurrent networks to more complex recurrent networks particularly due to the vanishing gradient problem inherent in simpler networks. The LSTM, current state-of-the-art has been widely applied for a number of tasks, more specifically for Covid-19 forecasting [38–40,42,43]. However, there are inherent limitations with the LSTM for example, lack of adequate memory mechanism and overly complex gating mechanism [48,50]. Current work compared the performance of varying deep learning models and some of these models have been compared with mathematical and statistical models. However, there currently exist no study that compares and assess simpler RNNs to complex RNNs for the Covid-19 forecasting task. Therefore, the MRN, a much simpler and less computationally intensive class of model is applied for Covid-19 forecasting and its performance is compared to the LSTM, which it outperforms.

In particular, the MRN's superiority is attributed to its memory mechanism which employs different types of memory banks to encourage strong information latching. This encourages and enables the network to identify and 'remember' the spatio-temporal relationships within the signal. As stated in the methodology, employing different types of memory provides a descriptive overview of the historical information and enhances performance as shown from the results obtained in this paper. In addition, the results in this chapter along with results obtained by [6,52–55] particularly indicate that the shift to more complex mechanisms might be premature. As such, the MRN should be further explored and endowed with additional features as with other models (for example, as seen in *(see* [19]*))* in order to further enhance performance.

6 Conclusion

The Multi-recurrent Network is presented to model and predict Covid-19 confirmed and death cases in the USA. Current state-of-the-art, the LSTM and its variant have been widely applied for this task. In this paper, we show the MRN has strong abilities as it models and predicts cases leading up to the first peak of the virus spread using monthly data and then the second peak using weekly data. Its performance is benchmarked against the LSTM and the MRN with fewer parameters obtained better results than the LSTM. The results show that the MRN is a suitable and superior model for the Covid-19 prediction task. More specifically, the MRN should be endowed and explored to further enhance its performance. These findings are indicative of the usefulness of the MRN to aid the fight to mitigate the spread of this deadly virus. In addition, these findings should be explored for more Covid-19 related task *(such as contact tracing, screening and treatment)* to harness the strength of the MRN to inform decision-making. Future research would include endowing the MRN with explanatory power to provide understanding of the model predictions. Appropriate techniques will be applied to review the hidden states in response to the input stimuli to identify localised clusters and transitions.

References

1. Cucinotta, D., Vanelli, M.: Who declares COVID-19 a pandemic. Acta Bio Med.: Atenei Parmensis **91**, 157–160 (2020)
2. Yahaya, S.W., Lotfi, A., Mahmud, M.: A consensus novelty detection ensemble approach for anomaly detection in activities of daily living. Appl. Soft Comput. **83**, 105613 (2019)
3. Fabietti, M., et al.: Neural network-based artifact detection in local field potentials recorded from chronically implanted neural probes. In: Proceedings of IJCNN, pp. 1–8 (2020)
4. Mahmud, M., Kaiser, M.S., McGinnity, T., Hussain, A.: Deep learning in mining biological data. Cogn. Comput. **13**(1), 1–33 (2021). https://doi.org/10.1007/s12559-020-09773-x
5. Noor, M.B.T., et al.: Application of deep learning in detecting neurological disorders from magnetic resonance images: a survey on the detection of Alzheimer's disease, Parkinson's disease and Schizophrenia. Brain Inform. **7**(1), 1–21 (2020). https://doi.org/10.1186/s40708-020-00112-2
6. Orojo, O., Tepper, J., McGinnity, T.M., Mahmud, M.: A multi-recurrent network for crude oil price prediction. In: Proceedings of IEEE SSCI, pp. 2953–2958. IEEE (2019)
7. Rabby, G., et al.: TeKET: a tree-based unsupervised keyphrase extraction technique. Cogn. Comput. **12**(4), 811–833 (2020). https://doi.org/10.1007/s12559-019-09706-3

8. Kaiser, M.S., et al.: Advances in crowd analysis for urban applications through urban event detection. IEEE Trans. Intell. Transp. Syst. **19**(10), 3092–3112 (2018)
9. Mahmud, M., Kaiser, M.S.: Machine learning in fighting pandemics: a COVID-19 case study. In: Santosh, K., Joshi, A. (eds.) COVID-19: Prediction, Decision-Making, and its Impacts, Lecture Notes on Data Engineering and Communications Technologies, vol. 60, pp. 77–81. Springer, Singapore (2021). https://doi.org/10.1007/978-981-15-9682-7_9
10. Dey, N., et al.: Social-group-optimization assisted Kapur's entropy and morphological segmentation for automated detection of COVID-19 infection from computed tomography images. Cogn. Comput. **12**(5), 1011–1023 (2020). https://doi.org/10.1007/s12559-020-09751-3
11. Aradhya, V.M., et al.: One shot cluster based approach for the detection of COVID-19 from chest x-ray images. Cogn. Comput. 1–9 (2021). https://doi.org/10.1007/s12559-020-09774-w
12. Kaiser, M., et al.: iworksafe: towards healthy workplaces during COVID-19 with an intelligent phealth app for industrial settings. IEEE Access **9**, 13814–13828 (2021)
13. Bhapkar, H.R., Mahalle, P.N., Shinde, G.R., Mahmud, M.: Rough sets in COVID-19 to predict symptomatic cases. In: Santosh, K., Joshi, A. (eds.) COVID-19: Prediction, Decision-Making, and its Impacts, Lecture Notes on Data Engineering and Communications Technologies, vol. 60, pp. 57–68. Springer, Singapore (2021). https://doi.org/10.1007/978-981-15-9682-7_7
14. Kaiser, M.S., Al Mamun, S., Mahmud, M., Tania, M.H.: Healthcare robots to combat COVID-19. In: Santosh, K., Joshi, A. (eds.) COVID-19: Prediction, Decision-Making, and its Impacts, Lecture Notes on Data Engineering and Communications Technologies, vol. 60, pp. 83–97. Springer, Singapore (2021). https://doi.org/10.1007/978-981-15-9682-7_10
15. Chimmula, V.K.R., Zhang, L.: Time series forecasting of COVID-19 transmission in Canada using LSTM networks. Chaos, Solitons, Fractals **135**, 109864 (2020)
16. Tomar, A., Gupta, N.: Prediction for the spread of COVID-19 in India and effectiveness of preventive measures. Sci. Total Environ. **728**, 138762 (2020)
17. Ayyoubzadeh, S.M., Zahedi, H., Ahmadi, M., Kalhori, S.R.N.: Predicting COVID-19 incidence through analysis of google trends data in Iran: data mining and deep learning pilot study. JMIR Public Health Surveill. **6**(2), e18828 (2020)
18. Barman, A.: Time series analysis and forecasting of COVID-19 cases using LSTM and ARIMA models (2020)
19. Shastri, S., Singh, K., Kumar, S., Kour, P., Mansotra, V.: Time series forecasting of COVID-19 using deep learning models: India-USA comparative case study. Chaos, Solitons Fractals **140**, 110227 (2020)
20. Siettos, C., Russo, L.: Mathematical modeling of infectious disease dynamics. Virulence **4**, 295–306 (2013)
21. Huppert, A., Katriel, G.: Mathematical modelling and prediction in infectious disease epidemiology. Clin. Microbiol. Infect. **19**(11), 999–1005 (2013)
22. Keeling, M.J., Danon, L.: Mathematical modelling of infectious diseases. Br. Med. Bull. **92**(1), 33–42 (2009). https://doi.org/10.1093/bmb/ldp038
23. Kyrychko, Y., Blyuss, K.B., Brovchenko, I.: Mathematical modelling of dynamics and containment of COVID-19 in Ukraine. medRxiv (2020)
24. Ahmad, Z., Arif, M., Ali, F., Khan, I., Nisar, K.S.: A report on COVID-19 epidemic in Pakistan using SEIR fractional model. Sci. Rep. **10**, 1–14 (2020)
25. He, S., Peng, Y., Sun, K.: SEIR modeling of the COVID-19 and its dynamics. Nonlinear Dyn. **101**, 1–14 (2020). https://doi.org/10.1007/s11071-020-05743-y

26. Tiwari, V., Deyal, N., Bisht, N.S.: Mathematical modeling based study and prediction of COVID-19 epidemic dissemination under the impact of lockdown in India. Front. Phys. 8, 443 (2020). https://www.frontiersin.org/article/10.3389/fphy.2020.586899

27. Singhal, A., Singh, P., Lall, B., Joshi, S.D.: Modeling and prediction of COVID-19 pandemic using gaussian mixture model. Chaos, Solitons Fractals. 138, 110023 (2020). http://www.sciencedirect.com/science/article/pii/S0960077920304215

28. Bekiros, S., Kouloumpou, D.: SBDiEM: a new mathematical model of infectious disease dynamics. Chaos, Solitons Fractals. 136, 109828 (2020). http://www.sciencedirect.com/science/article/pii/S0960077920302289

29. Ankarali, H., et al.: A statistical modeling of the course of COVID-19 (SARS-CoV-2) outbreak: a comparative analysis. Asia Pac. J. Public Health. 32(4), 157–160 (2020). pMID: 32450712, https://doi.org/10.1177/1010539520928180

30. Zuo, M., Khosa, S.K., Ahmad, Z., Almaspoor, Z.: Comparison of COVID-19 pandemic dynamics in Asian countries with statistical modeling. Comput. Math. Methods Med. **2020** (2020)

31. Richardson, B., Joscelyn, K.B., Saalberg, J.: Limitations on the Use of Mathematical Models in Transportation Policy Analysis. UMI Research Press, Ann Arbor (1979)

32. Subudhi, S., Verma, A., Patel, A.B.: Prognostic machine learning models for COVID-19 to facilitate decision making. Int. J. Clin. Pract. **74**, e13685 (2020)

33. Khuzani, A.Z., Heidari, M., Shariati, S.: COVID-classifier: an automated machine learning model to assist in the diagnosis of COVID-19 infection in chest x-ray images. medRxiv (2020)

34. Punn, N.S., Sonbhadra, S.K., Agarwal, S.: COVID-19 epidemic analysis using machine learning and deep learning algorithms. medRxiv (2020)

35. Parbat, D., Chakraborty, M.: A python based support vector regression model for prediction of COVID-19 cases in India. Chaos, Solitons Fractals. 138, 109942 (2020). http://www.sciencedirect.com/science/article/pii/S0960077920303416

36. Muhammad, L.J., Algehyne, E.A., Usman, S.S., Ahmad, A., Chakraborty, C., Mohammed, I.A.: Supervised machine learning models for prediction of COVID-19 infection using epidemiology dataset. SN Comput. Sci. **2**, 1–13 (2021). https://doi.org/10.1007/s42979-020-00394-7

37. Kirbaş, I., Sözen, A., Tuncer, A.D., Kazancıoğlu, F.S.: Comparative analysis and forecasting of COVID-19 cases in various European countries with ARIMA, NARNN and LSTM approaches. Chaos, Solitons Fractals. 138, 110015 (2020)

38. Wang, P., Zheng, X., Ai, G., Liu, D., Zhu, B.: Time series prediction for the epidemic trends of COVID-19 using the improved LSTM deep learning method: case studies in Russia, Peru and Iran. Chaos, Solitons Fractals. 140, 110214 (2020)

39. Yan, B., et al.: An improved method for the fitting and prediction of the number of COVID-19 confirmed cases based on LSTM. Comput. Mater. Continua. 64(3), 1473–1490 (2020). http://www.techscience.com/cmc/v64n3/39440

40. Shahid, F., Zameer, A., Muneeb, M.: Predictions for COVID-19 with deep learning models of LSTM, GRU and Bi-LSTM. Chaos, Solitons Fractals **140**, 110212 (2020)

41. ArunKumar, K.E., Kalaga, D.V., Kumar, C.M.S., Kawaji, M., Brenza, T.M.: Forecasting of COVID-19 using deep layer recurrent neural networks (RNNs) with gated recurrent units (GRUs) and long short-term memory (LSTM) cells. Chaos, Solitons Fractals **146**, 110861 (2021)

42. Arora, P., Kumar, H., Panigrahi, B.K.: Prediction and analysis of COVID-19 positive cases using deep learning models: a descriptive case study of India. Chaos, Solitons Fractals **139**, 110017 (2020)

43. Vadyala, S.R., Betgeri, S.N., Sherer, E.A., Amritphale, A.: Prediction of the number of COVID-19 confirmed cases based on k-means-LSTM (2020)
44. Silva, R., Ribeiro, M.H.D.M., Mariani, V., Coelho, L.: Forecasting Brazilian and American COVID-19 cases based on artificial intelligence coupled with climatic exogenous variables. Chaos, Solitons Fractals **139**, 110027 (2020)
45. Gautam, Y.: Transfer learning for COVID-19 cases and deaths forecast using LSTM network. ISA Trans. (2021). https://www.sciencedirect.com/science/article/pii/S0019057820305760
46. Demir, F.: DeepCoroNet: a deep LSTM approach for automated detection of COVID-19 cases from chest X-ray images. Appl. Soft Comput. **103**, 107160 (2021)
47. Nabi, K.N., Tahmid, M.T., Rafi, A., Kader, M.E., Haider, M.A.: Forecasting COVID-19 cases: a comparative analysis between recurrent and convolutional neural networks. Results Phys. **24**, 104137 (2021)
48. Chen, Y., He, K., Tso, G.K.: Forecasting crude oil prices: a deep learning based model. Procedia Comput. Sci. **122**, 300–307 (2017)
49. Le, X.H., Ho, H.V., Lee, G., Jung, S.: Application of Long Short-Term Memory (LSTM) neural network for flood forecasting. Water **11**(7), 1387 (2019)
50. Danihelka, I., Wayne, G., Una, B., Kalchbrenner, N., Graves, A.: Associative long short-term memory. In: 33rd International Conference on Machine Learning, ICML 2016, vol. 4, pp. 2929–2938 (2016)
51. Yu, Y., Si, X., Hu, C., Zhang, J.: A review of recurrent neural networks: LSTM cells and network architectures. Neural Comput. **31**(7), 1235–1270 (2019)
52. Ulbricht, C.: Multi-recurrent networks for traffic forecasting. In: Proceedings of the National Conference on Artificial Intelligence, vol. 2, pp. 883–888 (1994)
53. Tepper, J.A., Shertil, M.S., Powell, H.M.: On the importance of sluggish state memory for learning long term dependency. Knowl. Based Syst. **96**, 104–114 (2016)
54. Binner, J., Tino, P., Tepper, J., Anderson, R., Jones, B., Kendall, G.: Does money matter in inflation forecasting? Physica A **389**(21), 4793–4808 (2010)
55. Orojo, O., Tepper, J., McGinnity, T.M., Mahmud, M.: Time sensitivity and self-organisation in multi-recurrent neural networks. In: 2020 International Joint Conference on Neural Networks (IJCNN), pp. 1–7 (2020)

Correction to: Mixed Bangla-English Spoken Digit Classification Using Convolutional Neural Network

Shuvro Das, Mst. Rubayat Yasmin, Musfikul Arefin, Kazi Abu Taher, Md Nasir Uddin, and Muhammad Arifur Rahman

Correction to:
Chapter "Mixed Bangla-English Spoken Digit Classification Using Convolutional Neural Network"
in: M. Mahmud et al. (Eds.): *Applied Intelligence and Informatics*, **CCIS 1435,**
https://doi.org/10.1007/978-3-030-82269-9_29

The caption of figure 9 in the original version of chapter 29 contained erroneous data and typographical errors. The wrong value and typographical errors have been corrected.

The updated version of this chapter can be found at
https://doi.org/10.1007/978-3-030-82269-9_29

M. Mahmud et al. (Eds.): AII 2021, CCIS 1435, p. C1, 2021.
https://doi.org/10.1007/978-3-030-82269-9_31

Author Index

Printed in the United States
by Baker & Taylor Publisher Services